Where to Watch Birds in

SCOTLAND

SECOND EDITION

Mike Madders and Julia Welstead

Christopher Helm
A&C Black · London

Dedicated to our parents

Line illustrations by Philip Snow and David Pullan
Maps by Julia Welstead

Christopher Helm (Publishers) Ltd, a subsidiary of
A & C Black (Publishers) Limited, 35 Bedford Row,
London WC1R 4JH

ISBN 0–7136–3704–8

A CIP catalogue record for this book is
available from the British Library

Typeset by Florencetype Ltd, Kewstoke, Avon
Printed and bound in Great Britain by Biddles Ltd, Guildford

CONTENTS

ACKNOWLEDGEMENTS

Adult and juvenile Pied Wagtails

We wish to record our especial gratitude to the many Scottish birders who contributed detailed information about their local sites. Foremost amongst these were: Mr R. Anderson, I. Andrews, N.K. Atkinson, A. Bachell, C.O. Badenoch, A. Barclay, D. Bell, Dr M.V. Bell, Z. Bhatia, C.J. Booth, W.R. Brackenridge, A. Bramhall, R.A. Broad, A.W. and L.M. Brown, Prof D.M. Bryant, Ian Bullock, Michael Callan, E.D. Cameron, Graham Christer, Tim Clifford, P. Collin, M.J.H. Cook, L. Cranna, W.A.J. Cunningham, Ian Darling, Bob Davis, D.E. Dickson, Tim Dix, Tim Dunbar, A. Duncan, B. Etheridge, Keith Fairclough, Dr E.C. Fellowes, I. Finlay, William Fraser, S. Gibson, R. Goater, P.R. Gordon, Martin Gray, Paul Harvey, Les Hatton, J. Hawell, R. Hawley, Dr C.J. Henty, A. Hilton, A. Hogg, J. Holloway, D. Jardine, Dr A.R. Jennings, R. Johnson, Alan Lauder, Brian Lightfoot, B. Lynch, T. Keating, D. McAllister, D. Macdonald, Chris McGuigan, J. McNish, J. Malster, Mrs W. Mattingley, E. Maughan, Peter Mayhew, R. Mearns, E. Meek, C. Miller, C. Mitchell, Mrs. C. Munro, R.D. Murray, J.S. Nadin, D. Nethersole-Thompson, R. Nisbet, Peter Norman, S. North, Dr M.A. Ogilvie, J.D. Okill, Dr I.D. Pennie, P. Potts, D. Pullan, K. Rideout, R.J. Robertson, M. Robinson, Miss D.E. Rowling, David Sexton, T. Shannon, R.A. Schofield, G. Shaw, K. Shaw, Dr J.C. Sheldon, G. Smith, T.C. Smout, J. Stevenson, D.R. Stewart, I. Strachan, Dave Suddaby, S. Taylor, V.M. Thom, D. Thorogood, M. Trubridge, Dr L.L.J. Vick, D. Warnock, D. Watson, K. Watson, A. Whitfield, Elizabeth Wiffen, J. Wiffen, Dr K.F. Woodbridge, R.E. Youngman and B. Zonfrillo.

The following organisations gave us invaluable help: Borders Regional Council, Clackmannan District Council, Countryside Commission for Scotland, Forestry Commission, North East Fife Ranger Service, National

Trust for Scotland, Royal Society for the Protection of Birds, Scottish Natural Heritage, Stirling District Council and Scottish Wildlife Trust.

The completed manuscript for each region was checked and improved upon by Ray Murray (Borders), Paul Collin (Dumfries and Galloway), Dougie Dickson (Fife), Ken Shaw (Grampian), Roy Dennis (Highland), Peter Gordon (Lothian), Eric Meek (Orkney), Tim Dix (Uists), Dave Okill (Shetland), Roger Broad (Strathclyde and Central) and Wendy Mattingley (Tayside). We are grateful to these people for their time and effort. We must stress, however, that the selection of sites included in the book and any mistakes that remain in the site accounts are entirely our own.

For the superb line drawings we thank Philip Snow and Dave Pullan. We would also like to thank Pam Grant, Lynn North and Bill Wales for giving us some useful cartographical advice.

Mention must also be made of the support and encouragement of many friends, who have proof-read scripts, researched details, lent books, provided us with accommodation or been otherwise invaluable: our thanks to you all. In particular, we would like to single out David Sexton, Fay Wilkinson, Steve Newton, John-the-Post, Ken and Kathy Shaw, Cathy MacLean, Alan Stewart and Jamie, Diane, Megan and Hannah Welstead.

The authors will be pleased to receive any information and ideas which might be usefully incorporated in future editions of this guide. Any correspondence should be addressed c/o Christopher Helm (Publishers) Ltd, 35 Bedford Row, London WC1R 4JH and marked for the attention of the authors. (Please enclose an s.a.e. if a reply is required.)

INTRODUCTION

Peregrine Falcon and Hooded Crows

Scotland is a vast and varied country: covering approximately 30,000 sq. miles (48,000 sq. km) of land, it ranges from the scenic splendour of mountain and moorland in the highlands to the subtle charm of lowland vales and rolling hills of the border country. There is over 6,400 miles (10,300 km) of coastline, characterised by the rocky and heavily indented north and west coast with its steep-sided sea lochs and bold sea-cliffs, and the wide estuarine firths typical of the east coast. A galaxy of islands lie off the west and north coasts, varying from fertile, low-lying ones like Tiree to the rugged and mountainous, such as Rum, and from small stacks and skerries to the large inhabited archipelagoes of Orkney and Shetland.

More than 60 per cent of Scotland can be considered upland habitat and this hill ground is predominantly used for sheep grazing although some is maintained as grouse moor or inhabited by deer. An increasing proportion of these upland tracts is being surplanted by commercial forest (this currently accounts for about 10 per cent of land use in Scotland). About 20 per cent of the country is given over to more intensive agricultural use; the most productive areas being concentrated along the east coast, especially adjacent to the estuarine firths. The southern uplands of Dumfries and Galloway and the Borders are also quite fertile.

A large proportion of the country's human population lives in the lowlands, in particular the central industrial belt which includes the two major cities of Edinburgh and Glasgow. Areas to the north and south of this are predominantly rural and the highlands and islands are but sparsely populated (only 126 of Scotland's 790 islands being currently inhabited).

Over 450 species of bird have been recorded in Scotland and 175 or so regularly breed. Clearly, Scotland is an important place for birds – many of the species that occur achieve breeding or wintering population levels that exceed those necessary to qualify for international importance (seabirds and raptors for instance). Scotland's northerly location and the presence of large tracts of relatively undisturbed ground enable a number of species to breed which would otherwise be absent from Britain: a total of 19 British breeding birds nest only north of the border.

The northern isles and the east mainland coast are well placed to receive continental migrants and rarities are regularly recorded amongst these every year. North American vagrants are occasionally recorded on the west coast and Hebrides and many more must go undiscovered. In winter, divers and sea-duck gather offshore; Scotland hosts large numbers of offshore divers, wildfowl and waders, as well as important population of thrushes, finches and buntings.

To do adequate justice to such a huge area and such diversity of birdlife in a single volume is scarcely possible. The selection of sites has been a major problem and ultimately, whatever criteria for inclusion are used, the final choice tends to be subjective. We have taken into consideration the views of many local birdwatchers around the country, in an effort to select sites that are both good birding locations and that are suitable for public access. Inevitably, we encountered a wide and often conflicting range of advice and probably the best we can hope is that everyone will be displeased equally with our final selection! Foremost among considerations when deciding whether or not to include a particular site were: (1) Is its inclusion likely to be in any way detrimental to the birdlife of the area? (2) Are there any problems relating to the site's access which may be exacerbated by increased visitor pressure? (3) Are there adequate vantage points, parking areas and accessible routes (either driveable or walkable) within or overlooking the area of interest?

The sites which survived this selection procedure were then graded according to their overall bird interest, importance and suitability and then assigned to either 'main site' or 'additional site' status. We make no apologies for having ensured a reasonable distribution of sites, even if this means that a good birding site in south-east Scotland has been usurped by a site in north-west Scotland with a more restricted bird interest. A few sites have been included for no better reason than that they are personal favourites.

Certain aspects of birdwatching are outside the scope of this guide. The most obvious is bird identification: there are many good field guides available and it would have been both inappropriate and a waste of valuable space to include any identification advice here. Similarly, information concerning individual species' behaviour, feeding methods, breeding cycle, distribution, migration etc. is left to the wide range of books now available on these subjects.

HOW TO USE THIS BOOK

Sand Martins – nest site, late spring

The site accounts in this book are divided into the regions of Borders, Central, Dumfries and Galloway, Fife, Grampian, Highland, Lothian, Strathclyde and Tayside, with the Uists, Orkney and Shetland completing the picture. For the most part each site is described under the sub-headings of 'Habitat', 'Species', 'Access', 'Timing' and 'Calendar' – the same format that has been adopted in other guides in this series. Instead of applying this system rigidly, however, we have adapted both the order and the layout to suit the site, where appropriate. This was particularly necessary in the case of island sites, where a large number of disparate access points are often grouped together under one site heading. Also, for several sites we have amalgamated the 'species' and 'calendar' sections in order to reduce repetition in the text. We hope that readers will find these changes logical.

At the end of each regional section is a list of additional sites with information relating to habitat, bird interest and timing given in note form. Unfortunately, lack of space prevents us from giving detailed access instructions for these sites, so the pertinent Ordnance Survey Landranger map is given together with a grid reference.

Following the site accounts is a 'Systematic List of the Birds of Scotland'. This lists all birds recorded in Scotland from 1900 to 1991 inclusive, with a very brief indication of each species' status and distribution. For species of local or restricted distribution a selection of sites where they are likely to be found is listed.

Habitat

Here a short general description of the area is given with the onus on the major bird habitat regions. The size of the area is given, where appropriate, and its status quoted (for instance: Site of Special Scientific Interest,

National Nature Reserve, Scottish Wildlife Trust Reserve, RSPB Reserve, etc.). Any relevant botanical, geological, historical or other information about the area completes this section.

Species

This details the species for which the site is primarily of interest with an indication of their abundance/occurrence. This is not by any means an exhaustive list of all the species that may be seen, but an attempt to summarise the area's specialities and where they might be seen.

Access

The most practicable routes to the site from nearby towns or main roads are detailed here. Accessible tracks and available parking around the area are noted and any available public transport to the site mentioned. Many of the main sites have an accompanying map showing access routes. In cases where there are several areas of interest, each one is listed with numbers corresponding to those on the site map.

For each site we have detailed any access restrictions known to us – these may be seasonal or perhaps applicable just to certain specific areas. Within some reserves sanctuary zones are often established to prevent disturbance to breeding birds and others are only accessible by prior arrangement with the warden. Many of the hides on Scottish Wildlife Trust reserves are kept locked and the keys are made available only to its members (not that you should need this incentive to join!). In a few cases the area of interest is also used for military purposes and occasional access restrictions are imposed. An important point to bear in mind when visiting upland areas is that access may be severely curtailed by stalking activities (Red Deer stalking is between 1 August and 30 April). We trust that readers will comply with whatever conditions of access are required.

Timing

A badly timed visit to any site can result in great disappointment so prior planning should always take this into consideration. This section outlines the optimum times to visit the site, with reference to season, weather conditions (wind direction, etc.), lighting (morning/evening sunlight can sometimes be a problem), tides at coastal sites and so on. Opening times of those reserves not permanently open and of visitor centres are also given.

However, do keep an open mind when visiting a particular site – just because the book doesn't mention that a particular time of year/direction of wind/state of tide, etc. is very good, doesn't mean that there will be nothing to see. The best birds are often the unexpected ones!

Calendar

For most of the important sites an analysis of the changing bird interest over the year is given. Again, this is not a comprehensive account of all the birds to be seen, but a selection of the highlights that are likely to occur. As with the 'timing' section, this should be interpreted as a guide rather than a definitive statement.

The Maps

Many of the site descriptions have accompanying maps. These are essentially locatory, with little, if any, attention given to topography or vegetation. For each site, numbers on the map correspond to those in the text, where a description of that area and its bird interest is given. As a rule, maps have not been included for sites at which there is an information notice board or for reserves with visitor centres, as it was felt that these would be superfluous. A general key to the maps is provided below.

In many cases the use of an Ordnance Survey map is recommended, especially where walks in remote, upland areas are suggested. At the head of each site account reference is given to the relevant Ordnance Survey Landranger Series (1:50,000) sheet. A four- or six-figure grid reference is also given to locate the site on that sheet. (Guidance on the use of grid references can be found on the side panel of every Ordnance Survey 1:50,000 series map sheet.)

In addition to individual site maps, general maps at the beginning of each regional section locate the sites described for that region. Encircled numbers correspond to main sites while lower-case letters correspond to additional sites. Finally, the map of Scotland on page xvi locates each region.

Key to Maps

Motorways, 'A' and 'B' roads are labelled appropriately on each map.

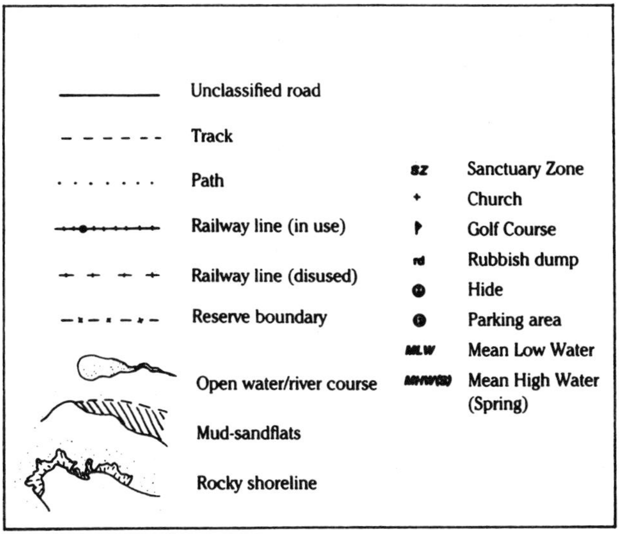

Unclassified road
Track
Path
Railway line (in use)
Railway line (disused)
Reserve boundary
Open water/river course
Mud-sandflats
Rocky shoreline

SZ Sanctuary Zone
Church
Golf Course
rd Rubbish dump
Hide
Parking area
MLW Mean Low Water
MHW(S) Mean High Water (Spring)

SOME NOTES FOR VISITORS

Male Ring Ousel – nest site

Accommodation and Transport

Detailed information concerning accommodation and transport is well beyond the scope of this book, already hard-pressed for space. Bus and train routes are mentioned in the 'access' section of each site account, however, where these are extant and accommodation suggestions are given for some islands where this is very restricted. The best overall advice that we can give regarding both accommodation and transport, however, is for the reader to contact the relevant Tourist Information Centre.

In General

Scotland's climate is extremely unpredictable and at any time of year visitors should be prepared for a wide range of conditions. For those venturing into the hills warm and waterproof clothing is essential, even if most of it remains packed in a rucksack all day. Strong, comfortable footwear is also important, with wellingtons often being necessary in the wetter terrain characteristic of north-western Scotland. Hill walkers will also require spare food, the relevant Ordnance Survey map and a compass. If possible leave word of your intended route and estimated time of return with someone and if conditions are against you, turn back.

With increasing numbers of people taking an interest in Scotland's wildlife and especially birdlife, care is needed to ensure that the pursuit of these interests does not in itself conflict with wildlife conservation. Please refer to the 'Code of Conduct for Birdwatchers' on page 280 and follow the good advice which is given there in order to make your visit responsible as well as pleasurable.

As a final plea, can we stress the importance of sending details of bird sightings to the local/county recorder (see page 273). Even sightings which you consider of little note in your own area can be important elsewhere. Visiting birdwatchers can undoubtedly provide valuable information on areas which are perhaps visited only on an irregular basis by local watchers.

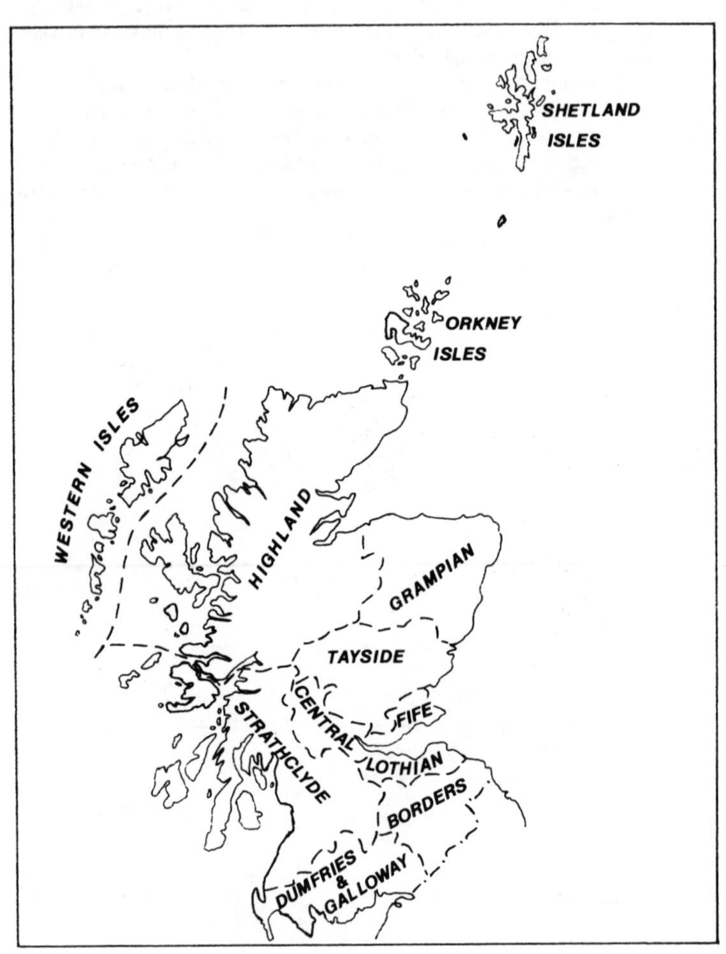
SHETLAND ISLES
ORKNEY ISLES
WESTERN ISLES
HIGHLAND
GRAMPIAN
TAYSIDE
CENTRAL
FIFE
STRATHCLYDE
LOTHIAN
BORDERS
DUMFRIES & GALLOWAY

BORDERS

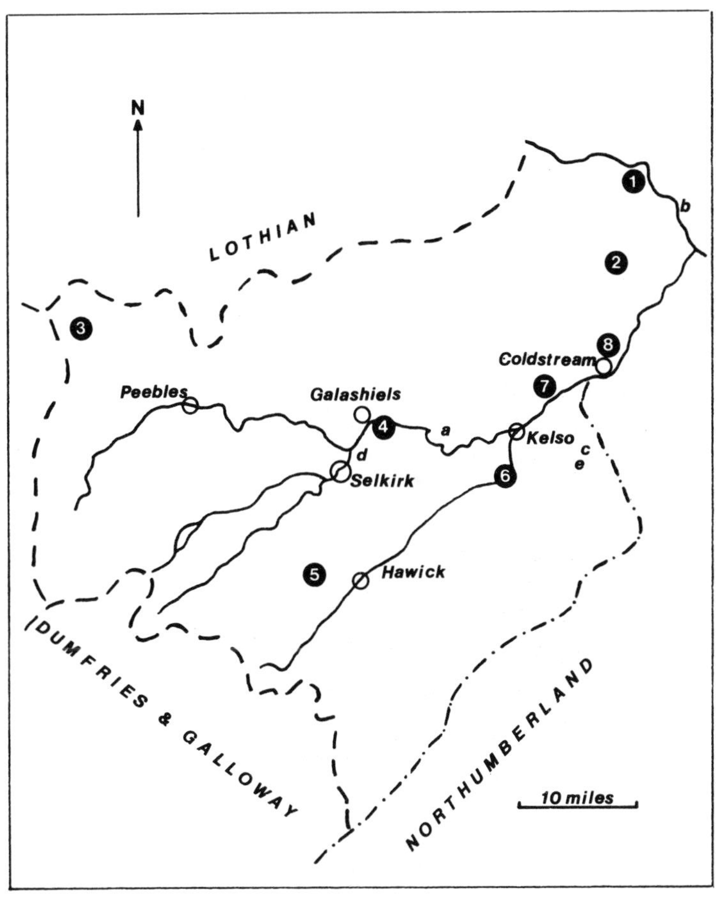

Main sites
B1. St Abbs Head
B2. Duns Castle
B3. West Water Reservoir
B4. Gunknowe Loch and Park
B5. Alemoor Reservoir
B6. River Teviot Haughlands
B7. River Tweed
B8. The Hirsel

Additional sites
a. Bemersyde Moss
b. Burnmouth
c. Hoselaw Lock
d. Lindean Reservoir
e. Yetholm Loch

B1 ST ABBS HEAD

OS ref.: NT 915690
OS map: sheet 67

Habitat

St Abbs Head is a rocky headland situated some 13 miles (21 km) north of Berwick-upon-Tweed. The sheer cliffs, up to 100 metres high, plunge dramatically into the North Sea and provide nest sites for around 60,000 seabirds. Inland from the cliff top, the habitat largely comprises grazed grassland with a man-made freshwater loch and trees/scrub in a sheltered valley. The National Trust for Scotland and the Scottish Wildlife Trust jointly manage 81 hectares of the cliffs and inland habitats, which are designated a National Nature Reserve.

Species

Around 350 pairs of Fulmar and 320 pairs of Shag nest on the cliffs; both species can be seen virtually all year. The cliffs also hold an impressive total of around 16,000 pairs of Kittiwake, 26,000 Guillemot, 1,500 Razorbill and 20 or so pairs of Puffin. Herring Gull, Rock Pipit, Wheatear and Raven also breed.

Shags – breeding plumage

The trees and scrub surrounding Mire Loch attract migrant passerines such as the commoner chats, flycatchers and warblers, as well as the occasional rarity. Spectacular numbers of passage thrushes are sometimes witnessed, whilst the area is probably the most reliable in Scotland for passage Firecrest.

Offshore, passage seabirds can be seen in April/May and especially in September/October (see Calendar).

Small numbers of wildfowl occupy the loch in winter, including up to 30 Goldeneye and a few Wigeon. Divers, particularly Red-throated, can be seen at sea. Good waterfowl passage is often a feature of seawatches.

Quail are annual visitors to the roadside fields north of Coldingham.

Access

Turn off the A1 onto the A1107 at either Burnmouth (from the south), or Cockburnspath (north) and continue until Coldingham is reached. Here, take the B6438 to St Abbs.

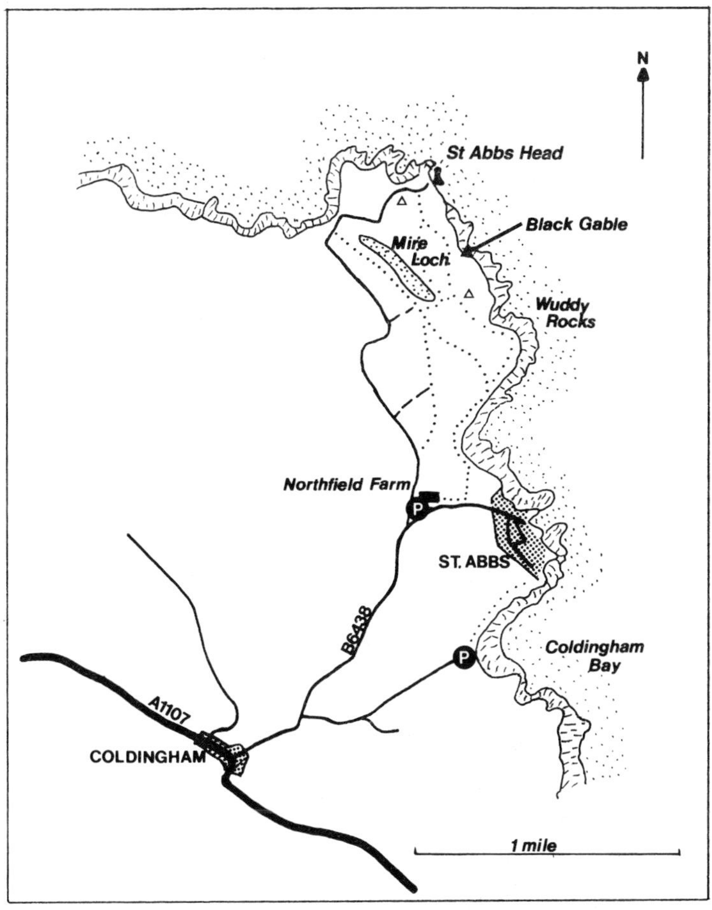

There is free parking at Northfield Farm Steading; also a visitor centre and coffee shop. A path leads east for 300 metres, then north around the cliffs towards the lighthouse. It is possible to return inland to the visitor centre using footpaths, making a 3-mile (4.8-km) circuit. There are many good vantage points along the cliff top; the best seawatching point is from Black Gable, the lowest point on the cliffs between Kirk and Lighthouse Hills and level with the dam end of Mire Loch. To the south of St Abbs, the scrub at Coldingham Bay is well worth checking in spring and autumn – rarities such as Pallas' Warbler and Olive-backed Pipit have been found here in recent years.

Buses to Coldingham run from Berwick and Edinburgh.

Timing

The reserve is an interesting location at any time of year. For nesting seabirds, visit between April and July. Migrants are most likely in April/May and again from August to October – easterly winds combined with poor visibility provide the ideal conditions for passerines, north to east winds for sea passage. Winter wildfowl and coastal sea-fowl should be present from October through to March/April.

Calendar

Some of the more interesting species likely to be seen.

All year: Little Grebe, Fulmar, Gannet, Shag, Mute Swan, Tufted Duck, Yellowhammer and Linnet.

March–May: Seabirds arrive back at nest sites. Migrants include Wheatear, Whinchat, Redstart and common warblers. Turtle Dove, Wryneck, Black Redstart, Bluethroat and Red-backed Shrike are annual whilst Night Heron, King Eider, Hoopoe, Water Pipit, Rose-coloured Starling, Golden Oriole, Great Reed, Sub-alpine and Dartford Warblers, Red-breasted Flycatcher and Rustic Bunting have been recorded.

June–July: Nesting seabirds, breeding Wheatear, common warblers (including Lesser Whitethroat). Shearwater passage starts.

August–November: Frequent Manx Shearwater, Great and Arctic Skuas, Common Scoter and divers with smaller numbers of Sooty Shearwater, Little Gull, Black Tern and Pomarine Skua. Cory's, Balearic and Great Shearwaters, Long-tailed Skua and Mediterranean Gull have also been recorded.

Return passage of passerines usually includes excellent, sometimes spectacular numbers of Goldcrest, common warblers, thrushes, Redstart and flycatchers. Water Rail, Siberian Chiffchaff, Yellow-browed and Reed Warblers, Red-breasted Flycatcher, Firecrest, Wryneck and Red-backed Shrike are annual, whilst rarities include Honey Buzzard, Richard's Pipit, Greenish, Pallas's, Dusky, Radde's, Aquatic and Icterine Warblers, Siberian Lesser Whitethroat, Siberian Stonechat and Little Bunting.

December–February: Wigeon and Goldeneye on Mire Loch; Scaup, Long-tailed Duck and Smew are occasionally recorded. Red-throated and occasional Great Northern and Black-throated Divers, Eider and small numbers of Common Scoter can be seen offshore. Sparrowhawk, Kestrel, Merlin and Peregrine frequently seen hunting over the reserve.

Warden

Ranger's Cottage, Northfield, St Abbs, Berwickshire TD14 5QF. Tel: 08907 71443.

References

Borders Bird Report 1985, pp. 53–7, ed. Ray Murray.
'The Seabirds of Berwickshire', S.R.D. da Prato and E.S. da Prato, *Scottish Birds*, vol. II (1980).

B2 DUNS CASTLE

OS ref.: NT 778544
OS map: sheets 67/74

Habitat

Both the shallow loch of Hen Poo and the nearby Mill Dam (sometimes known as Oxendean Pond) were created in the eighteenth century, as part of the landscaping works carried out to the Duns Castle estate. The Scottish Wildlife Trust currently manages 77 hectares of the estate, including the two lochs and the surrounding mixed policy woodland.

Access

The reserve is well signposted from the main square in Duns, which lies some 15 miles (24 km) west of Berwick-upon-Tweed on the A6105.

Several tracks and rides lead through the estate and there is a bird hide on the west bank of Hen Poo.

Species

Emergent vegetation around the loch fringe provides nesting cover for Mute Swan and Mallard, but the loch is more important as a wintering site than a breeding one. Over-wintering duck include Pochard and Goosander. In the woods, Great Spotted and Green Woodpecker, Jay, Redstart, Lesser Whitethroat, Garden Warbler, Blackcap and Chiffchaff all breed. Five species of tit have been recorded, including Marsh Tit. Pied Flycatcher have been encouraged to breed by the provision of nest boxes.

Timing

The grounds are open all year but the area is best visited during either the spring, when the woodland breeding species are of interest, or in winter for wildfowl on the lochs.

B3 WEST WATER RESERVOIR

OS ref.: NT 117523
OS map: sheet 72/65

Habitat

West Water reservoir lies at 320 metres above sea level in the Pentland Hills, 2 miles (3.2 km) west from West Linton. The site is very exposed and is surrounded by wet peatland, marsh grassland, rough pasture and heathland, principally used for sheep grazing and as grouse moor. Variations in the level of water in the reservoir can produce extensive areas of exposed mud in autumn, with smaller areas of sand and shingle.

The reservoir covers 51 hectares, including a main island and two others exposed at low water levels. It is designated a Site of Special Scientific Interest, being of regional significance for breeding wildfowl, gulls and waders, as well as an important location for wintering wildfowl.

Species

Since the reservoir was formed in the 1960s, 120 species have been recorded. Several pairs of Mallard, Teal (up to ten broods) and Tufted Duck breed and these species can be seen throughout the year at the reservoir. Mallard and Teal usually number about 300 birds each in late autumn/early winter, whilst peak counts of Tufted Duck can exceed 50 birds in early winter.

Up to five pairs of Ringed Plover, ten or so pairs of Lapwing, five pairs of Dunlin and small numbers of Snipe nest along the shoreline and in adjoining areas, together with Curlew and Redshank (10+ pairs each) and at least six pairs of Common Sandpiper.

Heron, Kestrel, Red Grouse, Black-headed, Common and Great Black-backed Gulls can be seen all year. Dipper frequent the reservoir outflow.

Wader passage can be very good in the autumn if there is sufficient exposed mud: Oystercatcher, Ringed Plover and Knot are frequently recorded. Little Stint, Dunlin, Ruff, Greenshank, Green Sandpiper and Turnstone may occur in small numbers, but are not recorded annually. The best areas of mud for these waders are in the south-western bay. Up to 20,000 Common Gull roost at the reservoir in spring and autumn.

West Water is a major Pink-footed Goose roost site and birds are present from mid-September until early May; 10,000 birds are regularly recorded, with peak counts in recent years of over 25,000. Up to 100 Greylag Geese can occur and small flocks of Barnacle Geese have been recorded on passage and in winter. White-fronted, Brent and Snow Geese have also been reported. Ten or so Goldeneye and a maximum of 20 Goosander are present in winter.

Timing

The area is worth a visit at any time of year. We do not advise a dawn or dusk visit to see roosting geese: this would involve a relatively long walk in the darkness and could well result in disturbance to the roost. Resting geese can generally be seen on a daytime visit during September and October, or again in April. We must stress, however, that regardless of the time of day, any geese present *must on no account be disturbed.*

Access

West Linton is situated on the A702, 15 miles (24 km) from Edinburgh. Turn off towards Baddinsgill at the south end of the bridge over Lyne Water and park at the entrance to West Linton Golf Course, ½ mile (0.8 km) later. From here, walk along the road across the golf course for 1 mile (1.6 km) to the waterkeeper's cottage, then on to the reservoir.

There is a regular bus service from Edinburgh.

Access to the dam is restricted and visitors are not encouraged to walk around the reservoir. It is advisable to contact the waterkeeper before proceeding to the reservoir. The hillside adjacent to either end of the dam is probably the best vantage point. *Care must be taken not to disturb geese at dawn and dusk – do not stand above the skyline on the hillside, or go near to the shoreline. The geese roost right up to the dam, so extra caution is needed if approaching at dawn.* This is currently one of the least disturbed goose roosts in the area, with only a limited amount of fishing and shooting activity.

Note: a new management plan is currently being developed that will probably result in a permit system for birdwatchers (administered by

Lothian Water and Drainage). Please therefore look out for any new access notices that may be erected.

References

Based upon information kindly supplied by A.W. Brown.

B4 GUNKNOWE LOCH AND PARK

OS ref.: NT 525351
OS map: sheet 73

Habitat

This area is situated beside the River Tweed near Galashiels and is at the junction of four river systems: the upper and lower Tweed valley, the Gala Water valley, and the Ellwyn Water valley. It is a housing and industrial development area, but retains a large area of parkland, scrub, developing and established woodland and river bank. The dismantled railway now carries part of the Southern Upland Way. The parkland is managed by Ettrick and Lauderdale District Council.

Species

Gunknowe Loch attracts a small wintering flock of Mute Swan, plus occasional Whoopers. Passage Wigeon, Mallard, Tufted Duck, Pochard and Goldeneye occur.

The area holds a variety of woodland species, including Great Spotted and Green Woodpeckers, Wood Warbler, Blackcap, Marsh Tit, Redpoll and Siskin. Sand Martin breed, Sedge and Grasshopper Warblers can be found in the scrubland areas, whilst Whinchat and Wheatear are seen on passage. Grey (and occasionally Yellow) Wagtail frequent the riversides; Dipper and sometimes Kingfisher can be seen. The River Tweed holds Little Grebe, Goosander and Moorhen.

Large night movements can occur, principally of waders, geese and thrushes, in spring and autumn, the birds presumably using the valley systems for navigation. In winter, Redwing, Fieldfare and Brambling may be seen.

Access

Access to the area is possible from the main A6091 road, 2 miles (3.2 km) from Galashiels. There is a car park at Gunknowe Loch. Several paths and tracks lead into the area.

Timing

The area is worth a brief visit at any time of year, although spring and autumn are likely to be the most productive times.

B5 ALEMOOR RESERVOIR

OS ref.: NT 397148
OS map: sheet 79

Habitat

This upland reservoir lies at about 300 metres altitude, some 8 miles (13 km) to the west of Hawick. It covers just under 6 hectares and is divided into two by the B711, with a narrow channel linking the two halves. The East Loch is surrounded by conifers, which eventually open out onto moorland, whilst the West Loch is only partially enclosed by conifers and includes an area of scrub and heather, again giving way to open moorland. The site is owned by the Water and Drainage Department of Borders Regional Council.

Species

Great Crested Grebe, Mute Swan, Teal, Mallard, Tufted Duck and Coot have bred at Alemoor. Both Whooper Swan and Goldeneye have lingered late or over-summered in recent years. The reservoir is an important assembly site for the Ettrick Forest Wigeon breeding population. Wigeon assemble there in April with most dispersing to neighbouring lochs to breed soon afterwards. From late June onwards fledged broods arrive to augment the existing population of males and failed breeders – up to 50 birds can be seen in summer.

The surrounding coniferous plantations hold Short-eared Owl, Siskin and Crossbill, whilst Redstart and Grasshopper Warbler have bred in recent years.

Common Sandpiper – spring

In winter, dabbling duck numbers vary according to the water level; the peak count of Teal is 230 birds, but other species are much less numerous. The East Loch is generally better for diving duck, including Tufted Duck, Pochard, Goldeneye and Goosander. Whooper Swan are regular visitors.

Passage waders are recorded only in small numbers, but have included Golden Plover, Knot, Sanderling, Little Stint, Curlew Sandpiper, Ruff, Spotted Redshank, Greenshank, Green and Wood Sandpiper, and Turnstone.

Timing

Wintering wildfowl provide the main interest and a visit between October and March is recommended. Passage waders occur during spring and late summer/autumn.

Access

The reservoir can be reached by taking the A7 from Hawick towards Carlisle, turning off right after about 2 miles (3.2 km) onto the B711 to Roberton. Park and view the lochs from the road 2½ miles (4 km) beyond the village. The West Loch is generally the most productive for birds.

References

Borders Bird Report 1982, pp. 32–4, ed. Ray Murray.

B6 RIVER TEVIOT HAUGHLANDS

OS ref.: NT 675255 to 709275
OS map: sheet 74

Habitat and Access

This area comprises the arable and pasture land bordering the River Teviot between Nisbet Village and Kalemouth, to the north-east of Jedburgh. Most of the area can be seen from the A698 Jedburgh–Kelso road and the B6400 Crailing–Nisbet road. The period October to April is the best time to visit.

Species

The haughlands are productive for Mute, Whooper (up to 250 have been recorded) and occasionally Bewick's Swan in winter. Pink-footed and Greylag Geese are also numerous, with a total of up to 1,500 present on occasion, whilst Barnacle Geese are sometimes seen. Wintering duck include up to 700 Mallard (usually in severe winters), 150 Goldeneye and lesser numbers of Wigeon, Tufted Duck and Goosander.

The area is a good place in which to observe the spring migration of Oystercatcher, whilst movements of Lapwing, Golden Plover, thrushes and finches can be conspicuous in spring and autumn.

Breeding birds include Mute Swan, Mallard, Goosander, Ringed Plover, large numbers of Sand Martin and several pairs of Yellow Wagtail.

B7 RIVER TWEED, BETWEEN KELSO AND COLDSTREAM

OS ref.: NT 724343 to 849401
OS map: sheet 74

Habitat and Access

An area with similar characteristics to the Teviot haughlands, the interest is again in wintering wildfowl and passage birds. There are several good vantage points along the two roads that traverse the area – the A698 Kelso to Coldstream road on the north bank of the Tweed and the B6350 Kelso to Cornhill road on the south bank. A circular tour can be devised using these roads, taking in the Hirsel (B8) at the same time. Birgham Haugh (NT 790380), viewed from the south side, is a good site for a variety of species representative of the area. Access to the north bank of the river at NT 795391 is from Birgham village – walk west and re-join the main road via the anglers' footpath to the west of Birgham.

Species

As many as 350 Whooper Swan and up to 50 Mute Swan winter in the Wark/Coldstream area. Goose numbers usually reach about 2,000 (maximum 4,000), mostly composed of Greylag, but with some Pink-footed in addition. The river and adjacent haughland are used by dabbling duck such as Teal, up to 250 Wigeon and 1,400 Mallard. The peak counts are generally during hard winters. Tufted Duck, up to 300 Goldeneye and 150 Goosander have been recorded. This is one of the few sites in the Borders which receives regular visits of Smew. Miscellaneous wintering species include inland feeding Cormorant and small numbers of Golden Plover, Lapwing and Redshank.

Breeding birds include those species listed for the Teviot Haughlands with Yellow Wagtail a particular speciality of Birgham/Springhall Haughs, where there is a population of 5–10 pairs, including breeding birds of the *flava*-type. The riverside and adjacent fields at Birgham are the best area; Ringed Plover and Sand Martin also breed here, whilst passage waders such as Greenshank, Ruff and Green Sandpiper are a possibility in July/August.

B8 THE HIRSEL

OS ref.: NT 827403
OS map: sheet 74

Habitat

The Hirsel is a 1,214-hectare private estate located 1 mile (1.6 km) north and east of Coldstream. It is of outstanding importance for both waterfowl and woodland species. The main attraction is Hirsel lake, a shallow water body (averaging less than 1.5 m) that occupies about 17 hectares, fringed by reeds along its north shore and wooded to the south. The lake was created from a damp hollow in 1786 and with the exception of Yetholm and Hoselaw Lochs in the Cheviot foothills, Hirsel lake is the largest inland lowland open water body in the Borders.

The adjacent policy woodlands at Dundock Wood were planted in the late eighteenth century and comprise mostly Oak, Ash and Pine, with a dense understorey of Azalea and Rhododendron which provides excellent warbler habitat. Selective thinning and re-planting have formed a mixed and structured woodland, with good canopy, understorey and shrub layers. The strips of woodland to the south of the lake probably date from the later nineteenth century.

Leet Water, a small tributary of the Tweed, meanders through wet pasture land to the east, bordered by more deciduous woodland.

Despite its man-made origins, the diverse mixture of high quality habitats at the Hirsel mean that it supports one of the highest breeding bird diversities in south-east Scotland. The lake is of regional, if not national, importance for passage and wintering wildfowl (especially Whooper Swan, Mallard, Shoveler and Goosander). The area is designated a Site of Special Scientific Interest.

Species

Nearly 150 species have been recorded at the Hirsel. Mallard and Coot are the dominant species on the lake, whilst Little Grebe, Heron, Mute Swan, Canada Goose, Shoveler, Tufted Duck, Pochard and Moorhen have all bred in recent years; Ruddy Duck are usually present in summer. Sedge Warbler and Reed Bunting nest in the reed beds.

Great Spotted Woodpecker

Because of the proximity of the River Tweed, many waterfowl use Hirsel lake as a roost, especially if the river is in spate or disturbed by anglers. Peak counts are usually recorded in late autumn and early winter. Waders are scarce due to the absence of extensive mud around the edges of the lake. Water Rail are present throughout the year and may possibly breed, but they are more numerous in winter.

Dundock Wood holds breeding Great Spotted Woodpecker, Redstart, Garden Warbler, Blackcap, Pied and Spotted Flycatchers, together with two species which have become something of a speciality at the Hirsel: Marsh Tit and Hawfinch.

The Leet has breeding Common Sandpiper, Grey Wagtail, Dipper and Kingfisher. Goosander, Sand Martin and passage Yellow Wagtails occur. Grassland areas along the Leet are used by hunting raptors. The adjacent mixed woodland with many over mature trees is an ideal passerine habitat; Green Woodpecker and Jay can be seen here, Pied Flycatcher breed and Nuthatch have been recorded (bred in 1989). The fruit trees that grow between the stable block and the house are especially attractive to Hawfinch.

Swifts annually occupy nest-boxes sited below the windows of the mansion.

Access

The main entrance to the Hirsel is signposted off the A698 Kelso to Coldstream road at the south-east Lodge (NT 837934), on the outskirts of Coldstream. There is a car park near to a stable block (NT 827401) which is being developed as a visitor centre, about 1 mile (1.6 km) from the road. From here, signposted paths lead off around the estate. Route leaflets and bird lists are available.

A second car park is situated on the A697 Coldstream to Edinburgh road, next to Dundock Wood (NT 820395).

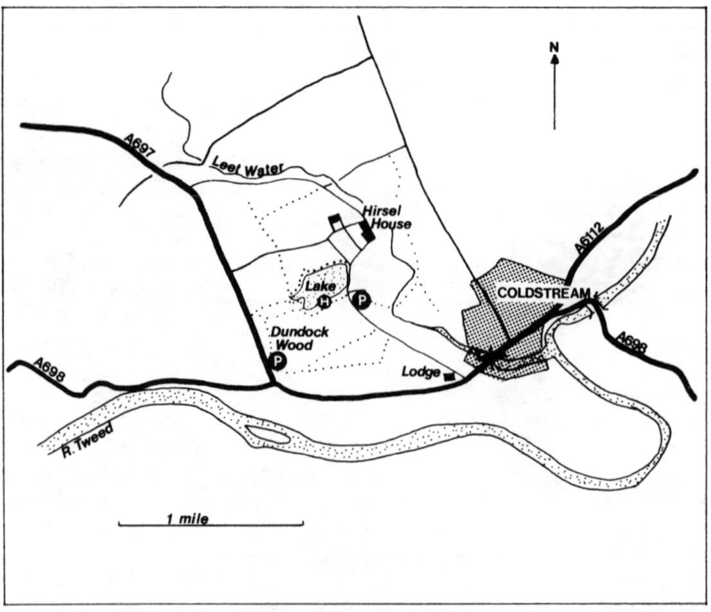

Several paths are open to the public and provide good views of most of the best bird areas. It is possible to walk around the lake (3/4 mile (1.2 km)), although the height of the reeds reduces visibility around much of the shore. A recently constructed hide, the result of the labours of the Borders SOC branch, has overcome this problem to an extent and the dam shore also provides some good vantage points.

Another path (1 1/4 miles (2 km)) leads between the main house and the old stable block and down to Leet Water. This crosses the River Leet and heads southwards, re-crossing the river and returning back to the Visitor Centre car park.

There is a bus service connecting Coldstream with Kelso, Berwick-upon-Tweed and Edinburgh.

Timing

The bird interest at the Hirsel is sustained throughout the year. Both the lake and the woods have considerable populations of breeding species and a spring or early summer visit is therefore very rewarding. Waterfowl numbers increase after the end of the breeding season as passage birds move through and large numbers use the lake as a roost during autumn and winter.

Access is possible virtually all year, except at Christmas and New Year.

Calendar

Some of the more interesting species likely to be seen.

April–June: Breeding bird activity on the lake and in the woods dominates the interest. Mid-June is the best time for Shoveler and Pochard ducklings. Dundock Wood is very colourful at this time due to the flowering Rhododendron and Azaleas.

July: Duck enter eclipse plumage. Mid-summer is perhaps the least exciting time to visit.

August–October: Waterfowl numbers start to build up; Mallard and Coot are the most numerous species, but peak counts have included 165 Mute Swan, 400 Wigeon and 300 Goosander. Shoveler numbers usually reach about 100 by October. Passage Green and Wood Sandpiper have been recorded along the Leet.

November–December: Large numbers of Whooper Swan (maximum count 120) sometimes join the over-wintering waterfowl. Up to 1,000 Greylag and 400 Pink-footed Geese, 4,000 Mallard, 150 Teal, 100+ Wigeon and *c.* 90 Shoveler have been recorded. Diving ducks, especially Goldeneye, tend not to build up until late winter/early spring: counts of 100 Pochard and 350 Goosander have been made. Coot numbers have exceeded 300 birds on occasion, but have declined greatly in recent years.

Scaup, Smew and Pintail are seen annually, whilst Slavonian and Black-necked Grebes, Canada Goose, Mandarin, Gadwall, Red-crested Pochard and American Wigeon have been known to occur. March is the best month in which to see Marsh Tit and Hawfinch.
For further information contact: The Estate Office, The Hirsel, Coldstream TD12 4LF, or visit the Information Centre.

References

'Birdwatching at the Hirsel', Ray Murray, *Scottish Bird News* (December 1987).
Borders Bird Report 1986, pp. 54–6, ed. Ray Murray.
Birds of the Borders, R.D. Murray (1986).

ADDITIONAL SITES

Site and Grid Reference	Habitat	Main Bird Interest	Peak Season
a. Bemersyde Moss SWT reserve NT 616339 Sheet 74	Shallow ponds & marsh with surrounding emergent vegetation and Willow carr	Over 10,000 prs. Black-headed Gull breed. Also 10–12 pr Tufted Duck & Grasshopper Warbler	June–Aug.
		Water Rail, Shoveler, Pochard, Moorhen	All year
		Wintering wildfowl, inc. Greylag Geese & Whooper Swan	Oct.–Mar.

Permit required – contact David Grieve, Forleys Park, Goslawdales, Selkirk TD7 4FP. There is an observation hide at this site.

Site and Grid Reference	Habitat	Main Bird Interest	Peak Season
b. Burnmouth NT 959610 Sheet 67	Coastal migration pt, in ESE facing cleft. 2 steep gullies & coastal slopes with gardens & thick scrub.	Passage warblers, Robin, thrushes etc. Occasional rare passerine migrants. Also, passage seabirds	Mar.–May & Aug.–Nov.
	Cliffs to north	Breeding seabirds, inc. Fulmar, Kittiwake, Guillemot & Razorbill	May–July
c. Hoselaw Loch SWT reserve NT 808318 Sheet 74	Freshwater loch, peat bog & surrounding farmland	Wintering wildfowl, inc. large numbers of roosting Greylag Geese	Oct.–Mar.
		Large assemblies of male Goosander in May	

Permit required – contact Keith Robeson, 12 Albert Place, Kelso, Roxburghshire TD5 7JL

Site and Grid Reference	Habitat	Main Bird Interest	Peak Season
d. Lindean Reservoir Borders RC NT 502292 Sheet 73	Small inland waterbody with sanctuary area & hide. Path around edge	Common waterfowl. Little & Great Crested Grebes, Tufted Duck, Whinchat, Sedge Warbler	Apr.–Aug.
		Wigeon, Teal, Pochard, Goldeneye, Goosander & Whooper Swan	Oct.–Mar.
e. Yetholm Loch SWT reserve NT 803279 Sheet 74	Shallow loch and fen	Feeding waterfowl, inc. Great Crested Grebe, Shoveler & Pochard	May–June
		Wintering wildfowl, inc. Whooper Swan, Pink-footed Geese and Teal	Oct.–Mar.

CENTRAL

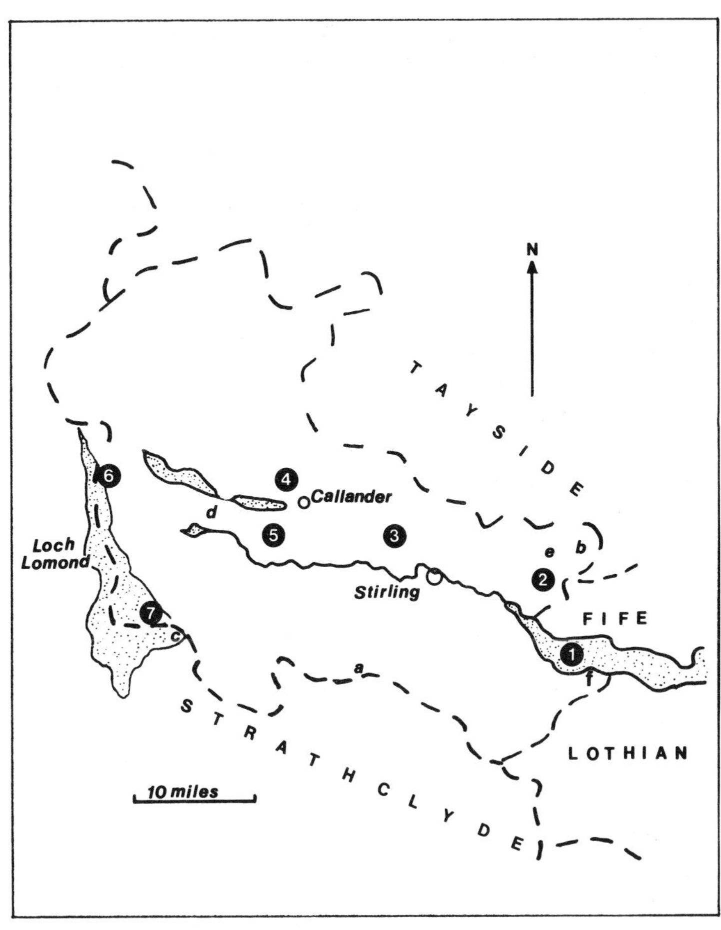

Main sites
C1. Forth Estuary
C2. Gartmorn Dam Country Park
C3. Doune Ponds
C4. Pass of Leny
C5. Lake of Menteith
C6. Inversnaid RSPB Reserve
C7. Inchcailloch

Additional sites
a. Carron Valley Reservoir
b. Dollar Glen
c. Endrick Mouth
d. Queen Elizabeth Forest Park
e. Tillicoultry Glen
f. Blackness Castle

C1 FORTH ESTUARY **OS map: sheets 57, 58 & 65**

Habitat

This is the section of the Forth extending from Stirling eastwards to the road bridge at Queensferry. The area is largely an industrial domain and the banks of the river are lined with various factories, chemical plants and power stations. Grangemouth docks lie on the south shore of the middle reaches of the estuary. Although aesthetically uninspiring, the area is of major importance for passage and wintering birds, especially ducks and waders. Large areas of invertebrate rich inter-tidal mud are available for feeding birds.

Timing

The estuary is at its most productive for birds during the autumn and winter; August/September and December–February are probably the optimum periods for most of the sites detailed below. A visit to the sites around Grangemouth, however, is likely to be rewarding at any time of year. Ideally, visits should be within three hours of high water.

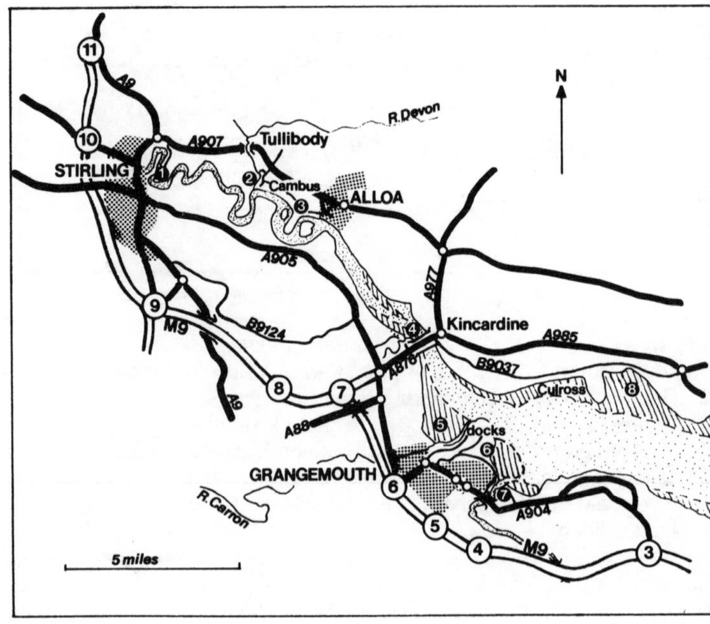

Access

1 Cambuskenneth

OS ref.: NS 808939

This section of river is tidal more by virtue of the water 'backing up' at high tide, rather than by saline water coming this far upstream. It is not a particularly rich feeding area, but does attract winter wildfowl such as Pochard, Tufted Duck, Goldeneye and Goosander, especially when static freshwater bodies begin to freeze over.

Cambuskenneth can be easily reached on foot from the centre of Stirling, by way of a footbridge across the river, or by car along a minor road to the Abbey, off the A907 road between Stirling and Alloa.

Cornton, immediately west of the Auld Brig near the town centre, is another good location.

2 Cambus Pool

OS ref.: NS 847936

This is a flood pool from the River Forth, trapped behind the embankment and is managed by the Scottish Wildlife Trust as a wildlife management area. The water is slightly brackish and tends to dry out at the margins in late summer. Recent conservation work has established a shingle spit, areas of reeds and screening trees and shrubs. It is of particular interest during the spring and autumn and now has a fairly impressive bird list. Access to the site is gained from the A907 Alloa to Stirling road: turn off south onto an unclassified road to the distillery, signed 'Cambus' just west of the turning to Tullibody. Cross the disused railway line, turn right at the junction ahead, then bear left over the bridge across the River Devon – there is room for a few cars to park on the roadside here, near to the road end. From here, follow the (often muddy) right of way that leads along the right-hand bank of the River Devon, until it joins the River Forth. Dipper and Grey Wagtail often frequent this area in winter. A track alongside the River Forth leads to Cambus Pool.

There is a bus service to the Cambus turn-off from Stirling and Alloa.

The optimum times to visit are probably from mid-April to late May and again from late June to early September. Wader migration should be at its peak during these periods. The pool is best watched at high tide, if possible in the early morning before disturbance by local dog walkers and shooters (Sept.–Jan.) occurs.

Heron, Cormorant, Kestrel, Sparrowhawk and Black-headed Gull are present all year. Small numbers of Mallard, Coot, Moorhen and Lapwing breed; up to three pairs of Sedge Warbler and one or two pairs of Reed Bunting nest in scrub and emergent vegetation. Gadwall, Teal, Shoveler and Red-breasted Merganser (spring only) occur on passage. The area is most notable for migrant waders, however, including occasional rarities. Ringed Plover, Dunlin, Ruff, Black-tailed Godwit, Whimbrel, Spotted Redshank, Greenshank, Green, Wood and Common Sandpipers are all regular on passage. The pool is also an excellent place for watching hirundines in late summer. In winter, Little Grebe, Whooper Swan, Tufted Duck, Goldeneye, Goosander, Peregrine, Water Rail, Jack Snipe, various gulls, Guillemot, Short-eared Owl and Kingfisher (up to three individuals) are regularly seen.

3 Tullibody and Alloa Inches

OS ref.: NS 86/92 & 87/91

This section of river lies between Cambus and Alloa and holds large concentrations of wildfowl and a variety of wader species during the winter. The site is particularly important for wildfowl during severe winter weather.

Tullibody Inch can be viewed by walking eastwards along the north bank of the Forth from the village of Cambus: take the turn off the A907 mentioned above for Cambus Pool, but turn left then right in Cambus village, along Forth St. There is room for one or two cars to park at the end of this lane. A track beyond the locked red gate leads onto the river bank. The small pool upstream, at the mouth of the Devon, sometimes holds passage waders.

Access is also possible from Alloa, by taking a right turn off the A907 immediately after the cricket ground when travelling into the town, then the second right turn afterwards. Continue until the road degenerates into a rough track, then park and walk on a right of way to the shore at Longcarse Farm. The surrounding farmland here holds good numbers of Grey Partridge. Where the dismantled railway crosses the River Forth there is a large Cormorant roost of approximately 100 birds. The area also has a resident population of between 50 and 70 Shelduck. Several hundred Pink-footed Geese sometimes frequent the area in March/April.

4 Kincardine Bridge

OS ref.: NS 92/87

This comparatively undeveloped part of the estuary can hold moderate numbers of both wildfowl and waders. If approaching from Kincardine, turn left off the A876 immediately before the bridge and park ¼ mile (0.4 km) later under the bridge itself. A small pier on the other side of the railway line makes a good vantage point, or walk westwards along the sea wall. Access to the south bank here is possible by crossing the bridge and then taking the first turning on the right. Keep right at the corner ahead, cross over Pow Burn ½ mile (0.8 km) later and park on the right; a public path leads to the Forth foreshore. Waders roost on the salting below the Pow Burn.

5 Skinflats

OS ref.: NS 92/83

The inter-tidal and foreshore areas at Skinflats, situated on the southern shore of the estuary between Kincardine and Grangemouth Docks, are some of the most important of all those on the Forth estuary.

Over 140 species have been recorded at Skinflats and it is of great significance for wintering duck and waders: almost all of the Forth's Pintail winter here and very large numbers of Shelduck occur; peak wader counts include over 2,000 Knot, 1,200 Redshank, 5,000 Dunlin and

2,000 Golden Plover. Passage birds include a wide variety of species, amongst which hundreds of Grey and Ringed Plover are significant. Raptors that regularly hunt over the area include Sparrowhawk, Kestrel, Merlin, Peregrine and Short-eared Owl. Black Tern are possible in spring and autumn. Twite and Snow Bunting sometimes frequent the seaward side of the embankment in winter, and this is a reliable site for small numbers of Lapland Bunting.

The RSPB lease 413 hectares here from the Crown Estate Commissioners and a private landowner. The reserve was established primarily to underline the importance of the area and to help ward off threats of reclamation for industry, rather than as a public site with viewing facilities, since feeding birds tend to be very distant and at roost they are easily disturbed. Inland from the reserve at its southern end is an area of subsidence pools and farmland known as Skinflats Pools which is currently in Local Authority ownership. These saline lagoons have produced records of many outstanding waders in the past, whilst the bushes around the lagoons can be good for migrant passerines such as Whinchat, Redstart and various warblers.

At the present time, however, the future of the pools is uncertain and problems of access along the north bank of the River Carron and of disturbance both here and on the saltmarsh mean that the only access to Skinflats that can be recommended is to view the area from Grangemouth Docks, looking west across the River Carron. This is reached by taking the A904 into Grangemouth and taking the West Docks Road from the roundabout at the western end of town. There are several vantage points along this road where parking is possible and it is feasible to obtain good views of the large flocks of Shelduck, Pintail, Knot, Redshank and Dunlin.

6 Grangeburn

OS ref.: NS 95/82–3

This burn mouth discharges into the Forth to the south-east of Grangemouth Docks and is approached along the East Docks Road. (A permit is required from the Forth Port Authorities.) It should be worked on a rising tide, when any waders will be pushed up into the burn and may roost on the adjacent reclaimed land. This is one of the more reliable sites for Curlew Sandpiper in early autumn. Up to 1,000 Teal are amongst a number of duck species that can be found on the open pools here, whilst the reed-fringed pool within the docks area may have Pintail, Shoveler and Snipe. Black-tailed Godwit and Ruff are faily regular through the autumn and the godwits can often be seen in winter also. Arctic, Great and occasionally Pomarine Skua occur in September and October; other seabirds include Gannet, Kittiwake and auks in late summer.

7 Kinneil

OS ref.: NS 96/81

The mudflats and reclaimed land at Kinneil lie between Grangemouth Docks and Bo'ness. Take the A904 east out of Grangemouth, turning left onto a small road to the sewage works, signed 'Kinneil Kerse', 1½ miles

(2.4 km) out of the industrial area. Park on the road verge *c.* ½ mile (0.8 km) further along, from where it is possible to walk along a rough track to the sea wall, about 300 metres distant. This is an excellent vantage point at high tide, although care should be taken to avoid the sludge on some parts of the embankment. Large numbers of Great Crested Grebe are present in autumn and late winter, whilst Shelduck can be seen year round – a flock of over 2,000 moulting birds gather in August and September, although they tend to congregate well offshore. Many of these birds remain right through the winter. Scaup are sometimes also present. The sewage settling tank immediately east of the Avon mouth is now largely overgrown and attracts few waders, although it is a good place for pipits and wagtails. Many of the waders now use the large lagoon behind the sea wall; the composition of the flocks varies through the year, but Knot, Dunlin and Redshank numbers are usually high and Black-tailed Godwit are regular in autumn and winter, whilst the marshy ground around the lagoon is good for Jack Snipe. In autumn, over 20 species of wader can be seen in this area and it is probably the best place in Scotland for seeing Little Stint. The best time to visit is on a rising tide; beware of disturbing the roosting/feeding waders here at high tide, however. Up to 20 Pintail occur in the lagoon and offshore; 1,000 Teal (the same ones as at Grangeburn) are sometimes present in the estuary. Sparrowhawk, Kestrel, Merlin, Peregrine and Short-eared Owl often hunt over the area.

The Falkirk District Council tip attracts many gulls, including Glaucous. Large flocks of Linnet and lesser numbers of Twite are not uncommon in winter. The sea wall sometimes harbours migrant passerines, for instance Whinchat and Wheatear; Sedge Warbler migrate through the lagoon area in autumn; several vagrant species have also been recorded here. Small numbers of Rock Pipit over-winter.

8 Torry Bay

OS ref.: NT 01/85

This bay, situated on the north shore of the estuary five miles (8 km) west of Dunfermline, actually lies within Fife but is included here for the sake of completeness. It is approached via the B9037 road to Culross; a track along the northern perimeter of the bay affords excellent views of the varied foreshore. The area holds important numbers of wintering Mallard, Wigeon, Red-breasted Merganser, Knot, Dunlin, Black and Bar-tailed Godwits, Curlew and Redshank. Passage Brent Geese sometimes occur in small numbers.

Between Torry Bay and Kincardine Bridge lie two major wader roosts, located on the ash settling pans of Kincardine and Longannet Power Stations. However, access to both of these sites is possible by permit only. Telescope viewing is also possible from the railway bridge at NS 965857, a short walk from the Culross Road. On very high tides, these sites can hold several thousand waders; Longannet also boasts a regular autumn roost of over 1,000 Sandwich Tern and is a good location in which to see Little and Glaucous Gulls.

Calendar

Some of the more interesting species likely to be seen.

April–May: Passage waders can be good; Curlew Sandpiper and Spotted Redshank have been a feature of recent years; Pectoral Sandpiper have also been recorded. White Wagtail passage in late April.

June–July: In common with most estuarine areas, the Forth has a relatively restricted breeding bird community: Shelduck and about 50 pairs of Common Tern breed, but there is little else to interest the birder here in summer. The return passage of waders, especially involving small numbers of Whimbrel and Greenshank, generally starts during July.

August–October: Large numbers of terns and skuas sometimes enter the estuary during late summer and early autumn. Other seabirds also occur, especially during easterly gales, the species most frequently involved being Manx Shearwater, Gannet and Kittiwake.

Passage waders such as Ruff, Black-tailed Godwit, Whimbrel and Spotted Redshank may occur during August, but the prime month for migrant shorebirds is September, when many thousands of birds can be seen. Wildfowl numbers also build up at this time, although the huge moult-flock of Shelduck will already be complete.

November–March: The very large numbers of over-wintering waterfowl and waders dominate the interest, although birds of prey and flocks of finches and buntings in the sparse vegetation are also important. White-winged gulls can usually be found at Kinneil and Culross/Torry Bay.

References

'Birdwatching on the Forth estuary', D.M. Bryant, *Scottish Birds*, vol. 11, no. 3, 1980.

C2 GARTMORN DAM COUNTRY PARK

OS ref.: NS 920943
OS map: sheet 58

Habitat

Gartmorn Dam was constructed in 1713 and is one of the oldest man-made reservoirs in Scotland. It is a shallow, rich water body with a great diversity of aquatic plant and invertebrate animal life. As a consequence of this, Gartmorn is extremely attractive to wildfowl. The 75-hectare Country Park includes not only the freshwater reservoir, but also a small amount of woodland and unimproved grassland. It incorporates land designated a Site of Special Scientific Interest and a Local Nature Reserve. Clackmannan District Council manage the site and employ a full time Ranger Service.

Timing

The Country Park is open from dawn to dusk throughout the year. There is a visitor centre near to the park entrance, open daily between April and September and open at weekends only from October to March. The birdlife is of interest all year, although peak activity is during the breeding season and in winter.

Access

From Alloa, take the A908 to Sauchie – the Country Park is clearly signposted thereafter. There are three car parks near to the entrance. A bus service from Alloa passes within ¼ mile (0.4 km) of the park. A 3-mile (4.8 km) footpath circuits the reservoir and two bird observation hides provide excellent views over the local nature reserve.

Species

Two or three pairs of Great Crested Grebe, about ten pairs of Little Grebe, three or four pair of Tufted duck and a couple of pairs of Heron breed at Gartmorn Dam. Passage birds have included Red-necked and Slavonian Grebes, various wildfowl and waders, and occasional Osprey. In winter up to 80 Whooper Swan occur, whilst 1,200–1,600 Wigeon, around 600 Teal, 2,000 Mallard, 60 Pochard, 200–300 Tufted Duck and 40 Goldeneye can be present. Pintail, Shoveler, American Wigeon, Scaup, Smew, Goosander and Red-crested Pochard are all occasional winter visitors.

Calendar

Some of the more interesting species likely to be seen.

March–April: Wintering waterfowl disperse, leaving resident species, such as Little and Great Crested Grebe, Mute Swan, Mallard, Tufted Duck, Coot and Moorhen. Reed Bunting take up territory in scrub areas.

May–June: Breeding season – waterside birds as above. Seven species of warbler breed in the surrounding woodland and scrub; Woodcock can be seen roding at dusk; Great Spotted Woodpecker and a variety of other woodland species breed.

July–September: Wildfowl enter eclipse plumage and are at their least impressive during July and August. Possibility of passage waders occurring.

October–March: Large numbers of over-wintering wildfowl (see above). Herons, Snipe and Water Rail can be seen; Waxwing, Brambling, Redwing and Fieldfare use the surrounding area.

Ranger

Michael Callan, Senior Countryside Ranger, Clackmannan District Council, Gartmorn Dam Country Park, Alloa. Tel: Alloa 214319.

C3 DOUNE PONDS

OS ref.: NN 726019
OS map: sheet 57

Habitat

Doune Ponds is a recently created reserve managed by Stirling District Council and is located immediately north-west of the village of Doune, on the Stirling to Callander road. Although not, as yet, a particularly notable birding location, on-going conservation work is helping to establish a varied and interesting mixture of habitats and the area has the potential to become a wildlife site of considerable local importance.

A series of pools occupy what was once a sand and gravel pit, closed in the mid-1970s. The largest of these is only 1.5 metres deep, although this may deepen in winter. This is linked, in the west, to a small silt pond which is now surrounded by a prolific growth of emergent vegetation. To the north, a small scrape has been constructed for wading birds.

A plantation of Scots Pine, Larch and Beech was established along the western edge during the early 1970s to screen the site; Willow and Birch have colonised much of the reserve, whilst mixed plantations surround a recently formed marshy pool.

Access

Doune Ponds are reached by taking the A820 Dunblane road east from its junction with the A84 Callander–Stirling road. Turn left onto Moray Street immediately before Doune church is reached, then take the second left to a car park beside the ponds. There is an information board at the reserve entrance.

There is a bus service to Doune from Stirling and Callander; the ponds are within easy walking distance.

Spotted Flycatcher

The reserve is open at all times. A nature trail, slightly over ½ mile (0.8 km) long, links the principal areas of interest. Please keep to this trail and note that dogs must be kept on a lead. Hides overlook the central and west ponds – keys can be obtained from the 'Spar' shop, 36

Main Street, Doune. The eastern hide is accessible to wheelchair users. Please note that access around the north pond is not permitted. A leaflet describing the reserve is available from local tourist information offices.

Species

All year: Heron, Mute Swan, Tufted Duck, Buzzard, Coot, Moorhen, Snipe, Coal Tit, Goldcrest, Siskin. Hawfinches have been recorded in the area.

In spring and summer the reserve holds Oystercatcher, Common Sandpiper, Whitethroat, Sedge Warbler and Reed Bunting.

To date, over 90 species have been recorded since 1980. This is a developing reserve and hopefully will attract more birds and bird-watchers in the future. Records from the reserve are therefore of great importance and should be entered in the reserve log-book in the east hide, or forwarded to the Stirling District Council Countryside Ranger Service, Beechwood House, St Ninian's Road, Stirling FK8 2AD.

C4 PASS OF LENY

OS ref.: NN 595089
OS map: sheet 57

Habitat

The Pass of Leny is the narrow gorge containing the fast-flowing outflow from Loch Lubnaig, to the east of Ben Ledi. It lies mostly within the extended boundary of the Queen Elizabeth Forest Park (see Additional Sites) and is one of the better sites within the park for birds. Oak woodland adorns the valley sides, with some alder growing nearer to the river and conifer plantations on the higher slopes.

Species

Resident woodland birds include Buzzard, Sparrowhawk, Great Spotted Woodpecker, Siskin and Redpoll. Crossbill can usually be found at the western end of the glen. Dipper and Grey Wagtail frequent the river.

In spring and summer, Tree Pipit, Redstart, Wood Warbler, Garden Warbler, Whinchat, Spotted Flycatcher and Cuckoo are present. Goosander and Common Sandpiper breed along the watercourses.

Redwing and Fieldfare are common during October and November; a winter visit should produce the resident species, good numbers of tits, Redpoll and Bullfinch.

From Coireachrombie, at the north-western end of the glen, it is possible to ascend Ben Ledi (879 metres). Capercaillie are occasionally glimpsed on the lower section of this path (especially early in the morning), but they are very scarce here. Above the tree line, Wheatear, Ring Ousel and Raven can be found in spring, with occasional Snow Bunting in winter. A few Ptarmigan occur near the summit. (Please note that adequate clothing and footwear are essential for this climb.)

Access

The best way to approach the Pass of Leny is to take the cycleway and footpath which runs south of the river between Kilmahog and Coireachrombie: the oakwood area mid-way along this track is particularly good. Kilmahog lies 1 mile (1.6 km) west of Callander on the A84. There are car parks at both Kilmahog and Coireachrombie.

A steeper climb through oak woodland and conifer plantation, following FC trails, is possible from the Falls of Leny car park, located on the A84, 1 mile (1.6 km) west of Kilmahog. This area is less interesting for birds, however.

A bus service connects Callander/Kilmahog with Stirling.

The Stirling District Ranger Service operates over the cycleway and organises guided walks in the area – contact Beechwood House, St Ninians Road, Stirling FK8 2AD for details.

C5 LAKE OF MENTEITH

OS ref.: NN 57/00
OS map: sheet 57

Habitat

A large, low-lying water body situated at the foot of a ridge of hills that run from Aberfoyle to Callander. A narrow belt of emergent vegetation fringes the lake, which is surrounded by arable ground, a small area of lowland heath to the west, with deciduous and coniferous woodland to the south. A wooded peninsular extends into the lake from the south shore, with a small wooded island, Inchmahome, just off its north-west tip. The lake is heavily fished and the disturbance caused by the small outboard-engined boats probably explains the paucity of breeding waterfowl.

Species

Three or four pairs of Great Crested Grebe are usually present on the lake from April through to September; they attempt to nest in most years, but their breeding success is poor.

Lake of Menteith is primarily of interest during the winter, when around 50–100 Mallard (exceptionally up to 500), small numbers of Tufted Duck and Pochard, 15–20 Goosander (mid-winter) and up to 50 Goldeneye (late winter) can be present. The lake is an important roost site for Pink-footed Geese, with up to 2,000–3,000 having been recorded, plus small numbers of Greylag Geese.

In early spring the lake attracts good numbers of hirundines.

Access

Lake of Menteith is reached via the A873 Stirling–Aberfoyle road, which passes alongside its northern shore. There are three useful vantage points from which to scan the lake:

Port of Menteith car park

OS ref.: NN 583009

The jetty here affords the most comprehensive views. Weather permitting, there is a boat service across to the priory on Inchmahome between April and September.

North shore

OS ref.: NN 568010

There is room for a few cars to park on the A873 roadside, 1 mile (1.6 km) west of Port of Menteith. A stile gives access to the shore. This is a useful viewpoint for the western part of the lake.

East shore

OS ref.: NN 588003

This layby and public access point is a good vantage point for the south-east corner of the lake.

There is a bus service connecting Port of Menteith with Stirling and Aberfoyle.

C6 INVERSNAID RSPB RESERVE

OS ref.: NN 337088
OS map: sheet 56

Habitat

The RSPB reserve at Inversnaid is situated on the east shore of Loch Lomond, some 4 miles (6.4 km) south of its apex. Deciduous woodland growing on the steep hillside above the loch leads to a ridge of crags with moorland beyond. A part of the 374-hectare reserve is classified as a Site of Special Scientific Interest.

Access

Inversnaid is reached by taking the B829 westwards from Aberfoyle. Turn left at the junction with an unclassified road after about 12 miles (19 km) – this road terminates at the Inversnaid Hotel car park some 4 miles (6 km) later. An alternative approach that may be feasible during the summer is to take the pedestrian ferry across Loch Lomond from Inveruglas on the west bank. Contact Inversnaid Hotel for details (tel: 087 786 223).

From the north-west corner of the hotel car park, the reserve is entered by walking northwards along the West Highland Way, which closely follows the lochshore for 600 metres. Just beyond the boathouse, the trail branches off to the right. At first it climbs through an area of open birch wood, before pasing into more dense oak woodland. The trail emerges onto the open hill and, after crossing a small burn, climbs to a viewpoint affording a superb vista of Loch Lomond and the surrounding mountains. The trail then descends to another burn followed by a second viewpoint. From here the path leads steeply downhill through more open woodland to rejoin the West Highland Way at the lochshore – turn left to return to the car park. Please note that Inversnaid Lodge and grounds are privately owned.

There is a daily postbus and newspaper bus service from Aberfoyle.

Wood Warbler

Timing

Inversnaid is accessible at all times and a warden is present throughout the year. The resident woodland birds make a visit worthwhile at any time of year, but the reserve is best visited between May and July, when the summer migrants make the place exceptionally interesting. Migrating wildfowl and waders can be seen using Loch Lomond during spring and autumn.

Calendar

Some of the more interesting species likely to be seen.

All year: Goosander, Buzzard, Black Grouse, Woodcock, Great Spotted Woodpecker, Grey Wagtail and Dipper, Raven, Siskin. Golden Eagle can sometimes be seen over the ridge to the east of the reserve.

May–July: Red-breasted Merganser, Common Sandpiper, Tree Pipit, Redstart, Whinchat, Wood Warbler and Spotted Flycatcher. The provision of nestboxes led to an increase in the breeding population of Pied Flycatcher, with 46 pairs nesting in 1988. However, numbers are now much reduced due to predation by Pine Marten.

October–March: The resident woodland species are joined by Fieldfare and Redwing; Goldeneye are present on loch.

Warden

Mike Trubridge, Garrison Cottage, Inversnaid, Aberfoyle, Central FK8 3TU. Tel: 087 786 244.

C7 INCHCAILLOCH

OS ref.: NS 410904
OS map: sheet 56

Habitat

The 56-hectare island of Inchcailloch is situated in the south-eastern part of Loch Lomond and is part of the much larger National Nature Reserve that includes four other islands and an area of mainland at Endrick Mouth.

Although quite small, Inchcailloch is a hilly island, rising to a maximum of 85 metres. It is largely covered with oak woodland that was mostly planted in the early nineteenth century, but alder grows around the shore and in wetter areas, whilst there are stands of Scots pine and larch on the higher ground. Greater woodrush forms a thick carpet on the woodland floor in places.

Access

At its nearest point, the island lies only 200 metres offshore and can be reached via Balmaha, on the B837, 3 miles (4.8 km) from Drymen. A ferry service and boat hire business is operated by McFarlane and Son, Balamaha Boat Yard.

There are no access restrictions, except that groups of 12 or more persons are requested to contact the Scottish Natural Heritage, Balloch Castle Country Park, Balloch, Dumbartonshire in advance (tel: 0389 58511).

There is a 2½-mile-long (4-km) nature trail around the island. Dogs must be kept on a lead.

Timing

Inchcailloch is best visited between May and July, when the breeding woodland birds provide the main interest. A mid-winter trip across to the island as part of a day's general exploration of the area can also be recommended.

Species

Buzzard, Great Spotted Woodpecker and Jay can be seen year round at Inchcailloch. During the summer the woods hold strong breeding populations of Tree Pipit, Wood Warbler, Garden Warbler and Spotted Flycatcher. Small numbers of Redstart and Blackcap are also present.

On Loch Lomond, Mallard and small numbers of Teal, Wigeon, Shoveler, Tufted Duck and Red-breasted Merganser occur at any time of year. Shelduck can be seen in spring and summer.

In winter, Greylag and Greenland White-fronted Geese can be seen in the area; these roost at Endrick Mouth (Cc.), to the south-east. Other regular wintering wildfowl include Pochard and Goldeneye.

References

Inchcailloch, leaflet published by SNH South West Region.

ADDITIONAL SITES

Site and Grid Reference	Habitat	Main Bird Interest	Peak Season
a. Carron Valley Reservoir NS 69/83 Sheet 64	Reservoir surrounded by coniferous woodland	Winter wildfowl, inc. visiting flock of 40–80 Bean Goose in Oct.	Oct.–Apr.
		Crossbill & Siskin breed	

Note: The water level of the reservoir was raised summer 1988, submerging much of the vegetation previously important for feeding wildfowl. It is not yet known what effect this will have on the numbers and variety of roosting wildfowl.

Site and Grid Reference	Habitat	Main Bird Interest	Peak Season
b. Dollar Glen NS 962989 Sheet 58	Oak woodland in steep gorge. Owned by NTS	Wood Warbler, Redstart, Spotted & Pied Flycatchers, Dipper	May–June
c. Endrick Mouth NS 42/87 Sheet 56	Swamp, lagoons, fen & willow carr at SE corner of L Lomond	Wintering wildfowl, inc. up to 100 White-fronted Geese Small numbers of passage waders in spring/autumn	Oct.–Mar.
d. Queen Elizabeth Forest Park Sheets 56 & 57	Vast and diverse area owned by FC. Conifers, Oakwoods, heather & bracken moorland, mtn summits	Woodland & Moorland species. Ptarmigan on some summits	Apr.–Oct.

Information about the Forest Park is available at the David Marshall Lodge Forest Park Visitor Centre near Aberfoyle. Open 11 am to 7 pm daily, mid-March to mid-October. See also QE Forest Park Guide, available from FC.

Site and Grid Reference	Habitat	Main Bird Interest	Peak Season
e. Tillicoultry Glen NS 914975 Sheet 58	Open valley/fast-flowing stream	Grey Wagtail, Dipper, Whitethroat	May–June
f. Blackness Castle NT 056803 Sheet 65	Estuarine foreshore on either side of Blackness Castle (park in Blackness village).	Wildfowl & waders	Oct.–Mar.

DUMFRIES AND GALLOWAY

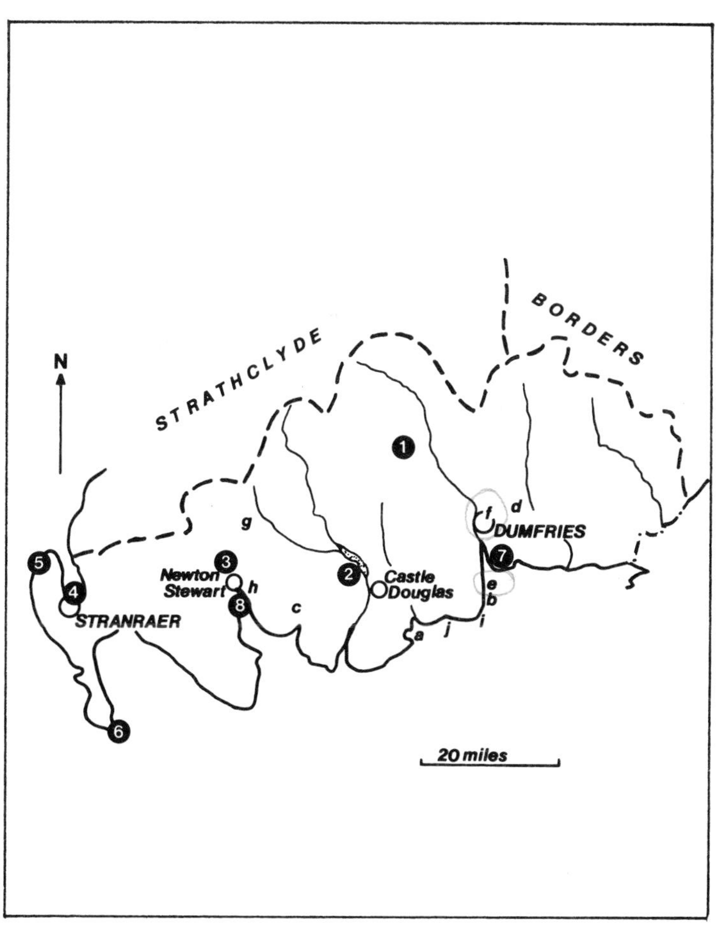

Main sites
DG1. Stenhouse Wood
DG2. Loch Ken/River Dee
DG3. Wood of Cree
DG4. Loch Ryan
DG5. Corsewall Point
DG6. Mull of Galloway
DG7. Caerlaverock
DG8. Wigtown Bay

Additional sites
a. Auchencairn Bay
b. Carsethorn
c. Carstramon
d. Castle Loch
e. Drummains Reedbed
f. Fountainbleau and Ladypark
g. Glen Trool
h. Kirroughtree
i. Southerness Point
j. Southwick Coast

DG1 STENHOUSE WOOD

OS ref.: NX 795930
OS map: sheet 78

Habitat

This lowland woodland is situated on a north-east facing hillside and contains deciduous trees of many types, including oak, ash, hazel, beech and willow. Stenhouse Wood covers 18 hectares and is owned by the Scottish Wildlife Trust. It is designated a Site of Special Scientific Interest.

The wood has two main components: the lower wood is an area of mature broadleaves and is the best area for birds, whilst the upper section of the wood has recently been replanted with deciduous species following clearance of a coniferous plantation. Open scrubland with emergent trees therefore characterises the upper slopes, leading onto open hillside. The whole site is botanically very rich and the rare ground flora is easily damaged by trampling.

Species

Sparrowhawk, Buzzard, Great Spotted and Green Woodpecker, Willow Tit and Siskin are amongst the resident birds likely to be seen. Breeding visitors include Redstart, Chiffchaff and Wood, Garden and Willow Warblers. In winter, Woodcock, Redwing and Fieldfare may be found.

Access

The reserve is approached from the village of Tynron, which lies about 1½ miles (2.4 km) to the north of the A702 Penpont to Moniaive road. Once in Tynron, cross the river and turn right at the war memorial. After ⅓ mile (0.5 km) turn right into a 'no through road'. The reserve is on the left after about ½ mile (0.8 km). There is a layby half way along the road beside the reserve on the left side.

The reserve is open to members and non-members of the SWT alike.

Timing

The reserve is always open, but please take care to avoid disturbance to nesting birds. Most migrants arrive late April/early May; May and June are the best months to visit.

DG2 LOCH KEN/RIVER DEE

OS ref.: NX 63/76 to 73/60
OS map: sheet 84 & 77

Habitat

The construction of a hydro-electric dam across the River Dee at Glenlochar, north of Castle Douglas, in 1935, has resulted in the formation of a shallow-sided loch system, just over 9 miles (14.5 km) long, flanked by marshland and meadows. Technically speaking, the southern part of the loch is still the River Dee and it is only the part to the north of the confluence of the Black Water of Dee, just below the old railway viaduct, that is referred to as Loch Ken. Extensive mudflats are revealed when the water level falls, especially along the south-western shore. The loch is bordered by hillside farmland and deciduous woods, adding to the diversity of the area.

The RSPB manages a total of over 162 hectares of marsh, meadow and broad-leaved woodland in five separate areas, although the most import-

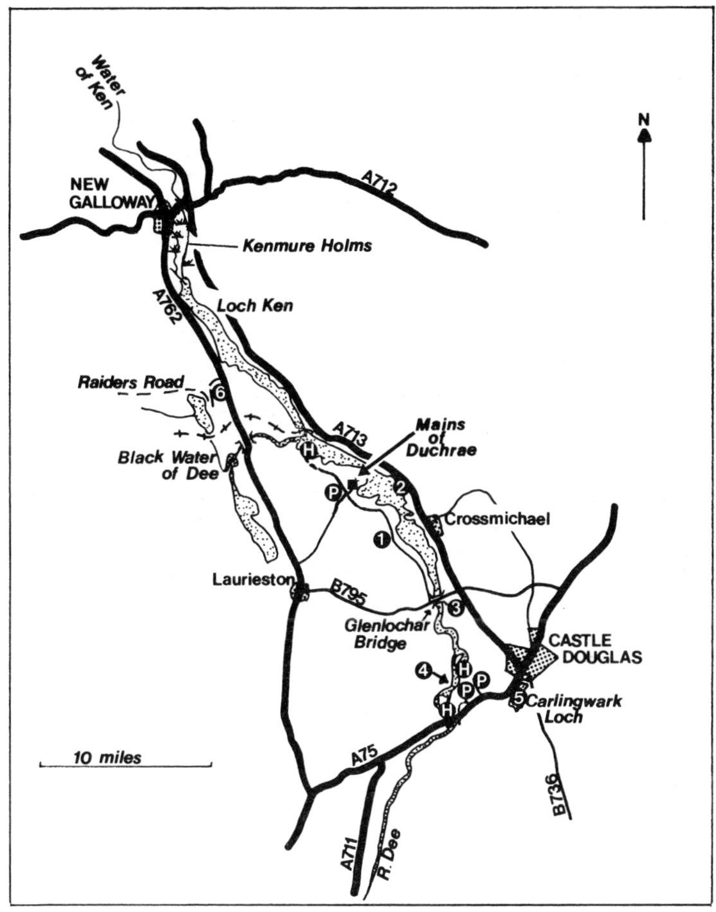

ant holdings are at Kenmure Holms near New Galloway and also that between Mains of Duchrae and Black Water of Dee. In addition, at Threave, immediately west of Castle Douglas, the National Trust for Scotland has a 348-hectare Estate of considerable ornithological interest. Three sites of Special Scientific Interest have been designated on the Ken-Dee system, between New Galloway and Glenlochar, with others at Threave and Carlingwark Loch.

Access

Good views over the area can be obtained from the roads encompassing the loch: the A762 Laurieston–New Galloway road on the west bank, the A713 New Galloway–Castle Douglas road on the east, and the road connecting these in the south, the B795 from Townhead of Greenlaw to Laurieston. The best road for viewing the River Dee marshes is the C50 from Glenlochar Bridge (see point 1, below).

The RSPB have built a car park at the entrance to the Mains of Duchrae Farm (NX 699684) and from here visitors may walk to a hide on the lochshore. The round walk is 3 miles (5 km) and affords good opportunities to see the birds in this, the most varied, part of the reserve. Fields, hedgerows, deciduous scrub and woodland and finally marshland is encountered en route. The area is good throughout the year for Willow Tit and in the breeding season for Pied Flycatcher, various warblers, field-nesting waders and breeding duck. In autumn/winter, ducks, hunting Hen Harrier and Barn Owl (always present) provide the main interest. Large groups should liaise with the RSPB warden in advance to arrange an escorted visit. Contact Ray Hawley, Midtown, Laurieston, Castle Douglas, DG7 2PP (tel: 064 45 236).

Outside the RSPB reserve, the following areas are recommended:

1. A minor road (C50) leaves the B795 northwards, immediately west of Glenlochar Bridge, 1 mile (1.6 km) from Townhead of Greenlaw; this road affords views of the south-west part of the loch, before curving back to join the A762, ½ mile (0.8 km) north of Laurieston. Please park considerately and do not cause an obstruction to other traffic. The area is a good one for wintering geese, especially at Mains of Duchrae, which is much favoured by Greenland Whitefronts and Greylag.

2. The east shore between Crossmichael and Parton, especially the pasture around Cogarth, is another regular Whitefront haunt.

3. Culvennan/Mains of Greenlaw area, south of the B795 between Glenlochar and the A713. This area is sometimes frequented by a large herd of Whooper Swan in winter; although these birds are more often seen at Threave.

4. Threave Estate (OS ref.: 74/62) is an area of farmland and marshes alongside the River Dee, providing good feeding grounds for wildfowl in autumn and winter. The Estate is entered from the A75 Castle Douglas–Bridge of Dee road, at Kelton Mains Farm, 1 mile (1.6 km) west of Castle Douglas. Maps showing the location of paths and hides are displayed at the car park. There are five hides: two on the disused railway line give good views across the fields where the geese feed, one on an island overlooks fields and the river, whilst another two on the riverbank afford views of the river and marshes. Goosander are fairly common on the river, Kingfisher are present all year.

The Estate is open all year: there is no charge. A leaflet and further information are available from a visitor centre at Threave Gardens, although this is closed in winter.

Ranger: Peter Norman, Threave Gardens, Castle Douglas, Dumfries & Galloway, DG7 1RX. Tel. Castle Douglas 2575.

5. Carlingwark Loch, on the south-west outskirts of Castle Douglas, can be comprehensively viewed from the A75, ½ mile (0.8 km) from the town centre. The loch is particularly good for diving duck in winter, such as Goldeneye and Goosander.

6. Bennan Forest (Forestry Commission). The conifers to the west of Loch Ken, north of Mossdale, are good for Siskin, Redpoll and Crossbill. The area also has a scattered population of Black Grouse, although these are now very scarce.

Access can be gained via the Raiders Road, a 10-mile (16 km) drive through the forest which starts from the A762, about 1 mile (1.6 km) north of Mossdale and emerges onto the A712 Newton Stewart–New Galloway road at Clatteringshaws Loch. It is open from late May through to October and costs £1.

Timing

There is bird activity throughout the year in this area, although mid-summer is probably the slackest time to visit. A winter visit can be strongly recommended.

Calendar

Some of the more interesting species likely to be seen.

All year: Great Crested Grebe, Goosander and dabbling ducks. Peregrine, Buzzard and Barn Owl regularly hunt over the area. Willow Tit can be found in areas of scrub Birch, Hazel and Willow; Great Spotted Woodpecker and a few Green Woodpecker frequent the more mature deciduous woodland, although the latter are very localised.

White-fronted Geese, November

March–May: Swans and geese usually depart in mid-April, although the occasional Whooper remains into early May. Marshland breeding birds include Great Crested Grebe, Teal, Shoveler, Snipe and Redshank. Sedge and Grasshopper Warblers take up territories in emergent vegetation around the lochshore. In the scattered deciduous woods Tree Pipit, Redstart, Wood Warbler and Pied Flycatcher breed. About three pairs of Common Tern usually breed. A few waders may stop over on their way north; a passage Osprey is an outside possibility.

June–July: The start of return migration in late July generally brings a few waders to the exposed mud around the south-western fringes of the loch. Breeding duck assume their nondescript eclipse plumage.

August–November: Wader passage continues and tern are occasionally present. Pintail are usually visible among dabbling duck in the River Dee marshes around the Mains of Duchrae; most Shoveler depart as winter approaches. A few dabbling duck can be found at Kenmure Holms, at the north of Loch Ken. Whooper Swan may turn up at any time from late September onwards; Greenland White-fronted Geese start to arrive in early October.

December–February: Up to 300 Greenland White-fronted Geese visit the valley, together with Greylag Geese, Wigeon, Pintail, Teal, Mallard, Goosander and Goldeneye. Whooper Swan and Greylag Geese winter in the vicinity of Threave and are joined by Pink-footed Geese from Christmas onwards. The formerly common Bean Geese are now very rare visitors to the Threave area, usually during severe weather in January and February. There is some fall-off in swan numbers by mid-winter as birds disperse further, possibly into Ireland. Hen Harrier hunt over the marshes and farmland; Great Grey Shrike are occasionally seen in mid-winter.

DG3 WOOD OF CREE

OS ref.: NX 382708
OS map: sheet 77

Habitat

An extensive area of deciduous woodland, situated on the eastern slopes above the River Cree and consisting mainly of sessile oak, birch and hazel. The RSPB owns 266 hectares of woodland and some of the riverside meadows and flood-plain on the opposite side of the river. Much of the area is designated a Site of Special Scientific Interest.

Species

Sparrowhawk, Buzzard, Woodcock, Great Spotted Woodpecker and Willow Tit are resident breeders in the woods. Characteristic summer visitors to the oakwoods include Wood Warbler, Pied Flycatcher and Redstart; Tree Pipit are common in areas of scattered trees and on the upper woodland fringe.

Along the stream courses and riverside Grey Wagtail and Dipper nest, joined in spring by Common Sandpiper. The wet meadowland adjacent to the River Cree is good for Teal, Mallard, Oystercatcher and Snipe; Water Rail breed. The surrounding countryside is a particularly good area in which to see Barn Owl.

Access

Wood of Cree is approached from Newton Stewart via the adjacent village of Minnigaff. From here follow the unclassified road on the east side of the River Cree, running parallel with the A714 Newton Stewart–Girvan road on the opposite bank. The reserve is reached some 4 miles (6.4 km) later – a parking area is marked by RSPB signs and from here a woodland track leads into the reserve. Access is possible at all times, but visitors are requested to keep to marked trails.

There are regular buses as far as Newton Stewart, just over 4 miles (6.4 km) away.

Timing

The reserve can be of interest at any time, but a May/June visit will be the most productive.

Warden

Paul Collin, Gairland, Old Edinburgh Road, Minnigaff, Newton Stewart DG8 6PL.

DG4 LOCH RYAN

OS ref.: NX 05/65
OS map: sheet 82

Habitat

Loch Ryan is a very large and mostly enclosed sealoch located in southwest Galloway. The dimensions of the loch are approximately 8 miles (13 km) from the head of the loch to the open sea and 1½–2½ miles (2.4–4 km) in width. The loch is a deep one and the shore shelves steeply with only limited inter-tidal areas, principally at the south end and at The Wig, a small bay to the west.

Species

Wintering sea-fowl provide the main interest; Red-throated and occasional Black-throated and Great Northern Divers can be seen; small numbers of Slavonian and Black-necked Grebes are also generally present, with the occasional Red-necked too. Eider are numerous, with over 300 birds often present; other sea-duck include large flocks of Scaup, Red-breasted Merganser and smaller groups of Common Scoter and Goldeneye. Long-tailed Duck are sometimes present and King Eider have been recorded on occasion. Wigeon and Mallard are the most numerous dabbling duck.

Moderate numbers of Oystercatcher and Lapwing over-winter and the area can be good for passage waders, including Golden Plover and Knot.

Both Iceland and Glaucous Gulls are likely in winter and small numbers of Black Guillemot can be seen.

Access

Loch Ryan is easily worked from the surrounding roads: the A77 on the east and south shores, and the A718 along the west shore. There are many suitable stopping places/vantage points. Recommended areas to scan are the Cairnryan area to the east (NX 06/68), the entire south shore and The Wig (NX 03/67).

Timing

A visit between October and March is recommended. Strong afternoon sunlight can restrict viewing from the east shore of the loch.

DG5 CORSEWALL POINT

OS ref.: NW 98/72
OS map: sheet 76

This excellent seawatching point is located about 3 miles (5 km) west of the entrance to Loch Ryan. It can be reached from Stranraer by taking the A718 northwards for 8 miles (13 km), turning off right onto an unclassified road to Corsewall lighthouse, 3 miles (4.8 km) away.

The optimum time to visit is in the autumn, from mid-August through to late October, when passages of large numbers of Manx Shearwater, Gannet, Shag, Kittiwake and auks can be seen. Smaller numbers of Storm and occasional Leach's Petrels, and Arctic and Great Skuas are likely, especially in westerly winds. There have been several sightings of Sabine's Gull recently.

Manx Shearwaters

DG6 MULL OF GALLOWAY

OS ref.: NX 157304
OS map: sheet 82

Habitat

A rocky headland, some 22 miles (35 km) south of Stranraer, at the tip of the Rhins peninsula. This RSPB reserve consists of ¾ mile (1.2 km) of rugged granite cliff, rising to a maximum height of just over 80 metres. The site is designated a Site of Special Scientific Interest.

Species

Nesting seabirds include Fulmar, Cormorant, Shag, Kittiwake, Guillemot, Razorbill and Black Guillemot. A few Puffin are seen in most years, but they no longer nest here. An offshore Gannet colony, currently numbering over 800 nests, is located on Scare Rocks, some 7 miles (11.3 km) east of the Mull. Large numbers of Manx Shearwater regularly pass the headland in September. Passerine migrants also occur, including various warblers and occasional Black Redstart. Stonechat and Twite are resident. The Mull of Galloway is one of the few places in Dumfries and Galloway where Corn Bunting can be seen.

Access

The reserve is reached from the Stranraer–Newton Stewart road by taking the A715 or A716 south to Drummore, then on the B7041 toward the Mull lighthouse. Access is possible at all times, but there is no warden present. Good views can be obtained from near the lighthouse; visitors are warned that the cliff edge is dangerous.

Timing

The breeding seabirds provide the principal interest here, so the best time to visit is between May and mid-July.

DG7 CAERLAVEROCK

OS ref.: NY 03/65
OS map: sheets 84 & 85

Habitat

The 5,500-hectare National Nature Reserve at Caerlaverock stretches for 6 miles (9.7 km) along the north Solway coast between the estuary of the River Nith and that of Lochar Water to the east. The extensive foreshore, saltmarsh and mud flat habitats are internationally important for wintering wildfowl, particularly Barnacle Geese. The Wildfowl and Wetlands Trust Refuge at Eastpark (NY 05/65) covers 524 hectares of saltmarsh and farmland, with excellent viewing facilities. These include 20 hides, an observatory and two observation towers. The pond immediately in front of the observatory enables up to 17 species of wildfowl to be watched at very close range.

Controlled shooting is allowed over parts of National Nature Reserve.

Species

The principal attraction is the very large numbers of wintering Pink-footed and Barnacle Geese. The inner Solway holds the entire Svalbard breeding population of Barnacle Geese – these start to arrive at Caerlaverock in late September/early October and build up to a peak of around 12,500 by mid-November. Pink-footed Geese are most numerous in late winter, usually from January through to March, when up to 5,000 roost on the merse. Both these and the smaller flocks of Greylag Geese feed on farmland managed deliberately for geese by the Wildfowl and Wetlands Trust.

As well as the geese, up to 350 Whooper Swans over-winter with smaller numbers of Bewick's Swan (usually in late October) and up to 70 Mute Swan.

Wintering dabbling duck include large numbers of Wigeon, Teal, Mallard and Pintail, with small numbers of Shoveler and Gadwall. Up to 400 Shelduck are present in late winter. Hen Harrier, Sparrowhawk,

Peregrine and Merlin regularly hunt over the saltmarsh for wintering duck, waders or passerines.

Very large numbers of Oystercatcher (up to 15,000), Golden Plover, Lapwing, Dunlin (over 5,000) and Curlew (over 3,000) roost on the saltmarsh, smaller numbers of Grey Plover, Knot and Redshank are also recorded. Passage waders include large numbers of Sanderling in May and occasional Little Stint, Curlew Sandpiper, Black-tailed Godwit, Whimbrel, Ruff and Spotted Redshank in autumn.

Access

The B725 from Dumfries to Bankend affords good general views of the merse and the eastern side of the Nith estuary. There is a parking area at NY 018653.

The Wildfowl and Wetlands Trust Refuge at Eastpark is reached by taking the signposted turning from the B725 1 mile (1.6 km) south of Bankend. Visitors should report to the observatory on arrival. A modest admission charge is levied.

Timing

Caerlaverock is an excellent area for birdwatching throughout the winter, from October to March. The Eastpark refuge is open daily; the warden conducts escorted tours at 11 am and 2 pm daily.

SNH Warden

Tadorna, Hollands Farm Road, Caerlaverock, Dumfries.

Wildfowl and Wetlands Trust Warden

Eastpark Farm, Caerlaverock, Dumfries DG1 4RS. Tel: 038777 200.

DG8 WIGTOWN BAY

OS ref.: NX 45/56 etc.
OS map: sheet 83

Habitat

Wigtown Bay is an area of merse and inter-tidal mud/sand flats formed by the estuaries of the rivers Cree and Bladnoch. A 3500-hectare Local Nature Reserve was established in 1992. In addition, the area is a Site of Special Scientific Interest and has been proposed for Ramsar and SPA designation. A sanctuary area is to established in winter 1992/93 and there are longer term plans to build birdwatching hides.

The area is bordered to the west by the Moss of Cree, whilst to the north-east lie the hills of Cairnsmore of Fleet. Newton Stewart lies upstream on the River Cree; the smaller towns of Wigtown and Creetown lie on the west and east shores of the Bay respectively.

Species

The area is an important one for wintering wildfowl and waders, including up to 10,000 Pink-footed Geese from January to May, plus up to 1,000 Greylag. Around 2,500 Oystercatcher and 2,000 Curlew winter, with lesser numbers of Shelduck, Pintail, Wigeon, Dunlin and Knot. Winter is a good time to see various raptors hunting over the area, also, especially Hen Harrier, Merlin and Peregrine.

Access

Birding is difficult owing to limited access points, long distance observation and disturbance problems. Good views of the geese can often be obtained from the Moss of Cree road, however. Turn off the A75 Newton Stewart to Creetown road 1 mile east of Newton Stewart and follow this loop road until it re-joins the A75 2 miles (3.2 km) later. The unclassified road leading east from the A714 Newton Stewart to Wigtown road, circa 2 miles (3.2 km) south of Newton Stewart affords good general views of the west side of the estuary.

Warden

Tim Adkin, Wigtown Town Hall, Wigtown, Wigtownshire.

ADDITIONAL SITES

<table>
<tr><th>Site and
Grid Reference</th><th>Habitat</th><th>Main Bird Interest</th><th>Peak Season</th></tr>
<tr><td>a. Auchencairn Bay
NX 82/50
Sheet 84</td><td>Large & Sheltered inter-tidal area</td><td>Large numbers of wintering wildfowl and waders</td><td>Oct.–Mar.</td></tr>
<tr><td colspan="4">View from unclassified road from Auchencraig to Balcary Bay. Path from road end to seabird cliffs at Balcary Heugh: nesting Fulmar, Cormorant, Shag, Kittiwake, Razorbill, Guillemot & Black Guillemot.</td></tr>
<tr><td>b. Carsethorn
NX 98/60
Sheet 84</td><td>Rocky coastline & creek</td><td>Migrant & wintering waders. Offshore Scaup very common</td><td>Aug.–May.</td></tr>
<tr><td colspan="4">See also Southerness Point.</td></tr>
<tr><td>c. Carstramon
SWT reserve
NX 592605
Sheet 83</td><td>Mixed woodland</td><td>Wood Warbler, Redstart & Pied Flycatcher, Green & Great Spotted Woodpecker</td><td>Apr.–July.</td></tr>
<tr><td>d. Castle Loch,
Lochmaben
NY 08/81
Sheet 78</td><td>Loch, fringing reedbeds & woodland</td><td>Roosting Greylag Geese & other wintering wildfowl</td><td>Jan.–Mar.</td></tr>
<tr><td>e. Drummains
Reedbed
SWT reserve
NX 984610
Sheet 84</td><td>Reedbed and marsh</td><td>Breeding Common Tern, Sedge Warbler & Reed Bunting</td><td>Apr.–July.</td></tr>
<tr><td></td><td></td><td>Wintering wildfowl & waders</td><td>Oct.–Mar.</td></tr>
<tr><td>f. Fountainbleau
and Ladypark
SWT reserve
NX 986772
Sheet 84</td><td>Wet Birchwood. Hide overlooks a newly created pond. Small visitor centre.</td><td>Willow Tit, Sedge Warbler, Redpoll & Reed Bunting</td><td>Apr.–July.</td></tr>
<tr><td>g. Glen Trool
FC
NX 400790
Sheet 77</td><td>Part of Galloway Forest Park. Loch, coniferous & oak woodland</td><td>Hen Harrier, Peregrine, Siskin & Crossbill</td><td>All year</td></tr>
<tr><td></td><td></td><td>Wood Warbler, Redstart & Pied Flycatcher</td><td>May–July.</td></tr>
<tr><td colspan="4">A 4½-mile (7.2-km) trail circuits Loch Trool. Leaflet available from Forestry Commission.</td></tr>
<tr><td>5. Kirroughtree
FC
NX 451645
Sheet 83</td><td>Streamside meadows scrub & broadleaved woodland, various conifer rotations</td><td>Buzzard, Tawny Owl, Dipper, Grey Wagtail, Wood & Garden Warblers, Jay, small numbers of Willow Tit. Also Golden Pheasant</td><td>May–July.</td></tr>
<tr><td colspan="4">From the visitor centre, the 'Papy Ha' bird trail leads through the valley of the Palnure Burn (trail length is 3½ miles or 5 miles (5.6 or 8 km) depending on route). Leaflet available from Centre.</td></tr>
<tr><td>i. Southerness Pt.
NX 97/54
Sheet 84</td><td>Peninsula extending into Solway Firth</td><td>Good seawatching vantage pt. Offshore divers, Scaup, C/V Scoter & auks. Also roosting & feeding waders, inc. large nos. Bar-tailed Godwit</td><td></td></tr>
<tr><td></td><td></td><td>Purple Sandpiper & Turnstone common on rocky shoreline</td><td>Nov.–Mar.</td></tr>
<tr><td colspan="4">Leave A710 1 mile (0.8 km) south of Kirkbean & park at end of minor road to Southerness. See also Carsethorn.</td></tr>
<tr><td>j. Southwick Coast
SWT reserve
NX 91/55
Sheet 84</td><td>Saltmarsh, fen & ancient oakwood on inland cliff</td><td>Very large numbers of over-wintering Greylag, Pink-footed & Barnacle Geese & other wildfowl & waders</td><td>Oct.–Mar.</td></tr>
<tr><td colspan="4">Car park off A710. Follow track to Needle's Eye.</td></tr>
</table>

FIFE

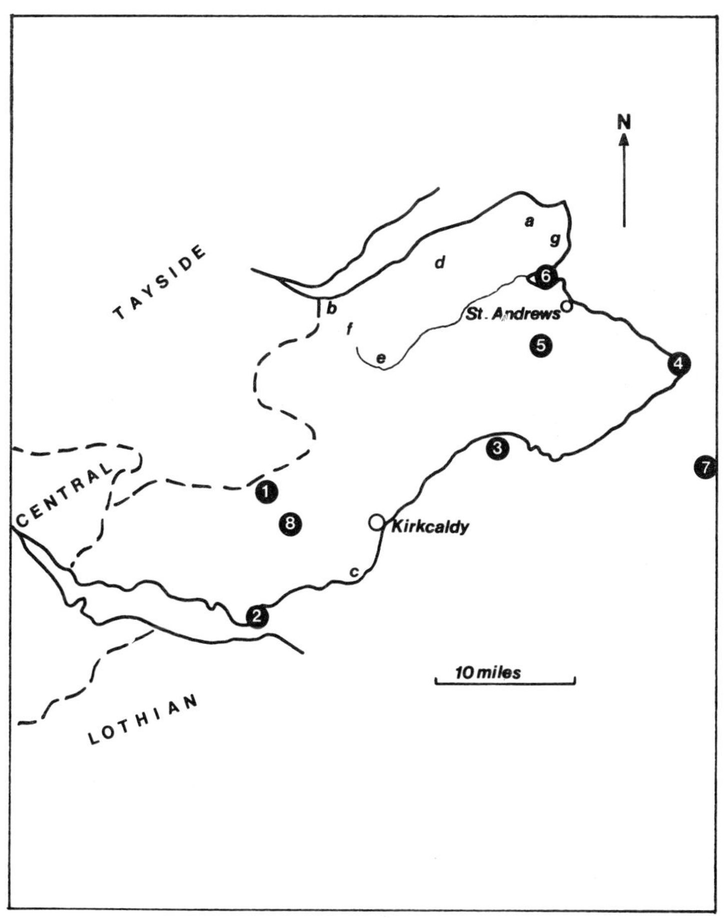

Main sites
F1. Lochore Meadows Country Park
F2. North Queensferry and Inverkeithing
F3. Largo Bay
F4. Fife Ness
F5. Cameron Reservoir
F6. Eden Estuary
F7. Isle of May
F8. Loch Gelly

Additional sites
a. Morton Lochs
b. Newburgh
c. Pettycur Bay
d. Moonzie
e. Rossie Bog
f. Lindores Loch
g. Tentsmuir Point

F1 LOCHORE MEADOWS COUNTRY PARK

OS ref.: NT 16/95
OS map: sheet 58

Habitat and Access

Lochore Meadows Country Park covers an area of about 400 hectares, including the 105-hectare Loch Ore. It lies at the centre of a reclamation scheme that has transformed a former coal mining wasteland into a landscaped area of open grassland and young woodland. The park incorporates a nature reserve at the western end, which can be reached by exiting the M90 at junction 4 and driving east past Kelty on the A909; turn left onto the B996 Cowdenbeath-Kinross road after 1 mile (1.6 km) and then take the first right to a car park. There is a bus service to Kelty from Cowdenbeath/Dunfermline.

From the car park, a track leads to the meadows – take a left turn at the junction approximately ¼ mile (500 metres) later to reach the Kon Lipphardt hide. Both the track and the hide have been constructed in such a way as to be accessible to wheelchair users. The other tracks here form a circuit that circumnavigate the main water body (the total distance of this walk is about 3½ miles (5.6 km)).

Species

Birds that are present on or just adjacent to the park during the breeding season include Little and Great Crested Grebes, Mute Swan, Pintail, Wigeon, Tufted Duck, Pochard, Moorhen, Coot, Snipe, Green Woodpecker, Grasshopper Warbler, Wood Warbler, Sedge Warbler, Whitethroat, Whinchat and Reed Bunting. Common Sandpiper, Redshank and Curlew can also be seen and the loch attracts many hirundines in late summer.

Wildfowl numbers are swelled in winter by the arrival of visiting Whooper Swan, Mallard, Pintail, Wigeon, Teal and Pochard. Other notable wintering species include Redwing, Fieldfare, Redpoll, Siskin and Goldfinch. This is a relatively new birdwatching location and conse-

Male Siskin

quently any records from visitors would be much appreciated by the Fife Ranger Service. Recent additions to the bird list of the park include Night Heron, American Wigeon, Ruddy Duck, Red-crested Pochard and Smew.

For more information contact: Fife Ranger Service, Lochore Meadows Country Park, Crosshill, Lochgelly, Fife. Tel: 0592 860086.

F2 NORTH QUEENSFERRY AND INVERKEITHING

OS map: sheet 65

Habitat

On the north shore of the Firth of Forth, immediately east of the Forth Bridge, exist a number of good, but relatively little-known birding locations. At Inverkeithing, a sheltered bay provides good feeding for both waders and wildfowl, whilst the more open coastline at Port Laing and St Davids Harbour is important for wintering divers/grebes and for fishing terns in summer.

Access and Species

Inner Bay

OS ref.: NT 132822

Wildfowl numbers are generally at their highest at Inverkeithing when birds are frozen out of their inland haunts. Several hundred Tufted Duck, over 100 Goldeneye and Pochard and good numbers of Shelduck, Teal and Eider occur. In addition, small numbers of Red-throated Diver, Great Crested Grebe, Cormorant, Scaup, Long-tailed Duck, Common and Velvet Scoters are often present. Other species take refuge in the bay during and after strong easterly winds: Great Northern Diver, Red-necked Grebe, Little Gull and even Little Auk have been recorded in this way. Moderate numbers of wintering waders also frequent this area, including small numbers of Ruff in recent years.

The best vantage points over the inner bay at Inverkeithing are West Ness, at the southern entrance to the bay, or from near the wooden pier.

Port Laing

OS ref.: NT 134813

Common, Arctic, Sandwich and occasional Roseate Terns can be seen fishing inshore during the summer and early autumn. Two White-winged Black terns were recently recorded off North Queensferry. Fulmar and Kittiwake are present further offshore. From late summer, Arctic Skua may be observed harassing the terns; Great and Pomarine Skuas are usually recorded later in the autumn. Large passages of Kittiwake, with lesser numbers of skuas, sometimes occur in autumn and these birds may be moving up the Forth and across to the Firth of Clyde. Seawatching is best from the high ground above the old pier around from Port Laing, reached from Carlingnose. In recent years, passage skua numbers have been very good and have included up to 50 Long-tailed Skua off Inverkeithing Bay.

Red-throated, Great Northern and occasional Black-throated Divers are recorded offshore in winter, along with five species of grebe and many auks.

Inverkeithing is accessible by bus and rail from Edinburgh, Dunfermline and Kirkcaldy.

References

'Coastal Birdwatching in West Fife', John S. Nadin, *Fife and Kinross Bird Report 1986*, ed. D.E. Dickson.

F3 LARGO BAY

OS ref.: NO 420010
OS map: sheet 59

Habitat

Largo Bay is situated on the south Fife coast, immediately east of Leven. It is approximately 3½ miles (5.6 km) wide and consists of a fairly deep tidal bay, backed by extensive sand dunes. The inter-tidal substrate is largely sand and mud, although a rocky area exists near the middle of the bay at Lower Largo and there is a muddy shingle area at the east end where the Cocklemill burn runs into the sea. Inland from the dunes lies rough grassland and improved pasture.

Just under a mile (1.6 km) inland from Elie, to the east of Largo Bay, lies Kilconquhar Loch, a 55-hectare shallow freshwater body surrounded by trees and gardens.

Species

Largo Bay is notable for its wintering sea-fowl, which includes Red-throated, Black-throated and (occasionally) Great Northern divers, wintering grebes, particularly Slavonian and Red-necked, Scaup (up to 300 present in winter at Leven), Eider, Long-tailed Duck (up to 300 are regularly recorded off Methil Docks, adjacent to Levenmouth), Common and Velvet Scoter, Goldeneye and Red-breasted Merganser. Very large numbers of Eider and the two species of Scoter use the bay as a moult site. Surf Scoter is annually recorded – February to May is probably the best period for these birds.

The bay does not attract particularly large numbers of either passage or wintering waders, although moderate numbers of Grey Plover and Purple Sandpiper occur and several hundred Knot and smaller numbers of Sanderling can be seen. Levenmouth is an excellent location for Glaucous and Iceland Gulls; Mediterranean Gull have occurred and Little Gull sometimes occur on passage. Little Auk can be numerous in the outer bay during some winters.

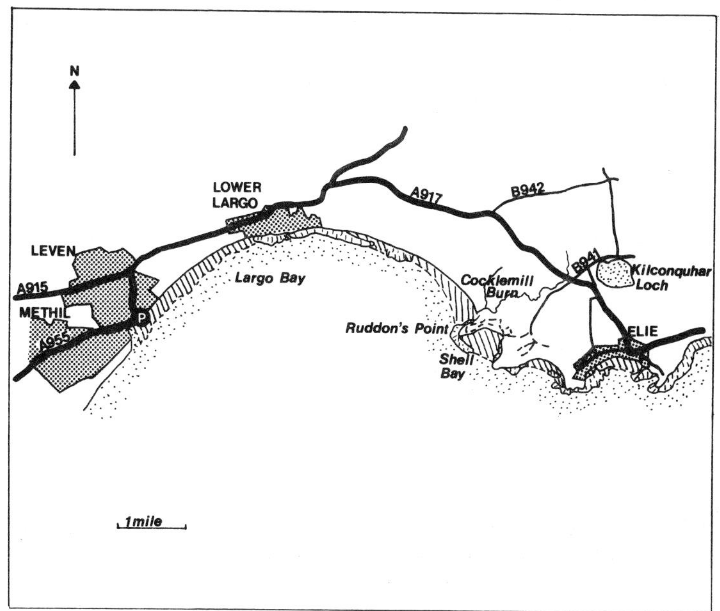

Kilconquhar Loch holds a variety of breeding waterfowl, including Little and Great Crested Grebes, Gadwall and Shoveler.

Access

The bay is easily accessible on foot from car parks at Levenmouth (opposite Methil Power Station) or Lower Largo. The free car park at the east end of Lower Largo affords a particularly good view of the Bay. Alternatively take the A917 eastwards from Lower Largo to a turn-off to Shell Bay Caravan Park, 1 mile (1.6 km) before Elie. From here, follow the minor road through the caravan site to Ruddon's Point (*c.* 2 miles (3 km)). Please note that between October and March the entrance gate to the caravan site is closed from 4 pm to 9 am daily.

Using shore paths and the beach, it is possible to walk the 4 miles (6.4 km) from Leven to Ruddon's Point, although Cocklemill Burn is difficult to cross at high tide. There is a bus service from Leven to Lower Largo and Elie.

Kilconquhar Loch can be viewed from the churchyard in Kilconquhar village, reached by taking the B941 turn-off from the A917 Elie to Leven road.

Timing

The best time to visit is from October through until April, although congregations of terns and sea-duck can be seen in late summer. High tide is best for seeing sea-duck and for waders at Ruddon's Point, low tide for white-winged gulls at Levenmouth.

Calendar

October–April: Offshore divers, grebes, sea-duck, wintering gulls (inc. occasional Little Gull in late winter).

May–June: Breeding wildfowl on Kilconquhar Loch; late wintering Goldeneye sometimes also present.

July–September: Variable numbers of Little Gull gather at Kilconquhar Loch during late July/August in some years. At sea, passage terns include Sandwich, Common and Arctic, together with the occasional Roseate Tern.

References

The Birds of Fife, A.M. Smout (1986).
Fife and Kinross Bird Reports 1981–, eds. M. Ware and D.E. Dickson.

F4 FIFE NESS

OS ref.: NO 638098
OS map: sheet 59

Habitat

Fife Ness lies at the eastern extremity of the Fife peninsula and is renowned for its migrant birdlife. The area is characterised by farmland, a golf course, coastal scrub and a few copses of sycamore-dominated woodland. Small areas of gorse and bramble are strewn along the coast, interspersed with sporadic pine trees. The shoreline is mostly rocky, with the exception of a sandy beach to the north. Inland, 1 mile (1.6 km) to the south-west, lies a disused airfield, now largely given over to cereal or root crops.

The Scottish Wildlife Trust manages just over ½ mile (0.8 km) of coast to the south-west at Kilminning, and also a small enclosed area of gorse, shrubs and trees immediately inland from the tip of the peninsula, called Fife Ness Muir. This contains several artificial pools created by Dr Jim Cobb and is probably the best place for passerine migrants.

Access

1 Fife Ness Muir

OS ref.: NO 638098

Take the minor road east out of Crail (a continuation of the main street) and follow it to the car park at Balcomie Golf Course, 1½ miles (2.4 km) later. From here, walk through the gate to the right of the road and then immediately left, down towards the sea. Fife Ness Muir is on the hill to the right and can be reached *only from the east* from the cottage on the shore.

2 Kilminning Coast

OS ref.: NO 63/08

Turn right off the golf course road, 1 mile (1.6 km) out of Crail, parking at the far end of this track. The Fife long-distance coastal footpath, slightly overgrown in places, affords access in both directions along the coast. This path can also be joined at Crail or Fife Ness.

There is a bus service from Leven to Crail.

Most areas of vegetation are suitable cover for migrant birds in spring and autumn. In addition to the above sites, Crail Airfield is worth checking out for waders, pipits, larks and buntings, whilst the quarry immediately below the golf club house may hold passerine migrants.

In the past, there has been some animosity shown towards birders by one or two local people, who have felt that their privacy has not been properly respected. In order that this tension is not exacerbated, it is very

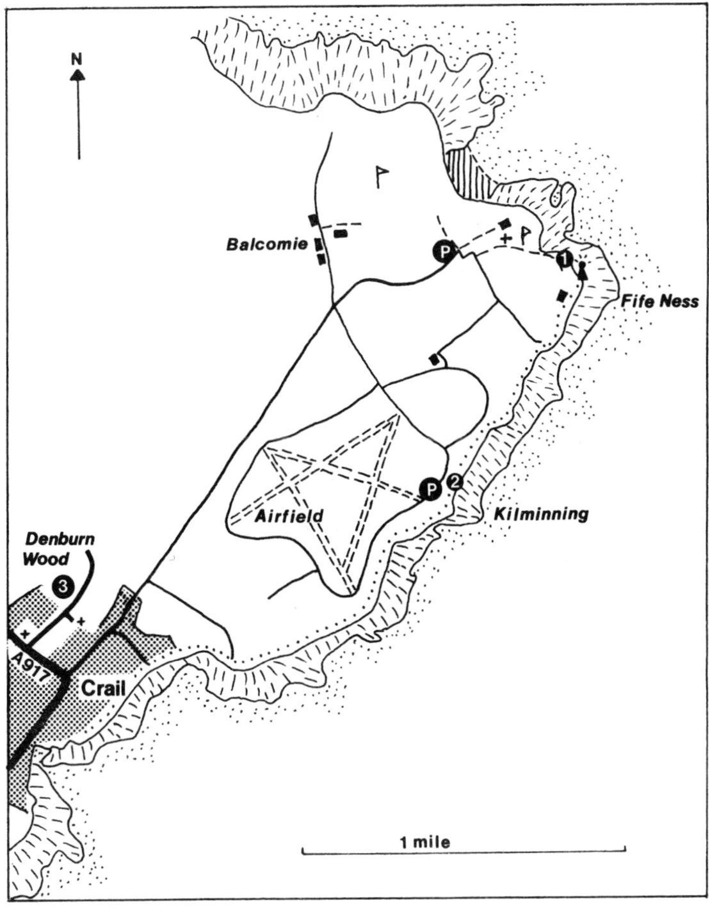

important that visitors behave responsibly; in particular, permission should be sought before entering the land around Balcomie Farm; Craighead Farm is an even more sensitive area and is probably best avoided altogether.

3 Denburn Wood

OS ref.: NO 614080

A mature copse bordering the churchyard; the wood has a variety of different shrubs and trees, a stream and some grassy areas at the top of the wood.

The wood has produced some very good passage migrants in recent years, including Yellow-browed, Pallas's and Barred Warblers, Golden Oriole, northern-race Treecreeper and Rose-coloured Starling. It is well worth visiting, especially after the birds have filtered through from Fife Ness after 1 or 2 days.

Timing

Fife Ness is primarily of interest for its migrant birds and both spring and autumn are excellent times to visit. Offshore sea-fowl provide some mid-winter interest; however, south-east, east or north-east winds are best for migrants.

Species

Offshore, Gannet, Cormorant, Shag, auks and several species of the commoner waders can be seen year-round. Sandwich, Common, Arctic and sometimes Little Tern occur in spring and autumn. Small numbers of passage waders frequent the shore and the tidal pool adjacent to the sixteenth tee.

Sedge Warbler, Corn Bunting and very occasionally, Stonechat, breed. An impressive number and variety of passerine migrants make landfall at Fife Ness (see Calendar) during spring and autumn.

Calendar

Some of the more interesting species likely to be seen.

March–May: Common and scarce migrants fairly regularly recorded include Long-eared Owl, Wryneck, Bluethroat, Black Redstart, Ring Ousel, occasional Firecrest, Red-backed Shrike; rarer visitors include Nightingale and Common Rosefinch; Ortolan Bunting and Subalpine Warbler have occurred.

Offshore, passage seabirds such as shearwaters, skuas and terns occur during April and May. This is a good time for divers, too.

June–July: A quiet time of year, although Gannet, large numbers of Eider, Kittiwake, terns and auks can usually be seen offshore. A few marauding skuas may occur in July.

Local breeding species include Corn Bunting and (rarely nowadays) Stonechat.

August–October: Offshore, Manx and Sooty Shearwaters, Arctic, Great and Pomarine Skua, terns and auks may be visible. Small numbers of Little Gull are often present; Little and Black Tern are recorded annually and Sabine's Gull have been seen. A few divers are usually present, mostly Red-throated. Groups of Barnacle and occasional Brent Geese may be seen in late September and through October, en route to their wintering grounds.

Migrant chats, thrushes, warblers and flycatchers can be abundant, especially during easterly winds.

Yellow-browed Warbler are seen annually, whilst Icterine, Barred, Pallas's, and Radde's have been recorded. Red-breasted Flycatcher are also occassionally reported.

November—February: Red-throated occassional Black-throated and Great Northern Divers, Shag, Cormorant, occassionāl skuas, white-winged gulls and auks can be present inshore. Little Auk are occassionally seen, especially after persistent northerly winds. Purple Sandpiper and Turnstone frequent the rocky shoreline.

Geese, Han Harrier, Golden Plover, various finches, Lapland and Snow Bunting are all possible.

Yellow-browed Warbler and Firecrest, autumn

References

The Birds of Fife, A.M. Smout (1986).
Fife and Kinross Bird Reports 1981–, eds. M. Ware and D.E. Dickson.
'Seawatching at Fife Ness', J. Steele in *Fife and Kinross Bird Reports 1986*, ed. D.E. Dickson.

F5 CAMERON RESERVOIR

OS ref.: NO 470113
OS map: sheet 59

Habitat

Cameron Reservoir is a water body of approximately 40 hectares lying at 150 metres above sea level, some 4 miles (6.4 km) south-west of St Andrews. The north bank is now largely grassland, following the felling of conifers there in the 1950s. To the east is the stone containing dam, whilst the south shore is still mainly afforested with spruce, larch and Scots pine. Sallows form a thick cover at many points along the water's edge. There is another stone and concrete containing wall to the west, with marshland beyond. The surrounding upland farmland is given over to sheep pasture, with some tillage.

The reservoir, owned by the local water board, is designated a Site of Special Scientific Interest. Problems over the upkeep of the dam have led to fears that it might be drained.

Species

Little and Great Crested Grebes, Mute Swan, Mallard, Tufted Duck, Moorhen and Coot can be seen all year at Cameron Reservoir, but it is in late autumn/early winter that the area becomes especially important for birds. Around 6,000 Pink-footed Geese (and up to 13,000 on occasion) roost on the reservoir in October and November; these can be easily watched as they arrive at sunset from the hide on the north shore, without fear of disturbance. The odd White-fronted and Snow Goose can often be seen amongst the Pink-feet. A few hundred Greylag Geese are also generally present and the reservoir holds good populations of a variety of wintering wildfowl, including Whooper Swan, Wigeon, Teal, Pochard, occasional Gadwall and even Smew. Ruddy Duck are regular autumn visitors.

Short-eared Owl often hunt over the grassland area on the north bank. Recent records show this to be without doubt one of the best passage wader sites in Fife. Although obviously dependent upon water levels, Greenshank and Spotted Redshank are regular spring and autumn migrants; Wood, Green and Common Sandpiper numbers fluctuate from year to year; Little Ringed Plover has also been recorded. A Crane was seen here in the mid-1980s.

Small numbers of Shoveler occur in spring/summer. The emergent and scrub vegetation around the edge of the reservoir holds breeding Sedge Warbler and Reed Bunting.

Timing

The reservoir is worth visiting throughout much of the year, although July is probably the least inspiring time. An autumn or winter visit can be strongly recommended: the best time for watching the geese flight-in is from one hour before sunset until dark, using the hide as a vantage point (see below). Calm conditions are preferable for identifying waterfowl; in strong sunlight the south bank will afford better views.

Access

From the A915 St Andrews–Leven road, turn west along the track to Cameron Kirk and drive on past it to a left turn down to the car park at the reservoir keeper's house.

There is a bus service along the A915 from St Andrews.

It is possible to walk around the entire perimeter of the reservoir (*c.* 2½ miles (4 km)), but the south bank is very marshy. Elsewhere, the tracks are good. The east and west dams, the hide on the north shore, and various locations along the south shore, all provide good vantage points.

Please note that dogs are not allowed except on a lead.

(Note: the hide, dedicated to John Wiffen, belongs to the Scottish Wildlife Trust and is kept locked: the key is available *only* to SWT/SOC members – contact Brian Gill, 45 Irvine Crescent, St Andrews. Tel. 0334 72053. For membership details of both of these organisations see addresses section.)

References

Based upon information kindly supplied by Chris Smout and the late John Wiffen.
The Birds of Fife, A.M. Smout (1986).
Fife and Kinross Bird Reports 1980–, ed. D.E. Dickson.

F6 EDEN ESTUARY

OS ref.: NO 485195
OS map: sheet 59

Habitat

This 891-hectare Local Nature Reserve lies immediately to the north of St Andrews. The habitat mainly comprises inter-tidal mud-flats and sand-banks, with extensive mussel and cockle beds. There is a small area of saltmarsh on the south shore. To the east, a series of low sand dunes extend northwards from St Andrews, sheltering the estuary. The area is a Site of Special Scientific Interest and is managed by North-east Fife District Council. There are plans to construct a visitor centre in Guardbridge, next to the paper mill (see map). In addition, the Fife Bird Club are hoping to build a hide at the Edenside Stables, halfway between Guardbridge and Coble Shore.

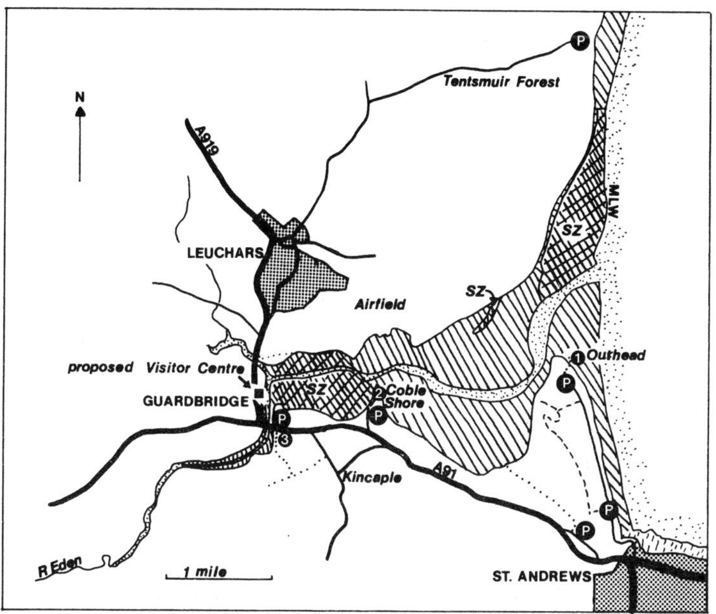

* Species exceeds1 per cent of the European/British population.

Species

The Eden estuary is a relatively small area, yet it is of outstanding importance for passage and wintering wildfowl and waders. Shelduck and Red-breasted Merganser are sometimes present in internationally important numbers*, whilst Scaup, Common and Velvet Scoter, Eider and Long-tailed Duck achieve nationally significant levels* on occasion. The most numerous winter waders are Oystercatcher, Knot, Dunlin, Bar-tailed Godwit and Redshank. Two specialities of the area are Grey Plover (500+) and Black-tailed Godwit (100+), the latter favouring the Edenside area on the south shore. Sanderling can be numerous around the estuary mouth and flocks of Golden Plover, Lapwing and Curlew are a common sight. In autumn the estuary can host an array of passage waders, regularly including Little Stint, Curlew Sandpiper, Ruff and Spotted Redshank.

Red-throated Diver are regular offshore wintering birds, whilst Black-throated and Great Northern are occasionally seen. Small numbers of Great Crested Grebe are present on passage and during winter. Red-necked and Slavonian Grebes are scarce, however.

Passage and wintering Merlin, Peregrine and Short-eared Owl frequently hunt over the area.

Access

Please note that access is not allowed to the north shore without a permit and that the sanctuary zones (see map) must not be disturbed. These zones have been designated in order to minimise disturbance to the principal wildfowl and wader roosts. Outside the sanctuaries wildfowling takes place between 1 September and 20 February. It is recommended that visitors contact the North-east Fife Ranger Service (address below) for information about the estuary and for the key to the hide in Balgove Bay. There are three publicly accessible vantage points that enable most of the estuary to be worked:

1 Outhead

OS ref.: NO 495198

This lies at the end of the sandy peninsula that extends into the estuary mouth from the south shore. Take the shore road north from St Andrews, signposted for West Sands. There is a car park at the end of this and it is only a short walk to Outhead. There are also tracks from this road across to Balgove Bay.

2 Coble Shore

OS ref.: NO 468194

Turn off the main A91 St Andrews–Cupar road 3½ miles (5.6 km) east of Guardbridge. There is a parking area at the end of this short track.

3 Guardbridge

OS ref.: NO 455189

There is an extensive layby by the L.N.R. noticeboard immediately east of the bridge on the A91; this gives good views of the inner estuary. On the opposite side of the A91 a footpath to Kincaple Den provides a good vantage point for the tidal reaches of the River Eden above the road bridge. This is a likely location for Black-tailed Godwit, Greenshank and Goosander in the winter.

There are regular buses between Cupar and St Andrews.

Timing

The vantage points detailed below are accessible all year; there are relatively few breeding birds here, however, and the main interest lies in passage and wintering species. A visit during the period August to May is recommended. A rising or falling tide is best for seeing most birds. Duck numbers are often much higher after strong easterly winds and both wildfowl and wader populations can increase dramatically in severe weather.

Calendar

Some of the more interesting species likely to be seen.

April–May: Large Ringed Plover passage can be observed during May, mainly at Balgove Bay. Other spring passage waders may also be present.

June–August: Gannet are sometimes seen in the outer estuary. Large flocks of Red-breasted Merganser congregate at Edenmouth in July and August, joined by Sandwich, Common and Arctic Terns, which often attract marauding Arctic Skua.

Early passage waders, such as Whimbrel, pass through.

September–October: Wader passage continues. Small numbers of Barnacle Geese pass through.

November–March Whooper Swan are regular, if unpredictable, visitors. Several hundred Greylay Geese roost on the estuary. Wigeon, Teal, Mallard, Goldeneye, Red-breasted Merganser and Goosander are common over-wintering species. Pintail, Shoveler and Tufted Duck are regular visitors. Sea-duck, including spectacular numbers of Common and Velvet Scoters, gather at Edenmouth – in recent years these have included Surf Scoter.

Very large numbers of waders feed and roost (see above).

Shelduck numbers peak in February/early March and some remain to breed.

Snow Bunting are frequently seen, whilst large numbers of Reed Bunting have roosted at Guardbridge in previous winters.

North-east Fife Ranger Service

Craigtoun Country Park, by St Andrews, Fife KY16 8NX. Tel: 0334 73666.

References

The Birds of Fife, A.M. Smout (1986).

F7 ISLE OF MAY

OS ref.: NT 65/99
OS map: sheet 59

Habitat

The Isle of May is situated at the mouth of the Firth of Forth, some 5 miles (8 km) south-east of the Fife coast. The 57-hectare island consists of hard volcanic rock, rising to 55 metres on the west side, which is largely vertical sea-cliff and sloping gradually to sea level to the east. Vegetation is sparse and the trapping areas of the Bird Observatory, established in 1934, offer the best cover for migrant birds. It has been designated a National Nature Reserve by Scottish Natural Heritage, who have recently purchased the island from the Northern Lighthouse Board.

Timing

Migrants are the primary attraction of the Isle of May and therefore April/May and August to October are the optimum periods to visit. However, breeding seabirds also provide much interest between May and July.

Access

During the summer it is possible to arrange a day trip to the island from Anstruther, depending on tides and weather (tel: Jim Reaper, 0333 310103). All who wish to stay at the Observatory must complete an application form, obtainable from the bookings secretary, Mrs Rosemary Cowper, 9 Oxgangs Road, Edinburgh EH10 7BG (tel: 031 445 2489). Details of the boat crossing from Anstruther are supplied when the booking has been confirmed. Visitors must take their own sheets or sleeping bag and sufficient food for the duration of their stay – this can be obtained in Crail or Anstruther daily, except Sundays. The cost of accommodation is modest and a maximum of six people can stay at any one time. The usual period of stay is one week, starting and finishing on a Saturday, although bad weather can delay plans.

Species

Large numbers of seabirds breed on the island: over 1,000 pairs of Shag, several thousand pairs each of Kittiwake and Guillemot, about 1,000 pairs of Razorbill and an estimated 10,000 occupied Puffin burrows have been counted. There is an increasing number of Fulmar and large populations of Herring and Lesser Black-backed Gulls. Other breeding species of interest include Eider (*c.* 500 pairs), Oystercatcher, a few Common and Arctic Terns, Rock Pipit and Wheatear.

Over 240 species have been recorded on the Isle of May, an impressive total partly due to the fact that the island has been studied during migration periods for more than 50 years. Large 'falls' of migrants are most likely when strong east or south-easterly winds coincide with poor visibility. In autumn, spectacular numbers of relatively common birds can occur, en route to their winter quarters; thrushes are probably the most usual of these, but other species are sometimes involved, for instance 15,000 Goldcrest were once recorded and over 1,000 Brambling appeared on another occasion. Scarcer species are regularly seen and Wryneck, Bluethroat, Icterine, Barred and Yellow-browed Warblers, Red-breasted Flycatcher, Great Grey and Red-backed Shrikes, Scarlet Rosefinch, Lapland and Ortolan Buntings are all almost annually recorded. Rarities such as Spoonbill, Red-footed Falcon, Pallas's Sandgrouse, Siberian Thrush, Daurian Redstart, Pied Wheatear, Paddyfield, Olivaceous, Melodious, Subalpine and Pallas's Warblers have all occurred at least once, as have Red-throated Pipit, Pine Grosbeak, Yellow-breasted and Rustic Buntings.

Seawatching can be worthwhile – divers, sea-duck, shearwaters, petrels and skuas can all be seen at various times (see Calendar).

Calendar

Some of the more interesting species likely to be seen.

April–May: Passerine migrants likely to occur, including possible rarities. Breeding seabirds return to nest sites; Manx Shearwater, Great and Arctic Skua usually visible offshore.

June–July: Fledged seabirds start to disperse during July. Common and Arctic Terns breed, and are occasionally joined by Sandwich Tern.

August–October: Peak migration period; large falls of migrants possible especially during easterly winds. Offshore, passage seabirds include Manx and Sooty Shearwaters, Storm Petrel, Great, Arctic and Pomarine Skuas.

Light phase Arctic Skua and Common Gulls, autumn

November–March: Offshore, divers, Black Guillemot and Little Auk are regularly seen; Merlin and Peregrine, Long-eared and Short-eared Owls, are frequently seen during this period. Woodcock pass through, whilst Purple Sandpiper and Turnstone frequent the rocky shoreline.

References

The Isle of May: a Scottish Nature Reserve, W.J. Eggeling, (1960, repr. 1985).

One Man's Island, Keith Brockie (1984).

F8 LOCH GELLY

OS ref.: NT 20/92
OS map: sheet 58

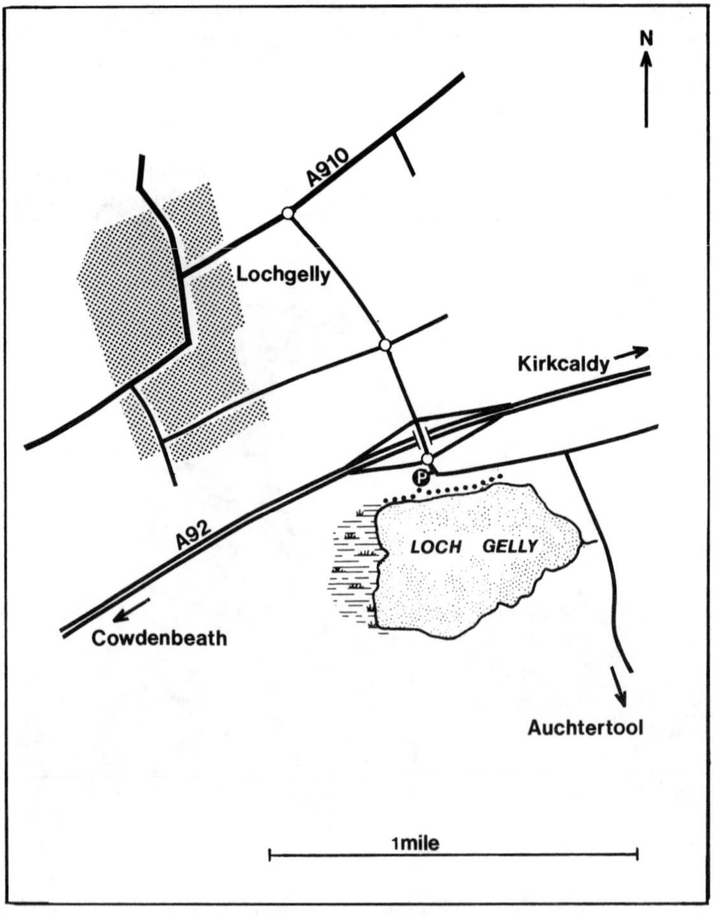

Habitat and Access

A freshwater loch bordered by mixed woodland, Phragmites swamp, willow carr and grassland habitats. The northern shore of this 79-hectare site is owned by the National Coal Board, whilst the south shore belongs to Wemyss Estate. Loch Gelly is leased by Fife Skiing Club.

Access to the loch is only from the A92 Cowdenbeath–Kirkcaldy road at the Lochgelly East Link Road interchange. At this junction take the road signposted to Auchtertool and park down a small, metalled track 20 metres along on your right. Steps lead from here down to a path on the north side of the loch. It is possible to walk right round the loch if you are prepared to negotiate long grass and mud in places.

Species

Over 108 species have been recorded. Loch Gelly attracts very good numbers of duck and waders (when the water level is low), especially in autumn. Breeding birds include Little Grebe, Mute Swan, Greylag Goose, Shelduck, Pochard, Shoveler, Teal and Grasshopper Warbler. Five species of grebe, three species of swan and 18 species of duck have been recorded here. Ruddy Duck are regular visitors; Garganey, Pintail and Ring-necked Duck have all been recorded. Passage waders likely to be seen include Wood, Green and Common Sandpipers, Ruff, Greenshank and Spotted Redshank. Other birds seen at Loch Gelly include Spoonbill, Corncrake, Black Tern and Little Gull. Hundreds of hirundines can be present in autumn, whilst Swift may be present in thousands in July.

The site is also important botanically; species of particular interest include Water Sedge, Tea-leaved Willow, Ivy Duckweed, Yellow Loosestrife, Horned Pondweed and Yellow Water Lily.

ADDITIONAL SITES

Site and Grid Reference	Habitat	Main Bird Interest	Peak Season
a. Morton Lochs NO 46/26 Sheet 54 or 59	Artificial lochs with surrounding marsh and woodland	Migrant wildfowl and waders	Aug.–Nov.
b. Newburgh NO 22/18 Sheet 58	Offshore island & inter-tidal habitats	Roosting geese	Oct.–April.
c. Pettycur Bay NT 27/86 Sheet 66	Sandy, tidal bay	Waders, terns and gulls	Aug.–Oct.
d. Moonzie NO 34/17 Sheet 59	Open water fringed by reedbed	Waders, gulls and geese	Aug.–Mar.
e. Rossie Bog NO 27/10 Sheet 59	Reed-fringed bog with drainage of streams	Grasshopper Warbler	May–June.
		Hen Harrier, Short-eared Owl, finches	Sep.–Dec.
f. Lindores Loch NO 26/16 Sheet 59	Open water fringed by farmland and reedbed	Geese, ducks, Water Rail	Oct.–Mar.
g. Tentsmuir Pt. NO 500242 Sheet 59	Sandy shore	Terns (inc. L. tern), gulls, waders, ducks.	Aug.–Nov.
		Snow Bunting	Oct.–Nov.

GRAMPIAN

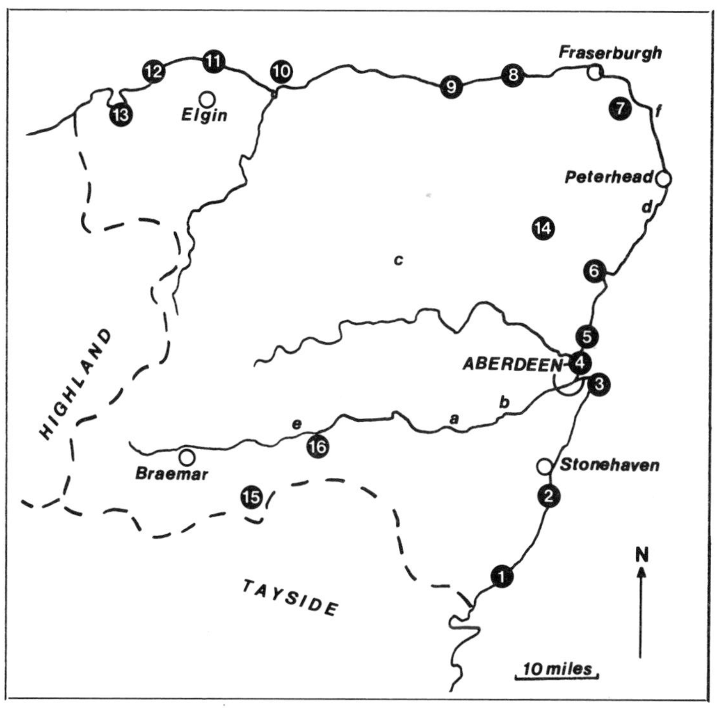

Main sites

G1. St Cyrus
G2. Fowlsheugh
G3. Girdle Ness
G4. Mouth of Dan
G5. Black Dog
G6. Ythan Estuary and Sands of Forvie
G7. Loch of Strathbeg
G8. Troup Head
G9. Banff/Macduff Harbour
G10. Spey Bay
G11. Lossiemouth
G12. Burghead
G13. Findhorn Bay
G14. Haddo Country Park
G15. Glen Muick and Lochnagar
G16. Glen Tanar

Additional Sites

a. Crathes Castle
b. Drum
c. Leith Hall
d. Longhaven Cliffs
e. Muir of Dinnet
f. Rattray Head

G1 ST CYRUS

OS ref.: NO 75/64
OS map: sheet 45

Habitat and Access

This 92-hectare National Nature Reserve lies at the mouth of the River North Esk and comprises foreshore, dune and cliff habitats. The reserve can be reached by turning off the A92 3½ miles (5.6 km) north of Montrose and following the north bank of the river to a track entering the reserve at the sharp bend 1½ miles (2.4 km) later (NO 743635). Alternatively, an approach may be made from St Cyrus village, by turning off the A92 6 miles (9.7 km) north of Montrose. A path from the church leads to the cliff-top.

Species

The reserve boasts a total of 47 breeding species, including a locally important colony of Little Tern at the south end of the reserve. These often suffer heavy losses to predators, however. In order to reduce disturbance, the colony is fenced off from May through to August. Fulmar and Herring Gull nest on the cliffs, whilst Eider breed in the dunes. Other noteworthy breeding birds include Stonechat, Grasshopper Warbler and Whitethroat. Large concentrations of Eider, Goosander and Red-breasted Merganser occur offshore in spring and autumn – the river mouth is the best place to see these.

Three species of diver have been recorded offshore in winter, although Red-throated are by far the most numerous. Common and Velvet Scoter, Eider and Long-tailed Duck winter in the bay, there being much interchange between the sea-duck here and at Lunan Bay further south.

Passage birds include offshore shearwaters, skuas and terns, a good range of shorebird species (less common species such as Curlew Sandpiper, Wood Sandpiper and Spotted Redshank occur every autumn) and passerines such as Wheatear, Whinchat and (after easterly winds) Black Redstart.

Dipper and Grey Wagtail frequent the river; Short-eared Owl frequently hunt over the dunes in winter.

Timing

Breeding birds provide the interest from April to July; migrants are best watched from September to November.

Further information is obtainable from SNH area officer, The Old Lifeboat Station, Nether Warburton, by Montrose, DD10 OAD. Tel: 0674 83736.

G2 FOWLSHEUGH

OS ref.: NO 880798
OS map: sheet 45

Habitat

The RSPB reserve at Fowlsheugh is the home of one of the largest and most accessible seabird colonies in Britain. An approximate total of 80,000 pairs of six different species breed on the 1½ miles (2.4 km) of Old Red Sandstone cliffs. These cliffs, up to 65 metres high in places, are deeply indented, making it possible to closely observe nesting birds without causing disturbance. The reserve is a Site of Special Scientific Interest of international importance.

Access

The reserve is reached via a minor road leading eastwards off the A92, 3 miles (4.8 km) south of Stonehaven, signposted for Crawton. There is a bus service along the A92, between Montrose and Stonehaven. The nearest railway station is at Stonehaven, on the Perth–Aberdeen line. From the car park at Crawton, walk north along the cliff-top footpath for ½ mile (0.8 km). Visitors are warned to take care at the cliff edge.

Superb views of the nesting seabirds can be obtained at several vantage points. The reserve is open at all times, but there is no full-time warden present although an information warden may be in post in future.

Timing

The seabirds are ashore from April to mid-July; there is little of interest during the remainder of the year.

Calendar

Some of the more interesting species likely to be seen.

May–July: Fulmar, Herring Gull and small numbers of Puffin occupy the upper cliff, whilst the niches and ledges lower down are crammed with about 30,000 pairs each of Kittiwake and Guillemot, and circa 5,000 pairs of Razorbill. Recent studies indicate that just over 2 per cent of the Guillemot are of the bridled form. Many Shag nest in the caves at the foot of the cliffs and small numbers of Eider can be seen close inshore.

Fowlsheugh is not noted for seawatching, but passage shearwaters and skuas can be seen offshore, especially during onshore winds in late summer/autumn.

G3 GIRDLE NESS

OS ref.: NJ 973054
OS map: sheet 38

Habitat and Access

This promontory lies on the south side of the mouth of the River Dee, in Aberdeen. A lighthouse is situated at its end, about 1½ miles (2.4 km) from the city centre. This is backed by a golf course, with short grass, some rough areas and gorse bushes.

Travelling south through Aberdeen, cross the River Dee on the A956 to Torry, then take the second road on the left, which leads past the docks and golf course to the lighthouse. There are two car parking areas – both of these can be good sea-watching vantage points.

Species

Passage seabirds are the main attraction. Arctic and Great Skua are numerous, whilst Pomarine are annual and Long-tailed have been recorded. Shearwaters are common in the autumn; sea-duck (especially Eider), white-winged gulls and waders provide interest in the winter. King Eider have been recorded on 3 occasions in recent years.

Large numbers of passage Wheatear sometimes occur on the short grasslands of the golf course. The limited amount of cover provides temporary shelter for migrant passerines such as Whinchat and Redstart and occasionally scarcer ones too, for instance: Bluethroat (recorded annually), Lesser Whitethroat and Yellow-browed Warbler (six records in 1988).

Purple Sandpipers and Oystercatchers, winter

On the rocky foreshore, Purple Sandpiper are present well into spring, whilst Turnstone can be seen year-round.

Timing

Northerly winds are best for seabird passage. In spring, a south-easterly might produce passerine migrants, especially Bluethroats.

Calendar

Some of the more interesting species likely to be seen.

March–May: Passage skuas, Iceland Gull, one or two Little Gull, possible Bluethroat, Wheatear, Whinchat and Redstart.

August–November: During late August and through September, passage

Manx and some Sooty Shearwaters can be seen, together with up to four species of skua and occasional Little Gull. Barnacle Geese may appear from late September onwards. Wader passage includes Ruff (up to 80), Black-tailed Godwit and Curlew Sandpiper. During August and September, the site is increasingly used by about 200 Eider coming out of eclipse plumage.

Miscellaneous species that can also be seen at this time include infrequent Blue Fulmar, Velvet Scoter and Snow Bunting.

December–February: Up to 300 Goldeneye used to over-winter in Greyhope Bay but this number has now reduced to perhaps only 40 birds due to a change in the sewage outflow into the bay. Iceland and Glaucous Gulls can be seen in the river mouth. On the rocky foreshore excellent views of Purple Sandpiper and Turnstone can be obtained.

G4 MOUTH OF DON

OS ref.: NJ 951095
OS map: sheet 38

Habitat and Access

A 'green-belt' area on the northern outskirts of Aberdeen, soon to become a Local Nature Reserve. The river mouth is situated 3 miles (4.8 km) north of the city centre, on the A92. On reaching the Bridge of Don, turn right onto Beach Boulevard, where there are plenty of parking places. It is possible to walk from here along the estuary 'foreshore' down to Aberdeen beach. On the opposite side of the Bridge of Don lies Seaton Park; this continues along an embankment high above the river, affording excellent views of ducks and waders.

Timing

There is year-round interest, owing to the attraction of the area for terns in summer, migrants during spring and autumn, and duck in winter.

Calendar
Some of the more interesting species likely to be seen.

All year: Sparrowhawk and Grey Wagtail can usually be found in the area.

May–July: Feeding Sandwich, Common and Arctic Terns can be seen (Little and Black Tern have been recorded). Towards the end of summer, Arctic and Great Skuas sometimes harass the terns in the estuary mouth. Riverside bushes provide cover for passerine migrants and Redstart, Goldcrest, Chiffchaff, Willow Warbler and Blackcap are recorded every year. During May Spotted and even Pied Flycatcher are possible, whilst Yellow Wagtail should be sought on the short grasslands.

August–October: Passage Manx Shearwater, Gannet and skuas can be seen offshore. Wader passage can be good (especially for an urban site!) and includes large numbers of Ringed Plover, plus occasional rarities. Pectoral Sandpiper and Greater Sand Plover have been recorded here in recent years.

November–April: Diving duck present; Goldeneye numbers are nationally important, whilst Tufted Duck and Goosander can be relatively common. Scaup (up to 15 at any one time) and Long-tailed Duck are possible in mid-winter and Smew are occasional visitors.

G5 BLACK DOG

OS ref.: NJ 965137
OS map: sheet 38

Habitat
A sandy shore backed by a Marram-dominated dune system with a few boggy dune slacks; these have been largely 'improved' for a golf course. To the south, the beach stretches for 3 miles (4.8 km) to the Don estuary, whilst the Ythan estuary lies some 7 miles (11 km) northwards.

Access
The beach at Black Dog is reached by way of the A92, turning off eastwards onto a driveable track about 5 miles (8 km) north of Aberdeen at NJ 955143. There is room for a few vehicles to park near the cottages after 1 mile (1.6 km). From here, walk 100 metres down to the beach. Offshore duck can be 'scoped from anywhere along the beach.

There is a bus route from Aberdeen to Ellon/Peterhead, along the A92.

Species
The principal attraction here is a large flock of moulting sea-duck, present during summer and early autumn.

Calendar
Some of the more interesting species likely to be seen.

June–September: From late June to early September, up to 10,000 Eider, 2,000 Common Scoter and perhaps 250 or so Velvet Scoter may be seen. King Eider and Surf Scoter are present most summers. In autumn, Scaup may also appear, whilst Sandwich, Common and Arctic Terns from nearby colonies feed at sea and rest on the beach, attracting marauding Arctic and Great Skuas.

November–March: Sea-duck numbers are much reduced, but many Red-throated Diver occur and Long-tailed Duck should be present. Sanderling may be found on the shoreline, whilst Short-eared Owl and Snow Bunting frequent the dunes.

Timing

Calm sea conditions are needed for 'scoping sea-duck. The afternoon is the best time to visit on a bright day, so that the light is behind you.

G6 YTHAN ESTUARY AND SANDS OF FORVIE

OS ref.: NK 00/24
OS map: sheet 38

Habitat

The Ythan estuary is around 5 miles (8 km) long by 300 or 400 metres wide and is situated some 12 miles (19 km) north of Aberdeen. It is bordered by agricultural land to the west and by the dunes and moorland of the Sands of Forvie to the east. The estuary is composed of inter-tidal mud and sand flats, with pebbles, shingle and mussel beds largely confined to the areas of faster moving water, especially below Waterside Bridge. Areas of saltmarsh occur mainly at the mouth of the Tarty Burn and near Waterside Bridge.

The area is a National Nature Reserve totalling some 1,018 hectares and includes the best example of coastal moorland in northern Britain. Although generally undisturbed, the outer estuary in particular is becoming increasingly popular as a wind-surfing location.

Access

The estuary can be reached by taking the A92 northwards from Aberdeen, then turning east onto the A975 Newburgh road after about 10 miles (16 km). This road crosses the estuary some three miles later.

Access to the foreshore and along footpaths is allowed at all times. Visitors are not permitted in the ternery or to enter the moorland area during the period April to August.

There are a number of good vantage points.

1 Newburgh

OS ref.: NJ 997252

Heading north along the A975, turn right immediately after the Ythan

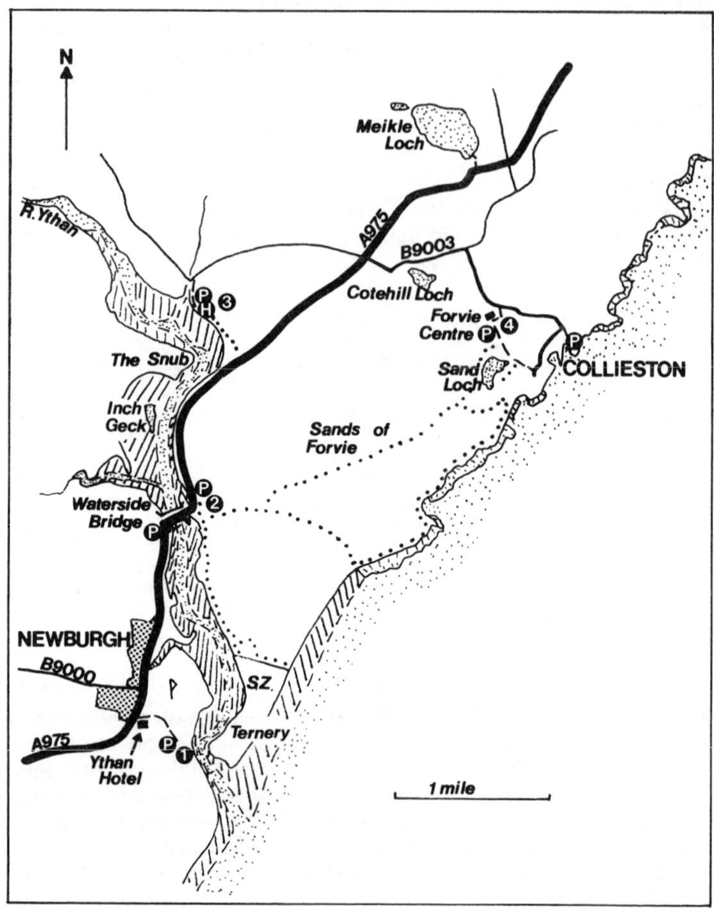

Hotel at the southern end of Newburgh (signposted to beach) and follow this track to the car park near the golf course. Good views over the river mouth and the tern breeding area opposite can be obtained by walking 100 metres across the dunes here.

2 Waterside Bridge

OS ref.: NK 002268

There are several laybys on the A975 north of Newburgh, both near the bridge and beyond, where the road follows the river for a mile or so. These are good viewpoints for feeding and roosting waders. From a parking area near the east end of the bridge, two tracks lead into the Forvie NNR. SNH wardens are at hand during the breeding season to impart information about the birds and the reserve.

3 Waulkmill Hide

OS ref.: NK 003290

Follow the A975 northwards from Newburgh for 3 miles (4.8 km); turn left along an unclassified road (opposite B9003 turn for Collieston) and after 1½ miles (2.4 km) take another left onto a track on the east side of a stream leading into the Ythan. A car parking area and large comfortable hide with wheelchair access will be reached within 200 metres. This hide, built by Gordon District Council, affords excellent views of the inner estuary.

4 Forvie Centre

OS ref.: NK 034289

Take the B9003 turn, 3 miles (4.8 km) north of Newburgh, towards Collieston. After 1½ miles (2.4 km) a track on the right leads to a car park and the Forvie Centre, where information about the reserve is displayed. Tracks lead from here into the moorland areas and Sands of Forvie National Nature Reserve. The nearby Sand Loch sometimes has Shoveler, Gadwall and (very rarely) spring Garganey and perhaps Ruddy Duck.

There is a regular bus service to Newburgh.

Timing

Apart from the restrictions mentioned above, the area is accessible at all times. The bird interest is sustained throughout the year (see Calendar). A rising or falling tide, two hours either side of high water, is best for observing the waders using the river at close quarters. High tide should be avoided, since waders will probably either be feeding in the surrounding fields, or roosting on the inaccessible Inch Geck Island. Note that high water above Waterside Bridge occurs approximately one hour later than at the estuary mouth. The Eiders at Newburgh are most easily watched at low tide, however, while they feed on the submerged mussel beds.

Species

The numbers and diversity of birds are outstanding at all times of the year. To date, 225 species have been recorded on the reserve with 43 of these as regular breeders. Approximately 2,000 pairs of Eider breed on the moor, making this the largest breeding concentration in Britain. Around 50 pairs of Shelduck also breed, using abandoned rabbit burrows.

At the southern end of the Sands of Forvie there is a large mixed tern colony of about 1,500 pairs of Sandwich, 200 pairs of Common, 50 or so pairs of Arctic and 25 plus pairs of Little Tern.

Curlew, Skylark and Meadow Pipit also breed on the moorland, whilst Oystercatcher and Ringed Plover prefer shoreline sites for their nests. Cliffs in the northern part of the reserve are colonised by Fulmar, Herring Gull, Kittiwake and (in recent years) Razorbill.

The Ythan is a major staging post for migrating geese. Up to 10,000 Pink-footed, 3,000 Greylag and smaller parties of Brent, Barnacle and White-fronted Geese can be seen during late autumn and early spring.

Lesser numbers over-winter. In addition, moderate numbers of Whooper Swan may also be present. Large numbers of duck also pass through, including Teal, Wigeon and Mallard with smaller numbers of Goldeneye and Long-tailed Duck. Drake King Eider have been recorded in both summer and winter in recent years.

The estuarine part of the reserve is an excellent feeding and roosting site for a variety of wader species and during spring and autumn passage counts of up to 1,500 each of Golden Plover and Lapwing have been recorded, as well as 1,000 each of Curlew and Redshank, whilst smaller, but significant numbers of Ringed Plover, Knot, Dunlin, Bar-tailed Godwit and Whimbrel occur. Scarcer, but still regular, passage waders include Curlew Sandpiper, Ruff, Black-tailed Godwit, Spotted Redshank, Greenshank and Green Sandpiper.

Wildfowl are generally most numerous around the Snub, whilst large high tide roosts of waders occur at Inch Geck, a favoured roosting site for Cormorant also.

Calendar

Some of the more interesting species likely to be seen.

All year: Eider, Shelduck, and Red Grouse.

March–May: Courting Eiders are prominent on the river and by early May most of the ducks will have laid. Goosander move into the river during late spring. Passage waders may stop over on the river. Skeins of northbound geese arrive and depart throughout April and into early May. Sandwich Tern arrive in late March and from April onwards the area at the southern end of the Sands of Forvie is fenced off to allow Sandwich, Common, Arctic and Little Terns to breed undisturbed.

June–July: Large numbers of Eider ducklings can be seen on the water, often in large crêches. Shelduck also take their young down to the estuary within a few days of their hatching. The four species of breeding tern can be viewed from the golf course vantage point near Newburgh. A rising tide brings shoals of herring fry and sand-eels into the estuary, resulting in frenzied tern activity. In July, skuas (mainly Arctic) enter the estuary mouth to harry the terns.

Snow Buntings and immature male Merlin, winter

August–November: Eider numbers decline, as many depart for their moulting grounds. About 1,000 remain and over-winter, however. The return passage of waders means that there is usually much activity on the river. Migrant geese can start to appear from mid-September onwards and numbers peak during late autumn.

December–February: Over-wintering geese use the fields and estuary, large herds of Whooper Swan are sometimes present. Wigeon, Teal, Goldeneye and Red-breasted Merganser are present on the river, whilst Long-tailed Duck may be seen in the estuary mouth, especially in rough sea conditions. Offshore, Red-throated Diver, Common and Velvet Scoters can usually be found in small numbers.

Short-eared Owl are a common sight over the moor whereas Hen Harrier are rare. Rough-legged Buzzard are occasional winter visitors. Peregrine and Merlin can regularly be seen hunting over the river. Snow Bunting are common winter visitors to the coast; look for Sanderling on the sea beaches.

SNH Reserves Manager

Forvie Centre, Collieston, Ellon, Aberdeenshire. Tel: 035887 330.

Adjacent sites

Cotehill Loch

OS ref.: NK 027293

This loch is visible from the B9003 road to Collieston, mentioned above, 1/4 mile (0.4 km) or so after the turn off from the A975. It is worth having a quick check for passage waders during spring and autumn and it can hold wildfowl (sometimes including Garganey) in spring. Ruddy Duck are frequently present. It is also a good northern Gadwall site.

Collieston

OS ref.: NK 043287

At the end of the B9003. The car park here can be a good sea-watching vantage point.

Meikle Loch

OS ref.: NK 028309, sheet 30

This is reached by continuing north on the A975 for 1 mile (1.6 km) past the Collieston turn-off. A rough track on the left leads down to a viewpoint of the loch, immediately before the next crossroads.

The loch is the main roost for wintering Pink-footed Geese, but also holds Whooper Swan, Tufted Duck and Goldeneye. In May/June and from late July until autumn it is sometimes visited by Black Tern; Little Gull is possible in autumn. Passage waders also occur, but they can be hard to find around the vegetated edges.

Pink-footed numbers in the area can reach tens of thousands in early autumn, whilst several thousand Greylag Geese are present in spring. A visit to the loch just before sunset for the roost flight can be spectacular; in good light the odd Snow, White-fronted or Brent Goose may be discernible.

References

'Birdwatching around the Ythan Estuary, Newburgh, Aberdeenshire', Sandy Anderson, in *Scottish Bird News 24*; December 1991.

G7 LOCH OF STRATHBEG

OS ref.: NK 063564
OS map: sheet 30

Habitat

A very large, shallow loch, on the north-east Grampian coast approximately midway between Peterhead and Fraserburgh. The 222-hectare loch is separated from the North Sea by an area of sand dunes only a few hundred metres wide. The RSPB own or manage the loch and much of the surrounding marsh, dune, farmland and wooded habitats, totalling 1,012 hectares. Extensive areas of reed-grass and other emergent vegetation fringe much of the loch; there are also scattered areas of Willow scrub. Widely fluctuating water levels mean that much of this surrounding land is frequently flooded. Loch of Strathbeg is listed as a Site of Special Scientific Interest by Scottish Natural Heritage. The reserve has a visitor centre, several hides and a lochside boardwalk. Some of the hides overlook the loch, whilst others provide views of wader scrapes.

Species

The size and location of Loch of Strathbeg combine to make it of great importance for staging and wintering wildfowl; at times more than 35,000 swans, geese and duck can be present, using the area for both feeding and roosting. Greylag and Pink-footed Geese are predominant, but smaller numbers of Barnacle Geese also visit. Small numbers of Barnacle Geese now winter, whilst Brent and White-fronted Goose are seen every year at the beginning and end of the winter. Snow Geese are regular visitors.

Breeding duck include Shelduck, Shoveler, Teal, Tufted Duck and Eider and Garganey have attempted to breed; Water Rail breed in the marshland, whilst Sedge Warbler and Reed Bunting nest in the reedbeds at the north-west end of the loch. An island supports an expanding colony of Sandwich Tern, whilst Common Tern also breed. A newly acquired part of the reserve has a rookery containing over 150 nests. Marsh Harrier and Black-tailed Godwit are present in summer. Loch of Strathbeg is an outstanding site for wader passage, especially in August when large numbers of Ruff and Black-tailed Godwit pass through, plus several species of rarer wader. Both the marshes and scrub attract migrant passerines, and Sparrowhawk, Merlin and Short-eared Owl often hunt over the reserve. Rarities are regular and in recent years have

Whooper Swans

included Bittern, Glossy Ibis, American Wigeon, Ring-necked Duck, Honey Buzzard, Lesser Yellowlegs and White-winged Black Tern.

Access

The reserve is entered from the A952 Peterhead to Fraserburgh road, some 7 miles (11.3 km) north-west of Peterhead, at the village of Crimond. The nature reserve is Thistle signposted from here.

Buses from Peterhead to Fraserburgh pass the turn-off to the reserve near Crimond.

Timing

The prime period to visit for wildfowl is between October and April, but May and June are of interest for breeding species. The nature centre and hides are open daily throughout the year. Please note that there are no public toilets on the reserve. Note also that dogs are not welcome.

Calendar

Some of the more interesting species likely to be seen.

March–June: Pink-footed and Greylag Geese begin to move north in late March and April, with all but a very few gone by the beginning of May. Other wildfowl disperse, leaving only breeding species by mid-May. Terns and warblers arrive. Spring wader passage occurs in May and continues until early June. Up to 6 Wood Sandpipers have been recorded in some years, whilst Temminck's Stint is annual.

July–August: Breeding species present; ducks enter eclipse plumage. Wader passage can be very good, especially in August; large numbers of Ruff (up to 140), Black-tailed Godwit (up to 60) and Greenshank (up to 12) can occur, whilst small numbers of Spotted Redshank, Green Sandpiper, Wood Sandpiper, Curlew Sandpiper and Little Stint are regularly recorded. Pectoral Sandpiper are annual visitors.

September–November: The first Pink-Footed Geese generally arrive during the first part of September and their numbers increase steadily towards the end of the month. From September onwards diving duck numbers start to build up, followed by an increase in the dabbling duck during October. Barnacle Geese often stage at Strathbeg during early October, on their way from Spitzbergen to wintering grounds on the Solway. Flocks of several hundred Whooper Swan are present in early November. More unusual wildfowl species, including Snow Goose, White-fronted Goose and Gadwall are seen annually in small numbers.

December–February: All over-wintering wildfowl present, including Whooper Swan, Pink-footed and Greylag Geese, Wigeon, Teal, Mallard, Pochard, Tufted Duck, Goldeneye, Red-breasted Merganser and Goosander. Smew have been regular winter visitors in recent years.

RSPB Warden

Jim Dunbar, The Lythe, Crimonmogate, Lonmay, Fraserburgh, AB4 4UB. Tel: 0346 32522.

Reference

Strathbeg Reserve, RSPB leaflet.

G8 TROUP HEAD

OS ref.: NJ 825673
OS map: sheets 29 or 30

Habitat

The rocky north-facing sea-cliffs of Troup Head extend for 5 miles (8 km) between Aberdour Bay and Crovie, some 10 miles (16 km) east of Banff. Large numbers of seabirds are present during the breeding season and the bays hold wintering divers and sea-duck. The area includes Troup and Lion's Head to the west of Pennan village and Pennan Head to the east. Rising to around 100 metres in height, the cliffs and steep, vegetated slopes consist mainly of sheer gritstone in the west and spectacularly eroded sandstone/conglomerate to the east. Agricultural land extends to the cliff edge along virtually the whole length, although there are some interesting areas of maritime heath and grassland vegetation. The coast is designated a Site of Special Scientific Interest.

Access

All of the cliff top is privately owned and the only public access points are at Lion's Head and Aberdour Bay. These are approached from either the New Aberdour or Macduff directions along the B9031. If visiting Lion's Head, there is a car park at Cullykhan, between the Gardenstown and Pennan turn-offs, or alternatively, car parking is possible at Northfield Farm, 1½ miles (2.4 km) east of the Gardenstown signpost (please ask at the farm for permission to park). From here the coast can be reached by walking northwards to the head of a large gully, then by following its left bank to the headland. The car park at Aberdour Bay lies immediately north of New Aberdour on the B9031.

There is a vague path along the cliff top. Several promontories between Lion's Head and Troup Head provide good views of nesting seabirds. There are fewer good vantage points on the eastern cliffs.

Timing

The optimum time to visit would be between May and mid-July, when seabird activity is at its peak. Relatively calm conditions are essential for viewing seabirds here, owing to the exposed situation of the vantage points.

Species

About 1,500 pairs of Fulmar breed, scattered throughout both the eastern and western cliffs. West of Pennan, approximately 125 pairs of Shag, over 16,000 pairs of Kittiwake, 16,000 Guillemot and 1,200 Razorbill have been counted. In excess of 60 Puffin and one or two pairs of Black Guillemot also occur, mainly to the east of Pennan village. Eider are visible throughout the year.

Calendar

Some of the more interesting species likely to be seen.

April–June: Breeding seabirds dominate the interest (see above).

July–August: Breeding birds start to disperse; Great and Arctic Skuas visible offshore.

November–March: Offshore divers and sea-duck join the Eider in the sheltered bays.

Reference

'Seabirds of Troup and Pennan Heads 1979–86', C.S. Lloyd and S.G. North, *Scottish Birds* vol. 14, no. 4 (1987).

G9 BANFF/MACDUFF HARBOUR

OS ref.: NJ 69/64
OS map: sheet 29

Habitat and Access

This is a renowned location for winter sea-duck and gulls. Banff is situated on Grampian's north-facing coastline, some 25 miles (40 km) west of Fraserburgh. The harbour and rocky coastline around Banff can be viewed from any number of vantage points along the coastline.

Species

Winter: Red-throated Diver, Velvet Scoter, Eider, Iceland and Glaucous Gulls, with Purple Sandpiper and Turnstone on the rocky foreshore. Great Northern and Black-throated Divers are sometimes present.

Passage birds include divers, both Common and Velvet Scoters, Eider and skuas. Little Auks are numerous during late autumn in some years.

Great Black-backed Gulls and Glaucous Gull – adults, winter

G10 SPEY BAY

OS ref.: NJ 335658
OS map: sheet 28

Habitat

This very wide, shallow bay is situated to the east of Lossiemouth. There are about 6 miles (9.7 km) of shoreline on each side of the mouth of the River Spey at Kingston. The inter-tidal area is predominantly sand and shingle in the western half of the bay, whilst rocky substrates characterise the eastern part.

Lossie Forest, to the east of Lossiemouth, is a mixed plantation of Scots and Corsican Pine.

Long-tailed Duck, winter

Species

The numbers of wintering sea-duck in Spey Bay are substantially lower than was formerly the case. Currently up to 1,000 Common Scoter and Long-tailed Duck over-winter, with around 500 Velvet Scoter. A few hundred Eider and small numbers of Scaup, Red-breasted Merganser and an occasional Surf Scoter are recorded most years. Up to 700 Red-throated Diver have been counted in late autumn/early winter, whilst very small numbers of Great Northern and Black-throated Diver are sometimes present.

The tidal area at the mouth of the Spey can be good for passage waders in autumn. To the east, the rocky shoreline around Portessie can hold up to 300 Purple Sandpiper and large numbers of Turnstone.

Large flocks of Snow Bunting may be found along the shoreline in winter, particularly towards Lossiemouth.

Goosander can be seen offshore during the summer months and large numbers of Sandwich Tern may be present in late summer/early autumn.

Crested Tit and Scottish Crossbill are present throughout the year at Lossie Forest.

Access

The following access points are recommended:

1 From Lossiemouth

OS ref.: NJ 238705

(See G11.) Cross the wooden footbridge over the River Lossie and walk east along the shore. The Lossie estuary is best worked for waders at low tide.

2 Boar's Head Rock

OS ref.: NJ 285678

Take the B9013 from Lossiemouth for 2 miles (3.2 km) to NJ 255670, (just over the River Lossie at Arthur's Bridge). From here a forestry track leads

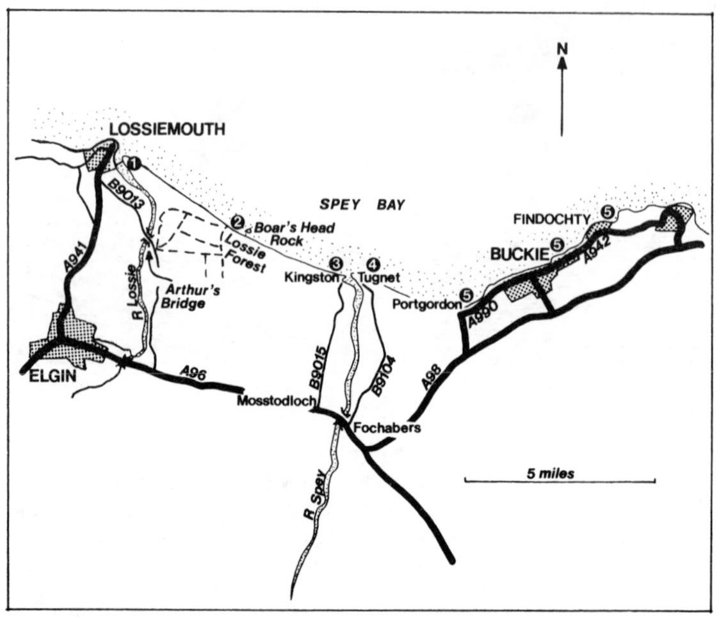

through Lossie Forest to Boar's Head Rock, a favourite feeding area for wintering sea-duck. This is a 2-mile (3.2 km) walk and there are a number of potentially confusing tracks – an OS map is therefore essential.

3 Kingston

OS ref.: NJ 340657

One mile (1.6 km) west of Fochabers take the B9015 turning off the main A96 at Mosstodloch. Kingston is reached 3½ miles (5.6 km) later. The tidal area at the mouth of the river is good for migrant waders. Access is easily obtained from the picnic site overlooking the estuary. A low tide is essential for watching birds in the estuary. Calm conditions are preferable for the sea-duck, which may be rather distant from the shore.

4 Tugnet

OS ref.: NJ 348656

This is on the opposite side of the river to Kingston and is reached via the B9104 from Fochabers. Again, the river mouth should be checked for waders, then walk eastwards along the shore.

5 Portgordon, Buckie and Findochty

The harbours along the A990/A942 are worth checking in winter for white-winged gulls and sheltering sea-fowl.

Timing

Spey Bay is mainly of interest between autumn and spring, although many sea-duck are present throughout the year.

G11 LOSSIEMOUTH

OS ref.: NJ 239712
OS map: sheet 28

Branderburgh pier and harbour at Lossiemouth are excellent sites for observing wintering sea-fowl and passage seabirds. The area is reached from Elgin by taking the A941 northwards for 5 miles (8 km).

Species

Sea-duck, especially Eider and Long-tailed Duck, enter the harbour in winter, whilst small numbers of Red-throated (and occasional Great Northern) Divers, Common Scoter and a few Velvet Scoter can be seen offshore.

Glaucous Gulls are regularly seen amongst the flocks of bathing and loafing gulls at the edge of the river.

Guillemot and Razorbill also enter the harbour; Little Auk have been known to take shelter there in some winters.

Large flocks of Snow Bunting are sometimes present and can usually be found either in the dunes or on the shoreline east of the town, reached via the wooden footbridge across the River Lossie (see G10).

The fields between Elgin and Lossiemouth usually hold Greylag Geese and occasionally Whooper Swan, together with large flocks of Greenfinch and Linnet. Corn Bunting occur here throughout the year.

Wader passage can be good in the tidal reaches of the River Lossie. Rarities in recent years have included Marsh and Pectoral Sandpipers.

Seawatching from the north side of the harbour can produce good numbers of Great, Arctic and occasional Pomarine Skuas. Little Auk are occasionally reported during autumn and early winter.

G12 BURGHEAD

OS ref.: NJ 110690
OS map: sheet 28

Burghead lies to the west of Lossiemouth and has a similar range of species. It can be reached by taking the A96 west from Elgin, turning north after 3 miles (4.8 km) onto the B9013. Burghead is reached 4½ miles (7.2 km) later.

Species

Eider and Long-tailed duck regularly enter the harbour and in late winter the latter can be watched displaying at very close range. Glaucous and Iceland Gulls can be found amongst the commoner gulls that frequent the harbour. A few Black-Guillemot are generally present and in some winters Little Auk use the harbour for shelter.

Both Common and Velvet Scoter flocks occur offshore and Surf Scoter are seen in most winters. Small numbers of Red-throated (and occasionally Great Northern) Divers are usually present. The harbour and headland make good viewpoints. The headland itself is an excellent place for watching Purple Sandpiper, although at high water they roost on the harbour wall.

G13 FINDHORN BAY

OS ref.: NJ 045625
OS map: sheet 27

Habitat and Access

This large tidal basin is almost completely land-locked, there being only a narrow northern outlet into the Moray Firth. The most straightforward approach to the bay is along the B9011 from Forres, via Kinloss. After 2 miles (3.2 km) this road more or less follows the eastern side of the bay and good views can be obtained from the roadside. Continue to Findhorn village, where it is possible to walk to the mouth of the bay – offshore is the best area for wintering sea-duck in winter and terns in summer.

Access to the western side of the bay is more complicated: 1 mile (1.6 km) west of Forres an unclassified road turns north off the A96, immediately after the bridge over the River Findhorn. Follow this road, without turning off, for 2½ miles (4 km) until just past Wellside Farm. Park here, taking care not to obstruct access, and walk about ¾ mile (1.2 km) along the track to the bay.

Species

Small numbers of Eider, Oystercatcher and Ringed Plover breed nearby, whilst Sandwich, Common and Arctic Terns can be watched feeding in the entrance to the bay in summer. The bay is also a favourite fishing haunt of Osprey. Crested Tit breed in the forest to the west.

Migrant waders include large numbers of Oystercatcher, Redshank, Knot, Ringed Plover and Dunlin, with smaller numbers of Greenshank, Whimbrel, Curlew Sandpiper and Black-tailed Godwit. Spotted Redshank and Little Stint are occasionally recorded. Sandwich Tern can be seen in the bay during late summer/early autumn, whilst offshore, Gannet and skuas occur.

Wintering sea-fowl are represented by large numbers of Long-tailed Duck, Common and Velvet Scoters, Red-breasted Merganser and Eider. Divers, especially Red-throated but also Great Northern and Black-throated, are regular offshore, particularly in late autumn.

Timing

Findhorn Bay has year-round attractions, although the large numbers of sea-fowl that gather offshore and in the entrance to the bay between autumn and early spring, or the passage waders that move through in spring and autumn, tend to be the prime lures for birders.

G14 HADDO COUNTRY PARK

OS ref.: NJ 875345
OS map: sheet 30

Habitat

Formerly part of the policies of Haddo House, this 73-hectare country park comprises parkland, woodland and wetland (including a loch and several ponds). Both broadleaved and coniferous trees are present and in recent years over 2,000 trees (mainly broadleaved) have been planted, greatly enhancing the wildlife potential of the area.

Species

A few pairs each of Heron, feral Greylag Goose, Mallard, Tufted Duck and Stock Dove breed at Haddo. One pair of Mute Swan occupies the Middle Lake throughout the year. Other resident species include Buzzard, Sparrowhawk, Kestrel, Grey Partridge, Pheasant, Moorhen, Great Spotted Woodpecker, Grey Wagtail and Goldcrest.

In spring and summer these are joined by around seven or eight pairs of Sedge Warbler and one or two pairs of Blackcap and Chiffchaff. Small numbers of Oystercatcher and Lapwing breed. Osprey are regular visitors to the loch.

The area is not particularly noted for migrants, although significant records in recent years have included Wood Sandpiper in spring and small flocks of Crossbill in the pine woods during July and August. In late summer, Sand and House Martins gather in large numbers over the Middle Lake.

Wintering wildfowl are dominated by large numbers of roosting Greylag Geese, especially in November/December when staging birds are present. Depending on the weather conditions, up to 5,000 Greylag can be present throughout much of the winter. In addition, over 100 Teal are usually present, mostly frequenting the reed bed areas. Fifty or so Wigeon and up to ten Pochard and a similar number of Goldeneye can be seen amongst the Tufted Duck, which number about 40 strong during the winter. The Middle Lake can host as many as 60 Goosander in the late winter.

Water Rail have been seen in the reed beds during winter, whilst small numbers of Brambling and Siskin have been recorded.

Access

Take the A92 from Aberdeen to Peterhead, turning off onto the B999 after Bridge of Don, 3 miles (4.8 km) later. Follow this road to Tarves (*c.* 13 miles (20 km)), then follow signs for Haddo House. There is ample parking space. Two bird hides overlook the loch and wetland parts of the park and there are a number of paths through the woodlands. A leaflet describing the park is available from the Ranger's Office and country park display at the Stables Block adjacent to Haddo House itself. Special facilities are available for handicapped visitors – contact Ranger Service in advance (see below).

Please note that dogs must be kept on a lead at all times.

There is a bus service from Aberdeen to Tarves, about two miles from the park entrance.

Timing

The country park is best visited between October and April, when a range of wintering wildfowl can be seen. Weekends, especially Sunday afternoons, can be very busy and are best avoided. The park is open daily from dawn to dusk.

For further information, contact Grampian Regional Council Ranger Service. Tel: Tarves 489.

G15 GLEN MUICK AND LOCHNAGAR

OS ref.: NO 300850
OS map: sheet 44

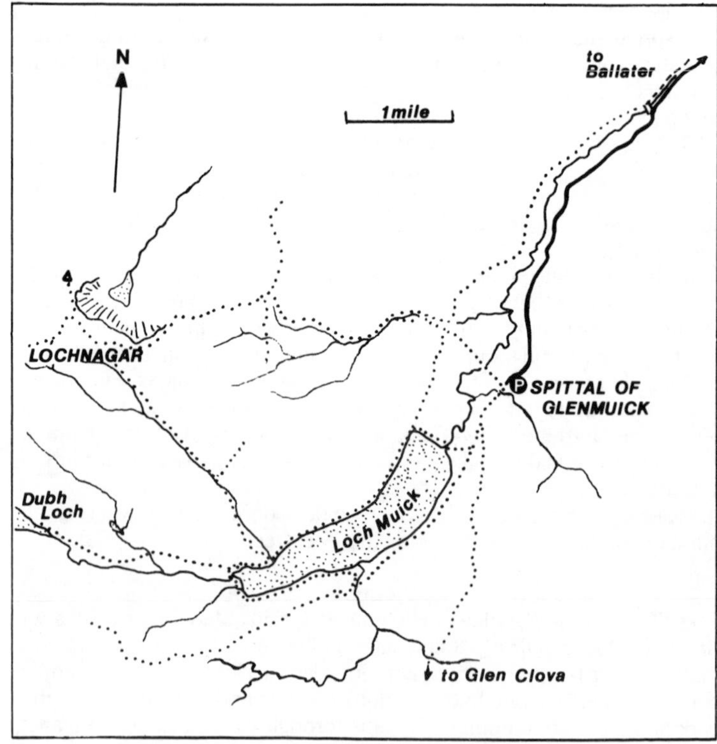

Habitat

The is one of the grandest parts of the eastern Grampians. Under an agreement with the Balmoral Estate, the Scottish Wildlife Trust manages a total of 2,570 hectares here, including Loch Muick, the plateau summit of Lochnagar and its spectacular northern corries, acres of open moorland and the craggy valley sides above Dubh Loch. The area has been designated a Site of Special Scientific Interest.

Further information is available at the visitor centre at Spittal of Glenmuick. The Estate operates a ranger service and has a reserve booklet on sale at the centre.

Species

Ptarmigan, Red and Black Grouse breed in the area. Breeding waders include Dotterel, Golden Plover and Dunlin, whilst Common Sandpiper frequent the shoreline of Loch Muick. Lochnagar is an excellent area for birds of prey and a regular eye should be kept on the skylines for Golden Eagle and Peregrine; Hen Harrier, and Merlin too, can be seen.

Access

Lochnagar is reached by taking the B976 westwards from Ballater, then turning left onto an unclassified road at Bridge of Glen Muick, just over ½ mile (0.8 km) further ahead. From here it is 8 miles (13 km) to a car park at the road end at Spittal of Glenmuick.

There are several paths leading away from the visitor centre, varying from the straightforward route along the shores of Loch Muick, to the more arduous climb to the summit of Lochnagar itself. A useful compro-

Meadow Pipit and Cuckoo, spring

mise is possible by tackling the moderate gradients of the track that leads southwards towards Glen Clova. Alternatively, cross the River Muick and take the track that leads northwards from Allt-na-guibhsaich through the woods.

Please note that all visitors are requested to keep to the paths, especially during the stalking season. Adequate footwear and clothing are essential if venturing onto the high ground.

Timing

The optimum time to visit Lochnagar is from May through until September, although a winter visit can be recommended for seeing large numbers of Red Deer.

G16 GLEN TANAR

OS ref.: 47/96
OS map: sheet 44

Habitat

The Glen Tanar National Nature Reserve covers 4,185 hectares of pine forest and moorland habitats, managed jointly by the Glen Tanar estate and Nature Conservancy Council. The forest is an important remnant of the old Caledonian forest and contains many fine mature trees with an understorey of heather, bilberry and cowberry. Juniper, some rowan, aspen and birch also occur.

Extensive, high quality heather moorland blankets the lower flanks of the mountains, although there is much natural regeneration of Scots Pine in some places. To the south, the ground rises gradually to the Grampian/Tayside watershed, whose summits include Mount Keen (939 metres), Hill of Gairney (756 metres) and Hill of Cat (742 metres). This ancient massif is bisected by the Waters of Tanar, Gairney and Allachy, which combine to flow northwards into the Dee.

Red Grouse

Species

Capercaillie and Scottish Crossbill are both reasonably common in the pinewoods. Crested Tit, however, are noticeable by their absence – there were records of these birds from Deeside in 1973, 1974, 1975 and 1977, but none since. Other breeding species of interest include Sparrowhawk, Black Grouse, Woodcock and Siskin in the pinewoods, Dipper and Grey Wagtail on the rivers and Ptarmigan on the summits.

Regular scanning of the open ground and ridges should produce views of raptors, especially Hen Harrier, Golden Eagle and Merlin.

Access

From Aboyne, on the main A93 Banchory–Braemar road, turn south across the River Dee, then west on the B976, following the south bank of the river. At Bridge o'Ess, 1½ miles (2.4 km) later, take the minor road left to Braeloine (1½ miles (2.4 km)), where there is a car park. A visitor centre, open from April through to September, on the opposite bank of the Tanar, gives some background information about the reserve. A little further upstream there are a number of trails leading off from Glen Tanar House into the surrounding woods, any of which can be good for birds.

Two old high-level drove roads – the Mounth Road and the Firmounth Road – lead southwards along Glen Tanar and Water of Allachy respectively and eventually climb up to the Grampian/Tayside watershed. These are the best routes for seeing open country species such as raptors and grouse, but the full expedition onto the watershed, or the summits of Mount Keen, Cock Cairn or Hill of Cat, is a considerable undertaking and should only be undertaken by fit and experienced hill-walkers.

Please note that access is permitted only along way-marked trails and the drove roads. There may be other restrictions in force during grouse shooting/stalking seasons – details should be posted at the visitor centre.

A ranger is present during the summer months.

Timing

The best time to visit is between May and September.

ADDITIONAL SITES

Site and Grid Reference	Habitat	Main Bird Interest	Peak Season
a. Crathes Castle NTS NO 73/96 Sheet 38 or 45	About 600 acres of mixed woodland, ponds and farmland	Woodland species, inc. Buzzard, Woodcock, Green & GS Woodpeckers, Jay	All year.

A ranger service provides information and a guided walks programme. There are five way-marked trails, inc. one suitable for wheelchair users.

Site and Grid Reference	Habitat	Main Bird Interest	Peak Season
b. Drum NTS NJ 79/00 Sheet 38	About 117 acres of mixed woodland, inc. ancient oakwood	Resident woodland birds, inc. Green & GS Woodpeckers, Jay & *c*. 500 prs of Rook	All year.
		Breeding visitors inc. Blackcap & Garden Warbler	Apr.–July.
c. Leith Hall NTS NJ 54/29 Sheet 37	Farm and woodland, some hill ground, two ponds	Common woodland and open ground species. Small number of waterfowl	Apr.–Aug.

There are three trails through the grounds and a bird hide.

Site and Grid Reference	Habitat	Main Bird Interest	Peak Season
d. Longhaven Cliffs SWT reserve NK 117394 Sheet 30	Coastal granite cliffs	Breeding seabirds – a total of *c*. 23,000 prs of nine species	May–July.
e. Muir of Dinnet SNH reserve NO 43/99 Sheet 37 or 44	Moorland, woodland, lochs and bog	Wintering wildfowl, inc. Whooper Swan, Greylag & Pink-footed Geese, small numbers of Pintail, Gadwall & Shoveler	Oct.–Mar.
		Hen Harrier often present	
f. Rattray Head NK 10/58 Sheet 30	Coastal peninsula	Passage seabirds, inc. regular RT & GN Divers, Sooty & Manx Shearwater, Gannet, Arctic & Gt Skua	Apr.–May. & Sept.–Oct.
		Falls of passerines in Sept/Oct.	
		Long-tailed Duck in winter	

HIGHLAND

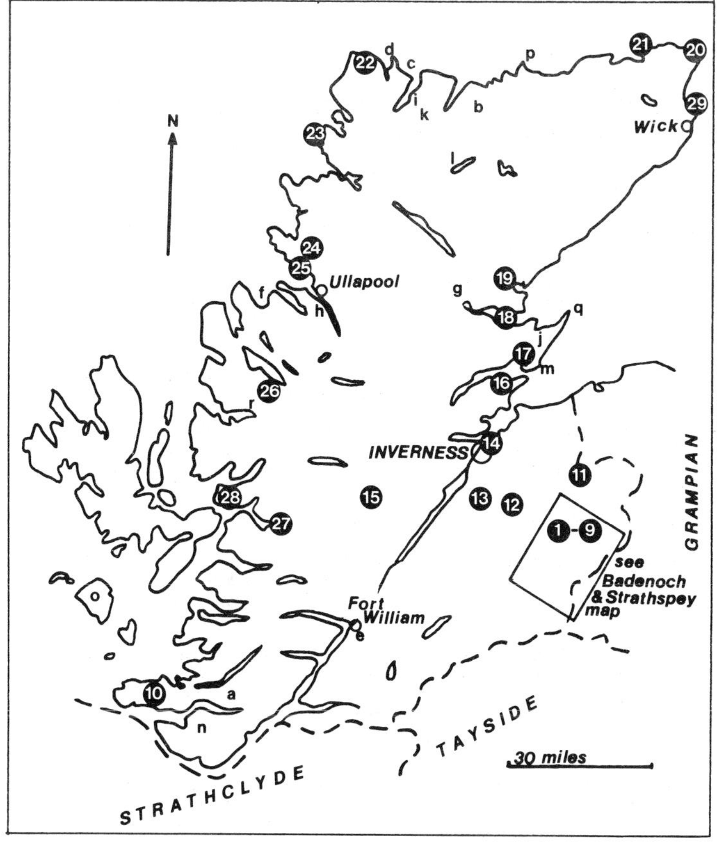

Main sites

H1. Aviemore
H2. Abernethy Forest – Loch Garten
H3. Rothiemurchus
H4. Pass of Ryvoan
H5. Cairngorm/Ben Macdui
H6. Carn Ban Mor
H7. Glen Feshie
H8. Insh Marshes
H9. Glen Tromie
H10. Glenborodale/ Ardnamurchan
H11. Lochindorb
H12. Findhorn Valley
H13. Loch Ruthven
H14. Longman Point
H15. Glen Affric
H16. Udale Bay
H17. Nigg Bay
H18. Dornoch Firth
H19. Loch Fleet
H20. Duncansby Head
H21. Dunnet Head
H22. Clo Mor
H23. Handa Island
H24. Inverpolly
H25. Ben Mor Coigach
H26. Beinn Eighe
H27. Kintail and Morvich
H28. Balmacara
H29. Noss Head

Additional sites

a. Ariundle
b. Borgie Forest
c. Eilean Hoan
d. Faraid Head
e. Glen Nevis
f. Gruinard Bay
g. Kyle of Sutherland
h. Loch Broom
i. Loch Eriboll
j. Loch Eye
k. Loch Hope
l. Loch Naver
m. North Sutor
n. Rahoy Hills
o. Rum
p. Strathy Point
q. Tarbat Ness
r. Torridon

H1 AVIEMORE

OS map: sheet 36

Three areas are of particular interest here:

Craigellachie

OS ref.: NH 88/12

Habitat and Access

This is a 260-hectare National Nature Reserve consisting mainly of Birch woodland situated below sheer cliffs and open heather moorland. The crags are a well-known and freely publicised site for breeding Peregrine, which can be watched from the public footpath below.

Craigellachie is on the very edge of Aviemore and can be reached from the car park next to the artificial ski-slope by walking along the path that goes under the A9 road. The Peregrine crag is now on the left. Several well-marked footpaths continue beyond this point and on into the woodland.

Species

The area is also notable for several woodland species: Great Spotted Woodpecker are resident, whilst migrant breeders include Tree Pipit, Redstart, Wood Warbler and Spotted Flycatcher. Siskin can usually be seen during autumn and winter.

Timing

The Peregrines should be present from April through to July, but it may be necessary to wait patiently for some time before the birds show themselves.

Inverdruie Fish Farm

OS ref.: NH 898117

Another site on the outskirts of Aviemore, this time famed for its Osprey, which fish over the ponds on a daily basis during the summer.

Access

The entrance to the farm is reached by taking the road east from Aviemore towards Coylumbridge, then turning into the car park immediately after the bridge over the River Spey. It is an easy stroll from the town centre and is best reached on foot via a footpath opposite the Tourist Information Office, which leads to the fish farm via Mac's pub and a footbridge over the Spey.

Species

A hide overlooks the large, well-stocked pool, which can attract three or four Osprey at a time, particularly in late summer, when adults are feeding young or the young themselves may come and feed.

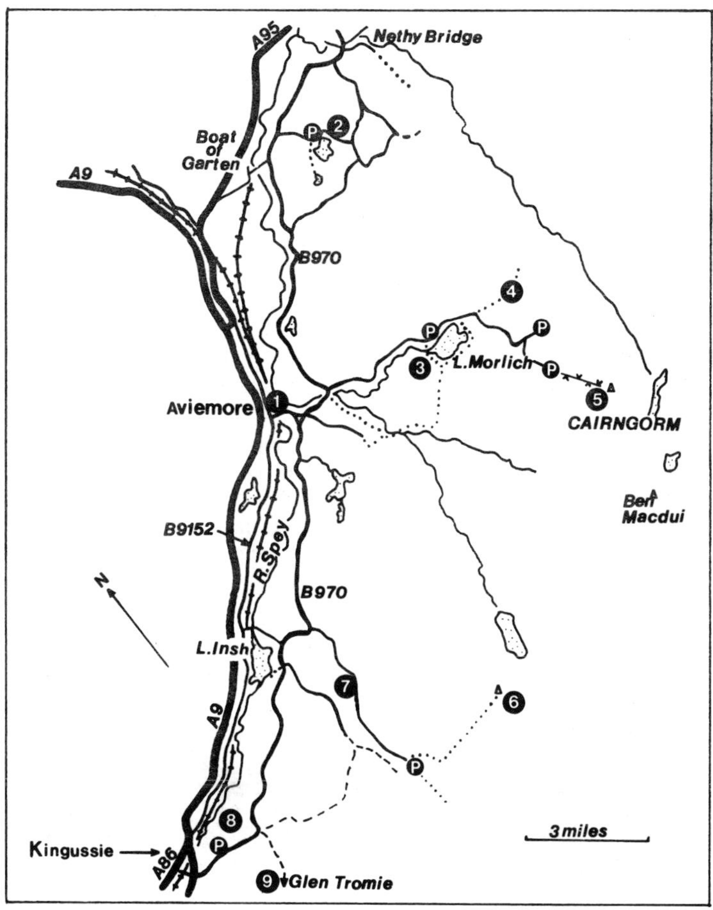

Tufted Duck and Goldeneye are often present on the pool, whilst Garden Warbler and Wood Warbler inhabit the surrounding scrub and trees.

Timing

The Ospreys can be seen throughout the summer. The Fish Farm is popular with tourists and the best time for birding is therefore early in the morning (before 8 am) or late evening (after 6 pm).

Loch An Eilein

OS ref.: NH 895075

This scenic loch is famous for its ruined castle, symbol of Scottish tourism, upon which Osprey once nested. It is reached by turning south onto the B970 at Inverdruie, 1 mile (1.6 km) from Aviemore. Take the unclassified road left 1 mile (1.6 km) later and follow this another ¾ mile (1.2 km) to the car park. From here a nature trail leads around the lochshore. Goldeneye are usually present and Red-throated Diver visit during summer. In the surrounding woodland, Redstart, Crested Tit, Siskin and Scottish Crossbill might be seen, whilst Green Woodpecker are present in some years.

H2 ABERNETHY FOREST – LOCH GARTEN

OS ref.: NH 975180
OS map: sheet 36

Habitat

Loch Garten is part of the RSPB's Abernethy Forest Reserve and is world famous for its breeding Ospreys. This 12,500-hectare reserve also holds several pine forest 'specialities'. The area, designated a Site of Special Scientific Interest, is a remnant of the once more extensive Caledon Forest. The habitat includes forest bogs, lochs, heather moorland, mountain plateau and crofting land.

Ospreys, spring

Species

Goldeneye can be seen on Loch Garten and Loch Mallachie throughout the summer. Crested Tit are common in the woods and Scottish Crossbill are usually present – the track to Loch Mallachie is probably as good a place as any to find them. Capercaillie are very scarce, but they can sometimes be encountered on the road early in the morning, or occasionally in front of the Osprey hide! Woodcock are plentiful and particularly conspicuous during early April–early June, when they can be seen (and heard) 'roding' in the evenings.

Other interesting breeding birds include Sparrowhawk, Great Spotted Woodpecker, Redstart and Siskin.

If travelling through Boat of Garten, it is well worthwhile briefly checking the River Spey as you cross the bridge – Goldeneye, Red-breasted Merganser and sometimes Dipper can be seen. Failing that, the view of the Cairngorms is terrific on a clear day.

In November–December, up to 1,500 Greylag Geese roost on Loch Garten (when not frozen), along with several of the larger gulls. From October to November, up to 100 Goosander have roosted, and Goldeneye are usually present. From early March, a gull roost of up to 4,500 Black-headed Gulls can be seen here, along with good numbers of the commoner ducks, including up to ten Red-breasted Merganser.

Access

Loch Garten lies mid-way between the villages of Nethy Bridge and Boat of Garten (about 2½ miles (4 km) from each) and is well signposted off the B970. Buses run from Aviemore and Grantown to Nethy Bridge and Boat of Garten – the best place to alight is at East Croftmore, about a mile (1.6 km) away from the loch. The nearest mainline rail station is at Carrbridge (8 miles (13 km) distant), but the Strathspey railway, which links Aviemore to Boat of Garten, may be of use.

Contrary to most people's expectations, the Osprey eyrie is not on the lochshore, but on the opposite side of the road.

Aside from the obvious restrictions in the vicinity of the Osprey nest, there is open access to the reserve. From the car park a short track leads to the Osprey observation hide, which affords excellent views of the eyrie and is equipped with telescopes and binoculars and closed circuit TV system. The hide is accessible to wheelchair users and assistance along the track is available – alternatively a post can be removed to enable cars with disabled occupants to drive up to the hide. Some of the other forest tracks are also negotiable by wheelchair.

During the summer, an RSPB warden conducts guided walks through the reserve: make arrangements with staff at the Osprey hide. Parties are limited to 12–15 people.

Timing

Provided that the Ospreys are nesting, the observation hide is open daily from late April to August, 10 am to 8 pm. (*Note:* the hide is not open until some time after the birds first arrive back, in order to give them a chance to re-establish themselves and settle down. Announcements in the press that 'the Ospreys are back' do not necessarily mean that they are yet on public view. If in doubt, contact the tourist information office in Aviemore, where up-to-date information is available. The most exciting time to visit is probably July and early August, when the birds should be feeding young.)

Warden

Richard Thaxton, Grianan, Nethybridge, Invernessshire PH25 3EF.

Adjacent sites

Loch Pityoulish

OS ref.: NH 920135

Visible from the B970 Coylumbridge to Boat of Garten road, this loch holds Goldeneye and Goosander in the summer and is occasionally fished by Osprey.

H3 ROTHIEMURCHUS AND LOCH MORLICH

OS ref.: NH 93/08
OS map: sheet 36

Habitat

A large area of the formerly extensive Caledonian pine forest, holding many of the characteristic native pinewood species. Loch Morlich is much disturbed by watersport enthusiasts, but is still a good location for waterfowl and fishing Osprey. Unfortunately, conifers have been planted right to the edge of the loch, making it unsuitable these days for nesting Greenshank. The loch is within the Forestry Commission's Glenmore Forest Park, a 2,644-hectare expanse of commercial woodland and heather moor. The birds of the Forest Park are similar to those of Rothiemurchus, but the area is not as inspiring scenically.

Species

Loch Morlich has Wigeon and small parties of Goosander throughout the year. Red-throated Diver and Goldeneye are regular in spring and summer and Osprey occasionally visit. Capercaillie are present in the woods, but are elusive and thought to be declining. Crested Tit are very common and can be found year-round, but Scottish Crossbill may need more effort to locate; they are nomadic and numbers fluctuate greatly from year to year.

Other species include Sparrowhawk, Black Grouse, Woodcock and Siskin. Redstart are common in spring.

Access

A network of footpaths lead through the area – the main access points to these are:

1. from Coylumbridge, 1½ miles (2.4 km) east of Aviemore on the A951. A track starts from near the telephone box.

2. from Whitewell, at the end of the minor road out of Inverdruie, 1½ miles (2.4 km) from Aviemore.

3. from the west end of Loch Morlich, 2½ miles (4 km) along the Glenmore road out of Coylumbridge.

Timing

A spring visit is highly recommended, although there is bird interest all year. Late March to early May is probably the best time to locate Capercaillie (mid-summer is probably the hardest) and a stealthy early morning walk in the forest is probably the only way that you are likely to see anything other than a huge black shape explode from amongst the branches ahead. With a lot of luck, a dawn visit may produce a displaying male or perhaps a female taking grit or drinking from a puddle.

H4 PASS OF RYVOAN

OS ref.: NH 999105
OS map: sheet 36

Habitat and Access

A small (121-hectare) reserve managed by the Scottish Wildlife Trust. The steep-sided valley has an attractive mix of open pinewoods, Juniper scrub, Willow, Birch and Rowan, with heather and bilberry slopes above.

From Aviemore, take the road to the ski-slopes as far as Glenmore. Park in the Forestry Commission car park and walk up the road past Glenmore Lodge. It is a 40-minute walk to the reserve and the track then carries on through Abernethy Forest and eventually to Nethybridge, a distance of some 11 miles (17.6 km).

Species

The species of greatest interest are Woodcock, Crested Tit, Siskin and Scottish Crossbill. Whinchat and Redstart can be seen in spring and summer.

Timing

The reserve makes a good excursion at any time of year, but between April and July is the most rewarding time for birds.

H5 CAIRNGORM/BEN MACDUI PLATEAU

OS ref.: NJ 005041
OS map: sheet 36

Habitat

This is the highest mountain plateau in Britain and includes the summits of Cairngorm (1,245 metres) and Ben Macdui (1,309 metres). Not only is the area scenically impressive, but the barren-looking boulder fields are the haunt of three specialist mountain birds: Ptarmigan, Dotterel and Snow Bunting.

Much of the area is a National Nature Reserve and also an RSPB reserve.

Access

Because of the Cairngorm chairlift the area is very easy to visit, although it must be stressed that the weather conditions can be arctic and the trip should not be taken lightly, even in summer. Extra clothing, food, a map and compass are all important if you intend to wander any distance from the chairlift. It would be safer, and a better use of time, to explore around Loch Morlich and in Rothiemurchus if the cloud base is low in the morning – often it will clear by the afternoon.

Take the Coylumbridge road from Aviemore and continue along the 'ski-road' which leads past Loch Morlich and on to the Cairngorm chairlift car park, 8 miles (13 km) later. There is a regular bus service from Aviemore at all times of the year. The chairlift itself operates in all but the worst conditions. Several paths also lead onto the plateau (see OS map). (Note: Jean's Mountain Refuge Hut, marked on all but the most recent OS maps as being in Coire an Lochain, no longer exists.)

From the chairlift station, head south towards Ben Macdui – in general, the chances of finding birds increase with distance from the chairlift station, although it should not be necessary to walk too far. A good

Ptarmigan, winter

technique is to scan the ground with binoculars every 30 or 40 metres or so. Also check out *any* bird calls, since at this altitude they are all likely to be interesting! It is disappointing that some groups of birdwatchers find it necessary to form a line and virtually beat across the plateau in order to locate birds – they are doing neither the birds nor birdwatching a service.

Timing

May to early July is probably the ideal time to visit, although Ptarmigan and Snow Bunting can be found year-round.

Species

Ptarmigan are resident on the plateau just about all year, but during the winter when there is a lot of snow cover, it is probably easier to locate them at lower altitude, at Coire an t-Sneachda and Coire an Lochain, for instance, Dotterel are present from early May through to late August; the adults' plumages start to look rather dowdy from late July onwards, although gatherings of adults and young during August can look quite impressive. Snow Bunting are perhaps the least predictable of the Cairngorm 'specialities', as their population tends to fluctuate from year to year. During the winter they are often numerous, however, and can be found feeding all around the chairlift stations and car parks.

Other species that occur: Golden Eagle and Peregrine can both be seen here, although the plateau is not an easy area in which to locate them. Although not seen annually, Snowy Owl has been seen during late summer in several years.

H6 CARN BAN MOR

OS ref.: NN 89/97
OS map: sheets 35/36

This is another good area for high mountain species; Ptarmigan and Dotterel are very likely to be seen here, but Snow Bunting are more elusive than on Cairngorm plateau. Golden Eagle also frequent the area.

Golden Plover, spring

Access

Take the B970 from Inverdruie, near Aviemore, or from Kingussie. At Feshiebridge, about 7 miles (11 km) from Kingussie, turn south onto the Lagganlia road and follow it to the end, some 5 miles (8 km) later, at Achlean. There is space to park a car here and the start of the well-worn track to the summit of Carn Ban Mor is obvious. This involves a long ascent of over 700 metres and once again, the weather conditions should not be underestimated. Quite apart from the birdlife, the scenery is dramatic, particularly the view down into Loch Einich.

H7 GLEN FESHIE

OS ref.: NN 850960
OS map: sheets 35/36/43

Habitat and Access

A long glen comprising open hill ground, patches of native pinewood and some Birch woodland. There has been much afforestation of the lower glen.

Two roads lead into Glen Feshie from the B970; one each side of the river. The best approach to the upper glen is from the road end at Achlean, the starting point for the ascent of Carn Ban Mor (H6). From here a path more or less follows the river. Alternatively, turn off the B970 at Insh House, 7 miles (11.3 km) from Kingussie, and follow the minor road for 2½ miles (4 km) until its end. Again, a track along the riverside leads into the upper valley.

Species

The glen is a good area for raptors: Hen Harrier, Golden Eagle, Merlin and Peregrine are all possible. Dipper and Grey Wagtail frequent the river and Ring Ousel call from the valley-sides. The pinewoods hold Crested Tit and Scottish Crossbill.

Timing

The period April to mid-July is recommended, but the area would make an interesting autumn or winter excursion as well.

Adjacent site

Vath Lochan

OS ref.: NH 946192

This Forestry Commission picnic area between Glen Feshie and Insh Marshes is a good site for Goldeneye, Great Spotted Woodpecker, Redstart, Crested Tit and Scottish Crossbill.

H8 INSH MARSHES

OS ref.: NN 77/99
OS map: sheet 35

Habitat

Insh Marshes occupy the floodplain of the River Spey between Kingussie and Loch Insh, some 5 miles (8 km) down-river. The reserve covers 850 hectares of wetland, farmland, moorland, scrub and woodland habitat, much of it designated a Site of Special Scientific Interest.

The marshes include several pools, areas of rough pasture and scattered Willow carr. They are regularly flooded in winter, sometimes to a depth of a metre or so. In summer, however, some of the shallower pools may dry out.

Species

The marshes and fens provide nesting habitat for a wide variety of wildfowl and waders, including Wigeon, Teal, Shoveler, Tufted Duck, Goldeneye, Greylag Goose, Snipe, Curlew and Redshank. Wood Sandpiper usually breed and Spotted Crake call in most years. Water Rail also breed and the emergent vegetation and scrub hold Sedge Warbler, Grasshopper Warbler and Reed Bunting.

In the drier Birch woodlands, Great Spotted Woodpecker, Tree Pipit, Redstart, Pied Flycatcher and Wood Warbler occasionally nest. Up to ten species of raptor have been recorded in July and August.

The principal attraction in winter are the large numbers of Whooper Swan that are usually present.

Access

The reserve reception centre and car park is entered off the B970 road from Kingussie to Insh village, 1½ miles (2.4 km) from Kingussie. The nearest railway station is at Kingussie, on the Edinburgh to Inverness line.

From the car park, access can be gained to two hides that overlook the western end of the marshes. Two nature trails, the Lynachlaggan and Invertromie, offer superb views over the reserve and are particularly recommended during late summer, when birds are often difficult to see from the hides. Good views of both the marshes and Loch Insh can be obtained from the B970 and B9152.

Timing

The reserve is open daily from 9 am to 9 pm (or sunset, if earlier). The reception centre, however, is open less frequently.

There is sustained bird interest throughout the year, with the peak activity during April–May and November–March.

Calendar

Some of the more interesting species likely to be seen.

April–August: Breeding wildfowl and waders, large Black-headed Gull colony. Marsh Harrier is recorded almost annually. Hen Harrier and Short-eared Owl regularly hunt over the marsh in late summer. Summer passerines include Tree Pipit, Redstart, Spotted and sometimes Pied Flycatchers, and Wood Warbler.

September–March: Migratory Greylag and Pink-footed Geese pass through during late September and throughout October. Up to 200 Whooper Swan, 500 Greylag Geese, plus a variety of duck over-winter. Hen Harrier are commonly seen, particularly in late afternoon. Great Grey Shrike are seen in some winters. Redwing and Fieldfare arrive in their hundreds during early October.

RSPB Warden

Zul Bhatia, Ivy Cottage, Insh, Kingussie PH21 1NT.

H9 GLEN TROMIE

OS ref.: NN 782972
OS map: sheet 35

Habitat and Access

An attractive valley containing a mixture of Birch woodland, some plantations and heather moorland.

Park on the track near Tromie Bridge on the B970, 3 miles (4.8 km) from Kingussie. Please take care not to block access for other vehicles. The track can be walked up the valley.

Ideally, the area should be visited on a spring day, perhaps in conjunction with a visit to the RSPB reserve at the nearby Insh Marshes.

Species

Dipper and Grey Wagtail frequent the river; Redstart, Siskin and Redpoll should be seen among the riverside trees. Merlin and Peregrine are occasionally seen; Hen Harrier attempt to breed each year, but usually have little success.

Female Grey Wagtail

Habitat

The Ardnamurchan Peninsula forms the most westerly landmass of mainland Scotland. It stretches out to the north of Mull, Morvern and Loch Sunart and to the south of the Small Isles (Rum, Eigg, Canna and Muck). The fantastic views from the Ardnamurchan Point lighthouse have made this a famous place to visit. Along its rocky shores are scattered oak woodlands – remnants of those which once dominated western Britain, from Devon to Sutherland. Rough heather moorland and hill lochans characterise the inland areas, with several coniferous forest plantations punctuating the landscape. Many sandy beaches and bays are dotted around the coastline. The peninsula is some 17 miles (28 km) east to west and approximately 7 miles (12 km) at its widest point. Ben Hiant (528 metres) and Ben Laga (512 metres) are the highest points on the peninsula. Slightly to the east is Beinn Resipol, an 845-metre mountain in the Sunart district.

Access

The peninsula has a single track road (B8007) along its southern shore, with minor roads branching off to the north and west. To reach the area, take the short (15 minutes) Corran Ferry crossing operated by Highland Regional Council (which runs frequently and is non-bookable) across

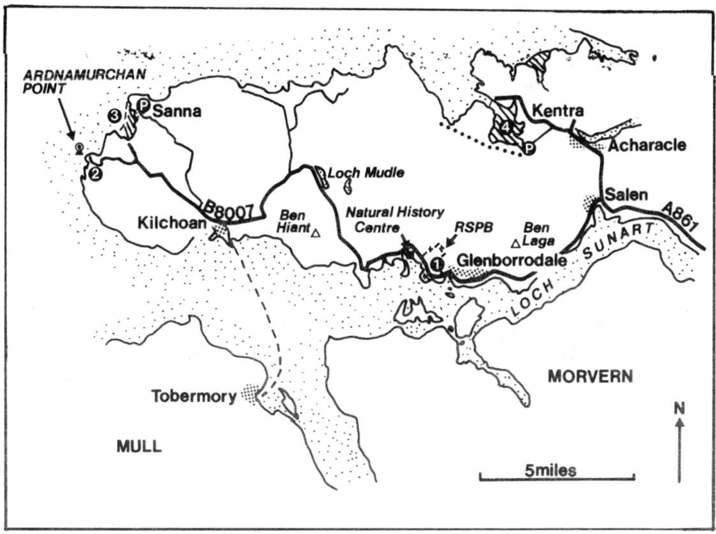

Loch Linnhe, off the A82 road from Glen Coe to Fort William. The ferry slipway is about 4 miles (6 km) north of the Ballachulish Bridge and 8 miles (13 km) south of Fort William. Once across the water, head south down the A861 through Strontian to Salen (some 23 miles or 37 km). Salachan Point, just over a mile to the south of Corran, is worth checking at any time of year for roosting waders, gulls and offshore divers and sea-duck. The B8007 is the left branch of the road at Salen. The road beyond here is single track and can be quite busy in the summer months. An alternative route to Ardnamurchan is by way of the Caledonian MacBrayne ferry from Tobermory on the Island of Mull. There is a regular (non-bookable) service to Kilchoan, on the south-west of Ardnamurchan, during the summer months only; this service now carries cars (but not caravans). The crossing takes 35 minutes and provides good sea-watching opportunities.

Species

A wide range of species are present, including wintering and passage wildfowl and waders, oak and coniferous woodland songbirds and upland heath and moorland birds. Breeding birds of particular importance include Red-throated Diver, Grey Heron, Teal, Hen Harrier, Golden Eagle, Buzzard, Merlin, Peregrine, Red Grouse, Golden Plover, Greenshank, Common Sandpiper, Short-eared Owl, Great Spotted Woodpecker, Tree Pipit, Dipper, Redstart, Whinchat, Stonechat, Wheatear, Ring Ouzel, Wood Warbler, Raven, Siskin and Redpoll.

In winter the area is notable for modest numbers of Great Northern Diver offshore, and a flock of wintering Greenland White-fronted Geese to the south of Loch Sheil. Good numbers of Wigeon and Teal can be present in Kintra Bay, along with a variety of wintering waders, including small numbers of Greenshank. Goldeneye are common on sea and freshwater lochs. Passage seabirds such as divers, shearwaters, petrels, Gannets, skuas, gulls and terns are easily watched from the western end of the peninsula, or from the Tobermory–Kilchoan ferry. Passage wildfowl includes Whooper Swan, White-fronted, Greylag and Barnacle Geese. Migrant waders are probably best looked for at Kintra, where Golden Plover, Dunlin, Snipe, Bar-tailed Godwit, Curlew, Redshank and Greenshank are likely. Less frequent passage waders include Grey Plover, Knot, Sanderling, Whimbrel and Green Sandpiper.

In addition to birds, the peninsula is an excellent place to see Pine Marten, Red Squirrel, Fox, Wildcat, Otter, Grey and Common Seals.

1 Glenborrodale RSPB Reserve

OS ref.: 60/61

This 250-acre (100-hectare) reserve comprises an interesting mosaic of habitats. About one quarter of the reserve is coastal oak woodland, with scrub areas leading up onto more open heather moorland. Two streams run through the reserve, the one to the west tumbling through a steep and inaccessible gorge. To the north-east is an over-mature conifer plantation, with extensive felled areas. Below the road, the reserve encompasses a short section of the rocky shoreline. Much of the oak woodland is being cleared of invading rhododendron.

The reserve lies immediately west of Glenborrodale village, with its eastern boundary adjoining that of Glenborrodale Castle. Driving west through the village, look out for the black railings of the Castle grounds to your right. The reserve starts where these end. A short distance beyond this the road crosses a stream running into a small bay. To your right is the start of a path which leads through the reserve, rejoining the road at its north-western boundary. As yet there are no parking facilities for visitors so it is best to drive further on, find a suitable parking spot (please do not park in the passing places), then walk back to the start of the path.

A reserve warden is usually in post between May and August, when regular reserve walks are organised: contact the Glenmore Natural History Centre or RSPB North Scotland Office for details.

Breeding woodland birds include Tree Pipit, Redstart, Wood Warbler and Willow Warbler. Great Tit, Blue Tit, Long-tailed Tit, Wren, Treecreeper, Robin and Buzzard are resident.

On the hill ground, Wheatear, Stonechat, Whinchat and Meadow Pipit are common in spring/summer. There is a traditional Raven territory on the crag overlooking the wood. Other birds occasionally seen include Golden Eagle, Kestrel, Merlin, Skylark and Twite.

Eider, Common Sandpiper and Heron frequent the main bay and this is also a good place to see Otter and both Grey and Common Seal. Common and Arctic Terns can be seen fishing further out in the loch.

The Ardnamurchan Natural History Centre at Glenmore, just west of Glenborrodale, is not to be missed. Mounted displays and marine tanks, illustrating the species and habitats to be found in the area, complement an audio-visual presentation on 'The Natural History of Ardnamurchan', produced by Michael MacGregor. General information on things to do and see and details of local events are available and the RSPB Reserve walks leave from here. The Centre also sells books, gifts, coffee etc. and excellent home baking! This is an ideal information point from which to explore Ardnamurchan.

2 Point of Ardnamurchan

OS ref.: NM 67/41

This is the most westerly point of mainland Scotland and a fantastic place to seawatch and to view the Small Isles to the north and Coll to the south-west. A walk along the cliff to the south of the lighthouse may give views of Raven and possibly Peregrine. To reach the Point, continue beyond the Glenmore Natural History Centre along the B8007 towards Kilchoan. A car park on the left after about 2 miles (3 km) affords fine views of Ben Hiant and an opportunity to scan the skyline for Golden Eagle, Buzzard and Raven. Continue on the B8007, stopping to check Loch Mudle after 4 miles (6 km), which often holds Red-throated Diver, plus Hen Harrier and Short-eared Owl hunting over the surrounding young conifer plantations. From Loch Mudle the road carries on for another 14 miles (9 km) until Achosnich, where a left fork will take you the remaining 3 miles (5 km) to Ardnamurchan Point. Park in the space available at the end of this road and walk up to the lighthouse. As well as seabirds, watch out for dolphins, porpoises, whales and basking sharks.

3 Sanna Bay

OS ref.: NM 69/44

To the north of the Point of Ardnamurchan is the tiny village of Sanna and an extensive sand dune system. In the summer, the bay can be a good place to watch diving gannets and other seabirds. From the B8007 take the minor road to Achnaha and Sanna about half a mile (1 km) out of Kilchoan. There is a large parking area at Sanna. As with the Point, this is a good place to see marine mammals and basking sharks.

4 Kentra Bay

OS ref.: NM 69/64

This is a large muddy/sandy bay in the north-east corner of the peninsula. To reach it, return to Salen and take the A861 north to Acharacle. Immediately after the church at the end of the village turn left onto the B8044 to Kentra. About half a mile (1 km) along this road there is a minor crossroads – take the left turn and drive to the end of the road, where you can go through a gate to a small parking area. From here walk along the track for good views of the south side of the bay. Continue on for just over one mile (2 km) through the conifer plantation to reach Camas an Lighe, a beautiful beach. The north side of the bay can be viewed from the road, by continuing along the B8044 beyond Kentra.

The bay is particularly good for passage and wintering waders and wildfowl (see Species).

Also see additional sites: Ariundle National Nature Reserve (Ha.) and Rahoy Hills SWT Reserve (Hn.).

H11 LOCHINDORB

OS ref.: NH 970360
OS map: sheet 27

Habitat

A large freshwater loch, approximately 2 miles (3.2 km) long, which is surrounded by open moorland managed for Red Grouse. The northern end of the loch has recently been cordoned off for wind-surfing, whilst the remainder of the loch is used by fishermen; neither activity appears to have any obvious detrimental effect on the birdlife, however, probably due to the size of the loch.

Species

Lochindorb is a very reliable place for Red-throated Diver, with up to four birds generally present. Small numbers of Wigeon and Red-breasted Merganser are usually to be found during the summer months, whilst Goldeneye are regular in April and May.

Careful scanning of the surrounding moorland and skylines should reveal some of the area's hunting raptors, which include Golden Eagle, Peregrine and Merlin. Hen Harrier are frequently seen in spring, but do not breed as successfully as might be expected. One or two pairs of Short-eared Owl usually breed in the area. Red Grouse are plentiful and in April the territorial males give excellent opportunities for roadside viewing. Both Golden Plover and Dunlin breed on the moors and can be watched from the road; Dunlin can often be seen feeding along the lochshore. Other wading species include Lapwing, Curlew, Common Sandpiper and Redshank.

Small numbers of Twite breed here and can often be picked up as they fly overhead calling.

In winter, the area is generally unrewarding, although Goldeneye may be present on the loch, whilst groups of Raven and the odd Golden Eagle (usually immature birds) may also be seen.

Access

Lochindorb is approached either (1) along the A938 road east from Carrbridge, turning north after 2 miles (3.2 km) onto the B9007. A single track road off to the right, 6 miles (9.7 km) later, heads down another mile (1.6 km) to the loch. Or (2) along the A939 road north from Grantown-on-Spey, turning left after 6 miles (9.7 km) onto the minor road signposted for Lochindorb.

Both routes lead one along the minor road that closely follows the south-east shore of the loch. There are several pull-offs that enable the area to be scanned without obstructing other traffic: the area immediately north from Lochindorb Lodge is probably the best general viewpoint.

Timing

This area is mainly of interest during the period April through to August.

H12 FINDHORN VALLEY

OS ref.: NH 710180
OS map: sheet 35

Habitat and Access

A very large area of open country given over to sheep and deer grazing, with some managed grouse moor and a scattering of plantations and Birch woodland.

The valley is reached from Tomatin (next to the A9, 15 miles (24 km) south of Inverness); a single-track road follows the River Findhorn upstream for about 9 miles (14.5 km), providing good views of the surrounding terrain. The ridges above the final 3 miles (4.8 km) of this road are particularly good for soaring Golden Eagle. It is possible to walk along the track from the road end at Coignafearn, but please *do not* take a vehicle – there is room to park here without obstructing access to the track. Various paths lead from the track, all of which are worth exploring for birds of prey, but do not venture into the hills during the stalking or grouse shooting seasons (i.e. early August through to February).

The Farr road, some 5 miles (8 km) after leaving Tomatin, crosses some excellent moorland areas and can be equally good for most species.

Species

The principal attractions here are the birds of prey. Sparrowhawk, Buzzard, Kestrel, Merlin and Peregrine all occur; Golden Eagle can usually be spotted with a bit of perseverance – frequent scanning of the skyline with binoculars is the tactic most likely to yield results. The eagles can be seen throughout the year and up to five individuals in a day have been known! Hen Harrier are scarce, and the Farr road is probably the best area for them. The moors hold Red Grouse and Golden Plover, whilst Ring Ousel are not uncommon on the hillsides in spring. Raven, however, are decidedly scarce.

The river itself is the haunt of small numbers of Goosander, Dipper and Grey Wagtail, joined in summer by Common Sandpiper. Osprey and Common Tern also occasionally fish the river.

Timing

The area has a good range of resident species and is worth visiting year-round.

H13 LOCH RUTHVEN

OS ref.: NH 63/28
OS map: sheet 26

Habitat

This 85-hectare RSPB reserve is situated to the east of Loch Ness, some 14 miles (22.5 km) south of Inverness. The relatively rich waters of the loch are backed by craggy moorland, with a narrow strip of Birch wood. To the north, much of the land has been recently afforested, although there is extensive farmland at Tullich to the north-east.

Slavonian Grebes, summer

Species

Slavonian Grebe are the speciality of this reserve;. they breed in the emergent vegetation around the loch edge and it is therefore essential not to stray closer to the shore than the path. Red-throated Diver use the loch for feeding, Tufted Duck and Coot are present all year, whilst small numbers of Common and Black-headed Gull breed. The Birch woods hold small but interesting bird communities, including Siskin and Redpoll; Sedge Warbler and Reed Bunting nest in the fringing scrub. Hen Harrier and Peregrine are regularly seen and Raven are present year-round; the area is a good one for Black Grouse.

In winter, Loch Ruthven attracts Pochard and Goldeneye, as well as the occasional Smew.

Access

Loch Ruthven can be reached from the A9 by turning west onto the B851, nearly 6 miles (9.7 km) from Inverness. Fork right 8 miles (13 km) later, onto a minor road that leads down to a parking area at the east end of the loch. Alternatively, approach directly from Inverness on the B862, turning left after about 12 miles (19 km) at the end of Loch Duntelchaig, onto the minor road to Loch Ruthven. Access is restricted to the south-east shore only – a 1½-mile-long (0.8 km) footpath leads to the hide, which overlooks the loch.

Timing

The optimum time to visit is in the spring or early summer. A summer warden is present from April to August.

H14 LONGMAN POINT, INVERNESS

OS ref.: NH 66/47
OS map: sheet 26

Habitat

Longman Point lies on the south side of the Beauly Firth, immediately east of the mouth of the River Ness. It is overshadowed by the Kessock Bridge which carries the A9 northbound out of Inverness and onto the Black Isle. Because of this proximity to the main road, it is a convenient place to stop off when heading further north. The mud and shingle shoreline here and the waters of the firth opposite provide excellent habitat for a representative selection of the birds that occur in Beauly Firth.

A sewage outfall discharges into the firth, attracting gulls and wildfowl. The shoreline is backed by a light industrial estate; to the west lies Inverness Harbour and to the east a rubbish tip and reclamation area (NH 678464).

Species

Mute Swan, Mallard, Oystercatcher and the commoner species of gull can be seen year-round. Breeding visitors are few, although one or two Shelduck and Ringed Plover nest. In winter the area is visited by a wide range of species, including up to 850 Tufted Duck, 400+ Goldeneye and large numbers of Teal. A few Scaup can usually be found amongst the Tufted Duck, which sometimes feed on the opposite side of the firth near Charlestown. Goosanders frequent the mouth of the River Ness (mostly in autumn) and a small number of Little Grebe and Long-tailed Duck are usually present in the harbour. Other wintering waterfowl regularly recorded include Cormorant, Wigeon, Pochard, Smew, Coot and Guillemot.

Passage waders include Knot, Dunlin, Bar and Black-tailed Godwits, Redshank and Turnstone. Up to 300 Redshank and a small number of Black-tailed Godwit over-winter.

Glaucous and Iceland Gulls occur every winter and commute between the outflow and the rubbish tip to the east.

Access

From the A9/A96 Milburn Interchange head north towards Kessock Bridge. Turn left at the next roundabout along Longman Road, then right at another roundabout onto Harbour Road. A right turn onto Cromwell Road then leads to Longman Drive, which affords good views of the foreshore.

Timing

Access is possible at all times. August through to March is the most interesting period. Visit one or two hours before high tide for shorebirds, although high water in mid-winter is best for ducks.

H15 GLEN AFFRIC

OS ref.: NH 24/24
OS map: sheet 25

Habitat

A picturesque combination of woodlands, hillsides, rivers and lochs make this into a classic highland glen and it is deservedly popular with visitors. The Forestry Commission have established a 1,265-hectare Native Woodland reserve here, which includes an important remnant of old Caledonian Pine forest. The area is designated a Site of Special Scientific Interest.

Male Capercaillie

Species

Small numbers of Capercaillie* and Black Grouse* breed in the pinewoods; Crested Tit and Scottish Crossbill are numerous all year, whilst Siskin and Redpoll are easier to find during the winter. Migrant breeders include Tree Pipit and Redstart.

On the lochs, Red and (occasionally) Black-throated Diver may be seen in spring/summer, whilst Red-breasted Merganser and Goosander occur regularly. Dipper and Grey Wagtail frequent the burnsides.

Various raptors hunt over the area, including Sparrowhawk, Buzzard, Golden Eagle and Kestrel; visiting Osprey and Merlin are seen occasionally.

Access

Approach via the A831 from Beauly or Drumnadrochit on OS sheet 26, turning off at Cannich onto an unclassified road leading westwards past Fasnakyle Power Station. There are several car parks along this road (see map), including one at its end, about 11 miles (18 km) later. Paths and trails, of a length varying from ½ mile (0.8 km) upwards, lead off from the parking areas: the routes to Dog Falls and to Coire Loch are particularly recommended. A longer excursion (approx. 11 miles (18 km)) around Loch Affric, or along the south shore of Loch Beinn a' Mheadhoin (7 miles (11.3 km) one-way) can be very rewarding.

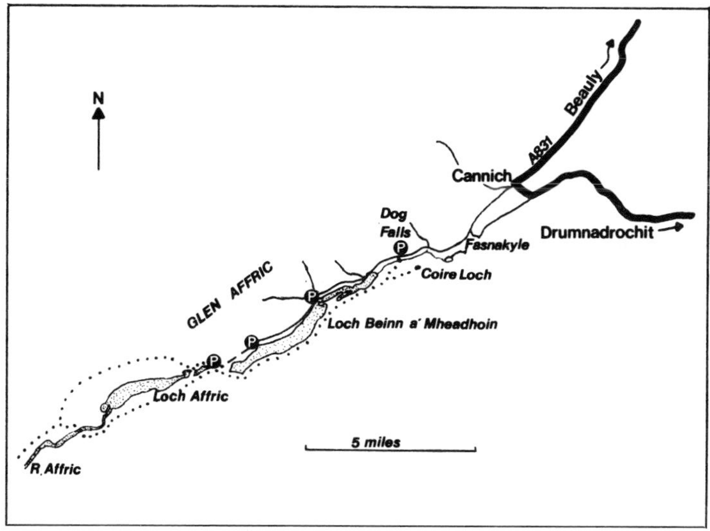

Timing

Access is possible at all times, although both the road and the paths can be treacherous in winter. Please take note of any specific restrictions that may apply during the stalking season.

The 'speciality' species found in the pinewoods are present all year, but many of the other interesting woodland species are summer visitors only.

* Please do not attempt to seek out leks of these two species as this will inevitably lead to disturbance – leks are in any case best watched from a good distance and generally a car is the best hide.

Reference

The Forestry Commission publishes a detailed booklet on the area, available from the FC or Inverness Tourist Office.

H16 UDALE BAY

OS ref.: NH 71/65
OS map: sheet 21/27

Habitat and Species

An open estuarine bay on the south shore of the Cromarty Firth. Like Nigg Bay on the north shore, Udale has extensive sheltered inter-tidal mud-flats which hold a large and diverse group of passage/wintering wildfowl and waders.

Udale Bay is best visited between September and March, during which time Wigeon are numerous and smaller numbers of Teal and Mallard can be seen. Shelduck over-winter. Large numbers of Greylag Geese sometimes come down to the bay from their feeding fields at high water. Waders include Oystercatcher, Knot, Dunlin, Curlew, Redshank and Bar-tailed Godwit. Small numbers of Grey Plover are often present. Sparrowhawk, Peregrine and occasional Merlin hunt overhead.

In the main channel of the Cromarty Firth, to the north of Udale Bay and visible from the unclassified road to Balblair, a flock of Scaup sometimes feed very close inshore and small numbers of Red-throated Diver, Slavonian Grebe and Long-tailed Duck can be seen.

Access

Udale Bay is situated between the small villages of Balblair and Jemimaville and can be approached from the A9 via the B9163, or from Fortrose on the A832 then the B9160. Excellent views of the bay are possible from the layby just west of Jemimaville, from the parking area between the road and the shore approximately 1 mile (1.6 km) east of Jemimaville, or from the unclassified road to Balblair just beyond the ruined church.

H17 NIGG BAY

OS ref.: NH 790730
OS map: sheet 21

Habitat

An open bay on the north side of the Cromarty Firth with extensive inter-tidal mud and areas of degenerate salt marsh, much reclaimed during the last century. Over a mile (1.6 km) of the eastern shore is taken up with oil storage and rig fabrication sites. Nigg Bay measures around 3 miles by 4 miles (4.8 km by 6.4 km) and has been designated a Site of Special Scientific Interest.

Species

The bay holds a significant selection of the internationally important populations of wintering/passage wildfowl and waders that occur on the Cromarty Firth. Nigg Bay holds a similar suite of species to that found on the Dornoch Firth (H18), but with larger numbers of most of the commoner birds. A good growth of eelgrass here attracts very large numbers of Wigeon as well as Mute and Whooper Swans. In addition, up to 2,000 Greylag and 1,000 Pink-footed Geese frequent the inner bay and between 200 and 400 Pintail can be found near the Meddat shore. The more typical waders using the bay include Oystercatcher, Knot, Dunlin, Curlew and Redshank. Moderate numbers of Scaup and Goldeneye winter on the firth.

Access

The best areas for birds are at the inner end of the bay between Pitcalnie and Meddat.

From Tain, take the A9 south for 4 miles (6.4 km), turning off onto the B9175 towards Nigg. After a further 4 miles an old coastguard station will be reached and this and the adjacent banks make good observation points. Parking is possible on the roadside, but care must be taken – the road can be extremely busy with traffic to the nearby fabrication yard.

All of the surrounding farmland is privately owned. The paths to the two old coastguard huts (NH 795739 and 803724) are rights of way to an old fording point.

Timing

Nigg Bay is a good birding location throughout the winter from late September to late March.

The best time to visit is from one to three hours before high tide, although good wader roosts can be seen at high water. A south-east wind is best if watching from the old coastguard station.

H18 DORNOCH FIRTH

OS ref.: NH 609915–900900
OS map: sheet 21

Habitat

The Dornoch is the only east-coast firth that has no industrial development. The combined flow of the rivers Shin, Oykel and Carron, plus their many tributaries, enter the firth via glaciated valleys. A series of points and promontories naturally divide the firth into several distinct areas and a complex of sand bars – Gizzen Briggs – guards the mouth of the estuary from the Moray Firth and almost connects Dornoch Point, on the north shore, with Morrich More on the south. This narrow mouth feeds into a wide bay cut off from the rest of the Moray Firth by the Tarbat Ness peninsula.

The Dornoch Firth is about 16 miles (26 km) long and varies in width from around ½ mile (0.8 km) at Bonar Bridge to almost 4 miles (6.4 km) across Tain Bay/Dornoch Sands. The outer bay from Embo to Tarbat Ness is approximately 10 miles (16 km) wide.

The extensive estuarine mudflats are the principal habitat of interest, there being little saltmarsh development. To the east of Tain lie the sand-dune and sand-flats areas of Morrich More, which are important for breeding waders but form a part of RAF Tain's bombing range. The Tarbat Ness coast of the outer firth is rocky, whereas that on the north side at Dornoch is sandy. There is a brackish water lagoon cut off from the estuary by the railway mid-way along the south shore (Mid-Fearn Mere).

Both Morrich More and the Outer Dornoch Firth are designated Sites of Special Scientific Interest.

The only noteworthy surrounding bird habitats are at Spinningdale, where there is a small and rather over-grazed oakwood and at Easter Fearn, opposite the base of the Struie Hill road, where there is a locally important area of juniper scrub.

Species and Calendar

The Dornoch Firth is of great importance for passage and wintering wildfowl and waders. Outstanding amongst the visiting duck populations are a flock of between 150 and 300 Shelduck in Tain Bay, up to 7,000 Wigeon and 1,000 Teal at Ardjackie/Tain Bays (peak numbers occur in October), up to 150 Pintail and up to 400 Scaup in Edderton Bay. Up to 1,000 Common and 400 Velvet Scoter winter off the Dornoch/Embo coastline; 2–3 Surf Scoter and (in recent years) a Black Scoter have also been present. The period late March to early May is probably the best time for these birds.

Oystercatcher numbers peak at around 2,000 birds in November, with a similar number of Redshank present in October. Approximately 3,000

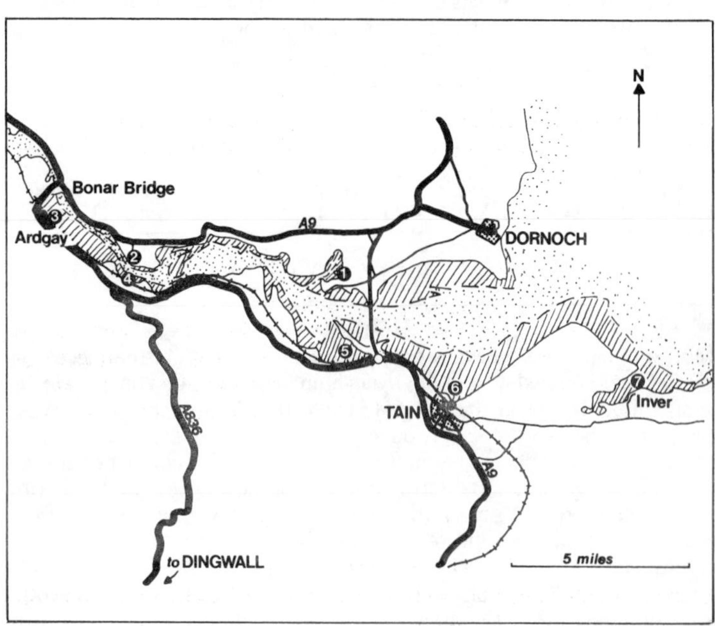

Dunlin can be found in September. Other passage waders include up to 50 Grey Plover, 100 Golden Plover, 400 Curlew, 200 Bar-tailed Godwit and around 70 Knot. Small numbers of Greenshank and occasional Black-tailed Godwit, Ruff and Spotted Redshank also occur. Modest numbers of Sanderling and Turnstone over-winter at Portmahomach and Dornoch.

The firth is very quiet from March through until July, although small numbers of non-breeding ducks and waders are present and there is often a good spring passage of geese and Whooper Swan.

Osprey are regularly seen fishing over the estuary during the late spring/summer.

Return wader passage commences in July, with the main arrival occurring between late August and early November.

Access

The A9 provides access to both the north and south shores and there are many good vantage points from roadside laybys. The new bridge across the Dornoch Firth to the west of Tain affords good views of the outer estuary.

1 Skibo Estuary

OS ref.: NH 73/88

Turn off the A9 at Clashmore, then take a right at the junction 1 mile (1.6 km) later to Ferrytown. Park in the gorse area and walk down to the pier, a good general vantage point. Large numbers of Teal can be present on the estuary in late autumn. Tufted Duck occur on Lochs Evelix and Ospisdale all year.

2 Newton's Point

OS ref.: NH 711877

Futher along the A9 towards Bonar Bridge turn off to Newton's Point, a good viewpoint up and down the estuary. There is space to park at the point and also by the inner bay west of the point.

3 Ardgay Station

OS ref.: NH 601904

The station platform is a useful vantage point. The railway line between Ardgay and Tain follows the south shore closely and gives good views of the firth; there are four trains per day during the summer, but fewer in winter. Tain Station is also a good vantage point, being conveniently situated on the edge of Tain Bay.

4 Mid-Fearn Mere

OS ref.: NH 638873

A lagoon visible from a layby on the A9 Bonar Bridge–Tain road immediately after the Dingwall turn-off.

5 Cambuscurrie Bay

OS ref.: NH 725852

Known locally as Edderton Bay. Turn off the A9 to Meikle Ferry 2 miles (3.2 km) west of Tain. This is an excellent viewpoint.

6 Tain Bay

OS ref.: NH 785840

From the car park on the seaward side of the railway in Tain (down the road to the golf course), cross over the footbridge and 'scope the bay from the opposite bank of the inlet. Morrich More lies to the east.

7 Inver Bay

OS ref.: NH 864832

Take the unclassified road out of Tain towards Tarbat Ness, turning off after 5 miles (8 km) to the village of Inver. A car park overlooks the sheltered inlet.

Timing

August to March is the best time to visit. Waders are most easily seen between one and three hours before high water. Southerly winds seem to be the most productive conditions. Disturbance is at its lowest on Sunday mornings, although afternoon light is preferable on sunny days.

References

Nature Conservation within the Moray Firth Area, NCC (1978).
'Birdwatching in Sutherland', T, Mainwood (1992), *Scottish Bird News* 27.

H19 LOCH FLEET

OS ref.: NH 79/96
OS map: sheet 21

Habitat

The large tidal basin of Loch Fleet is the most northerly inlet on the east coast of Scotland. Only a narrow channel between the shingle and dune bars of Ferry and Coul Links connects the loch with the open sea. At low tide, an extensive area of inter-tidal mud is exposed; this estuarine habitat is bounded by dunes and coastal heath to the east and pine-woods to the north. To the west, beyond the Mound, lies an area of alder carr which formed as a result of an abortive attempt to drain the loch.

The Scottish Wildlife Trust manages the loch and some of the surrounding habitats as a reserve, totalling 1,163 hectares. A summer warden is employed from April until August and organises guided walks to explore the woodland, estuary and sand dunes. Much of the site is designated a Site of Special Scientific Interest.

Eiders and King Eider

Species

Large numbers of dabbling duck over-winter in the loch, including over 2,000 Wigeon with lesser numbers of Teal and Mallard. The coastline between Embo and Golspie holds important concentrations of sea-fowl, including three species of diver, Slavonian and occasional Red-necked Grebes, up to 2,000 Eider and several hundred Long-tailed Duck, Common Scoter and Red-breasted Merganser. Smaller numbers of Goldeneye and Velvet Scoter can also be seen. Drake King Eiders have been annual since 1973 and at least one individual appears to be more or less resident. Up to 3 have been seen at once, although they have been a little more elusive in recent years. If not present in the entrance to the loch, try the coast off Embo or Brora, although they can be some distance offshore. Surf Scoter can also be seen year round, although their movements are less predictable. Green-winged Teal and American Wigeon have both been recorded in recent years.

A moderate-sized flock of Greylag Geese use the area and a flock of more than 50 Whooper Swan feed in the surrounding fields in winter.

Sparrowhawk and Buzzard are resident and seen often. Osprey may occur in summer, whilst Hen Harrier and Peregrine are seen occasionally. Short-eared Owl regularly hunt over the dunes and heathland.

Waders roost at 3 main places: Skelbo Point, the beach at the mouth of the Fleet and Balblair saltmarsh. Up to 1,800 Oystercatcher, *c.* 250 Curlew, 400 Redshank and 150 Ringed Plover can be present at Loch Fleet, with Dunlin numbers sometimes exceeding 1,000 and Knot and Bar-tailed Godwit numbers occasionally reaching 1,000.

The loch is not generally considered to be an especially good place for passage waders, but many species do pass through, including large

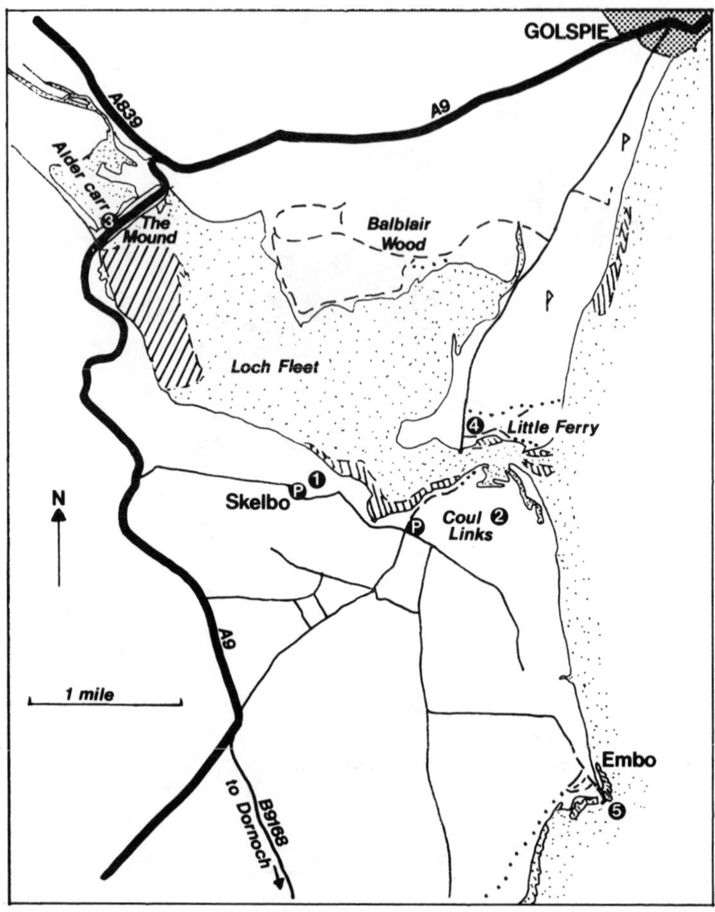

numbers of Curlew, Golden Plover and Knot. Greenshank are regular in spring and autumn at the Mound Pool.

Redstart, Goldcrest, Coal Tit, Siskin and Scottish Crossbill breed in the pinewoods at Balblair, but Capercaillie have probably now disappeared.

Access

Loch Fleet is situated 5 miles (8 km) north of Dornoch and is accessible from the A9 and by unclassified roads along the south shore and to Littleferry from Golspie. There are several good vantage points:

1 Skelbo

OS ref.: NH 790950

Take the minor road east off the A9 along the south shore of the loch. There is a car park and information board at Skelbo, 1½ miles (2.4 km) later.

2 Coul Links

OS ref.: NH 803952

Half a mile (0.8 km) east of Skelbo, take a track northwards onto the links and park overlooking the estuary. It is possible to explore the links on foot from here.

3 The Mound

OS ref.: NH 770979

There are two parking bays on the A9 at the head of the loch which overlook both the upper estuary and the freshwater pools and Alder carr to the west. Road improvements here may alter the parking arrangements.

4 Balblair and Ferry Links

OS ref.: NH 80/96

Take the minor road south from Golspie, past the golf course, towards Littleferry. There are car parks at Balblair Wood, where the road first comes alongside the estuary, and at Littleferry itself. Eider and Long-tailed Duck can sometimes be watched at very close quarters here; most sea-duck tend to congregate to the north of the loch mouth and can be viewed by taking the paths east from Littleferry.

A permit is required from the SWT in order to wander off the paths in Balblair pinewoods and at Ferry Links. *Please note that there is a very high fire risk on this reserve.*

5 Embo Pier

OS ref.: NH 820922

This is reached via the caravan site at Embo. It is probably the best place for close views of Velvet/Common Scoters and is a favourite resort of King Eider in some years. White-winged gulls are occasionally present in winter and Purple Sandpiper frequent the rocky shore adjacent to the pier. Other good vantage points include the pier at Golspie, Brora and at Dornoch caravan park.

There are bus and train services to Golspie from Inverness.

Timing

The reserve is of most interest to birders from October through to April, when large numbers of waterfowl and waders are present, although a summer visit is pleasant and can also be productive for birds.

Calendar

Some of the more interesting species likely to be seen.

March–May: Up to 2,000 Long-tailed Duck can be seen by late May, prior to their departure to breeding grounds.

June–July: Shelduck, Redshank and Oystercatcher feed on the inter-tidal mud; Eider are numerous right through the summer, feeding on the mussel beds in the river channel, Common and Arctic Terns can be seen fishing for Sand Eels.

August–November: Sea-duck numbers decline to mid-winter levels, following peak counts in October. Shelduck numbers start to build up from late November as they return from their moulting grounds. Moderate numbers of passage waders occur. Passage shearwaters and skuas are occasionally present offshore in autumn, especially when visibility is poor.

December–February: Red-throated and lesser numbers of Black-throated and Great Northern Divers occur offshore. Glaucous and the scarcer Iceland Gull, small numbers of Snow Bunting and Twite are occasionally present. Purple Sandpiper and Turnstone frequent rocky shorelines.

References

'Birdwatching in Sutherland', T. Mainwood (1992), *Scottish Bird News* 27.

H20 DUNCANSBY HEAD

OS ref.: ND 406733
OS map: sheet 12

This headland forms the extreme north-east corner of Caithness. Coastal cliffs are backed by maritime heath; the area is designated a Site of Special Scientific Interest.

An unclassified road off the A9 at John O'Groats covers the 2½ miles (4 km) to the Head. There is a car park near the light house – a rough path leads to the cliff top. The best vantage point for nesting seabirds is at the Geo of Sclaites.

Late April to mid-July is the optimum time to visit. Sea mist is not infrequent.

The cliffs hold breeding Fulmar, Shag, Kittiwake, Guillemot, Razorbill and Puffin.

H21 DUNNET HEAD

OS ref.: ND 20/76
OS map: sheets 12/7

Habitat and Access

The cliff-girt moors of Dunnet Head lie on the most northerly headland in Britain, some 13 miles (21 km) to the west of Duncansby Head. It can be reached by taking the B855 turning off the main A836 Thurso–John

O'Groats road in the village of Dunnet and following this northwards to the lighthouse, almost 5 miles (8 km) away.

Species

Fulmar, Kittiwake, Guillemot, Razorbill, Black Guillemot and Puffin all breed on the sea-cliffs on the north and east of the headland. A few Great Skua usually attempt to breed on the moors. Other miscellaneous breeding birds include Rock Dove, Raven and Twite.

Dunnet Bay, to the south-west, is an important winter resort for seafowl, including Red-throated Diver, a few Black-throated and Great Northern Divers, Common Scoter, Goldeneye, Eider, Long-tailed Duck and Red-breasted Merganser. Glaucous and Iceland Gulls can often be found here too.

Around 100 Greenland White-fronted Geese over-winter in the Loch of Mey area to the east of Dunnet.

Timing

There is year-round bird interest, with the seabird colonies of Dunnet Head being the main attraction from mid-May to mid-July and the divers, sea-duck and gulls providing the interest during autumn, winter and early spring.

H22 CLO MOR

OS ref.: NC 32/72
OS map: sheet 9

Habitat

Clo Mor is situated about 4 miles (6.4 km) east of Cape Wrath, in the extreme north-west of Sutherland. The Torridonian Sandstone cliffs here are the highest on mainland Britain, rising to nearly 300 metres; inland lie extensive tracts of open moorland and hills. The Ministry of Defence use the Cape Wrath area as a bombing range and access restrictions are sometimes in force.

Species

The cliffs hold considerable numbers of Fulmar (estimated 5,000 occupied sites), Kittiwake, Guillemot, Razorbill, Black Guillemot and one of the largest Puffin colonies in Britain. Other cliff-nesting species include Peregrine and Rock Dove. Inland, Red Grouse and even Ptarmigan occur; Greenshank can also be seen, but Golden Plover are scarce.

Access

Clo Mor is reached by taking the ferry across the Kyle of Durness (pedestrians and bicycles only) at Keoldale, 1 mile (1.6 km) south-west from Durness and just off the A838. A connecting minibus service on the far side operates to Cape Wrath, 11 miles (16 km) away (tel: 097181 287) – arrange to be dropped off at the Kearvaig track and picked up later at Inshore. Walk to the coast at Kearvaig, and then around the cliffs eastward for about 3 miles (5 km), cutting inland along the eastern flanks

Ravens

of Sgribhis-bheinn to the road at Inshore. This is a tough walk and should not be underestimated!

The ferry across the Kyle of Durness operates several times daily during the summer months, except in bad weather (tel: 097181 377 for details).

H23 HANDA ISLAND

OS ref.: NC 13/48
OS map: sheet 9

Habitat

Handa Island lies off the north-west coast of Scotland, some 18 miles (29 km) south of Cape Wrath. Near-vertical cliffs of Torridonian sandstone, over 120 metres high in places, bound the island on three sides; only in the south do these diminish and give way to lower cliffs and sandy bays. The interior of the island comprises 363 hectares of rough pasture, moorland and a few lochans, although there is a small plantation of lodgepole pine and alder near to the warden's bothy.

Handa is a Site of Special Scientific Interest and has long been a bird

Puffins – breeding cliffs

reserve, previously under the management of the RSPB, but now managed by SWT.

Species

Over 170 species have been recorded on/from the reserve; 30 are regular breeders and another 20 nest occasionally. An estimated total of 98,000 pairs of Guillemot and 9,000 pairs of Razorbill breed on the ledges and crevices of the cliffs, best seen on the Great Stack in the north-west of the island. Large populations of Fulmar (*c.* 3,000 pairs) and Kittiwake (*c.* 10,000 pairs) also occur, with about 200 pairs of Shag and 700–800 pairs of Puffin. Black Guillemot are often to be seen on the crossing to Handa, but do not regularly breed. Skuas have recently colonised Handa; currently about 30 pairs of Arctic Skua and 100 pairs of Great Skua breed on the moorland, although many non-breeders are also present.

No raptors at present breed on Handa, but visiting Buzzard and Peregrine are regular and passage Sparrowhawk and Merlin may be seen during spring and autumn.

Access

Boats for Handa leave from Tarbet, which is reached by way of an unclassified road off the A894 Laxford Bridge–Scourie road, 3 miles (4.8 km) north of Scourie.

Boats operate daily (except Sunday) between 1 April and 10 September (tel. William MacRae, 0971 2156). The first boat usually departs at around 10 am. Please note the crossing should be undertaken only in calm weather. The boat service is not connected with the SWT and the Trust accepts no liability for the safety of visitors whilst making the crossing. Once ashore on Handa, visitors are asked to keep to the waymarked paths and take care near the cliff edge. Very close views of nesting skuas are possible from the marked path which passes through what has now become a breeding area, the birds seemingly very tolerant of human visitors. There are many good vantage points from which to overlook cliff-nesting seabirds. A warden is present from April to August.

Timing

The best time to visit is between early May and mid-July.

Calendar

The auks start to come ashore in large numbers during April and lay their eggs in early May. Most of the young Guillemot and Razorbill will have left their nest ledges by late July, but the Puffin will be present until early August. Kittiwake lay in the third week of May and the first young start to leave their nests in mid-July. Apart from the breeding seabirds, many other interesting species frequent Handa.

Over-wintering Great Northern Diver are often still present in early May, and a few Black-throated Diver can be seen in the sound throughout summer. Small numbers of Red-throated Diver, Eider and Shelduck breed in the area, and can all be seen off Handa's south-east coast. The bays here hold small numbers of nesting Oystercatcher and Ringed Plover. A small colony of Common and Arctic Terns is located on the skerries in Port an Eilein, near the boat landing point. In addition to Kittiwake, four other species of gull breed on the cliffs, as do Rock Dove. Inland, breeding birds include Snipe, Wheatear, Stonechat and occasionally Red Grouse, Golden Plover and Reed Bunting.

Regular passage migrants include parties of Pink-footed and Greylag Geese flying north in April and early May; small numbers of waders such as Dunlin, Greenshank, Turnstone, Sanderling and Whimbrel which feed along the tideline during spring and autumn; Pomarine Skua offshore in early May and movements of Manx and a few Sooty Shearwaters in the autumn. The plantation in the east of the island provides useful cover for passerine migrants.

In winter a small flock of Barnacle Geese visit the island.

Warden

C/o Mrs A Munro, Tarbet, near Lairg IV27 4SS.

H24 INVERPOLLY

OS ref.: NC 13/12
OS map: sheet 15

Habitat

The 10,856-hectare Inverpolly National Nature Reserve is a vast wilderness area bordered to the east by the A835 Drumrunie–Elphin road and extending north-westwards to Enard Bay. The undulating moorland plateau is interspersed by a mosaic of freshwater lochs, lochans and boggy hollows, punctuated by the sharply defined sandstone peaks of Stac Pollaidh (613 m), Cul Mor (849 m) and Cul Beag (769 m).

Small remnants of the formerly extensive birch/hazel woodland cover cling to the valleysides in a landscape otherwise dominated by heather and grass moorland, excepting the relatively barren mountain summits.

Species

Black- and Red-throated Divers, Red-breasted Merganser, Goosander, Wigeon and small numbers of Greylag Geese can be seen on the freshwater lochs in spring and summer. These are best worked from the roadside so as to minimise disturbance to breeding species.

Repeated scanning of the skyline with binoculars should eventually produce views of Golden Eagle, and Buzzard, Merlin, Peregrine and Raven can also be seen.

Ptarmigan are present in small numbers on the high tops, with the more numerous Red Grouse occurring on the lower moors, Snow Bunting sometimes frequent the roadsides in winter and many linger on the summits until well into spring.

Moorland breeding birds include Golden Plover, Greenshank, Ring Ousel, Wheatear and Stonechat. A few Twite can often be seen around crofts.

In the birch woods, look for Woodcock, Wood Warbler, Treecreeper, Long-tailed Tit and Spotted Flycatcher.

Fulmar, Shag, Eider and Black Guillemot breed on the coast and small numbers of Barnacle Geese can be seen using the offshore island in winter.

Access

The challenging nature of the environment here requires that any exploration away from the roadside is taken very seriously – adequate clothing/footwear are necessary and experience in hill walking and navigation essential. Fortunately, many interesting birds can be seen either from the roadside (the A835, plus the unclassified road alongside Loch Lurgainn and the connecting road northwards to Lochinver), or from one of the few short tracks that lead into the area. One of the best of these is alongside the River Kirkaig in the west of the reserve. Please note that dogs are not allowed on the reserve.

There is an Information Centre at Knockan (NC 187904), 2½ miles (4 km) south-west of Elphin on the A835. Open Monday to Friday 10 am to 6 pm, between May and mid-September. The Knockan Cliff Nature Trail, adjacent to the centre, gives fine views over the area.

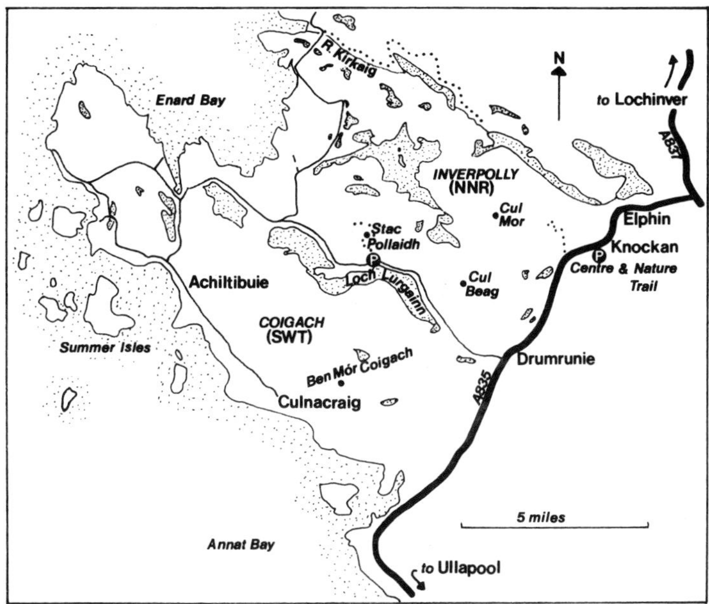

Timing

April to June is the best time for birds, although scenically the area is absolutely superb in the autumn and winter. There is unrestricted access to the hill ground for most of the year, except from 15 July to 21 October when permission should be sought from the Assynt Estate Office (tel: 05714 204) to visit the Drumrunie area. Between 1 September and 21 October it is advisable to contact one of the NCC wardens (see below) for advice on the access situation.

Skylark, spring

SNH Wardens

Knockan Cottage, Knockan, Ullapoll, Ross-shire. Tel: 085484 234.
Strathpolly, Lochinver, Ross-shire. Tel: 05714 204.

H25 BEN MOR COIGACH

OS ref.: NC 10/04
OS map: sheet 15

(See map of Inverpolly, H24.)

Habitat and Access

This is the largest of the Scottish Wildlife Trust's reserves, covering more than 6,000 hectares of mountain, moorland, coastline and islets on the north shore of Annat Bay. To the north, a chain of large freshwater lochs separate this area from the adjacent *Inverpolly National Nature Reserve*. The SWT reserve takes its name from, and is dominated by, the 743-metre-high summit of Ben Mor Coigach, which rises steeply above the moorlands and peat bog inland from the crofting township of Achiltibuie.

In common with Inverpolly, this area has few tracks and expeditions into the remoter parts of the reserve should not be taken lightly. Many of the birds characteristic of the area can be seen from the road to Achiltibuie and the continuation of this to the road end at Culnacraig.

Great Northern Divers, winter

Species

Breeding birds include Red Grouse, Ptarmigan, Golden Plover, Greenshank, Whinchat, Stonechat, Wheatear, Ring Ousel, Raven and Twite. Look for Golden Eagle over the skylines and check the roadside lochs for divers.

The fields and offshore islands at Achiltibuie are used by Barnacle Geese in winter, whilst Great Northern Diver are generally present in the bay from October through to May.

H26 BEINN EIGHE

OS ref.: NG 001650
OS map: sheets 19 & 25

Habitat

The Beinn Eighe National Nature Reserve covers 4,800 hectares of remote and rugged terrain to the south of Loch Maree. The area comprises a rich mixture of upland habitats, including about 182 hectares of natural pinewoods, which extend from the shores of Loch Maree up to about 300 metres. Birch, Rowan and Holly trees grow amongst the relic Scots Pines and the area has an understorey of heather and bilberry. In addition to this woodland, a further 486 hectares has been planted with native tree species.

Golden Eagles – immature and adult

The hills to the south of Loch Maree rise to around 1,000 metres altitude; heather, grass moorland and bog dominate this landscape, with dwarf shrubs on the high ground giving way to arctic-alpine heath on the summits.

Species

The woodlands hold limited but interesting bird communities, including Buzzard, Sparrowhawk, Great Spotted Woodpecker, Coat Tit, Goldcrest, Long-tailed Tit, Siskin, Redpoll and Crossbill all year, joined by Tree Pipit, Redstart, Wood Warbler and Willow Warbler in the summer. Above the tree line, Golden Eagle, occasional Merlin, Peregrine, and Raven occur; small numbers of Golden Plover, Ring Ousel, Wheatear and Whinchat are present during the breeding season. Red Grouse may be seen on the lower moorlands, whilst the summits have small populations of Ptarmigan.

Loch Maree is the haunt of Red- and Black-throated Divers, Red-breasted Merganser, Goosander and Greylag Geese. Common Sandpiper breed around the lochshore. Greenshank are occasionally seen, whilst Dipper and Grey Wagtail frequent the burnsides.

Timing

The optimum time to visit for birdlife is between May and July. From mid-August to 21 October Red Deer stalking is in progress and access to the hill ground is therefore restricted to the main footpaths and nature trails – for details contact Scottish Natural Heritage, Dingwall Business Park, Strathpeffer Road, Dingwall, Ross-shire.

Access

The A832 runs along the south shore of Loch Maree and there are several car parks that afford good views out across the loch. There are two nature trails: one is a short (*c.* 1-mile (1.6-km)), mainly woodland route, the other a long (*c.* 4-mile (6.4-km)) path that climbs above the tree line through a variety of upland habitats. Both of these commence from a car park at Glas Leitire (NH 000650), about 3 miles (5 km) north-west of Kinlochewe. If venturing further afield, please note that the terrain demands a high level of competence in hill walking ability and that adequate clothing and footwear are essential. Please also note that dogs are not allowed on the reserve.

Buzzard and Hooded Crow

The Aultroy Visitor Centre near Kinlochewe (tel: 044584 258) can supply trail leaflets, further information and advice. It is open daily between May and September.

SNH Reserve manager

Anancaun Field station, Kinlochewe, Ross-shire IV22 2PD. Tel: 044584 244 or 254.

H27 KINTAIL AND MORVICH

OS ref.: NH 00/19
OS map: sheet 33

Habitat and Access

The magnificent highland scenery on this 18,000-hectare National Trust for Scotland property includes the peaks of the Five Sisters of Kintail, rising from sea level at the head of Loch Duich to over 1,000 metres altitude. There is a Countryside Centre at Morvich Farm, just off the A87 north of Shiel Bridge; this is also the best access point into the hills. The centre is open from June until September and a ranger-naturalist leads guided walks in the area and can give advice on the best routes to take in the hills.

Species

Kintail is a particularly good place in which to see Golden Eagle and the mountain skyline should be scanned frequently. Peregrine are present year-round and again, regular vigilance should be rewarded. Ptarmigan breed on many of the summits, however, only experienced and adequately equipped groups should contemplate the ascent of any of the Kintail peaks.

Three or four pairs each of Red-breasted Merganser and Goosander breed and can be seen between March and July in Glen Lichd and Glen Shiel. The mergansers also frequent Loch Duich. Scarcer breeding visitors include Black-throated Diver and Greenshank.

The area is poor for passage birds, but the sea and freshwater lochs support modest numbers of wintering wildfowl, including occasional Whooper Swan. A few Crossbill are usually present in the Glenshiel forestry between December and March.

Ranger/Naturalist

William Fraser, Morvich Farm, Inverinate, Kyle, Ross-shire IV40 8HQ. Tel: 059 981 219.

H28 BALMACARA ESTATE

OS ref.: NG 79/29
OS map: sheet 33

Grey Heron

This is another National Trust for Scotland property, covering some 2,274 hectares of the Kyle/Plockton peninsula to the north of Loch Alsh. The habitat comprises sea coast, rugged moorland with scattered hill lochs and both deciduous and coniferous woodland. The woodland at Coille Mhor is a Site of Special Scientific Interest. There is a visitor centre at Lochalsh, open from April to October.

Although not an outstanding area for birds, there is good selection of woodland and moorland species that typify west coast birdlife. Hen Harrier have bred in recent years and Grasshopper Warbler can be heard in Coille Mhor. The area is poor for passage and wintering species.

Ranger/Naturalist

William Fraser, Morvich Farm, Inverinate, Kyle, Ross-shire IV40 8HQ. Tel: 059 981 219.

H29 NOSS HEAD

OS ref.: ND 388550

Habitat and Access

This important seawatching and migrant bird headland is situated some 3 miles (5 km) north of Wick, at the southern end of Sinclair's Bay. It can be reached by taking the unclassified road from Wick to Stoxigoe and then following the signs for Noss Head (note: the alternative route across Wick Airport is now closed to vehicles). Park at the car park approximately 400 metres from the lighthouse.

Species

The bird interest at the headland is divided between the migrant passerines that can sometimes be found in the numerous gorse overgrown ditches and the old lighthouse garden, and the passage seabirds that can be watched from the lighthouse.

Spring migrants have included Bluethroat, Red-backed Shrike, Great Reed Warbler and Thrush Nightingale. In autumn the area is good for passage thrushes, chats and warblers (especially Sylvia warblers); Bluethroat, Wryneck, Red-breasted Flycatcher, Yellow-browed Warbler and Little Bunting have all been recorded in recent years.

Seawatching can be very good for shearwaters, petrels and skuas. Possible species include Sooty, Great and Cory's Shearwater, plus Pomarine and Long-tailed Skuas.

ADDITIONAL SITES

Site and Grid Reference	Habitat	Main Bird Interest	Peak Season
a. Ariundle SNH/FC NM 830635 Sheet 40	Oakwood & pines, streamside	Woodland species, inc. Redstart & Wood Warbler Dipper & Grey Wagtail	May–July.
b. Borgie Forest FC NC 66/58 Sheet 10	Only large area of mature woodland on the north Sutherland coast	Common woodland birds	All year.
c. Eilean Hoan RSPB reserve NC 44/67 Sheet 9	Low-lying offshore island	Great Northern Diver gather in late winter Barnacle Geese	Apr.–May Oct.–Apr.

Access to this island is very difficult – the divers and geese can be 'scoped from the A838 Durness–Tongue road.

Site and Grid Reference	Habitat	Main Bird Interest	Peak Season
d. Faraid Head NC 38/71 Sheet 9	Headland/sea-cliffs	Breeding Fulmar, Kittiwake Black Guillemot, Guillemot Razorbill & Puffin	May–July.
		Passage seabirds, inc. Sooty Shearwater	Aug.–Oct.
e. Glen Nevis NN 16/69 Sheet 41	Mountain & steep valley	Golden Eagle	All year.
f. Gruinard Bay NG 95/93 Sheet 19	Open sealoch	Great Northern Diver	Oct.–May.
g. Kyle of Sutherland NH 59/93 Sheet 21	Enclosed tidal basin with surrounding conifer woodland	Wintering wildfowl Common woodland species inc. Scottish Crossbill	Oct.–Mar. All year.

There are a number of Forestry Commission trails in this area – booklet available from the Tourist Office in Dornoch.

Site and Grid Reference	Habitat	Main Bird Interest	Peak Season
h. Loch Broom NH 12/93 Sheet 19	Long deep sealoch, used by trawlers landing fish at Ullapool & visiting fish factory ships	Wintering divers and gulls esp. Glaucous & Iceland	Nov.–May.
i. Loch Eriboll NC 43/59 Sheet 9	Long, deep sealoch A838 follows shore	Divers & sea-duck	Oct.–May.
j. Loch Eye NH 830795 Sheet 21	Only large (*c.* 165 ha.) eutrophic loch in East Ross	Passage & wintering geese roost, inc. up to 20,000 Greylag & 2,000 Pink-footed. Also up to 700 Whooper Swan	end of Oct.

Note: all the land surrounding Loch Eye is privately owned. Reasonable views can be obtained from the road to the north and west of the loch. Visit in the last two hours of daylight (3.30 pm to 5.30 pm in October). During the day, many feeding geese and Whoopers can be found in the area between Arabella and Balmuchy (on stubble in autumn, winter wheat/barley in spring).

Site and Grid Reference	Habitat	Main Bird Interest	Peak Season
k. Loch Hope NC 46/54 Sheet 9	Long freshwater loch surrounded by open moor and birch scrub. Vegetated crags of Ben Hope (927m) to south-east	Divers, Golden Eagle, Merlin, Peregrine, Whinchat, Stonechat, Wheatear, Ring Ousel, Raven	May–Aug.

Good views of surrounding terrain and across loch from unclassified road along east shore.

l. Loch Naver NC 61/36 Sheet 16	Long freshwater loch with birch scrub on west shore. Heather, bracken & some conifers to east	Divers, raptors & moorland birds	May–Aug.

This loch can be easily 'scoped from the B873 along the north shore.

m. North Sutor NH 822688 Sheet 21 or 27	Steep 100m cliffs on seaward side of the entrance to the Cromarty Firth	Nesting Guillemot, Razorbill Black Guillemot & over 400 prs Cormorant	Jun.–July.

Access is by path across private farmland. There should be no objections provided that gates are closed etc. From Nigg Ferry, take the obvious but unsignposted road up the north Sutor. Turn right past a wood and go down the rough lane to some gun emplacements, then follow the path which runs to the right along the top of the cliff and descends steeply to the lower emplacements. Most of the seabird colonies can be seen from here.

Please note that this path is very steep and hard to follow through the gorse – *not recommended in wet weather.*

n. Rahoy Hills SWT reserve NM 690530 Sheet 49	Mountain, Oak woods, hill lochans	Red-throated Diver, Golden Eagle, Snipe, Common Sandpiper & Pied Flycatcher. Pine Marten & Wildcat present	May–July.

Permit required – contact Donald Kennedy, tel: 0967 421203.

o. Rum SNH reserve Sheet 39	Mountain & coastal habitats. Some woodland around Kinloch	Variety of upland species inc. Golden & Sea Eagles. Seabird colonies on south & north-east coasts	Apr.–Oct.

Permits are required in order to visit all areas away from the Loch Scresort area – contact SNH Inverness Office.

p. Strathy Point NC 82/69 Sheet 10	Exposed northerly peninsula	Sea-watching vantage point Sooty Shearwater regularly recorded	Aug.–Sept.
q. Tarbat Ness NH 949877 Sheet 21	Rocky promontory extending into Moray Firth	Excellent sea-watching pt. especially in SE gales. Fulmar, Sooty & Manx Shearwaters, geese, waders, Pomarine, Arctic & Great Skuas, gulls, terns & auks	Aug.–Sept.
r. Torridon NTS NG 90/59 Sheets 24 & 25	Vast mountainous areas adjacent to Beinn Eighe NNR	Breeding divers, birds of prey, Ptarmigan & moorland species	May–Aug.

Visitor Centre at Torridon, with resident ranger/naturalist. Tel: 044587 221. Guide books available.

LOTHIAN

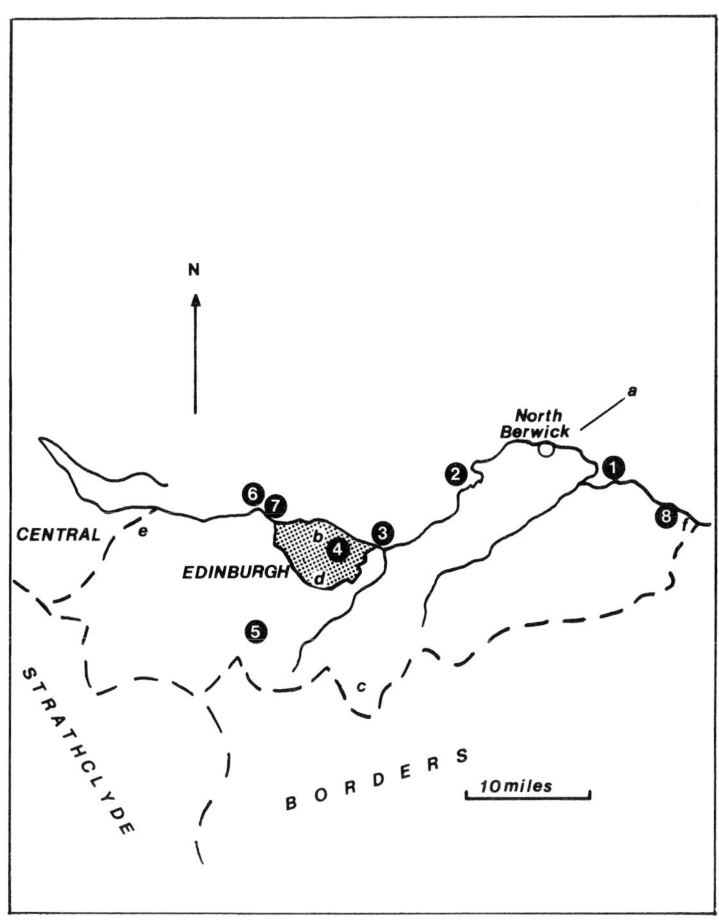

Main sites:
L1. Tyninghame and John Muir Country Park
L2. Aberlady Bay
L3. Musselburgh
L4. Duddingston Loch
L5. Threipmuir Reservoir
L6. Hound Point
L7. Dalmeny
L8. Barns Ness

Additional sites:
a. Bass Rock
b. Botanic Gardens, Edinburgh
c. Gladhouse Reservoir
d. Hermitage of Braid
e. Linlithgow Loch
f. Skateraw

L1 TYNINGHAME/JOHN MUIR COUNTRY PARK

OS ref.: NT 64/78
OS map: sheet 67

Habitat

Tyninghame, or the John Muir Country Park, lies to the west of Dunbar in East Lothian. The 704-hectare park is dominated by the estuary of the River Tyne, with its extensive inter-tidal mud-flats and saltmarsh habitats. Sandy substrates underlie the northern part of the estuary, which is bounded to the north by the rocky headland of St Baldred's Cradle. To the south-east of the river mouth, the sand shores are backed by the dunes of Spike Island with the rocky shoreline of Dunbar further east. A long narrow spit, Sandy Hirst, extends into the Tyne estuary from the north shore.

An extensive plantation of Scots pine is located to the north of the Linkfield car park. The area is otherwise vegetated by grassland and scrub.

The park has been accorded Site of Special Scientific Interest status in recognition of its biological and geological importance.

Species

Over 225 species have been recorded in the Tyninghame area, reflecting the rich diversity of habitat here.

Small numbers of Eider, Shelduck and Ringed Plover attempt to nest in the dunes and along the shoreline, but breeding success for all these species is low. Over 200 pairs of Kittiwake nest on the cliffs at Dunbar Harbour.

The Tyninghame Estate woodlands hold breeding Green and Great Spotted Woodpeckers and the commoner species of tit, warbler and finch. Hawfinch may possibly breed.

It is the large numbers of passage and wintering birds, however, that make this area so important. Up to 250 Mallard roost on the sea at the mouth of the Tyne in winter with over 600 Wigeon and around 70 Teal frequenting the estuary. Shelduck numbers usually peak at well over 100 birds in March. Up to 100 Common and a few Velvet Scoters winter offshore and small numbers of Eider are invariably present. Goldeneye regularly feed at the mouth of the Biel Water and a total of over 50 birds use the area in mid-winter. Long-tailed Duck and Red-breasted Merganser are often present; in late summer a moult flock of around 80 Goosander are usually present. Between 20 and 30 Mute Swan can be seen in any month of the year in the fields adjacent to the embankment at the west end of the estuary and in winter these are joined by up to 25 Whooper Swan and the occasional Bewick's Swan. Up to 500 Greylag and small flocks of Pink-Footed Geese feed in these fields in winter and occasionally roost on the mud-flats at night, but shooting disturbance probably prevents larger goose roosts from forming.

Wintering waders include over 700 Oystercatcher, a minimum of 40 Ringed Plover, around 100 Grey Plover, 250 Lapwing (late winter), 500–1,000 Dunlin, over 80 Bar-tailed Godwit, 200 or so Curlew and circa 300 Redshank. Two or three Greenshank usually linger right through the winter. Turnstone and Purple Sandpiper frequent the rocky shoreline below the cliffs at Dunbar and between 700 and 1,000 Knot can be found on the rocks around St Baldred's Cradle or at the mouth of the Biel Water. Small flocks of Golden Plover occasionally occur on the golf course at Winterfield.

Birds of prey that regularly visit the estuary include Sparrowhawk, Merlin and Peregrine; Hen Harrier and Short-eared Owl are less regular. Small numbers of Shore Lark are likely throughout winter, especially on the Spike Island saltmarsh. Snow Bunting and Twite also occur; Lapland Bunting are occasional.

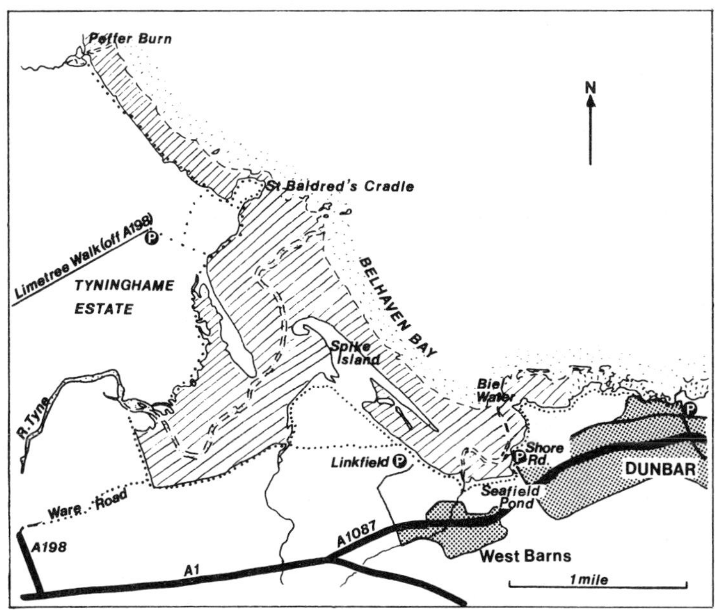

Access

The Country Park is reached by turning off the A1 onto the A1087 1 mile (1.6 km) west of Dunbar. Turn left 1/4 mile (0.4 km) later and follow this minor road to the Linkfield car park. Alternatively, continue on the A1087 through West Barns and into Dunbar, turning left to Shore Road car park. A coastal path links the two car parks and there are information boards giving details about the park. It is also feasible to continue westwards from the Linkfield car park along the south side of the estuary towards Ware Road. Parking at the west end of Ware road, just off the A198 is *not* recommended.

There are regular bus and train services to Dunbar.

Tyninghame Estate, to the north-west, is privately owned and access is possible only along certain paths. Park at Tyninghame Links car park at the end of Limetree Walk (off the A198 1 mile (1.6 km) north of the bridge over the River Tyne). See map for details.

Timing

The park is open at all times and can be interesting at any time of year. The prime time for bird activity, however, is from September through to May.

An ebbing or flowing tide is best for watching waders – the inner estuary and Spike Island areas in particular are best visited two hours either side of high water. The high tide roosts are rather variable and depend to a large extent on the degree of human disturbance – the main ones are at the north and south ends of Spike Island (spring tides) and during neap tides, on the north side of the inner estuary.

Calendar

Some of the more interesting species likely to be seen.

April–July: Some 400–500 Eider are present either offshore or within the estuary, whilst around 140 Shelduck can usually be seen. The wintering Wigeon and Teal have mostly dispersed by mid-April, but passage duck such as Gadwall, Shoveler, Pintail or even Garganey may put in an appearance in the river mouth or at Seafield Pond. Large numbers of Ringed Plover and Dunlin pass through at this time, together with smaller groups of Sanderling (May), Common Sandpiper and Spotted Redshank. Whimbrel are occasionally seen between April and early June.

Passerine migrants seen in spring include White Wagtail, Wheatear, Whinchat, Redstart and Ring Ousel, with Tree Pipit, Siskin and Crossbill occurring in the woods.

August–October: Large numbers of Gannet can be seen offshore in late summer, with passage Manx Shearwater, Kittiwake, and Great/Arctic Skuas also present. St. Baldred's Cradle is the best seawatching location. Brent and Barnacle Geese occur in small numbers during September/October and a few passage Pintail and Shoveler have also been recorded. Goosander are sometimes present in the river mouth. Less common passage waders regularly recorded in small numbers during the autumn include Greenshank, Little Stint, Curlew Sandpiper, Spotted Redshank, Green Sandpiper, Ruff and Black-tailed Godwit. These mostly frequent the north end of Spike Island until disturbed, when they generally move onto the less convenient northern saltmarsh.

Snow Bunting and Shore Lark can often be found around Spike Island in late autumn and often linger into winter. Short-eared Owl can sometimes be seen hunting over the dunes, both in autumn and winter.

Several hundred gulls gather in late autumn to feed, bathe and roost at the mouths of Peffer Burn and Biel Water. Little Gull and Black Tern are occasional visitors to the estuary at this time.

Around 100 Shag and 25 Cormorant fish in the outer estuary and can be seen loafing on the rocks at the mouth of the Tyne.

November–March: Wintering wildfowl and waders provide the main interest. Shelduck numbers build up to a peak of over 100 birds in late February/early March.

Offshore, modest numbers of Red-throated Diver and occasional Black-throated and Great Northern Divers are seen.

Adjacent Sites

Seafield Pond

OS ref.: NT 659784

This old clay pit between West Barns and Dunbar has been flooded to form a freshwater pond. Willow, alder and hawthorn have been established around the edge of the pond, providing nesting habitat for Willow Warbler, Sedge Warbler and Reed Bunting. The site is easily accessible from the Shore Road car park (see above).

Mute Swan, Mallard, Coot and Moorhen are resident, whilst Little Grebe, Pochard and Tufted Duck are present throughout the winter. Regular winter visitors include Whooper Swan, Pink-footed Goose, Shoveler, Scaup, Long-tailed Duck, Goosander and Kingfisher. Dippers frequent the nearby Biel Water in winter.

References

Birdwatching Sites in the Lothians, ed. I.J. Andrews (Lothian Branch of SOC).
John Muir Country Park, East Lothian, factsheet by R. Anderson.
Lothian Bird Reports 1987–90. Ed. I.J. Andrews/O. McGarry, SOC.

L2 ABERLADY BAY

OS ref.: NT 46/81
OS map: sheet 66

Habitat

Aberlady Bay lies on the south shore of the Firth of Forth, some 16 miles (26 km) east of the centre of Edinburgh. Extensive inter-tidal mud- and sand-flats provide rich feeding for wildfowl and waders, whilst a diverse mixture of saltmarsh, sand dunes, grasslands, open freshwater, scrub and mixed woodland habitat support a wide range of migrant and breeding species.

Aberlady is a Local Nature Reserve, covering 582 hectares (only 119 hectares lie above the high water mark, however), managed by East Lothian District Council, although most of the land is in fact in private ownership. The area is a Site of Special Scientific Interest and is notable not only for birds but also for its outcrops of limestone and sandstone and for its examples of dune and saltmarsh succession.

Access

Aberlady Bay is reached via the A198 Musselburgh to North Berwick road and can be viewed from the roadside immediately to the east of Aberlady village. There is a car park ½ mile (0.8 km) beyond the village. From here a track crosses the footbridge and heads northwards to Gullane point, with a left branch just beyond the sewage works which goes down to the coast. The point is an excellent place for seawatching. Please keep to the

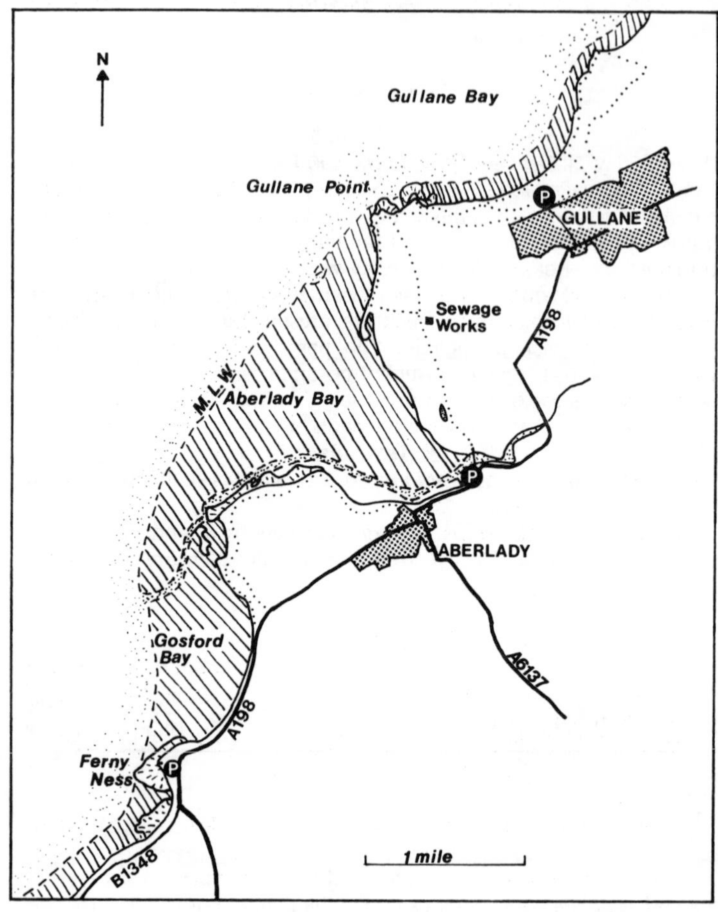

main paths, especially during the breeding season. Access to the saltmarsh is tolerated except from April to June. Dogs must be kept on a lead and are not allowed between April and July.

Other locations to try are:

Gosford Bay

OS ref.: NT 44/78

This can be viewed from the B1348, east of Port Seton, and the A198, which it joins immediately before Ferny Ness. There is a parking space at Ferny Ness, which makes a good vantage point.

A footpath leaves the A198 at the north end of Gosford Bay and follows the headland round into Aberlady Bay. The key to the hide mid-way along this path is available from the Aberlady warden. This is probably the best site in Britain for grebes. In August, up to 50 adult Red-necked Grebe in full summer plumage are regular (double figures are guaranteed!). In winter, up to 160 Slavonian Grebe can be present. Surf Scoter have been a feature during March–April every year between 1983 and 1990 inclusive.

Gullane Bay

OS ref.: NT 47/83

Gullane Bay lies immediately to the north-east of Aberlady Bay LNR, and can be viewed from Gullane Point (see Aberlady access details), or approached more directly from a large car park to the north of Gullane itself, reached by turning left off the A198 along Sandy Loan.

There are buses from Edinburgh to Aberlady car park and Gullane. The nearest train stations are 3 miles (4.8 km) away at Longniddry and Drem.

Timing

The area is interesting throughout the year, although from September through to March is probably the optimum time to visit for birds.

The area is best viewed from the A198 at low tides, but the saltmarsh on the east side of the bay is better at high tide. Strong sunlight can be a problem on afternoon high tides.

Relatively calm sea conditions are essential for viewing sea-fowl; a north/north-easterly wind is best for seabirds such as skuas and Little Auk.

Species

Around 250 species have been recorded at Aberlady, reflecting both the importance of the site and the high level of coverage given to the area by birdwatchers.

Breeding birds include Little Grebe, around 40 pairs of Shelduck, at least 200 pairs of Eider, also Partridge, Moorhen, Coot, over 30 pairs of Ringed Plover, and Lapwing, Snipe and Redshank.

Common breeding passerines include Skylark, Meadow Pipit, Dunnock, Sedge and Willow Warblers and Reed Bunting. Around five pairs of Lesser Whitethroat and a few pairs of Garden Warbler, Blackcap and Spotted Flycatcher over-summer.

Sparrowhawk and Kestrel are seen regularly throughout the year; Merlin, Peregrine and Short-eared Owl are chiefly seen in autumn and winter. Long-eared Owl sometimes breed and are joined by winter visitors.

Summering birds include Knot, Sanderling, up to 150 Lesser Black-backed Gull and (in late summer especially) large numbers of Sandwich Tern. Guillemot and Razorbill can be seen offshore at any time of year; Black Guillemot and Puffin are uncommon summer visitors.

Fulmar and Gannet can be seen throughout much of the year, but are commonest between April and September; small numbers of Manx Shearwater are recorded from March to October.

Common and Velvet Scoter can be seen year-round, although the latter are much scarcer than the former. Populations of both species peak in spring and autumn. Surf Scoter is almost annual in its occurrence on this coast.

Common passage and wintering waders include Oystercatcher, Ringed Plover, Golden and Grey Plovers, Knot, Sanderling, Snipe, Bar-tailed Godwit, Curlew, Redshank and Common Sandpiper. Migrant waders recorded less frequently are Little Stint, Curlew Sandpiper, Ruff,

Black-tailed Godwit, Whimbrel, Spotted Redshank, Greenshank, Green and Wood Sandpipers. Rarer waders recorded in recent years have included Avocet, Little Ringed, Kentish, Caspian and Greater Sand Plovers, American Golden Plover, White-rumped, Sharp-tailed and Broad-billed Sandpipers, and Wilson's Phalarope.

Passage Herring Gull and Kittiwake occur in great numbers during spring and autumn.

Red-throated Diver are common offshore in winter, whilst Black-throated and Great Northern Divers are seen on occasion. Great Crested, Red-necked and Slavonian Grebes are common passage and winter visitors; Black-necked Grebe are rare.

A flock of Whooper Swan, usually less than 40-strong, but on occasion comprising over 100 birds, roosts on the reserve at night from November until March, sometimes joined by a few Bewick's Swan, although in recent winters they have tended to roost inland. Large numbers of Pink-footed Geese over-winter and small parties of Greylag Geese occur, especially in severe weather and on spring passage. Canada and Barnacle Geese are rare in winter but are seen regularly on passage, especially in September/October. Brent Geese are seen occasionally on passage, or may linger in winter.

Moderate numbers of dabbling duck over-winter. Gadwall are very occasionally seen; Pintail and Shoveler are scarce visitors in spring and autumn. Visiting diving duck include occasional Pochard and Tufted Duck, Scaup and Goosander. About 100 Long-tailed Duck usually winter, with smaller numbers of Goldeneye. Black-headed, Common and Great Black-backed Gulls winter in large number; Glaucous Gull are seen annually.

Water Rail, Jack Snipe and occasionally, Greenshank, over-winter.

Calendar

Some of the more interesting species likely to be seen.

March–May: Red-necked Grebe are usually present in Gullane Bay during April/May. Small numbers of Shoveler may be seen; Marsh Harrier are almost annual May visitors; Wood Sandpiper are regular, if scarce, spring migrants.

Of the various passerine migrants passing through the reserve, Yellow Wagtail are particularly notable – up to nine have been seen around the pools at the edge of the saltmarsh, including individuals of the Blue and Grey-headed races. White Wagtail also occur.

June–July: Small numbers of Bar-tailed Godwit, Knot and Grey Plover over-summer. An influx of large numbers of Sandwich Tern in late summer augments the summer populations of Common, Arctic and Little Terns.

August–November: As many as 150 Red-throated Diver congregate in Gullane Bay from September through to April, with small numbers of other diver species. Red-necked Grebe assemble off Ferny Ness in late summer/early autumn (a maximum of 68 have been recorded), where up to 154 Slavonian Grebe are present from October through to March. Up to 120 Cormorant roost on the sandspit in late summer. Pink-footed Goose numbers peak in October/November – over 17,500 have been recorded at dawn and dusk, when these birds move between their roost on the mud-flats and their feeding areas in the fields around Drem.

Numbers of Wigeon, Teal and Mallard build up from September onwards; a moulting flock of Eider at Gullane Bay has reached nearly 7,000 birds in some years, with up to 6,000 Common and 600 Velvet Scoters, whilst a smaller concentration of Red-breasted Merganser occurs in early autumn. Shelduck return from their moulting grounds in November.

Large numbers of passage waders move through the area (see above); Whimbrel and Spotted Redshank, Greenshank, Green and Wood Sandpipers are regular autumn migrants; Little Stint and occasional Curlew Sandpiper are also seen.

Arctic, Great and, more rarely, Pomarine Skuas harass gulls and terns offshore. Little Gull and Black Tern are annual visitors in late summer/ early autumn.

Thrushes, including large flocks of Fieldfare and Redwing and occasional Ring Ousel, move through during October.

December–February: Wintering species still present; Shelduck numbers peak, with up to 200 birds present. Purple Sandpiper and Turnstone occupy areas of rocky foreshore.

There are usually several Short-eared Owls hunting over the reserve during the winter months (calm, sunny afternoons are best).

Flocks of up to 200 Tree Sparrow, 200 Greenfinch and 1,200 Linnet can be present on the saltmarsh and nearby stubble, with lesser numbers of Redpoll, Twite, Brambling and Snow Bunting. Shorelark and up to 70 Lapland Bunting have been recorded in some winters.

References

'A Checklist of the Birds of Aberlady Bay Local Nature Reserve', Peter R. Gordon in *Lothian Bird Report 1987*, ed. I.J. Andrews (Lothian branch of the SOC).

Warden

Ian M. Thompson, 4 Craigelaw Cottages, Longniddry, East Lothian, EH32 0PY. Tel: 08757 588.

L3 MUSSELBURGH

OS ref.: NT 345735
OS map: sheet 66

Habitat

Musselburgh lies on the eastern outskirts of Edinburgh, at the mouth of the River Esk. The coast here has been subjected to much industrial development, but although not a particularly scenic place, Musselburgh is justly famed for its birdlife. In the past, the flooded lagoons on the east bank of the Esk were renowned for attracting migrant waders, but they have now been infilled with ash from the nearby Cockenzie Power Station. The un-compacted parts of these ash lagoons have subsequently become major roost sites for many species of waders and gulls. East Lothian District Council ultimately intend to create a wader 'scrape' to compensate for the loss of the freshwater pools.

Species

The area is an exceptionally productive one for birds, with large numbers of offshore sea-fowl present during with winter, important populations of passage and wintering wildfowl and waders, huge numbers of roosting gulls and considerable seabird traffic in the Firth.

Offshore wintering sea-duck include nearly 1,000 Eider, over 500 Goldeneye, around 100 each of Long-tailed Duck and Red-breasted Merganser, up to 250 Common Scoter, around 50 Velvet Scoter and small numbers of Scaup (formerly very numerous).

Common and Velvet Scoters

Modest numbers of Red-throated and occasional Black-throated Divers are generally present in winter and, in addition, up to 200 Great Crested Grebe, small numbers of Slavonian Grebe, occasional Red-necked and even Black-necked Grebes can be seen.

Wintering Oystercatcher numbers sometimes exceed 2,000 birds, whilst between 1,000 and 3,000 Knot, up to 1,000 Bar-tailed Godwit, 300–400 Dunlin, 200–300 Curlew, over 150 Redshank, 100 each of Ringed Plover and Turnstone and small numbers of Grey Plover and Lapwing are not unusual.

Passage waders include large numbers of Golden Plover, Lapwing, Redshank and Turnstone, with lesser numbers of Sanderling, Ruff, Black-tailed Godwit, Whimbrel, Greenshank and Common Sandpiper. Little Stint and Curlew Sandpiper are recorded regularly, but Spotted Redshank, Green Sandpiper and Wood Sandpiper are scarce.

Very large numbers of gulls bathe and loaf in the mouth of the Esk, including up to 5,000 each of Black-headed and Common Gulls, 8,000 Herring Gull, smaller numbers of Great Black-backed Gull and occasional Glaucous, Iceland and Mediterranean Gulls (especially in spring).

Seawatching from July to October can produce sightings of Fulmar, Manx Shearwater (late summer), Gannet (main passage in September) and Kittiwake. Arctic Skua are seen regularly between August and October, with small numbers of Great Skua and occasional Pomarine and Long-tailed Skuas also recorded.

Sandwich Tern can be seen between April and October, with a peak of around 1,000 birds present in August. Smaller numbers of Common Tern are recorded and one or two Black Tern occur each autumn.

The long list of rarities that have been recorded at Musselburgh is as much a testament to the efforts of local observers as to the richness of the site; it includes Surf Scoter, Buff-breasted and White-rumped Sandpipers, Franklin's Gull, Forster's and Lesser Crested Terns, Citrine Wagtail and Red-throated Pipit.

Access

The offshore sea-fowl can be viewed from a number of points along the A199 Leith–Musselburgh road. To reach the outflow of the Esk, turn north off the main road east from Musselburgh immediately before reaching the racecourse, then right until the River Esk is reached; follow the river downstream and park at the road end (Goosegreen Crescent). The sea wall along the east side of the river is a good vantage point, especially at low tide, when most bird activity will be at the river mouth. Continue further along the sea wall as far as the sewage outfall (a distance of just over a mile), scanning for offshore sea-fowl. The land around the lagoons is mostly owned by Scottish Power and access on foot is allowed except to the active lagoons.

Timing

The timing of a visit is crucial in order to savour the full range of species to be found at Musselburgh. The optimum time to visit is about two and a half to three hours before high water (on spring sequences of tide – around an hour or so later on neaps). The waders feeding at the river mouth should then be gradually driven closer before they fly to the lagoons to roost. Offshore sea-fowl will usually be closer inshore at high water – relatively calm sea conditions are important. Strong afternoon sunlight can be problematic when birding at the river mouth in winter.

Birdwatching at Musselburgh can be exciting at any time of the year, although September–March is the period of most activity.

Calendar

Some of the more interesting species likely to be seen.

March–June: Goldeneye and Long-tailed Duck can be seen displaying prior to their departure north. Large numbers of Turnstone and Ringed Plover move through in late April/early May.

Lesser Black-backed Gull return in mid-March and there is a marked Common Gull passage. Mediterranean and Ring-billed Gulls have been recorded at this time.

Regular spring migrants include Sandwich and Common Terns, Common Sandpiper, hirundines, White Wagtail and Wheatear.

July–October: The return passage of waders such as Curlew, Golden Plover, Knot and Bar-tailed Godwit can be seen in early July. Small numbers of Grey Plover and occasional Ruff, Whimbrel and Spotted Redshank also occur. Little Stint and Curlew Sandpiper are likely after easterly winds.

Very large numbers of Sandwich Tern can be seen in August, with smaller numbers of Common Tern and the occasional Black Tern in

August/September. A few Little Gull pass through in October/early November.

By late autumn a moulting flock of around 400 Red-breasted Merganser has generally built up in the river mouth. Passage duck include Wigeon and Teal, with occasional Pintail and Shoveler occurring. Great Crested Grebe numbers peak in September, but Red-necked Grebe do not usually arrive until October.

Offshore, Manx Shearwater and a few Great and Arctic Skua are sometimes present, although Musselburgh is not particularly well situated for sea-watching.

November–February: Wintering divers, grebes, sea-duck, waders and gulls provide the main interest (see above).

In addition modest numbers of Guillemot and other auks can be seen offshore with regular Black Guillemot and Little Auk in recent years.

Skylark and Linnet frequent the rough ground surrounding the lagoons and Twite, Snow and Lapland Buntings are common along the foreshore habitats in some winters. Peregrine, Merlin and Short-eared Owl are seen regularly.

References

Birdwatching Sites in the Lothians, ed. I.J. Andrews, (Lothian branch of SOC).
'A Checklist of the Birds of Musselburgh Lagoons', I.J. Andrews.
Lothian Bird Reports 1987–90. Ed. I.J. Andrews/O. McGarry, SOC.

L4 DUDDINGSTON LOCH

OS ref.: NT 284725
OS map: sheet 66

Habitat

This excellent birding site lies at the southern edge of Holyrood Park, just below Arthur's Seat and only a short distance from the centre of Edinburgh. Both the loch and Bawsinch, a triangular piece of ground now supporting scrub, mixed woodland grassland and freshwater ponds, are managed by the Scottish Wildlife Trust.

Marshland, reed beds and Willow and Poplar woodland surround some of the shoreline. The reserve covers a total of 26 hectares and is designated a Site of Special Scientific Interest. One of the most important and long-term projects at the reserve is the re-introduction of indigenous Scottish broadleaved trees such as aspen, birch, ash, alder, cherry and hazel.

Species

Breeding birds include Little and Great Crested Grebes, Heron, Mute Swan, feral Greylag Goose, Mallard and Tufted Duck. Sparrowhawk breed in the woodland area and Sedge Warbler can be found in the reed beds. Cormorant, Teal and Pochard are seen regularly and a colony of a dozen or so Herons nest in the reedbeds. One or two Bitterns have been regular in recent winters and escaped Night Herons (often unringed) from the free-flying colony at Edinburgh Zoo are frequently noted.

A visit to Holyrood Park can be strongly recommended; Fulmar now breed regularly on Salisbury Crags, with up to 30 adults present in spring and summer; Meadow Pipit, Skylark and Linnet breed, whilst Wheatear and Ring Ousel can be seen on passage.

Timing

A visitor centre at Holyrood Park is open daily from 10 am to 5.45 pm between June and September; weekends only, 10 am to 4 pm, during April, May, and October to December.

Access

Duddingston Loch is located between Holyrood Park and Craigmillar and can be reached from the A1 along Old Church Lane. There are car parks on Duddingston Road and at Holyrood Park gates. Part of the northern shore, beside the public road through the Royal park, is open to the public.

A permit and key to the hide on the south-east shore are available from the visitor centre at Holyrood Park. There is a deposit payable on the key.

The car park by Holyrood Palace is a good base for exploring the park from the north side.

L5 THREIPMUIR RESERVOIR

OS ref.: NT 16/63
OS map: sheets 65/66

Habitat

Threipmuir Reservoir and the adjoining Harlaw Reservoir are situated at the foot of the Pentland Hills, approximately 10 miles (16 km) from the centre of Edinburgh, and lie within the Pentland Hills Regional Park. Between them, the reservoirs cover about 100 hectares, plus surrounding marshland, reed bed, scrub woodland, plantations arable land and improved pasture. Red Moss, a 23-hectare reserve managed by the Scottish Wildlife Trust, lies immediately north of Bavelaw Marsh, at the western end of Threipmuir, whilst the marsh itself is managed as a reserve by Lothian Regional Council.

This locality is one of the most important areas in Lothian Region for breeding and wintering waterfowl and yet it has so far received only limited attention from birders. The species information given below is based on regular visits over the last five years by Allan Brown, former SOC recorder for Midlothian.

Species

More than ten pairs of Little and five pairs of Great Crested Grebe attempt to breed in most years, mostly on Bavelaw Marsh. Feral Greylag Geese breed and Mallard are quite numerous. Summering duck records in recent years include Wigeon, Shoveler and Pochard. A moult flock of over 100 Tufted Duck use the main reservoir in July/August. Ruddy Duck are increasingly regular in spring/summer.

Red Grouse occur on Black Hill, to the south-east; Grey Partridge are widely distributed in the surrounding farmland.

Moorhen and Coot both breed on Bavelaw and Water Rail sometimes nest. Breeding waders of the area include Golden Plover on Black Hill and Common Sandpiper in the eastern part of the reservoir.

Over 2,000 pairs of Black-headed Gull usually breed at Bavelaw – the most important colony in the Lothians.

A few pairs of Spotted Flycatcher breed in the area; small numbers of Tree Pipit and Redpoll can be found in the birchwood at Red Moss; the Bavelaw Marsh area holds between 25 and 30 pairs of Sedge Warbler and around 20 pairs of Reed Bunting in spring.

Regular spring passage waders include Oystercatcher, Curlew, Redshank and Golden Plover (best late April). Whinchat and Wheatear are occasionally numerous at East Threipmuir, whilst Chiffchaff, Whitethroat, Blackcap and Garden Warbler are occasionally recorded. Small flocks of Siskin are seen in both spring and autumn.

Low water levels in the autumn often attract Ringed Plover and Dunlin or scarcer waders such as Ruff, Whimbrel, Spotted Redshank and Greenshank.

Flocks of several hundred Common Gull are a feature of both spring and autumn passage and Lesser Black-backed Gull may linger on into November.

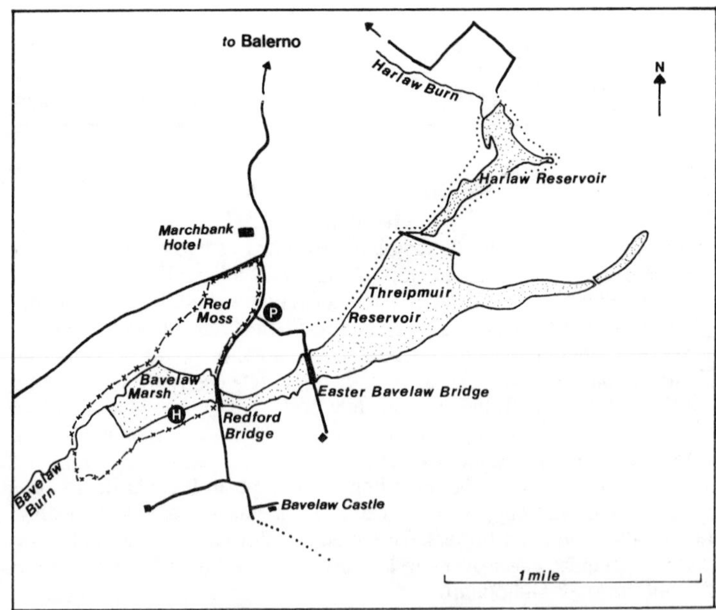

Redwing and Fieldfare are often abundant during the autumn, whilst mixed flocks of finches and buntings, sometimes including Brambling and occasional Snow Buntings, exploit the autumn stubble fields.

Small numbers of Whooper Swan visit in winter, whilst up to 600 Greylag Geese feed/roost at the main reservoir. Smew are occasionally recorded. Hen Harrier and Short-eared Owl are frequently seen hunting over Red Moss and Sparrowhawk, Kestrel, Merlin and Peregrine may occur.

Access

From the A70 Edinburgh–Lanark road, turn off south to Balerno, turning left immediately after crossing the Water of Leith. This road leads to a car park near Red Moss some 2 miles (3.2 km) further on (see map), past the Marchbank Hotel. From the car park, walk to Redford Bridge, which is one of the best general vantage points for birding. A hide overlooks Bavelaw Marsh, but the key must be obtained in advance from the Pentland Hills Ranger Service at Hillend Park, Biggar Road, Edinburgh EH10 7DU (tel: 031 445 3383). Access to the marsh itself is not permitted. It is also possible to walk to the north end of Easter Bavelaw Bridge from the car park; from here an extensive view of the main reservoir can be obtained. A path leads from here along the north shore and on to circuit Harlaw Reservoir.

Please note that access to the SWT reserve at Red Moss is by permit only – contact Brian Catley, 3 Greenfield Crescent, Balerno EH14 7HD.

In view of the relative paucity of coverage by birdwatchers at this site, records of bird observations would be very useful – there is a log book in the hide, but please also submit sightings to the Lothians recorder.

Timing

The area is of year-round importance; breeding waterfowl and a variety of passerines provide the interest between April and July, passage waders move through in April/May and August to October, whilst wintering waterfowl, thrushes and finches can be numerous from October through to March.

Reference

Threipmuir Reservoir, Allan W. Brown (1988). Unpublished.

L6 HOUND POINT

OS ref.: NT 158796
OS map: sheet 65

Habitat and Access

Hound Point extends into the Firth of Forth from its south shore just to the east of the Forth Bridge. It is an excellent, if rather unusual, seawatching vantage point and can be reached by walking east along the coast from South Queensferry (a distance of about 2 miles (3.2 km)).

Birds can approach from almost any direction (some seem to suddenly appear overhead!), but it is in the north and east quarters that effort should be concentrated, scanning the horizon frequently to pick up distant birds which can then be followed in.

Small numbers of seabirds may possibly continue up the Forth valley and cross over to the Clyde in the west, although to what extent this occurs is not entirely clear.

Species

A wide variety of seabirds can be seen at Hound Point, including Fulmar, Manx Shearwater, Gannet, Kittiwake, and Guillemot, as well as divers and the other auk species. The area is particularly good for skuas – Arctic Skua are seen regularly from late July through until November, both on passage and harassing terns for prey; in the right conditions (see Timing), very large movements of Pomarine and Long-tailed Skuas can occur in autumn. In addition, there is generally a regular passage of Pomarine Skuas in late autumn (October – November). Small numbers of Great Skua can also be seen, although these have been the rarest of the four skua species in recent years. Passage birds tend to gain height as they pass up the Forth and fly (often in flocks) west over the Forth

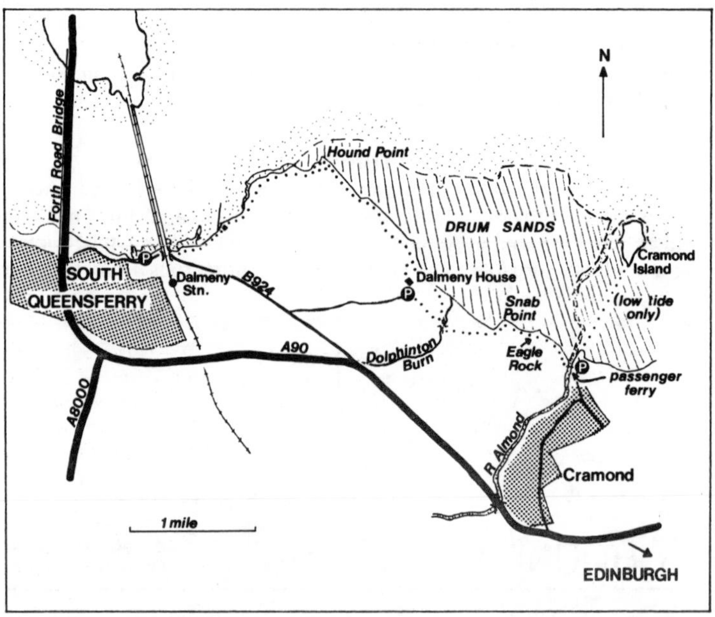

bridges. Large numbers of Sandwich Tern are present in August and very small numbers of Little Gull and Black Tern occur annually in autumn. In addition, occasional records of Leach's Petrel, Cory's Shearwater, Osprey, phalaropes, Sabine's, Mediterranean and Glaucous Gulls, and Caspian Tern have been a feature of recent years.

Small parties of Brent, Barnacle and Pink-footed Geese pass through in September and October.

Large numbers of Cormorant can be seen around Inch Garvie, to the west, in winter, whilst Shag tend to loaf on The Buchans, to the east. In some years, Little Auk are seen in early winter.

Timing

The best time to visit Hound Point is between August and October, although spring passage can be good and there may be considerable movements of birds in winter during gales. Light winds from the north-west through north and east to south-east produce the best sea-watching here, with few birds apparent during southerly or westerly winds. Onshore wind with clear weather and broken cloud, such as occurs after the passage of a front, are often productive, whilst a sudden clearing in sea mist that may have settled in for a few days also seems to stimulate activity.

Reference

Birdwatching Sites in the Lothians, ed. I.J. Andrews, (Lothian branch of SOC).

L7 DALMENY

OS ref.: NT 137784 to 190770
OS map: sheet 65

Habitat and Access

The shore path to Hound Point from South Queensferry (see L6 above) continues on around the coast, following the perimeter of the woods and farmland of the Roseberry Estate until the River Almond is reached, some 3 miles (4.8 km) beyond Hound Point. A passenger ferry across this river connects the walk with Cramond, where there is a large car park. The best vantage points for waders and wildfowl are at Eagle Rock, Snab Point and near Dolphinton Burn. Ideally, walk the entire length of the coast from Cramond to South Queensferry either by arranging to be picked up at the far end, or by using the bus services that connect the two access points with Edinburgh. Alternatively, the shore path can be joined by visiting Dalmeny House/gardens, open daily except Fridays and Saturdays from May to September, 2 pm to 5.30 pm.

Red-breasted Mergansers and male Wigeon

Species

Modest numbers of Shelduck and Eider breed in the area and their young can be seen on the water in late June/early July. Small numbers of Mallard are present in spring, but passage and wintering birds increase the population to over 200 individuals. Wigeon, Teal and small numbers of Pintail and Shoveler occur in autumn. Eider, Goldeneye and Red-breasted Merganser over-winter and Tufted Duck and Pochard are sometimes recorded in severe weather, when their inland haunts freeze over.

Drum Sands support very large numbers of passage and wintering waders, most of which roost on Cramond and other islands. Over 2,000 Oystercatcher and Dunlin, up to 700 Curlew and 400–500 Redshank can be found in autumn and winter; smaller numbers of Bar-tailed Godwit, Turnstone, Whimbrel, Greenshank and Black-tailed Godwit can occur on passage in autumn, whilst Little Stint and Curlew Sandpiper are occasional.

Woodland breeding species include Green and Great Spotted Woodpeckers, Jay and the commoner warblers and tits.

Timing

The passenger ferry across the Almond operates daily (except Fridays) between 9 am and 7 pm, April to September, and 10 am and 4 pm, October to March. There is a very modest charge. Note: check the ferry is running before committing yourself to a walk from South Queensferry to Cramond.

Many waders roost on Cramond Island, so the best time to watch birds here is some two to three hours before high water (depending on height of tide) when the waders will be gradually pushed off by the incoming tide. Any offshore duck will also tend to come closer.

References

Birdwatching Sites in the Lothians, ed. I.J. Andrews, (Lothian branch of SOC).
Lothian Bird Reports 1987–90. Ed. I.J. Andrews/O. McGarry, SOC.

L8 BARNS NESS

OS ref.: NT 723773
OS map: sheet 67

Habitat and Access

Barns Ness is one of the more accessible of the south-east coast migration watch points. It can be reached by turning off the A1 Dunbar–Berwick road some 3 miles (4.8 km) out of Dunbar and proceeding to the car park at the beach. There is a lighthouse near the end of the promontory and the area just to the north of it is the best sea-watching vantage point except in especially stormy conditions, when the higher ground near the wire dump (see map) is preferable. The campsite to the south of the road is backed by a small plantation and has buckthorn hedges and sycamore trees near its entrance, all of which can be good for migrant passerines. Please note that exploration of the campsite is possible only between October and March, when it is closed. Other good places for migrants are the wire dump and the lighthouse garden.

Calendar

Some of the more interesting species likely to be seen.

March–May: Early spring migrants such as White Wagtail, Black Redstart, Wheatear and Chiffchaff usually first appear at the beginning of April, with the passage of Meadow Pipit, hirundines, Robin, Wheatear, Blackbird, Willow Warbler, Goldcrest and various finches starting later and continuing through until late May. Small numbers of Tree Pipit pass through and a few Yellow Wagtail are regular. Less usual spring passage migrants include Wryneck, Bluethroat, Lesser Whitethroat, Pied Flycatcher and Red-backed Shrike.

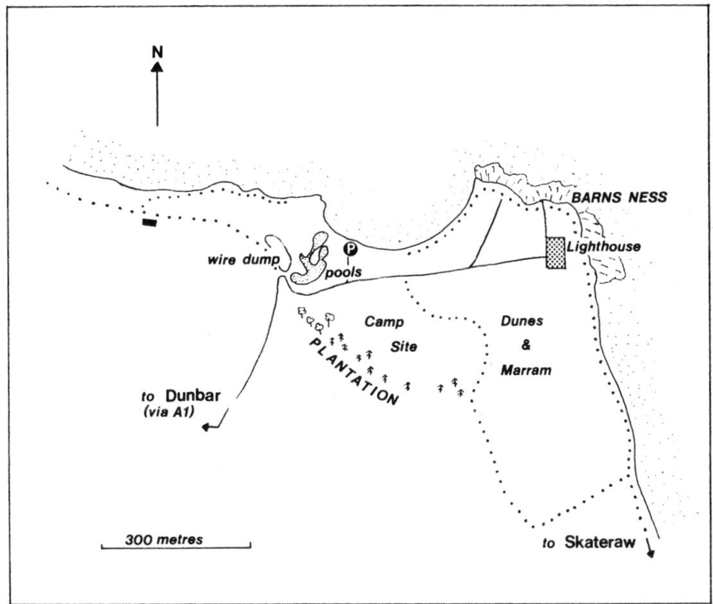

Offshore, Fulmar, Manx Shearwater, Gannet, Kittiwake, a few skuas, terns and auks are likely.

June–July: Breeding species at Barns Ness include Shelduck, Ringed Plover, Sedge Warbler and Linnet. Yellow Wagtail usually over-summer.

August–November: Wigeon, Teal and Goldeneye move past Barns Ness in good numbers, especially in westerly winds, with smaller numbers of diving duck such as scoters and Red-breasted Merganser.

Moderate numbers of waders migrate along the coast in August/early September, but few linger. A few Little Stint, Curlew Sandpiper, Ruff, Whimbrel, Spotted Redshank, Greenshank and Green Sandpiper are generally recorded at this time. A large flock of Golden Plover is regular on the rocks.

Strong north-easterly winds can produce large passages of Manx

Female Red-backed Shrike

Shearwater, Arctic Skua and Kittiwake, with smaller numbers of Great Skua and occasional sightings of Sooty Shearwater and (in October/November) Pomarine Skua. Black Tern are occasionally seen in August and Little Gull are possible later in the autumn.

Regular passerine migrants include Dunnock, Robin, Redstart, Whinchat, Blackbird, Whitethroat, Garden Warbler, Blackcap, Chiffchaff, Pied and Spotted Flycatchers and Goldcrest. Up to 40 Tree Sparrow pass through in August. Rarer species occasionally recorded in autumn include Richard's Pipit, Barred, Pallas's, Radde's, Icterine and Yellow-browed Warblers, Firecrest, Red-breasted Flycatcher, Great Grey Shrike, Scarlet Rosefinch and Little Bunting.

Redwing and Fieldfare are generally first seen in late September and continue to arrive throughout October. Small numbers of Brambling are likely at this time, too.

December–February: Purple Sandpiper and Turnstone frequent the rocky shoreline in winter.

Timing

Barns Ness is worth a visit at any time of year, although large 'falls' of migrants or good passages of seabirds obviously require very special conditions and do not occur often. April–June and August–November are the peak months for passage birds.

The best 'fall' conditions are probably light south-easterly winds with attendant drizzle, specially if clear conditions prevail on the continent. For sea-watching, strong north-easterly winds are best and in winter, northerly and easterly gales may bring divers close inshore, or produce views of Glaucous Gull or perhaps Little Auk. See also Skatelaw, additional site f.

References

Birdwatching Sites in the Lothians, ed. I.J. Andrews, (Lothian branch of SOC).

Lothian Bird Reports 1987–90, ed. I.J. Andrews/O. McGarry, SOC.

ADDITIONAL SITES

	Site and Grid Reference	Habitat	Main Bird Interest	Peak Season
a.	Bass Rock NT 602873 Sheet 67	Spectacular volcanic rock island	About 20,000 prs of Gannet, plus other breeding seabirds	May–June.
Contact Fred Marr (tel: North Berwick 2838) for details of boat trips.				
b.	Botanic Gardens, Edinburgh NT 244753 Sheet 66	Area of exotic trees & shrubs close to city centre	Hawfinch is a speciality	Apr.–May.
c	Gladhouse Res. NT 29/53 Sheet 66	Large reservoir in the Moorfoot Hills. Can be viewed from road along north shore Pink-footed Geese roost in autumn	Wintering wildfowl, inc. Wigeon, Teal, Mallard, Tufted Duck, Goldeneye & Goosander	Oct,–Mar.
d.	Hermitage of Braid NT 244703 Sheet 66	Ancient semi-natural woodland in the valley of the Braid Burn	Woodland & scrub species inc. Wood Warbler, Lesser Whitethroat, Green & Gt Spotted Woodpeckers	Apr.–June.
e.	Linlithgow Loch NT 010770 Sheet 65	Small inland loch adjacent to M9	Wintering wildfowl Displaying GC Grebe	Oct.–Mar. Spring.
f.	Skateraw NT 730759 Sheet 67	Steamsides with scrub/trees	Passage migrants	Apr.–Jun Aug.–Oct.

STRATHCLYDE

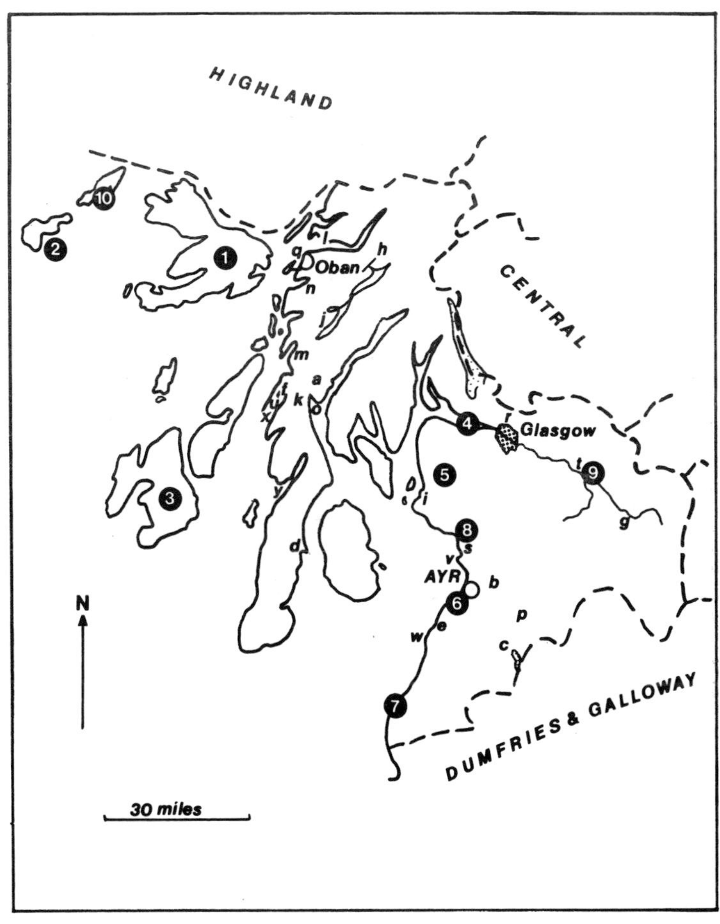

Main Sites
S1. Mull
S2. Tiree
S3. Islay
S4. Clyde Estuary
S5. Lochwinnoch
S6. Doonfoot
S7. Ballantrae Shingle Beach
S8. Bogside Flats
S9. Baron's Haugh
S10. Coll RSPB Reserve

Additional sites
a. Argyll Forest Park
b. Ayr Gorge
c. Dalmellington Moss
d. Carradale Point
e. Culzean Castle and Country Park
f. Fairy Is, L. Sween
g. Falls of Clyde
h. Glen Nant
i. Hunterston
j. Inverliever Forest
k. Knapdale
l. Ledaig Point
m. Loch Craignish
n. Loch Feochan
o. Loch Gilp
p. New Cumnock
q. Oban Harbour
r. Possil Marsh
s. Shewalton Sandpits
t. Strathclyde Country Park
u. Taynish
v. Troon & Barassie
w. Turnberry Point
x. Ulva Lagoons
y. West Loch Tarbert

Habitat

Mull is essentially a mountainous island; the highest of the peaks in the central body of the island, Ben More, is over 950 metres. A long, low-lying moorland peninsula extends out into the Atlantic to the south-west; the Ross of Mull. To the north, the island is characterised by fairly gentle, terraced moorlands, separated from the rest of Mull by only a narrow nexus of land between Salen Bay and Loch na Keal. Another isthmus connects the smaller, but more rugged land mass of Laggan. Three large glens divide the island: the steep-sided valleys of Glen More and Glen Forsa in the southern part, and the more gently profiled Glen Aros in the north. Loch Ba and Loch Frisa are the only substantial freshwater bodies.

The coastline is heavily indented, with four major west-facing sea-lochs: Loch Tuath, Loch na Keal, Loch Scridain and Loch Buie, plus several more sheltered lochs and inlets elsewhere. Off the west coast lies a plethora of islands, ranging from semi-submerged rocks and skerries to large inhabited islands such as Iona and Ulva.

Mull is approximately 25 miles (40 km) from north to south and varies from 3 to about 20 miles in width (4.8 to 32 km).

Access

Caledonian MacBrayne operate car and passenger ferries throughout the year from Oban to Craignure, and from Lochaline to Fishnish. There is also a summer-only car and passenger service between Tobermory and Kilchoan, on the Ardnamurchan peninsula. If approaching from the south, it is more convenient, if more expensive to take the ferry from

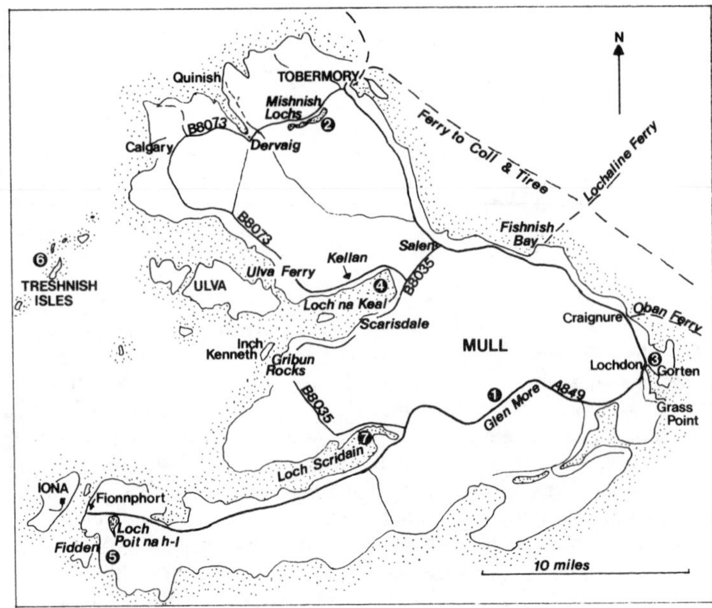

Oban. The 40-minute trip can be good for seabirds, especially during May/June and August/September. It is also possible to disembark at Tobermory on some crossings from Oban to Coll and Tiree.

For details of ferry services, contact Caledonian MacBrayne, The Ferry Terminal, Gourock PA19 1QP (tel: 0475 34531).

Public transport on Mull is limited to three regular bus services, operating between Tobermory and Calgary, Tobermory and Craignure, Craignure and Fionnphort. It is posible to hire cars, mopeds and bicycles on the island – details of these and of bus timetables are available from the Oban or Tobermory Tourist Information Centres.

There is a wide variety of bird habitats on the island, and space only for a few that typify Mull here:

1 Glen More

OS ref.: NM 64/32

Ten miles from Craignure on the A849 towards Fionnphort, Glen More is about 10 miles (16 km) long and rises to about 200 metres. The single-track road through it gives excellent opportunities for observing upland species: Hen Harrier and Short-eared Owl can often be seen hunting over the young plantations; scan the skyline for Buzzard, Golden Eagle, Kestrel and Raven. In the valley floor and on lower hillsides, Curlew, Cuckoo, Whinchat, Stonechat and Wheatear all breed. In winter, Snow Bunting can sometimes be seen by the roadside.

2 Mishnish Lochs

OS ref.: NM 47/52

Three miles (4.8 km) from Tobermory on the N8073 road towards Dervaig, the Mishnish Lochs are three contiguous lochs stocked with Brown Trout and popular with anglers. Little Grebe and Heron are present year-round and Red-throated Diver can often be seen April–October. Goosander can sometimes be seen also. Hen Harrier, Buzzard, Golden Eagle and Short-eared Owl all regularly hunt over the surrounding terrain. In winter look for Whooper Swan and Goldeneye. A number of laybys on the B8073 afford good views across the lochs.

3 Lochdon

OS ref.: NM 73/32

Lochdon is a small, but complex shallow sealoch 3 miles (4.8 km) south of Craignure on the A849 road to Fionnphort. Rich inter-tidal silt and muds attract a wealth of passage and wintering waterfowl and waders.

Resident birds include Heron, Mute Swan, Eider, Red-breasted Merganser, Hen Harrier, Buzzard and Redshank. Common and Arctic Terns feed in the outer loch during summer.

In winter, Red-throated Diver, Little Grebe and Cormorant can usually be seen. Wintering duck numbers build up to a maximum of about 300 Wigeon, 180 Teal and 50 Mallard. A few Goldeneye are generally present. Shelduck arrive back from their moulting grounds in November, and the flock usually increases to around 60 birds by March before dispersing to their breeding areas; only a few remain at Lochdon to breed.

Passage waders seen annually include small numbers of Grey Plover, Knot, Sanderling, Bar- and Black-tailed Godwits and Whimbrel. Pectoral Sandpiper, Ruff, Spotted Redshank and Green Sandpiper have all been recorded in recent years. Greenshank are regular in late summer/autumn and a few usually winter.

The area is best worked on rising or falling tides, ideally about an hour either side of high water. Good views can be obtained from the end of the tarmac road to Gorten, on the north side of the loch; from the main A849 where it runs alongside the inner loch; and from Grass Point, at the end of the road to the south of Lochdon.

4 Loch na Keal

OS ref.: NM 50/38

Three miles (4.8 km) west of Salen on the B8035, Loch na Keal is a large deep sealoch with varied coastline and several islets and skerries.

Shag, Eider, Red-breasted Merganser, Oystercatcher, Curlew and Redshank can be seen all year. During the summer, Common and Arctic Tern frequent Ulva Ferry and Gannet fish in the inner loch.

In winter, Loch na Keal is an excellent place for divers, with up to 20 Great Northerns, a few Red-throated and the odd Black-throated regularly present. Common and, very occasionally, Velvet Scoter may be seen, whilst Razorbill and Black Guillemot are invariably present. Small numbers of Slavonian Grebe winter; peak numbers are usually recorded in April when up to 20 can be present.

The loch can be scanned from both the N8073 Ulva Ferry road and the B8035 around the south shore. Good viewpoints are Kellan, on the north-east shore, Scarisdale on the south, and under Gribun Rocks, to the south-west. The last of these overlooks the island of Inch Kenneth and its satellite islets and skerries; this is an area much frequented by Barnacle geese in winter.

5 Fionnphort and Iona

OS ref.: NM 30/23

Fionnphort is at the end of the A849, some 40 miles (64 km) from Craignure. From here there are frequent ferry crossings to Iona, a mile (1.6 km) across the water. Around Fionnphort there are two main areas of interest:

(a) 1 mile (1.6 km) to the south is Fidden, a diverse mixture of inter-tidal habitats, coastal farmland, and lowland moor. The area is good for migrant waders and passerines, wintering Greenland White-fronted Geese and occasional raptors.

(b) 1 mile (1.6 km) east of Fionnphort is Loch Poit na h-I, which can be viewed from the main road along the north shore. Little Grebe are present year-round. In winter White-fronted Geese, Tufted Duck, Pochard and Goldeneye can be seen.

Iona comprises low-lying rocky moorland, fertile hay meadows, sandy bays and exposed sea cliffs. Fulmar, Shag and Kittiwake breed on the south-western cliffs; Rock Dove and Jackdaw nest on many cliffs elsewhere. Linnet, Twite and Yellowhammer are common all year. Common and Arctic Terns fish in the sound during summer. Iona is the most likely place on Mull that Corncrake will be heard – the fields around the Abbey and village being the best areas.

6 Treshnish Isles

OS ref.: NM 27/41

An uninhabited, basaltic archipelago lying between Mull and Tiree. During the summer, day-trips can be arranged from Quinish and Ulva Ferry. Views of the nesting seabirds are best obtained by circumnavigating the islands rather than landing on any particular one. The main island, Lunga, holds important breeding populations of Guillemot, Razorbill and Puffin, in addition to more widespread coastal species such as Fulmar, Shag, Kittiwake and other gulls.

Between May and September, Manx Shearwater, Storm Petrel, Gannet and Arctic Skua can be seen on the crossing to the islands; passage Great and Sooty Shearwaters, Pomarine and Great Skuas are also occasionally sighted.

7 Loch Scridain

OS ref.: NM 50/27

This loch is 20 miles (32 km) from Craignure, on the A849 road to Fionnphort. The loch is best viewed from either the B8035 along the north shore, or from various stopping places on the A849 along the south shore. Loch Scridain is similar in dimensions and character to Loch Na Keal (see above). The main interest is in winter, when Red-throated, Black-throated and Great Northern Divers can all be seen, the latter being the most numerous. Individuals of all three species are occasionally seen in summer.

Timing

There is year-round bird interest on Mull. April and May are the optimum months for combining breeding and migrant bird activity, but late May–July is better for seabirds, and August–early October for wader passage. Wintering species, such as Great Northern Diver and various types of wildfowl, start to build up in October and most linger until at least the following April. Midges can be a nuisance from late May until early August. An important consideration to be taken into account when planning an autumn or winter visit is that access to some upland areas may be restricted by stalking activities. Red Deer stalking is in progress during September and October – sometimes longer.

Calendar

Some of the more interesting species likely to be seen.

All year: Red-throated Diver, Fulmar, Eider, Red-breasted Merganser, Hen Harrier, Sparrowhawk, Buzzard, Golden Eagle, Kestrel, Merlin, Peregrine, Red Grouse, Ptarmigan, Ringed Plover, Snipe, Woodcock, Redshank, Greenshank, Common Gull, Guillemot, Razorbill, Black Guillemot, Rock Dove, Tawny Owl, Short-eared Owl, Great Spotted Woodpecker, Rock Pipit, Grey Wagtail, Dipper, Stonechat, Raven, Siskin, Twite, Redpoll, Crossbill, Yellowhammer.

April–July: Great Northern Diver and Goldeneye often remain in coastal waters until mid-May (the former in superb breeding plumage by this time). Breeding visitors include Manx Shearwater, Golden Plover, Common Sandpiper, Kittiwake, Common and Arctic Terns, Cuckoo, Sand Martin, Tree Pipit, Redstart, Whinchat, Wheatear, Ring Ousel, Sedge Warbler, Whitethroat and Wood Warbler. Gannet are common offshore from mid-May.

Whimbrel, spring

Spring passage birds include Pink-footed Goose, Golden Plover, Sanderling, occasional Spotted Redshank and Black-tailed Godwit, Whimbrel, Kittiwake and (in April) White Wagtail.

August–October: Passage birds include Merlin, Golden and Grey Plovers, Knot, Sanderling, Dunlin, Bar-tailed and occasional Black-tailed Godwits, Whimbrel, Redshank and Greenshank. Offshore, Manx and Sooty Shearwaters, Storm and occasional Leach's Petrel, Pomarine, Arctic and Great Skuas and Kittiwake occur.

November–March: Great Northern Diver are the commonest offshore diver, but small numbers of Black and Red-throated Diver also occur, other wintering species of interest include Slavonian Grebe, Whooper Swan, Greenland White-fronted Goose, Greylag Goose, Barnacle Goose, Wigeon, Teal, Pochard, Tufted Duck, Goldeneye, Water Rail, Purple Sandpiper, Turnstone, Iceland and Glaucous Gulls, Fieldfare, Redwing and Snow Bunting.

Shelduck numbers build up from late November.

References

Argyll Bird Reports 1980–91, ed. C. Galbraith/S.J. Petty (Argyll Bird Club).
Birds of Mull, Mike Madders and Philip Snow, Saker Press (1987).

S2 TIREE

OS map: sheet 46

Habitat

Tiree is mostly a low-lying, fertile island, some 15 miles (24 km) to the west of Mull. Covering approximately 8,400 hectares and measuring about 10 miles (16 km) from east to west and a maximum of 6 miles (9.7 km) north to south, the island has an irregular outline, much indented by a series of wide bays. These sandy beaches are interspersed with areas of rocky shoreline which generally form low headlands, although there are higher cliffs at Ben Hynish and more especially at Ceann a' Mhara in the south-west. The shoreline is backed by dune systems in several localities, particularly those on the west-facing coast.

Inland, Tiree is characterised by a mixture of machair and wet lowland moor. The machair is extensive and is the basis for Tiree's traditional yet highly productive agricultural regime, which is chiefly geared to cattle and sheep. More than 640 hectares of land are used for grass and cereal production in the summer, the livestock being put out to the communal grazings on the moorland and permanent pasture. Despite some shift towards silage production, the herb-rich grasslands are vitally important for many breeding birds, not the least of which is the Corncrake.

There are several large inland water bodies, such as Loch a' Phuill, Loch Bhasapoll and Loch Riaghain, which are of great significance for both breeding and wintering wildfowl. In addition, several small, shallow lochans and boggy hollows punctuate the moorland terrain.

Access

Tiree is reached by Caledonian MacBrayne ferry from Oban. The service operates four days a week in summer, plus Sundays between June 28th and August 30th. In winter there are three sailings per week. Visitors should check times with Caledonian MacBrayne, The Ferry Terminal, Gourock, PA19 1QP (tel. 0475 34531). Booking is essential for vehicles. The ferry calls at Coll en route and now has a roll-on/roll-off facility. It is also possible to board the ferry at Tobermory (Mull), although there is currently dispute about whether cars will be loaded in future. The crossing can be very good for seawatching, especially in May/June and August-early October.

Apart from a post-bus, there is no public transport on the island. Tiree is just too large for exploration solely on foot to be practical, although a bicycle would be a reasonable option. Both cars and bicycles may be hired locally.

Although the whole island is ornithologically interesting, a number of locations are exceptional:

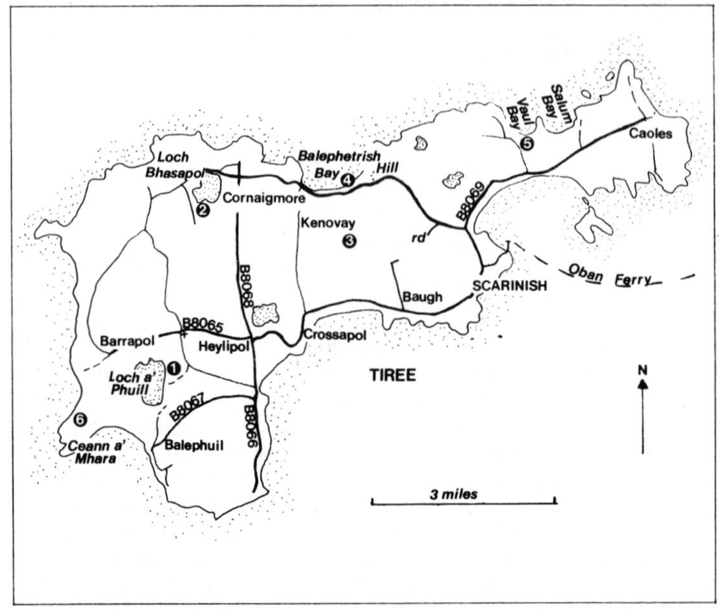

1 Loch a' Phuill

PS ref.: NL 95/41

This is the most productive of the inland water bodies for wintering wildfowl. The best viewpoint for this loch is reached from the church west of Heylipol, on the B8065, 7 miles (11.3 km) west of Scarinish. From the crossroads at the church, take the road heading south, towards Balemartine. After ½ mile (0.8 km) a rough track on the right leads down to the lochshore, affording a panoramic view of all but a tiny part of the loch. On clear days this vantage point is best visited in the morning, when the light will be behind you. Alternatively, walk ½ mile (0.8 km) along the track from Balephuil at the end of the B8067 road, 2 miles (3.2 km) from Balemartine. This gives good views of the southern half of Loch a' Phuill. A 'scope is more or less essential.

The loch holds large numbers of Mute and Whooper Swans in the autumn and winter; a flock of 50 or so Greenland White-fronted Geese frequent the area from October to April, whilst Greylag Geese are present year-round. Wintering ducks include Wigeon, Teal, Mallard, a few Pintail, occasional Shoveler, small numbers of Pochard, Tufted Duck, Goldeneye and Red-breasted Merganser.

2 Loch Bhasapol

OS ref.: NL 97/46

An easily accessible loch with a good variety of wintering wildfowl, including large numbers of Pochard and Tufted Duck.

Loch Bhasapol is best 'scoped from the road along the north shore, just west of Cornaigmore and 6 miles (9.7 km) from Scarinish. Closer views of waterfowl in the southern half of the loch (where most of the diving duck tend to occur) can be obtained from the Kilmoluag road, to the south-west. Again, a telescope is needed.

3 The Reef

OS ref.: NM 00/45

This area comprises the low-lying central part of the island and is an especially important area for wintering Greenland White-fronted Geese. This is a difficult area to overlook, owing to the flatness of the terrain. The only feasible vantage points are from the summit of Balephetrish Hill, reached by walking up a short track off the B8068, 2½ miles (4 km) from Scarinish, or from Kenovay on the unclassified road between Balephetrish and Crossapol. Both afford only distant views, and a telescope is essential. The B8065 road from Scarinish to Crossapol provides extensive views across the southern-most part of the Reef, but the short grasslands here are perhaps the least ornithologically interesting features of the area. It is possible to see the less cultivated eastern part of the Reef either by taking the mile-long (1.6 km) tarmac road from Baugh, 2 miles (3.2 km) west of Scarinish on the B8065, or walking the ½-mile (0.8 km) track to the rubbish dump, 1½ miles (2.4 km) out of Scarinish on the B8068. Groups of 20 or more Raven can sometimes be present at this tip.

Please note that walking onto the Reef is not advised – there is no access to the crofting land and walking elsewhere will only result in the disturbance of nesting or wintering wildfowl.

4 Balephetrish Bay

OS ref.: NM 00/47

View from the roadside at the western end of the bay. This is an excellent area for passage and wintering waders, such as Ringed Plover, Sanderling, Dunlin, Purple Sandpiper and Turnstone. Great Northern Diver, Eider and Long-tailed Duck frequent the bay during winter.

5 Salum and Vaul Bays

OS ref.: NM 05/48

Take the B8069 east towards Caoles, turning off left near the 'phone box after the Lodge Hotel. follow this road to the end, ¾ mile (1.2 km) later. Like Balephetrish Bay, the shoreline here is very good for feeding waders.

6 Ceann a' Mhara

OS ref.: NL 93/40

Approach from a track that leaves the B8065 at the Barrapol corner. It is possible to walk around this cliff peninsula, although the terrain is rugged and there is no obvious path. Several small headlands provide views of breeding seabirds, which include Fulmar, Shag, Kittiwake, Guillemot and Razorbill.

Timing

Tiree has year-round interest for the birdwatcher; breeding wildfowl, waders, seabirds and Corncrake are attractions during the spring and summer, large numbers of passage shorebirds can be seen in spring and autumn, whilst a variety of wildfowl, offshore sea-fowl and strong populations of waders make the winter an excellent time to visit.

Calendar

Some of the more interesting species likely to be seen.

All year: Fulmar, Mute Swan, Greylag Goose, Shelduck (except August–November), Wigeon, Teal, Pintail, Shoveler, Tufted Duck, Eider, Red-breasted Merganser, Buzzard, Kestrel, Peregrine, Moorhen, Ringed Plover, Lapwing, Dunlin, Snipe, Curlew, Redshank, Turnstone, Rock Dove, Skylark, Rock Pipit, Stonechat, Raven, Twite, Yellowhammer, Reed Bunting and a small and declining population of Corn Bunting.

April–June: Wintering geese depart in late April/early May. Gannet fish in coastal waters from May onwards. Corncrake can be heard at night (and quite frequently during the day also) from May until July, with up to 100 calling birds present.

Ringed Plover, Sanderling and Dunlin are prominent amongst spring passage waders.

The machair resounds to the song of Skylark, whilst Sedge Warbler and Reed Bunting take up territories in the denser vegetation.

July: At Ceann a' Mhara, breeding Fulmar, Shag, gulls and auks can be seen. Common, Arctic and Little Tern breed around the coast and fishing terns can often be seen harried by Arctic Skuas, in areas such as Hynish Bay and Gunna Sound. Great Skua are less common: the deck of the ferry is probably the best place from which to see them.

August–October: Manx and occasional Sooty Shearwaters, Storm and (rarely) Leach's Petrels can be seen offshore and from the ferry.

Large numbers of Whooper Swan arrive in late September/early October; a small influx of Mute Swan, presumably from the Outer Hebrides, also occurs. Greenland White-fronted and Barnacle Geese generally start to arrive in mid-October. Passage Brent Geese are occasionally recorded at this time.

Return passage waders can be seen from August onwards, and may include small numbers of Ruff, Black-tailed Godwit and Whimbrel.

In some years very large flocks of Redwing appear in October, with smaller numbers of Fieldfare.

November–March: Red-throated, Great Northern and occasional Black-throated Divers can be seen offshore, especially in Gott Bay, Balephetrish Bay and Gunna Sound. A few Little Grebe, around 100 Whooper Swan, *c.* 600–700 White-fronted and similar numbers of Barnacle Geese over-winter. Strong populations of inland wintering duck include Wigeon,

Teal, Mallard, Pochard, Tufted Duck and Goldeneye, with lesser numbers of Red-breasted Merganser, a few Pintail and occasional Gadwall and Shoveler.

Merlin and Peregrine are regularly seen in winter.

A total of between *c.* 3,500 and *c.* 5,600 shorebirds have been counted around the coast of Tiree in mid-winter. These are dominated by nationally important populations of Ringed Plover, Sanderling and Turnstone, although large numbers of Oystercatcher, Lapwing, Curlew, Redshank, Dunlin and Purple Sandpiper also occur. Small numbers of Grey Plover and Bar-tailed Godwit generally over-winter. Inland, very large flocks of Lapwing and passage Golden Plover feed in the fields, where Chaffinch and Twite are also numerous. A massive Starling roost at Scarinish sometimes attracts Merlin and Peregrine at dusk.

References

Argyll Bird Reports 1980–91, ed. C. Galbraith/S.J. Petty (Argyll Bird Club).
The Birds of Coll and Tiree, ed. D. Stroud (1989).

S3 ISLAY

OS map: sheet 60

Habitat

Islay is a large and varied island which lies 12 miles (19 km) or so off the Argyll mainland. The most southerly of the Inner Hebrides, it covers about 60,000 hectares and measures approximately 25 miles (40 km) from north to south and 20 miles (32 km) east to west. Although lacking the more spectacular mountains of islands such as Mull or Skye, there are quite large areas of upland ground on Islay, with several summits in excess of 300 metres. Most of these lie in the south-east of the island, where a ridge of open hills runs from Port Ellen in the south, towards Port Askaig in the east. The north-eastern part of Islay is a rugged and remote terrain of summits, small valleys and lochans, bordered by raised beaches and cliffs, whilst in the west, a wide ridge of low moor, The Rhinns, extends south-westward into the Atlantic.

Two large sealochs almost separate The Rhinns from the main body of the island Loch Gruinart to the north and the larger Loch Indaal in the west. Of the many magnificent sea-cliffs, those of The Oa and to the west of Sanaigmore are perhaps the most outstanding. The coastline elsewhere is extremely varied, encompassing rocky and shingle shores, sandy beaches and inter-tidal mud. Immediately inland from the shore at Ardnave, Killinallan, Laggan Bay and one or two other locations, extensive sand dune-systems occur.

Loch Gorm is the largest inland water body, although there are many smaller lochans and areas of marshland.

Elsewhere the landscape is characterised by areas of lowland pasture, croftland, peat bog, scrub, coniferous plantation and small deciduous woodlands.

To the birdwatcher, Islay is synonymous with geese; current censuses put the numbers of wintering Barnacle Geese at between *c.* 21,000 and *c.* 25,000 birds, with between *c.* 9,000 and *c.* 10,000 Greenland White-fronted Geese, the higher totals being recorded is October/November and March/April. These is much more to Islay than geese, however, and the island has good populations of breeding, wintering and migratory species. Over 100 species are present on the island in every month of the year, whilst around 105 to 110 species breed.

Access

Caledonian MacBrayne operate a car and passenger ferry service from Kennacraig, 7 miles (11.3 km) west of Tarbert, to Port Ellen and Port Askaig on Islay. There are two sailings a day, Monday to Saturday, with a single sailing on Sundays. Additional sailings operate during the summer. The trip takes approximately two hours and provides excellent opportunities for seawatching en route. West Loch Tarbert (see Additional Sites) is very productive for sea-fowl (especially divers), gulls and auks in winter, whilst the waters immediately north of the island of Gigha can hold modest concentrations of Great Northern Divers from October through to April.

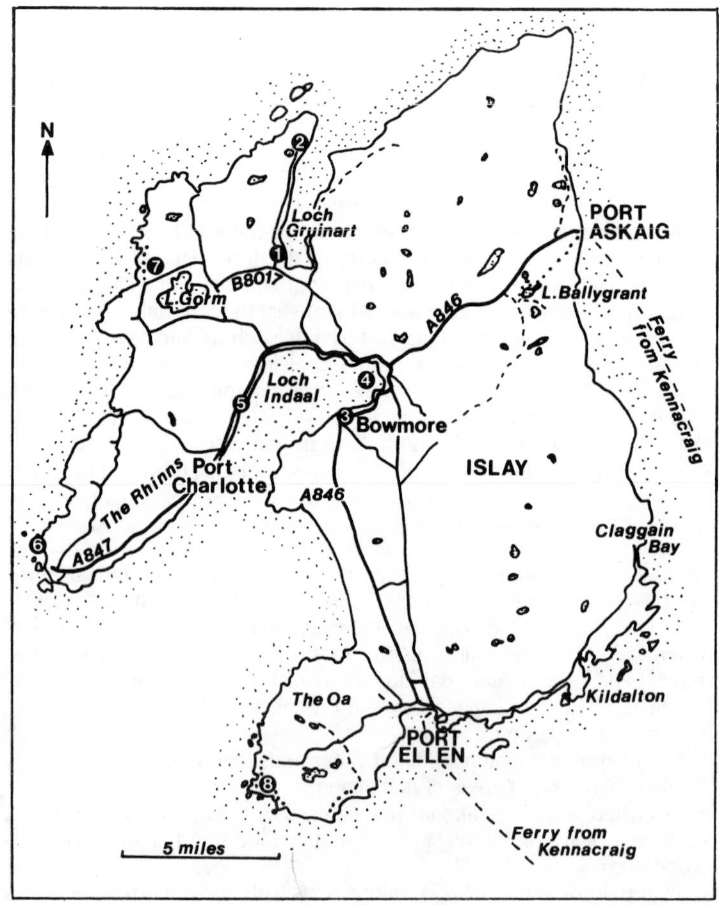

For details of ferry services, contact Caledonian MacBrayne, The Ferry Terminal, Gourock PA19 1QP (tel: 0475 34531).

It is possible to fly to Islay from Glasgow – Loganair operates two flights a day from Monday to Friday, with one on Saturdays. Contact Loganair at Glasgow Airport (tel: 041 889 3181).

Islay is well endowed with roads, making it possible to cover most of the island's bird habitats from a vehicle. This tends to minimise disturbance to the birds and often enables a closer approach (e.g. to feeding geese) than would otherwise be possible. Please be considerate to other road users, however, and do not obstruct access to gateways, etc. when parking. Flocks of feeding Barnacle and White-fronted Geese will be readily apparent in roadside fields; areas that can be particularly recommended are Gruinart Flats (see below), the Loch Gorm area, the fields bordering the main A846 Port Askaig–Bridgend road and beside the lanes leading south and south-east from Bridgend, as well as the saltmarsh at the head of Loch Indaal.

1 Loch Gruinart RSPB reserve

OS ref.: NR 28/67

This 1,667-hectare reserve comprises inter-tidal habitats, saltmarsh, farmland and moorland. It is situated on the south and west sides of Loch Gruinart and can be viewed from the B8017 and the unclassified road that branches off north to Ardnave. There is a visitor centre at Aoradh Farm open 10.00–17.00 hours seven days a week. Features include a large panoramic window, live TV pictures from the reserve, displays, video, information, guided walks and farm visits. Parking is available at Aoradh Farm. There is also a small hide that overlooks some of the best goose feeding and roosting grounds. This is reached by walking a short distance along the Ardnave road, until the path to the hide is indicated off to the right – a second car park is located opposite this path.

Gruinart is particularly important for its wintering Barnacle and Greenland White-fronted Geese. A wide variety of wildfowl and waders breed on the reserve; Black and Red Grouse can occasionally be seen and the area is an excellent place to watch hunting raptors such as Hen Harrier, Golden Eagle, Merlin and Peregrine. Wintering waders are best viewed from the road up the east side of the loch.

Please keep to the public roads during the period when the geese are present. Note also that the reserve is a working farm and that account may need to be taken of farm machinery and animals!

RSPB Warden: Mike Peacock, Grainel, Gruinart, Islay.

2 Ardnave Loch

OS re.: NR 28/72

A shallow exposed loch which can be viewed from the end of the minor road running north from the Gruinart reserve, on the west side of Loch Gruinart. From October through to May it holds a good variety of wildfowl, generally including Mute Swan, Wigeon, Teal, Mallard, Pochard and Tufted Duck.

The shoreline of Loch Gruinart, just to the east, is a good place to look for Otter.

3 Bowmore

OS ref.: NR 31/60

The stone pier at the end of the main street in Bowmore is a good general vantage point for inner Loch Indaal, although the elevated layby opposite the Hydroboard Generating Station ½ mile (0.8 km) north of Bowmore is probably even better (with room for several cars to park here). From October to April a good selection of sea-fowl are usually visible, including Red-throated Diver, small numbers of Great Northern Diver and occasional Black-throated Diver, Slavonian Grebe, Scaup (over 1,000 sometimes present in mid-winter), Eider, occasional Long-tailed Duck, Common Scoter, Goldeneye and Red-breasted Merganser. Dabbling duck and waders occupy the inshore shallows.

The rubbish tip to the south-west of Bowmore is worth checking out for glaucous and Iceland Gulls, whilst the shoreline between Raineach Mhor and Gartbreck is a good area for waders on ebbing and flowing tides.

4 Head of Loch Indaal

OS ref.: NR 32/61

The extensive inter-tidal area here is very important for estuarine birds and is one of the principal roost sites for the island's Barnacle Geese. Between November and April Shelduck, Wigeon, Teal, Mallard, Oystercatcher, Ringed Plover, Lapwing, Dunlin, Bar-tailed Godwit, Curlew and Redshank can be seen. Pintail are usually present in the river channel where it opens out into the sand flats. Small numbers of Shoveler are usually present, either in the river channel or the freshwater pools at Carnain, on the north side of the loch. A visit one hour either side of high tide is best for waders. The best vantage points are from the roadside at NR 335620 on the south shore, or NR 324627 on the north. Both of these places are suitable for watching the astonishing spectacle of thousands of Barnacle Geese coming in to roost at dusk.

5 Bruichladdich Pier

OS ref.: NR 265609

This is another good vantage point for wintering divers and sea-duck (especially Common Scoter which are present year-round: 50–100 in summer and 100–150 in winter) in Loch Indaal. Occurrences of Black-throated Diver have been more frequent here than off Bowmore. The rocks in front of the distillery are one of the best places on Islay for Purple Sandpiper in winter.

6 Frenchman's Rocks

OS ref.: NR 15/53

The peninsula of Rubha na Faing, opposite these offshore rocks, is the most westerly point on the island and has become a popular sea-watching location. There can be good passages of seabirds in April/May and August–October, including Manx Shearwater, Fulmar, small numbers of Sooty Shearwater, Gannet, Storm and occasional Leach's Petrels, a few Arctic and Great Skuas, large numbers of Kittiwake and auks, as well as divers and sea-duck.

Approach the coast from the minor road to Claddich, ½ mile (0.8 km) north of Portnahaven. The best time to watch is during the first hour or so after dawn – direct sunlight can be problematical in the evening.

7 Saligo Bay

OS ref.: NR 210663

A popular coastal walk, with fine views of the Atlantic Ocean to the west and the dramatic cliffs of Cnoc Uamh nam Fear to the north. There is room for the careful parking of a few cars at Saligo Bridge.

The area can be very productive for passage seabirds, especially from late August to early October. In addition, regular scanning inland with binoculars is likely to produce views of Buzzard, Golden Eagle, Peregrine, Chough and Raven Stonechat and Twite are resident, whilst Whinchat and Wheatear are common in spring/summer.

8 The Oa

OS ref.: NR 26/41

The sea cliffs at Mull of Oa rise sharply to over 130 metres above sea level. These are the most impressive cliffs on Islay and a walk from the Mull eastwards towards the even higher (though less vertical) cliffs at Beinn Mhor is a superb experience. If it is possible, arrange to be picked up at Risabus (NR 315439) and walk the entire cliff top from Mull of Oa to Inerval. Allow plenty of time – five or six hours ideally – for investigation of the cliffs and of the moors inland. The numerous wild goats are a special feature of these cliffs.

Fulmar, Shag, Herring Gull, Guillemot, Razorbill, Black Guillemot and a few Kittiwake breed on the cliffs. Noteworthy species likely to be encountered include Golden Eagle, Peregrine, Chough and Raven. In winter the cliff tops are a regular haunt of Snow Bunting.

There are many other good birding locations on Islay awaiting exploration and this brief list does little justice to such a rich and varied island. Other places that can be strongly recommended include:

(a) Loch Ballygrant (NR 40/66) for common woodland species and wildfowl.

(b) Port Ellen for white-winged gulls and sheltering sea-fowl.

(c) Claggain Bay (NR 46/53) for Great Northern Divers – present from October through until early May.

(d) Kildalton (NR 46/50 – the delightful woodlands, bog and coastline around here are not especially bird-rich, but make a very pleasant contrast to the more open habitats elsewhere on Islay.

Timing

One of great attractions of Islay as a birdwatching location is that there is plenty of interest throughout the year, since the island has strong populations of both breeding and wintering birds. For sheer diversity of species, however, September/October and March/April stand out – at these times both breeding and wintering visitors are present and their numbers are further supplemented by passage birds.

Species and Calendar

Some of the more interesting species likely to be seen.

All year: Eider, Red-breasted Merganser, Hen Harrier, Buzzard, Golden Eagle, Merlin, Peregrine, Black Grouse (now very rare), Water Rail (uncommon/under-recorded), Barn Owl, Stonechat, Chough, Raven and Twite.

April–June: Gannet can be seen fishing close inshore during the spring. The geese mostly depart in late April, with a few lingering into May; small numbers of passage Brent Geese occur in April/May, Shelduck, Teal, Eider and Red-breasted Merganser all breed.

Corncrake can be heard at night at a number of farms, especially on The Rhinns. Spring passage waders include Ringed Plover, Sanderling, Purple Sandpiper, Dunlin and Whimbrel. Common Sandpiper arrive in early April.

Breeding seabirds include Fulmar, Shag, Kittiwake, Arctic and a few Common and Little Terns, Guillemot, Razorbill and Black Guillemot.

Amongst the passerine visitors that breed are Whinchat, Sedge Warbler, Whitethroat, and small numbers of Tree Pipit, Wood Warbler and Spotted Flycatcher, Redpoll and Siskin breed and are possibly under-recorded.

June–July: A moult flock of male Red-breasted Merganser gathers in Loch Indaal and also at Claggain Bay during late June. Common Scoter

Barnacle Geese and Oystercatcher

summer in Loch Indaal. Fledged broods of Short-eared Owl are conspicuous over the moorland areas in some years.

August–October: Passage Manx Shearwater and a few Sooty Shearwater, Arctic Skua and occasional Great Skua can be seen from Frenchman's Rocks and from the ferry.

The first returning geese usually arrive in mid-September, with the main influx occurring in October. Small numbers of pasage Brent and Pink-footed Geese move through at this time. Whooper Swan numbers peak in late October/early November.

Regular autumn passage waders include Ringed Plover, Golden Plover, Dunlin, Redshank, a few Bar-tailed Godwit and small numbers of Grey Plover, Knot, Sanderling, Black-tailed Godwit and Greenshank.

Large thrush movements occur in some autumns, mostly involving Fieldfare, Redwing and smaller numbers of Blackbird and Song Thrush.

November–March: Great Northern, Red-throated and Black-throated Divers can be seen offshore; Slavonian Grebe, Scaup, Eider, Common Scoter, Goldeneye and Red-breasted Merganser tend to concentrate in Loch Indaal. Whooper Swan are present at a variety of inland water bodies, especially Loch Gorm, and occasionally around the coast too, although most have left the island by mid-winter.

Small numbers of Greylag Geese winter, especially near Bridgend, and one or two Pink-footed, Snow, Canada and Brent Geese are usually to be found in the larger flocks of wintering White-fronts and Barnacles.

Strong populations of Wigeon, Teal and Tufted Duck over-winter.

Wintering shorebirds, such as Oystercatcher, Ringed Plover and Curlew are common; around 200 Bar-tailed Godwit over-winter; Purple Sandpiper and Turnstone frequent areas of rocky shoreline.

Several Glaucous and a few Iceland Gulls are recorded in most winters, particularly at Port Ellen and in Loch Indaal. Brambling and Snow Bunting are not uncommon in some years.

Note

Bird records for Islay should be sent to Dr M.A. Ogilvie at the Islay Natural History Trust, Port Charlotte. The Trust funds the Islay Field Centre which shares a building with a Youth Hostel, combining low-cost self-catering accommodation with displays and information, including help for visiting groups with their birding itinerary. For details contact Dr Ogilvie (tel: 049685 288 or 218 evenings).

References

Argyll Bird Reports 1980–91, ed. C. Galbraith/S.J. Petty (Argyll Bird Club).
Birds in Islay, Gordon Booth (1981).
Birds of Islay, Richard Elliott (1989).
Birds of Islay, Malcolm Ogilvie (1992).
Islay Bird and Natural History Report 1986–1991, Malcolm Ogilvie.

Habitat

Although blighted by industrial and residential development, the Clyde Estuary is an exceptionally important place for birds. The extensive inter-tidal areas provide rich feeding grounds for passage/wintering waders and wildfowl, whilst the open water is frequented by diving duck, roosting wildfowl and small numbers of divers and grebes throughout the winter.

The estuary is considered here to extend seawards from Erskine to Inverkip, a distance of over 18 miles (29 km). The M8/A8 closely follows the south shore, connecting the western dockyard conurbations of Gourock and Greenock with the heartlands of Glasgow. On the north shore, the A92/A814 links the towns of Helensburgh and Dumbarton with Erskine Bridge and north-west Glasgow. In general, the northern shore is less developed than the south, especially around Ardmore, where the estuary is backed by fields and scattered woodland.

Species

Neither wildfowl nor wader totals compare with the numbers of birds recorded on the Firth of Forth or the Solway Firth, yet average peak counts in recent years have exceeded 4,000 wildfowl and 13,000 waders. Several of the diving duck species achieve nationally significant wintering populations.

Eider dominate the wildfowl totals for the estuary throughout the year; numbers peak in autumn, when over 4,000 birds can be present.

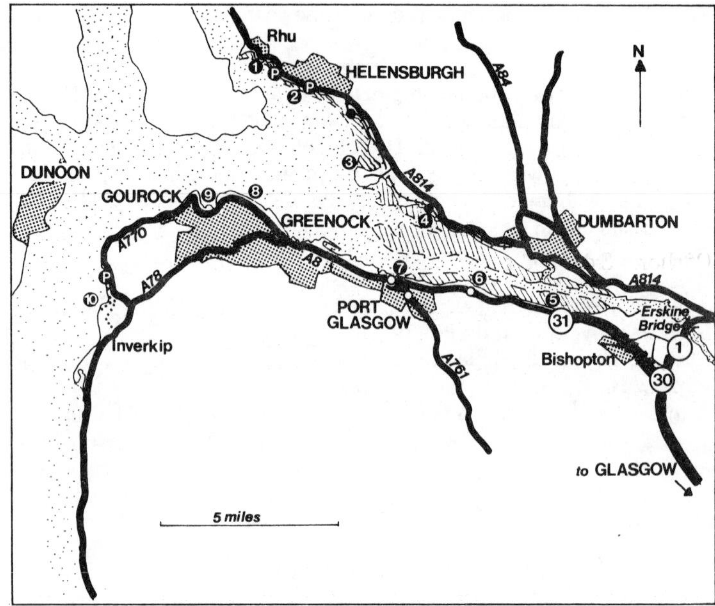

Maximum numbers of Goldeneye occur in late winter, when totals exceeding 800 birds have been recorded. Moderate numbers of wintering Pochard, Scaup and Red-breasted Merganser are also seen, along with a few Long-tailed Duck and Common Scoter.

Shelduck numbers build up during winter to a maximum of over 500 birds in February; up to 100 Mute Swan occur; dabbling duck include over 300 Wigeon and Mallard, with very small numbers of Pintail.

Other birds using the estuary in winter include small numbers of Red-throated Diver, up to 50 Great Crested and a few Slavonian Grebes. Around 200–300 Cormorant and a few Shag can be seen. Gannet occur regularly in the outer estuary in summer.

Wintering waders include over 3,000 Oystercatcher, 5,000+ Lapwing (peak in November), over 1,000 Redshank, moderately large numbers of Dunlin and Curlew (*c.* 700), with smaller numbers of Ringed Plover and Turnstone. Small numbers of Grey Plover, Knot, Black-tailed Godwit, Spotted Redshank and Greenshank are recorded each winter. Passage waders include Golden Plover, Bar-tailed Godwit, Whimbrel and Greenshank.

The estuary also holds very large numbers of wintering Black-headed Gull, substantial flocks of Common Gull and smaller numbers of Herring Gull. Small numbers of Common, Arctic and Sandwich Tern occur in July/August.

Small numbers of Black Guillemot may be seen throughout the year.

Access

The vastness of the area and the paucity of suitable access points tend to limit the birdwatching potential of the Clyde. The following vantage points can be recommended, however:

1 Rhu

OS ref.: NS 27/84

Two small bays with outflow burns to the east and west of Rhu Marina attract large numbers of feeding/roosting waders. Moderate tides are best – visit one hour either side of high water.

Oystercatcher, Dunlin and Redshank can be seen in the bays; Purple Sandpiper and Turnstone frequent the rocky islet near the Marina. Offshore, Eider and a few Goldeneye occur. Black-headed and Herring Gulls feed, bathe and loaf near the outflows.

The area is accessible from the A814 west of Helensburgh. The best vantage points are from the small car park to the east of the sailing club, or from the Marina visitors' car park. Please note that there is no vehicular access to the point west of Rhu.

2 Helensburgh

OS ref.: NS 29/82

The large sea-front car park gives a good overview of the outer estuary.

3 Ardmore Point

OS ref.: NS 319786

This rocky promontory, managed by the Scottish Wildlife Trust, makes an ideal vantage point for wildfowl and waders on the north side of the Firth. There are extensive foreshore areas both to the north and south of the point, attracting large numbers of waders and dabbling duck. In addition, the coastal bramble and gorse scrub here attract Whinchat, Linnet and Yellowhammer.

The reserve is open at all times and is accessible by taking a minor road down to the coast off the A814 Dumbarton–Helensburgh road, 1½ miles (2.4 km) west of Cardross. A footpath around the edge of the peninsula then cuts across the narrow nexus of farm and woodland that connects Ardmore Point to the coast, making a 2-mile (3.2-km) circuit of the reserve.

4 Cardross Station

OS ref.: NS 345773

Excellent foreshore habitat which attracts large numbers of feeding and roosting waders and dabbling duck. Turn south off the A814 to Cardross Station, parking in the station car park. Cross the footbridge and 'scope the burn outflow and inter-tidal areas. Rising and falling tides are best.

5 West Ferry

OS ref.: NS 40/73

This is the most useful of the south shore access points, giving extensive views of the inner estuary. Leave the M8 westbound from Glasgow at junction 31, the Bishopton exit. Follow around the roundabout to a parking space at West Ferry.

6 Woodhall

OS ref.: NS 35/74

Another good vantage point for the south shore. Exit from A8 at the roundabout five miles (8 km) east of Port Glasgow.

7 Newark Castle

OS ref.: NS 328746

A good viewpoint for the middle reaches of the Clyde – large numbers of Eider can usually be seen offshore. Turn off A8 at the roundabout in Port Glasgow and continue for ¼ mile (0.4 km) to a car park.

8 West Greenock

OS ref.: NS 26/77
The esplanade offers ample parking and birdwatching opportunities.

9 Gourock Bay

OS ref.: NS 24/77
Reached by taking a 'no through road' off the A770 Greenock–Gourock road. Limited parking is available at the road end.

10 Lunderston Bay

OS ref.: NS 20/74
The foreshore car park at the north of the bay, a part of the Clyde Muirsheil Country Park, affords excellent views of the outer Firth. A path leads southwards to the marina at Inverkip.

Timing
Large numbers of birds can be found from October through to March. In the late summer, small numbers of plunge-diving Gannet at the estuary mouth and fishing terns further upstream can be seen. Passage waders are best seen in May and again from August through to October.

Because of the volume of traffic using the roads that surround the estuary, weekday 'rush hour' periods are best avoided.

S5 LOCHWINNOCH

OS ref.: NS 359581
OS map: sheet 63

Habitat
The RSPB's Lochwinnoch Nature Reserve lies approximately 18 miles (29 km) southwest of Glasgow. The A760 Largs–Paisley road divides the reserve into two: the northern part, Aird Meadow, comprises an area of shallow open water and wetland, with Willow scrub and some mature woodland; the southern part contains a much more extensive and open water body – Barr Loch. The reserve covers a total of 158 hectares plus the shooting rights over another 78 hectares of adjoining land. Of great importance for both breeding and wintering wildfowl, it forms part of the Castle Semple and Barr Loch Site of Special Scientific Interest.

Access
The reserve and nature centre lie off the A760 Largs–Paisley road, ½ mile (0.8 km) east of Lochwinnoch village. Access to the reserve is possible

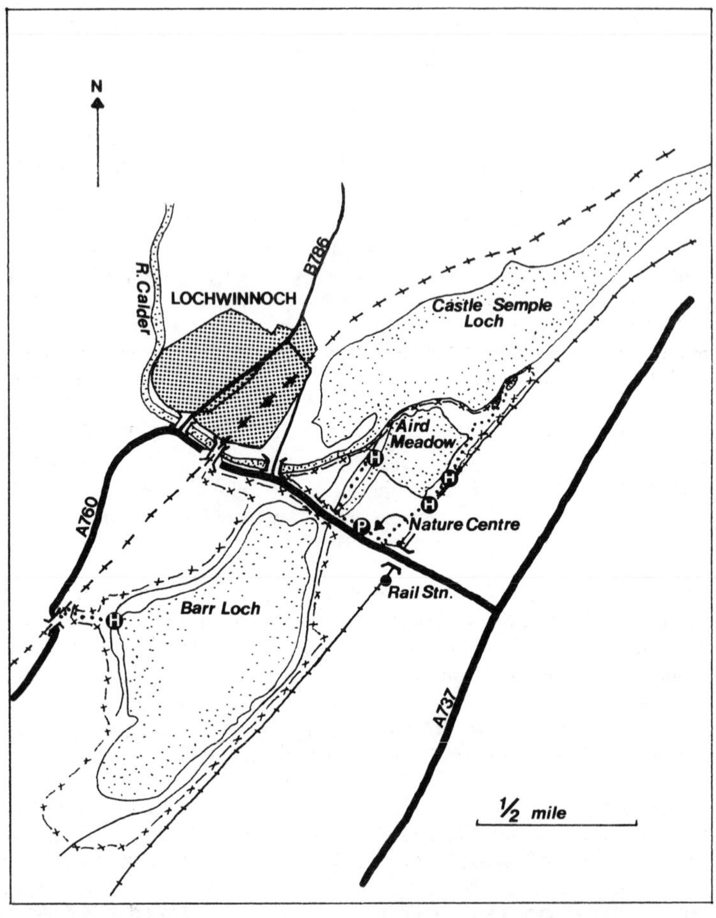

daily from 9 am to 9 pm (or sunset, if earlier) to RSPB and YOC members, but non-members may visit only during the opening hours of the Nature Centre: 10 am to 5 pm daily, except Thursdays. The Centre includes an observation tower, which affords comprehensive views of Aird Meadow and the surrounding farmland. There is a modest charge to non-members of the RSPB. Car parking is free. There is also a gift shop and (at weekends only) a tea room.

The Aird Meadow nature trails lead to three hides which overlook marsh and open water habitats. The trail and hide on the west of the meadow have been designed with wheelchair users in mind. Access to a hide overlooking Barr Loch is from a layby on the Kilbimie/Largs road, then by walking along the disused railway line (now re-surfaced as a cycle path). Please note that this hide is no longer kept locked, as was once the case.

Lochwinnoch Lochside Station, on the main Glasgow–Ayr railway line, is directly opposite the Nature Centre. Roughly speaking, there is an hourly service to and from Glasgow, Monday to Saturday, and a limited Sunday service in summer.

There are two buses an hour in each direction between Glasgow and Largs that pass the Nature Centre, Monday to Saturday. A regular, but reduced, service operates on Sundays throughout the year.

Species

Of the 173 or so recorded species from the reserve, 66 have bred in recent years. Lochwinnoch is one of the main Scottish strongholds of Great Crested Grebe, with up to eleven pairs breeding each year. Little Grebe also breed, as do Teal, Shoveler, Pochard and Tufted Duck. Ruddy Duck bred successfully in 1987, the first breeding record for western Scotland, but the birds are currently absent again. In the past, floating nest rafts have been anchored within view of the hides, enabling breeding species such as Great Crested Grebe and Black-headed Gull to be seen. It is hoped to re-establish these eventually, once the destructive problems of heavy rain and wave action have been overcome. The emergent vegetation surrounding Aird Meadow provides good nesting cover for a variety of waterfowl, as well as for a few pairs of visiting Grasshopper Warbler and the commoner Sedge and Willow Warblers.

Sparrowhawk, Kestrel and, occasionally, Peregrine hunt over the reserve. Otters are sometimes seen in the Aird Meadow.

Timing

There is lively activity for much of the year at Lochwinnoch – visit in April to June for breeding species; October to March for wintering wildfowl. Mid-summer is probably the least interesting time ornithologically, but botanically the reserve looks superb!

Calendar

Some of the more interesting species likely to be seen.

March–May: Breeding warblers should have all arrived by late April; wintering wildfowl have dispersed by early May. At any time in April, May or early June migrant waders may pass through the valley, although there is seldom enough exposed mud on the reserve to pull them down. Great Crested Grebes can be seen displaying, whilst wildfowl and gulls start to nest.

June–July: The breeding season continues; ducks enter eclipse plumage and return wader passage commences in July. Migrant Terns occasionally turn up.

August–November: Waders such as Whimbrel, Spotted Redshank, Greenshank and Ruff may stop off to feed if there is sufficient exposed mud (see comment for March–May). Redwing and Fieldfare pass through in October, often feeding on the Hawthorn and Rowan next to the nature centre. Wildfowl numbers build up during October, dominated by Mallard, but also including moderate numbers of Wigeon, Teal and Tufted Duck, with smaller numbers of Pochard and some Shoveler.

December–February: Moderate numbers of Whooper Swan, Goldeneye and Goosander are generally present throughout the winter; Greylag Geese usually peak at just over 500 individuals. Duck numbers decline slightly from their autumn peak, as birds disperse to wintering haunts.

Colder weather may encourage further immigration into the reserve providing the waters stay ice-free.

Warden

Graham Christer, Lochwinnoch Nature Centre, Largs Road, Lochwinnoch, Strathclyde. Tel: 0505 842663.

S6 DOONFOOT

OS ref.: NS 325195
OS map: sheet 70

Habitat

Doonfoot is located at the mouth of the River Doon, on the southern edge of Ayr. The raised beach here is fringed by a line of sand dunes and there is a short section of low cliff at Greenan. The foreshore includes extensive areas of sand, with small rocky outcrops and mussel beds. Grass fields and marsh border the site to the north of the estuary at Cunning Park. The coastal strip to the west of the Doon estuary is designated a Site of Special Scientific Interest.

Timing and Species

The area is primarily of interest from August through to May, when up to 1,000 duck, 2,000 waders and 10,000 gulls can be present. Visits are best timed for two hours before high water or from one hour after, i.e. a rising or falling tide. Calm sea conditions are helpful for looking at the offshore duck.

The most numerous wintering duck are Goldeneye (up to 400), which can be seen from November until March. Amongst the gulls, several Glaucous/Iceland are usually seen in late winter and rarer ones, such as Mediterranean and Ring-billed, occasionally occur. January to March is the best time to find these rarities. Waders such as Whimbrel and Sanderling frequent the foreshore on passage in May and again from July to September, whilst large numbers (250+) of Snipe and a few Jack Snipe can be found at Cunning Park between December and March.

Access

Doonfoot is accessible at all times and can be reached from Ayr by taking the A719 southwards, turning off right after crossing Doonfoot Bridge, onto the road to the shore on the south side of the river. There are three car parks along the south shore.

References

Birds of Ayrshire, Angus Hogg (1983).
Ayrshire Bird Reports 1976–91, ed. Angus Hogg.

S7 BALLANTRAE SHINGLE BEACH

OS ref.: NX 080820
OS map: sheet 76

Habitat and Species

The 22-hectare Scottish Wildlife Trust reserve at Ballantrae comprises a shingle bar, backed by a raised beach and enclosing an area of salt-marsh, mudflats and brackish lagoons, cut by the River Stinchar. Ballantrae is designated a Site of Special Scientific Interest.

Between 50 and 100 Eider and 20 to 50 Red-breasted Merganser are present offshore all year. In spring and summer, about 10–15 pairs of Arctic and up to four pairs of Little Tern breed – this is in fact the only mainland Strathclyde Little Tern site. To prevent disturbance to the terns, access to the shingle spit is not allowed between May and August. A warden is present from mid-May to July.

Arctic Terns – adult and juvenile, late summer

Moderate numbers of passage waders can be seen from April through until September, whilst offshore, hundreds of Guillemot and Razorbill congregate, with small numbers of usually Black Guillemot present. Passage seabirds can be seen in autumn.

Divers, including Red and Black-throated and Great Northern are present from January until April, with maximum numbers usually occurring in late March.

Access

Ballantrae is located at the southern end of the Ayrshire coast, some 12 miles (19 km) south of Girvan, 18 miles (29 km) north of Stranraer. The reserve is reached by parking at the Ballantrae Beach car park and walking southwards, taking care to stay *outside* the marked tern colony. The area can be viewed from the car park. There is a bus service to Ballantrae from Ayr and Stranraer.

Timing

There is year-round bird activity at Ballantrae, provided by breeding, passage and wintering species. The reserve can be interesting at any state of tide, although low tides are probably the least helpful. For offshore species, relatively calm conditions are important and a morning visit preferable in order to avoid direct sunlight.

References

Ayrshire Bird Reports 1976–91, ed. Angus Hogg.
Ayrshire Coastal Survey, SWT.
Birds of Ayrshire, Angus Hogg (1983).

S8 BOGSIDE FLATS

OS ref.: NS 310385
OS map: sheet 70

Habitat

Bogside Flats is an area of extensive saltmarsh, lying at the confluence of the rivers Garnock and Irvine. It is bounded to the east by the defunct Bogside racecourse (still used occasionally for local meets), and to the west by an ICI industrial complex. In addition to the large area of inter-tidal mud and the saltmarsh pool complex of the Garnock estuary mouth, the area includes a large central area of brackish marsh. Most of the site is privately owned and enjoys limited protection because of its proximity to the ICI explosives facility.

Species and Timing

The site is important primarily as a passage wader feeding area and an increasingly significant wintering wildfowl resort. Wader passage is best observed in the autumn – from August to late October large gatherings of Lapwing and Golden Plover occur, numbers of the latter species sometimes exceeding 3,500. In addition, large flocks of Redshank, Curlew and Dunlin can be present, often accompanied by small parties of Black-tailed Godwit, Ruff, Grey Plover, Curlew Sandpiper and Little Stint. Duck numbers increase as the autumn progresses, with Wigeon and Teal numbers regularly peaking at around 700; numbers start to decline from late February. Mallard are also common and a small number of Whooper Swan are usually present in the area. The concentration of such a large number of birds in this relatively small area inevitably attracts wintering predators such as Peregrine, Merlin, Sparrowhawk and Short-eared Owl. A short walk to the mouth of the estuary provides views of the large wintering flocks of Goldeneye and Eider. Rarer visitors are possible also – this was the location for Britain's first record of Barrow's Goldeneye, in 1979. Nearby, Irvine Beach Park also has a pool which regularly holds Scaup and Tufted Duck during the winter, affording the opportunity to study the differences and similarities between the females and immatures of these two species.

Access

Bogside is most conveniently reached from Irvine Railway Station or from the town centre in Irvine New Town. Follow the signs marked 'Harbourside' or 'Magnum Sports Centre' to the west. Upon reaching the harbourside, the large expanse of mudflat and saltmarsh lies across the River Irvine due north of the harbourside car parks. Best viewing times are from approximately two hours before high tide and from an hour after high tide. A telescope is advisable. A clear, calm day provides the best viewing conditions, although it is usually possible to find shelter in windy conditions.

The information on Bogside was kindly supplied by Angus Hogg.

References

Ayrshire Bird Reports 1976–91, ed. Angus Hogg.
Ayrshire Coastal Survey, SWT.
Birds of Ayrshire, Angus Hogg (1983).

S9 BARON'S HAUGH

OS ref.: NS 755552
OS map: sheet 64

Habitat

Baron's Haugh lies in the Clyde Valley, 1 mile (1.6 km) south from the centre of Motherwell. Despite its proximity to such an industrial area, Baron's Haugh is an excellent birdwatching site. The RSPB owns and manages a total of 107 hectares of marshland, woodland, scrub, meadows, and parkland, all alongside the River Clyde.

Four hides overlook the haugh, two of which are suitable for disabled visitors. In addition there is a one-hour trail around the reserve. People wishing access for wheelchairs should contact the warden.

Access

Motherwell can be reached from the M74 by exiting at junction 6 onto the A723 (east) and following signs to the town centre, or from the M8, also at junction 6 (south). Once in Motherwell, head for the Civic Centre and take the road opposite (Adele Street). After ½ mile (0.8 km), this leads to North Lodge Avenue and the reserve entrance.

The nearest railway station is 1½ miles (2.4 km) to the north, on the Glasgow Central–Edinburgh line.

Timing

The reserve is open at all times. There is year-round bird interest, although mid-summer is perhaps the least exciting time to visit. A winter visit is strongly recommended.

Species and Calendar

Some of the more interesting species likely to be seen.

All year: Little Grebe, Heron, Mute Swan, Teal, Mallard, Shoveler, Tufted Duck, Water Rail, Moorhen, Coot, Redshank, Grey Wagtail, Kingfisher, Reed Bunting. Willow Tit can also be found here: Baron's Haugh is at the very northern limit of its range in Britain.

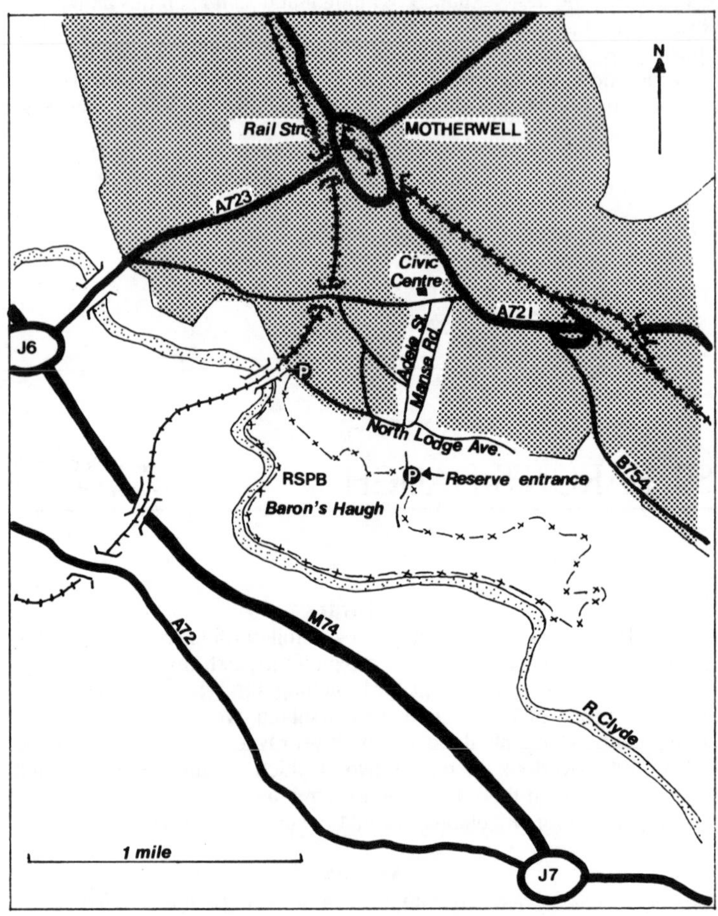

March–May: Breeding visitors arrive, starting with the Sand Martins which nest in the river banks, then birds such as Common Sandpiper, Whinchat, Grasshopper, Sedge and Garden Warblers.

June: Ducklings are much in evidence: most adult ducks enter their eclipse plumage. Ruddy Duck have been present in recent years.

July–October: Careful control of water levels in the muddy areas of the haugh provide optimum conditions for autumn passage waders; 22 species have been recorded, including Ruff, Black-tailed Godwit, Spotted Redshank, Green and Wood Sandpiper and up to 1,000 Lapwing. Wintering wildfowl start to build up.

November–February: Wildfowl provide the main interest, with over 50 Whooper Swan sometimes present, as well as good numbers of duck such as Wigeon, Teal, Shoveler, Pochard, Tufted Duck and Goldeneye.

A feature of the haugh in winter are the upwellings of tepid water around the Marsh hide. The water here therefore remains open even when the rest of the haugh freezes over, and concentrations of waterfowl can occur close by the hide. Such situations are ideal for glimpsing the shy Water Rail.

RSPB Warden

Russell Nisbet, 9 Wisteria Land, Carluke ML8 5TB.

S10 COLL RSPB RESERVE

OS ref.: NM 15/54
OS map: sheet 46

Habitat

This 1,012-hectare reserve was acquired by the RSPB in 1991. It is situated at the west end of the Isle of Coll, a rugged, largely heather covered island that lies some 5–6 miles (10 km) north west of Mull. The reserve comprises two huge dune systems, large areas of herb-rich grazing, heather moorland and some of the best hay meadows on the island. The moorland area occupies the central part of the reserve and in places grades into the machair, forming a low-lying marshy habitat favoured by many breeding waders. The machair itself is formed once sand dunes, composed of finely-ground shell sand, have stabilised and turfed over. It is by far the most fertile habitat on the island and holds a number of unusual plants, including Bloody Cranesbill.

The extensive dune system in the western part of the reserve separates two wide bays, both with superb sandy beaches flanked by rocky headlands: Feall Bay to the north and Crossapol Bay to the south. These are important resorts for wintering sea-fowl.

Species

The RSPB established the reserve specifically for Corncrake, which depend upon carefully managed grassland and are now largely confined to a few remaining strongholds in the Hebrides and parts of Ireland. Between 1988 and 1991, the British population of the Corncrake declined by a third, whilst over the same period, the Northern Ireland population went from 100 pairs to just over a dozen by 1992. On Coll and Tiree, however, numbers have remained reasonably stable, helped by RSPB initiatives advising crofters on ways to help the bird. On Coll, Corncrake numbers have remained at about 20 males in recent years. The Coll reserve now gives the RSPB an opportunity to experiment with different farming techniques in order to maximise the Corncrake potential here. This will probably involve removing livestock from the hay meadows earlier in the year than is currently the practice, to promote early cover for returning birds, delaying the cutting of fields for silage until late July or early August, and cutting fields in a 'Corncrake-friendly' way, to prevent the accidental mowing of adults and chicks.

Machair habitats hold some of the highest breeding densities of waders in Britain, and the machair – moorland interface on the reserve supports strong populations of breeding Snipe, Dunlin, Lapwing and Redshank. Shelduck and Wheatear nest in the numerous rabbit burrows in the drier machair. Other notable breeding birds on the reserve include Rock Dove, Raven and Twite. Hen Harrier, Peregrine, Merlin and Short-eared Owl also occur.

The moorland habitats of Coll are probably best observed en route to the reserve, from the Aringour road. Important breeding species include Red-throated Diver, native Greylag Geese, Teal and Arctic Skua.

Fulmar, Shag, Eider, various gulls, Common, Arctic and Little Terns all breed on Coll, whilst offshore, seabird activity is likely to include plunge-diving Gannet, marauding Arctic Skua, and possibly the odd summer-plumaged Great Northern Diver. Manx Shearwater, Razorbill, Guillemot and Puffin all breed on the nearby Treshnish Isles and are therefore frequently seen from the Coll coast. As well as birds, the coastline is also good for Otters, whilst Common Seal can be watched close inshore; Basking Shark, porpoise, dolphin and whales are also not uncommonly seen.

In winter, Coll holds 500–600 Greenland White-fronted, around 500 Barnacle and 100–300 Greylag Geese. The reserve hosts a flock of 40 or so feral Snow Geese that summer on nearby Mull. Offshore divers, mainly Great Northerns, can be seen in many of the bays and elsewhere around the coast. Feall Bay is a good area for watching wintering divers and more particularly for Long-tailed Duck (up to 100 in some winters) and occasional Common Scoter and Scaup.

Access

Coll is reached by Caledonian MacBrayne ferry from Oban. The service operates four days a week in summer, plus Sundays between June 28th and August 30th. In winter there are three sailings per week. visitors should check times with Caledonian MacBrayne, The Ferry Terminal, Gourock, PA19 1QP (tel: 0475 34531). Booking is essential for vehicles. The ferry also calls at Tiree and now has a roll-on/roll-off facility. It is also possible to board the ferry at Tobermory (Mull), although there is currently dispute about whether cars will be loaded in future. The crossing can be very good for seawatching, especially in May/June and August–early October.

Once on Coll, take the B8070 south from Aringour, for nearly 5 miles (8 km). This road affords fine views of Coll's moorland habitats – take time to scan the roadside lochans in particular, which often have Red-throated Divers in spring/summer. The reserve is entered after turning left at Arileod. Continue for just over a half mile (1 km) or so, keeping right at the turn-off towards Breachacha Castle, then park just beyond the next cattle grid. The track continues on towards Crossapol Bay, with the dunes lying to the west.

The reserve is open throughout the year. Visitors are asked not to take vehicles onto the machair, or to enter any of the hay meadows.

Timing

Corncrake are rarely seen and the best that most visitors can hope for is to hear one. They are present between April and August, but birds generally cease to call after the end of July. Calling activity is mainly confined to the hours between about 10 pm and 5 am, although in warm weather they may also call during the day. It is very important that visitors do not enter the hay meadows to try to locate birds – you are very unlikely to succeed in this way and may cause damage to vital Corncrake breeding habitat and unnecessary disturbance to the birds. Listening for calling birds from the road between Uig and Roundhouse is probably the best method. Patient watching of this area during the day may also reveal a glimpse of a bird or chicks, although it may be necessary to put in many hours!

Calendar

May–July: The best time to visit for Corncrake and other breeding birds (see Species). Young auks can be seen at sea, accompanied by single adults, from early July.

August–October: Passage waders and seabirds provide the main interest. Wintering geese generally arrive by early October.

November–April: Wintering divers, geese and seaduck present. Greylag Geese start to take up nesting territories in mid-March; White-fronted and Barnacle Geese usually depart in late April. Passage geese, duck and waders can also be seen in April.

RSPB Warden

Ian Bullock, Roundhouse, Coll. Tel. 087 93 309.

References

Argyll Bird Reports, 1980–91, eds. C. Galbraith/S.J. Petty (Argyll Bird Club).
The Birds of Coll and Tiree, ed. D. Stroud (1989).

ADDITIONAL SITES

Site and Grid Reference	Habitat	Main Bird Interest	Peak Season
a. Argyll Forest Park FC Sheet 56	Vast area of coniferous woodland, rugged mtn terrain & some deciduous woodland	Variety of moorland & woodland species	All year

See *Argyll Forest Park Guide*, available from FC or HMSO bookshops.

Site and Grid Reference	Habitat	Main Bird Interest	Peak Season
b. Ayr Gorge SWT reserve NS 457249 Sheet 70	Oak and Birch woodland; steep ravine	Common woodland birds, Dipper & Grey Wagtail	All year
c. Dalmellington Moss NS 460060 Sheet 70	Extensive wet, moss & willow scrub SWT reserve	Water Rail & Willow Tit, Sedge, G'hopper & Garden Warblers Fieldfare, Redwing & Brambling, Whooper Swan	All year May–Jun Oct.–Nov. Jan.–Feb.
d. Carradale Point SWT reserve NR 817372 Sheet 68 or 69	Coastal grassland & low cliffs.	Eider & Red-breasted Merganser Fishing Gannet	All year May–Aug.
e. Culzean Castle & Country Park NTS NS 234103 Sheet 70	Shoreline, park & woodlands, streams & ponds	Woodland birds, inc. Blackcap & Garden Warbler Winter shorebirds & offshore diver/sea-duck	May–July. Mov.–Mar.

Visitor Centre and ranger service.

Site and Grid Reference	Habitat	Main Bird Interest	Peak Season
f. Fairy Is. Sween SWT reserve NR 766884 Sheet 55.	Deciduous woodland, offshore islands	Common woodland birds, Heron, Eider, R-b Merganser, gulls & terns	Apr.–Aug.
g. Falls of Clyde SWT reserve NS 882425 Sheet 71	Mixed woodland, gorge & waterfalls Visitor Centre & ranger	Common woodland birds, inc. Willow Tit, Dipper & Grey Wagtail	All year
h. Glen Nant NNR NN 020273 Sheet 50	Oak & open birch woodland with adjacent mature coniferous ptns	Woodland bird community inc. GS Woodpecker, Tree Pipit & Redstart	Apr.–July.
i. Hunterston NS 20/53 Sheet 63	Extensive sand & mud flats, now partially reclaimed.	Wildfowl, inc. up to 200 Shelduck & 300 Wigeon	Jan.–Mar.
	Artificial lagoon in British Steel Works	Breeding Common Tern & Black-headed Gull	June–July.
j. Inverliever Forest FC NM 94/10 Sheet 55	Mature coniferous forest & Oak woodland. Open hill ground	Buzzard, Sparrowhawk, Jay & Crossbill, Hen Harrier & Golden Eagle seen on moors	All year
k. Knapdale FC NR 82/90 Sheet 55	Coniferous woodland, hill lochans & open moor	Buzzard, Sparrowhawk, Hen Harrier & Golden Eagle, Crossbill & Siskin	All year

Site and Grid Reference	Habitat	Main Bird Interest	Peak Season
l. Ledaig Point NM 902349 Sheet 49	Peninsula with sand & shingle foreshore	Passage waders & a few seabirds	Apr.–June. Aug.–Oct.
		Inshore R-t Diver, terns & B Guillemot	Apr.–Aug.
		GN Diver, Slav. Grebe & B Guillemot, Stonechat & Twite	Oct.–Mar.
m. Loch Craignish NM 79/01 Sheet 55	Wide SW facing sealoch with many islands. View from B8002 Ardfern road	Wintering divers & wildfowl	Oct.–Mar.
n. Loch Feochan NM 84/23 Sheet 49	Enclosed sealoch with varied foreshore. Large inter-tidal zone at head of loch	Breeding gulls & terns	May–Aug.
		Passage & wintering wildfowl & waders	Aug.–May.
o. Loch Gilp NR 85/86 Sheet 55	Extensive inter-tidal mud	Passage & wintering wildfowl & waders	Aug.–June.
p. New Cumnock NS 606135 Sheet 71	Shallow lagoons, Reed beds and lochs (Black Loch, Creoch Loch & Loch o' th' Lowes)	Breeding wildfowl plus Sedge & Grasshopper Warblers	May–June.
		Migrant wildfowl, waders & passerines	Aug.–Oct.
		Whooper Swan	Dec.–Feb.
		Water Rail	All year
q. Oban Harbour NM 85/29 Sheet 49	Fish quay & sheltered bay	Mute Swan, Eider, Black Guillemot	All year.
		White-winged gulls	Oct.–Apr.
r. Possil Marsh SWT reserve NS 585700 Sheet 64	Shallow loch, marsh & surrounding scrub	Breeding waterfowl Passage wildfowl, waders and passerines	All year
s. Shewalton Sandpits SWT reserve NS 327371 Sheet 70	Pools & lagoons, dune grassland, scrub & riverback	Passage waders	Aug.–Oct.
		Wintering wildfowl	Oct.–Mar.
t. Strathclyde Country Park NS 72/57 Sheet 64	Loch & nature reserve with trails & visitor centre	Wintering wildfowl, inc. Wigeon, Mallard, Pochard, Tufted Duck, Goldeneye Goosander & regular Smew	Oct.–Mar.
u. Taynish NNR NR 73/84 Sheet 55	Oak woodland, heath, bog & foreshore, Park at reserve entrance just S. of Tayvallich	Typical suite of Oak woodland birds, inc. GS Woodpecker, Redstart & Spotted Flycatcher	May–July.
v. Troon & Barassie NS 306314 & 322314 Sheet 70	Promontory with rock/ shingle foreshore	Seawatching vantage pt for shearwaters, petrels & auks	May & Aug.–Oct.
	Inter-tidal sand and mud	Passage waders	Apr.–May & July–Oct.
w. Turnberry Point NS 19/07 Sheet 70	Peninsula at northern end of open bay. Sandy foreshore with rock outcrop	Offshore Eider & Red-breasted Merganser	Aug.–Sept.
		Passage seabirds	Aug.–Oct.
		Late winter divers	Mar.–Apr.
x. Ulva Lagoons NR 71/82 Sheet 55	Small but complex area of tidal basins & pools	Modest waterfowl numbers inc. Whooper Swan	Oct.–Mar.
y. West Loch Tarbert NR 81/62 Sheet 62	Long, sheltered sea-loch with varied shoreline	Wintering divers, grebes and sea-duck. Dabbling duck frequent the head of loch	Oct.–May.

Further reading: *Birds of Mid-Argyll*, Mike Madders, Philip Snow and Julia Welstead (1992).

TAYSIDE

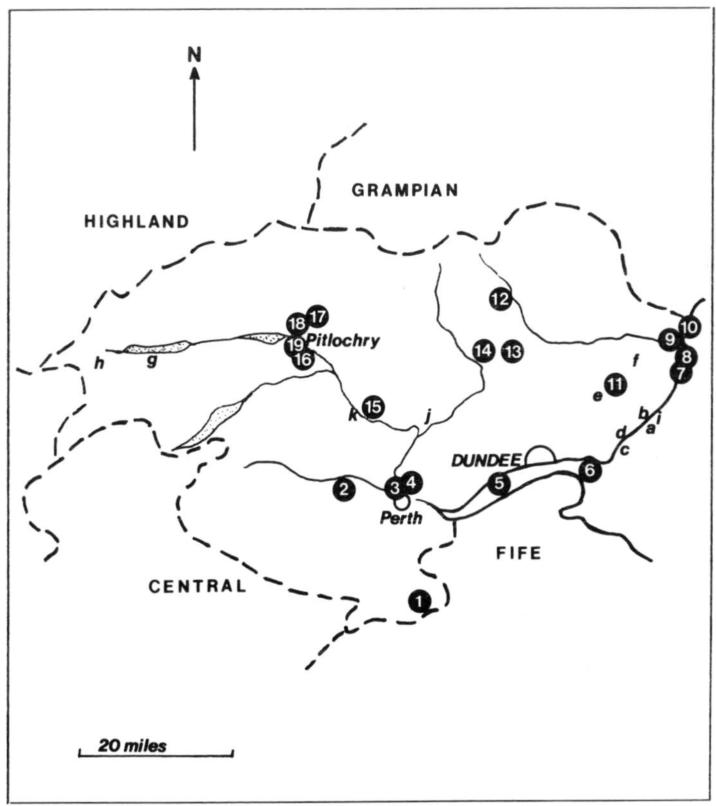

Main sites
T1. Loch Leven
T2. Strathearn
T3. River Tay at Perth
T4. Scone Den
T5. Tay Estuary
T6. Outer Tay
T7. Lunan Bay
T8. Fishtown of Usan
T9. Montrose Basin
T10. Kinnaber Links
T11. Balgavies Loch
T12. Angus Glens
T13. Loch of Kinnordy
T14. Loch of Lintrathen
T15. Loch of the Lowes
T16. Loch Faskally
T17. Ben Vrackie
T18. Killiecrankie
T19. Linn of Tummel

Additional sites
a. Arbroath
b. Auchmithie
c. Carnoustie
d. East Haven
e. Forfar Loch
f. Montreathmont
g. Rannoch Forest
h. Rannoch Moor
i. Seaton Cliffs
j. Stormont Loch
k. The Hermitage

Habitat and Species

Loch Leven is a National Nature Reserve managed by Scottish Natural Heritage. The 1,597-hectare loch and surrounding fertile farmland is internationally important as both a breeding and wintering wildfowl site. The loch is mostly shallow and contains seven islands, including St Serf's Island, where over 1,000 pairs of duck nest each year. These include Shelduck, Wigeon, Gadwall and Shoveler, although Mallard and Tufted Duck are by far the most numerous. The island is also a large Black-headed Gullery and has a small Common Tern colony.

Around the loch, Oystercatcher, Lapwing, Snipe, Curlew and Redshank nest in the few remaining wetland areas, whilst Ringed Plover and Common Sandpiper breed near to the shore.

Loch Leven is especially significant as a winter feeding and roost area

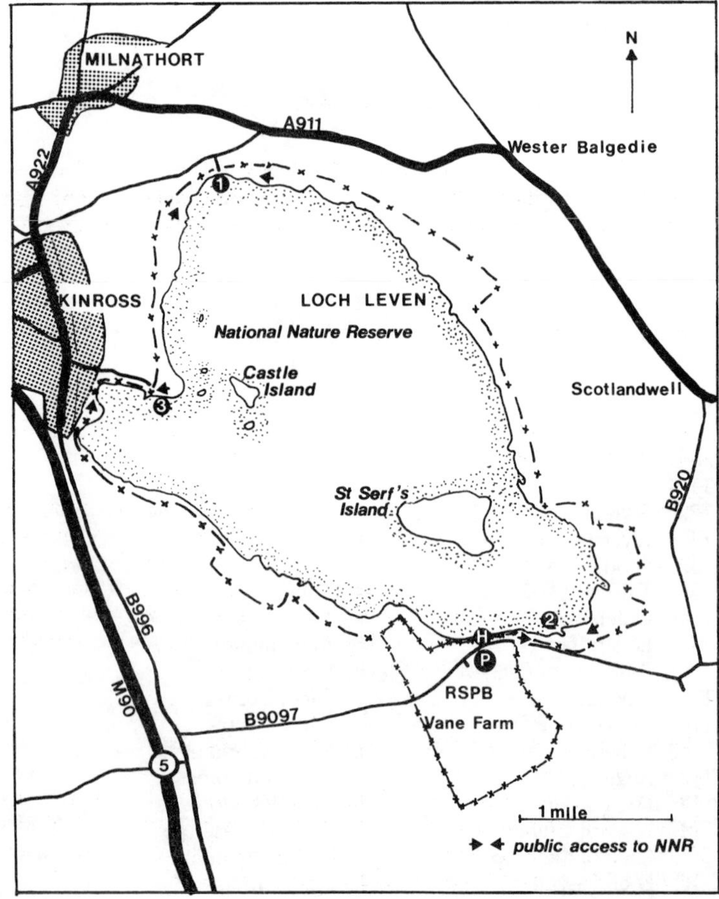

for Pink-footed Geese and is one of the major arrival points in Britain for these birds in the autumn. Many of these later disperse to wintering grounds elsewhere, but several thousand remain and move onto the surrounding farmland to feed and use the loch as a roost right through the winter. Between 1,000 and 5,000 Greylag Geese also winter here and varying numbers of Whooper Swan are often recorded. A few Canada, Barnacle, Brent and White-fronted Geese can sometimes be found amongst the goose flocks. Up to ten species of duck winter on the loch, including Wigeon, Gadwall, Shoveler, Pochard and Tufted Duck.

Access

Apart from the RSPB reserve at Vane Farm, there are three vantage points around the shore of the loch to which access is permitted:

1 Burleigh Sands

OS ref.: NO 134040

Reached via the unclassified road which turns east off the main Kinross–Milnathort road, immediately north of Kinross. Car park 1½ miles (2.4 km) after this turn.

2 Findatie

OS ref.: NT 171993

Car park and viewpoint on the B9097 road, 2½ miles (4 km) from junction 5 on the M90 and ½ mile (0.8 km) east of the RSPB reserve at Vane Farm.

3 Kirkgate Park

OS ref.: NO 128018

A half mile (0.8 km) out of Kinross, along Burns-Begg St. From April to September boats leave the jetty here for Loch Leven Castle.

There are information boards at all three places. Given calm conditions, many of the species found on Loch Leven can be 'scoped from these locations, but none of them compare with Vane Farm for variety or proximity to birds. Please note that access to the rest of the shore and islands is not permitted without prior consent of Scottish Natural Heritage, which will issue permits only to people engaged in scientific research. Small escorted groups can be arranged.

Calendar

Some of the more interesting species likely to be seen.

All year: Great Crested Grebe, Fulmar, Cormorant, Heron, Mute Swan, Wigeon, Gadwall, Teal, Mallard, Shoveler, Pochard, Tufted Duck, Ruddy Duck, Sparrowhawk, Moorhen, Coot, Lapwing, Snipe, Curlew, Black-headed, Lesser Black-backed Gulls, Jackdaw, Rook.

Breeding visitors: Shelduck, Common Sandpiper, Common Tern.

Regular migrants: Slavonian and Black-necked Grebes, Ruff, Black-tailed Godwit, Spotted Redshank, Greenshank, Green and Wood Sandpipers, Sand Martin.

Winter visitors: Whooper Swan, Pink-footed Goose, Greylag Goose, Pintail, Goldeneye, Goosander, Short-eared Owl, Fieldfare, Redwing.

SNH Reserve Manager

Loch Leven Laboratory, The Pier, Kinross, KY13 7UF. Tel: 0577 864439.

Vane Farm RSPB Reserve

OS ref.: NT 160991
OS map: sheet 58

Habitat

This 231-hectare reserve is located on the south shore of Loch Leven. There are a variety of habitats within the reserve, from the marshland and shallow lagoons of the lochshore, through mixed farmland. Birch and bracken slopes with scattered rocky outcrops, to the heather moorland 150 metres above. A series of lagoons and floods have been created to diversify the wetland part of the reserve; this attracts nesting duck and waders in the summer and wildfowl in winter. Gleanings from the reserve's two main arable crops, barley and potatoes, combined with the close-grazed sward created by cattle on adjacent land, provide conditions ideal for visiting geese. Vane Farm is designated a Site of Special Scientific Interest by Scottish Natural Heritage.

The Vane Farm Nature Centre incorporates an observation room, looking out over the reserve and providing a comprehensive view of Loch Leven, aided by tripod-mounted binoculars and telescopes. There is also a gift shop and tea room.

Access

The reserve entrance is located on the south side of the B9097 Glenrothes road, 2 miles (3.2 km) east of junction 5 on the M90.

Access to the car park and the nature trail to the summit of the Vane is possible at all times. There is a hide, reached via a tunnel under the B9097, overlooking the scrape. The nature centre and observation room are open from 10 am to 5 pm, April to Christmas, and 10 am to 4 pm January to March. Both are closed between Christmas and New Year. There is a resident teacher-naturalist at the Vane Farm Nature Centre; school parties are welcome, but please book well in advance. A short nature trail is suitable for wheelchair users and a ramp allows access to the observation room.

The nearest railway station is 5 miles (8 km) away at Lochgelly, on the Edinburgh to Dundee line, though Cowdenbeath is probably more convenient.

Timing

The most spectacular time to visit is between October and March, when the geese are present. However, passage and breeding birds provide alternative interest and the educational displays and activities at the nature centre continue throughout the year.

Species

Over 130 species have been recorded on the reserve, about 70 of which are winter visitors. The observation room at Vane Farm is a good place from which to see the large flocks of Pink-footed and Greylag Geese that use the Loch Leven area in winter. Likewise, Whooper Swan are also often visible on the loch; up to 400 have been recorded, but their appearances are rather unpredictable. As many as ten species of duck can be seen in winter and Wigeon, Teal, Mallard, Shoveler, Pochard and Tufted Duck may be seen year-round.

Pink-footed Geese

Sparrowhawk, Buzzard and Kestrel are occasionally seen over the reserve. Work is in progress to build a permanent dam to reverse some of the effects of past agricultural drainage; hopefully this will result in an increase in breeding Lapwing numbers.

The Birch woods have perhaps a rather limited bird community, but Tree Pipit, Whinchat and Spotted Flycatcher are present in spring and Long-tailed Tit, Redpoll and Siskin can be seen throughout autumn and winter. A small hide overlooking a stream flowing through the larch wood on the lower part of the nature trails affords the opportunity of watching many feeding and bathing woodland species.

See Loch Leven section for general species list.

Calendar

Some of the highlights likely to be seen.

March–May: Pink-footed Goose numbers peak in March, as birds from more southerly wintering haunts begin to move into the area. During April and early May, skeins of departing geese can be seen, leaving just a few individuals by mid-May.

June: Perhaps the quietest month, but Great Crested Grebe, Shelduck, Gadwall and Redshank should all be present.

July–October: Passage waders that may put in an appearance at the scrape include Knot, Black-tailed Godwit, Greenshank, Green and Wood Sandpipers.

The main influx of wintering geese occurs late in September and during early October; Pink-foot numbers can reach almost 15,000 before birds begin to disperse to their winter haunts. Smaller numbers of Greylag Geese and Whooper Swan also appear, although the latter can be very unpredictable.

December–February: By mid-winter, goose numbers have declined and stabilised. Whooper Swan are present in varying numbers and are sometimes joined by Bewick's Swan. Dabbling ducks that can generally be seen include Wigeon, Gadwall, Shoveler and the occasional Pintail; diving duck such as Tufted Duck, Goldeneye and Goosander are usually present.

At dusk, large numbers of Woodpigeon cross the reserve to their roost site.

Chaffinch, Greenfinch, Yellowhammer and occasionally Brambling, can be seen around the car park.

RSPB Warden

David Fairlamb, Vane Farm Centre, by Loch Leven, Kinross KY13 7LX. Tel: 0577 62355.

T2 STRATHEARN

OS map: sheet 58

Strathearn is a well-known area for wintering geese and has been covered extensively in earlier guides. However, a number of factors have persuaded us not to recommend the area wholeheartedly as a birdwatching site.

Numbers of Greylag are much lower than they were 10–20 years ago, probably reflecting the change to winter cereals and the resultant hostility of farmers towards the geese. After a big peak in early autumn, Pink-footed Goose numbers are also low throughout winter. Access is very problematical – all of the land is in private ownership and visitors are generally unwelcome. In a nutshell, there are better places in which to see geese in Tayside, such as Stormont Loch, Loch of Kinnordy, Loch Leven and Montrose Basin, where access is less of a problem and is less likely to cause friction between land-owners and birdwatchers.

Roadside views of feeding geese are possible at Tibbermore (NO 050237), best in late September and early October, and Kinkell Bridge (NN 932168), from November through to March. Parking is awkward at both places and care should be taken not to obstruct access.

T3 RIVER TAY AT PERTH

OS ref.: NO 120245
OS map: sheet 53

Habitat

This 2½-mile (4 km) section of the Tay upstream from Perth Bridge as far as its confluence with the River Almond is an interesting and easily accessible area for riparian birdlife. The west bank is largely short-turf grassland with scattered mature trees. At Woody Islands there is deciduous woodland, a small conifer plantation and areas of hawthorn/ blackthorn scrub. On the east bank, large houses with extensive gardens occupy the southern part of the riverbank, with the parkland of Scone Palace further north.

Species

In recent years, one of the great attractions of this section of river has been the small feral population of Mandarin Duck. These breed in nest boxes in Upper Springland and adjacent gardens, but in recent years few young have been reared. The autumn 1991 Wildfowl Counts revealed only 2 male and 3 female birds, compared with a maximum of 14 recorded in 1987. It therefore seems likely that the population will become extinct in the very near future. There are usually several 'winged' Pink-footed and Greylag Geese present; they have not been known to breed, however. Red-breasted Merganser, occasional Kingfisher, Dipper and Grey Wagtail all frequent the river throughout the year. Tawny Owl and Great Spotted Woodpecker are present in the woodland and garden habitats and Jackdaw nest in the stonework of Perth Bridge (which is also a year-round Starling roost). Other resident species include Herring and Great Black-backed Gulls, Rook, Carrion Crow and Goldfinch.

In the summer, Oystercatcher, Ringed Plover, Lapwing, Common Sandpiper, Common Tern, Skylark, Grey Wagtail, Sedge and Garden Warblers, Whitethroat, Blackcap and Spotted Flycatcher can be seen. Sand Martins nest in drainage holes in the retaining wall of Tay Street.

Lesser Black-backed Gull, hirundines, Whinchat and Wheatear occur on passage in spring, whilst Oystercatcher, Lapwing and Curlew move through in autumn. Over 500 Pied Wagtail roost in the salix scrub on an island against the pier at the east end of Perth Bridge during late summer.

Up to 500 Greylay Geese roost on the river below Scone Palace from November through to March/April. Other wintering wildfowl include Mute Swan, Wigeon, Tufted Duck and Goosander, although numbers depend largely on the severity of the weather, with more birds moving onto the river when nearby open water habitats freeze over. Little Grebe, Cormorant (over 100 birds have been recorded at a tree roost here) and Coot are all generally present in winter. Fieldfare, Redwing, Siskin and Redpoll utilise adjacent habitats.

Birds recorded only occasionally include Black-throated Diver, Great Crested Grebe, Whooper Swan, Canada Goose, Teal, Pochard, Golden Plover and Greenshank. It is also worthwhile checking the gulls for any less common species that may occur from time to time. Note: many of the Mallard on the River Tay here are of the 'Cayuga' strain, with variations from glossy black with white breast to almost pure Mallard. The Scottish Council for Spastics' Upper Springland complex has a wildfowl collection, elements of which wander on to the river and can be the cause of considerable confusion for the unwary!

Access

Access is feasible to the west bank only. Metered parking is possible in Perth city. There is a surfaced path, suitable for wheelchair users, for most of the route from Perth Bridge to the Almond confluence. Good views are also afforded by the bridges in Perth and from Tay Street.

Timing

The river is worth a look at any time of year, it's an interesting, convenient and brilliant place to go birding!

T4 SCONE DEN

OS ref.: NO 136258
OS map: sheet 53

Scone Den is a narrow valley nearly 1 mile (1.6 km) long with mature deciduous woodland, scrub and gardens. Den Road runs alongside the burn and gives access to an old quarry surrounded by ash trees and with hawthorn growing on its floor.

Access is off the A94 in Scone. Park at Cross Street or Burnside, on the outskirts of the town of Scone and about ¼ mile (0.4 km) south of Den Road. This road is unsurfaced, but negotiable by wheelchair users.

The resident birds are largely woodland/scrub species and include Great-Spotted Woodpecker, Jay, Tawny Owl and Hawfinch. The latter are most commonly seen between November and April, often in the vicinity of the old quarry – much of the quarry floor scrub has recently been cleared for house construction, so this may affect the attraction of the site to Hawfinch. Dipper can be seen along the burnside throughout the year.

In summer, breeding visitors include Mandarin Duck, Grey and Pied Wagtails, Whitethroat, Garden and Willow Warblers, Blackcap and Spotted Flycatcher.

In addition, Kingfisher, Green Woodpecker and Chiffchaff are occasionally recorded.

T5 TAY ESTUARY

OS map: sheets 58 & 59

Habitat

The inner Tay estuary is considered here to extend downstream from Perth as far as the rail bridge at Dundee, a total length of approximately

18 miles (29 km). This is one of the cleanest and least spoilt of the country's larger estuaries, having the highest volume of freshwater outflow of any in Britain. It is the extensive mud-flats on the north back of the estuary that will mainly interest the birder. The largest area of reedbed (*Phragmites australis*) in Great Britain can be found along this bank, much of it commercially harvested. Inland, the heavy clay soils support an intensive agricultural regime, giving way to rich sandstone loams and some wooded hillsides on the Braes of The Carse of Gowrie.

The area is of international significance for roosting geese, as well as of national importance for its numbers of wintering Goldeneye. The tidal flats are the feeding ground of the large local breeding Sheduck population and of other migratory, wintering and breeding wildfowl and waders. Much of the shoreline is designated a Site of Special Scientific Interest and is a proposed Local Nature Reserve.

Species

The Tay is particularly important for passage and wintering wildfowl and waders. Around 2,000 Greylay geese feed on the Carse of Gowrie and roost on the estuary; 500 or more Pink-footed Geese and small numbers of Whooper Swan are also present. Common wintering waders include Redshank, Dunlin, Bar-tailed Godwit, Curlew, Golden Plover, Lapwing, Common and Jack Snipe. Migrant waders regularly include Curlew Sandpiper, Ruff, Greenshank and Little Stint. Small numbers of Whimbrel and Green Sandpiper occur regularly in spring.

Very large mixed flocks of hirundines occur on passage, sometimes forming roosts (near Errol) in excess of 10,000 birds.

Shelduck breed along the inner fringe of the reed bed and inland on the 'Braes'.

In the reed beds, Water Rail and Reed Bunting are resident breeders, joined in summer by Sedge Warbler – the populations of all three of

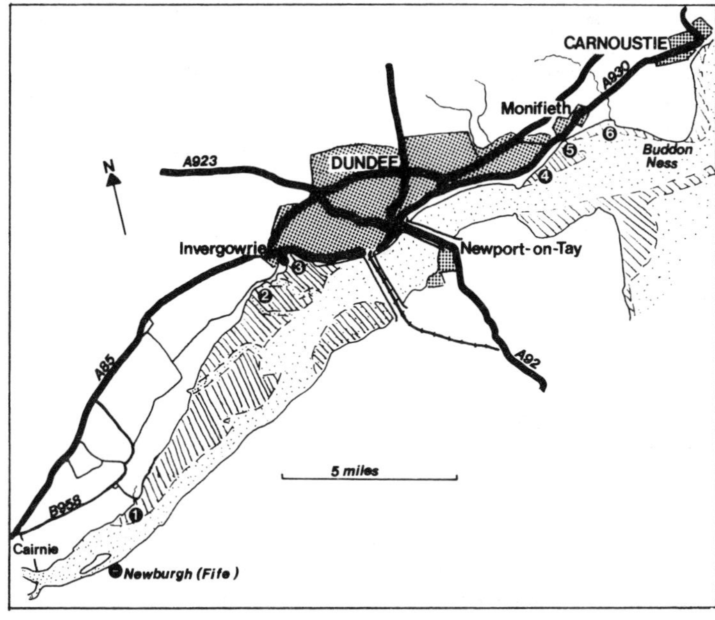

these species are amongst the largest in Scotland. The harvested areas allow Snipe, Redshank, Curlew and Lapwing to breed successfully within the reed beds.

Access

Access to this coast is difficult, there being few roads down to the shore and the generally narrow, but dense, reed beds effectively block visibility of much of the estuary. Parking, too, is problematical and care must be taken not to prevent access to gateways, impede traffic on roads and tracks, etc. if stopping on road verges. Please note that there is no access to Dundee Airport.

The following vantage points can be recommended:

1 Port Allen

OS ref.: NO 252212

Continue along the B958, past the Cairnie turn-off and take the minor road to the shore just beyond Mains of Errol, 3 miles (4.8 km) later. Please park considerately at the farm near the end of this road – do not block the track leading towards the shore. A series of mud banks, used by a variety of passage waders, can be viewed from the embankment on the west side of Port Allen. Late summer/early autumn is the best time of year.

2 Kingoodie

OS ref.: NO 33/29

This is by far the best general viewpoint for overlooking the estuary. An unclassified road, leading south from Invergowrie, runs along the foreshore immediately west of Kingoodie and there is a layby for parking. This area is best worked at high tide.

3 Invergowrie Bay

OS ref.: NO 35/29

Both the pier and Invergowrie Station make good vantage points from which to scan this busy and interesting bay.

Access is also possible at Cairnie Pier (NO 197192) via an unclassified road from St Madoes, and at Seaside (NO 283243) via a public right of way from Grange.

There are buses and trains from Perth/Dundee to Invergowrie.

Timing

It is the spring and autumn passage birds and the wintering wildfowl that provide the main interest on this picturesque estuary. Spring sequences of tides are best for bringing waders close up to vantage points, but with the exception of overcast days, early morning and late afternoon/evening are the best times of day to visit. Otherwise direct strong sunlight may make viewing difficult. Between September and January there is a great deal of wildfowling activity both on the embankments and in the reed beds – Sunday visits are therefore recommended.

Calendar

Some of the more interesting species likely to be seen.

March–May: This is the time of greatest species diversity and activity on the estuary, with both winter visitors and summer migrants present. Grey geese, wintering wildfowl and waders are joined by migrant thrushes, Swallow, Sand Martin, Sedge Warbler, Willow Warbler and other summer migrants.

July–September: Hirundines and migrant warblers move through the area. During the latter part of this period, Ruff, Greenshank, Spotted Redshank, Arctic Skua, Sandwich, Common and Arctic Terns occur regularly. Curlew Sandpiper and Little Stint also occur, but their numbers are more variable.

October–February: Greylag and Pink-footed Geese, Whooper Swan, Mallard, Teal, Pochard, Tufted Duck and Goldeneye are present. So too are small numbers of Great Crested Grebe and a few Pintail.

Over-wintering waders (see above) are abundant and sometimes include a few Black-tailed Godwit. Redwing and Fieldfare frequent the disused orchards and the hawthorn hedges/scrub along the length of the estuary. Kingoodie and Invergowrie usually attract Waxwing in years when irruptions occur.

T6 OUTER TAY

OS ref.: NO 434308–520320
OS map: sheet 54 or 59

Habitat

This area comprises the 5 miles (8 km) or so of urbanised north shore of the Firth of Tay, from Stannergate in the west to Buddon Burn in the east. The deepwater channel offshore contains large mussel beds, which are especially attractive to Eider. The inter-tidal zone of the north shore is characterised by a mixture of substrate-types, with areas of mussel beds and Eel Grass. Freshwater and sewage outflows discharge onto the sand and mud flats. A dune system extending out into the mouth of the Firth to the east is a rare example of a lowland heath bounded by dunes involving mobile sands.

Monifieth Bay and Barry Buddon Ranges are both Sites of Special Scientific Interest.

Species

Up to 300 Little Gull can be seen in Monifieth Bay and at Carnoustie, to the east. These birds can be seen year-round; the flock is mostly juvenile birds, but adults are generally also present.

In winter, over 20,000 Eider can sometimes be seen in the mouth of the Firth. In addition, small numbers of Red-throated Diver and occasional Black-throated and Great Northern Divers occur, with up to 250 Red-breasted Merganser; some Great Crested Grebe, Goldeneye and a few Long-tailed Duck. Common and Velvet Scoter are also seen occasionally.

Little Gulls – immature and adult, late summer

Wader numbers are equally impressive, with around 1,000 Oystercatcher, between 50 and 200 Ringed Plover, 300–400 Sanderling and 500–2,000 Bar-tailed Godwit. A few Black-tailed Godwit may also be present. Small numbers of Turnstone, Redshank and Dunlin also occur. Knot numbers vary considerably, but the species regularly over-winters.

The area is not especially noted for its passage birds, but Green Sandpiper are regular migrants in spring and autumn, whilst offshore, Great and Arctic skuas often enter the firth in late summer and autumn, pursuing the fishing terns, which at that time of year include Sandwich Tern.

Local passerines include Tree Sparrow, Linnet, Goldfinch, Redpoll and Yellowhammer. A few Snow Bunting can usually be found in the Carnoustie/Buddon area each winter.

Access

The area can be worked from the A930 Dundee–Carnoustie road; the foreshore is easily accessible at many points, using public roads and pavements. There are very good bus and train services between Dundee, Broughty Ferry, Balmossie, Monifieth and Barry Links.

Note that access to the Barry/Buddon MOD area is not permissible when the red flags are flying but is otherwise unrestricted to pedestrians. Park at Riverview (football pitches) and walk.

The following vantage points, as numbered on the Tay estuary map, page 195, can be especially recommended:

4. Broughty Ferry Harbour/esplanade (OS ref.: NO 462305).
5. Foreshore at Dighty Water outflow (OS ref.: NO 487318).
6. Buddon Burn/Monifieth Links (OS ref.: NO 516323).

Timing

The main interest here is during the winter, although Common, Arctic and Little Terns can be seen in summer. Spring sequences of tides are usually the best, especially when high water is around mid-day. Ideally, visit during slightly overcast conditions or in the morning and evening, thus avoiding having to look directly against the light.

Calendar

March–May: Displaying Eider, Goldeneye and Red-breasted Merganser are conspicuous, as too are many of the breeding plumaged waders.

June: This is the quietest month of the year, although breeding Eiders, terns and small numbers of Redshank, Curlew and Ringed Plover occupy territories on Barry Links.

July–September: Return passage of waders occurs, many of them (Bar-tailed Godwit, Sanderling and Dunlin for example) still in breeding plumage. Offshore, the terns and gulls are given a hard time by Great, Arctic and occasional Pomarine skuas. Other obvious passage migrants include Swallow and Meadow Pipit.

October–February: Wintering wader populations build up; large gull roosts (comprising Black-headed, Common, Herring and Great Black-backed Gulls) form; wintering wildfowl (Goldeneye, Scoters, Red-breasted Merganser, etc.) gather offshore; divers and auks move into the shelter of the outer Firth. Short-eared Owl hunt over Barry Links.

T7 LUNAN BAY

OS ref.: NO 69/51
OS map: sheet 54

Habitat and Access

This wide, sandy bay is located between Montrose and Arbroath on the Angus coast. The bay is backed by dunes and divided by Lunan Water, which enters the bay mid-way along the $2\frac{1}{2}$-mile (4 km) beach – at high tide the river here is unfordable. The Water is flanked by deciduous woodland and a small conifer plantation.

The bay is accessible at three points:

1. Car park at NO 692516, reached by private road (with speed ramps) just north of the entrance to Lunan Bay Hotel (now a hospital for the mentally handicapped).
2. On foot via Red Castle. Parking on the roadside is awkward, but feasible, at NO 688510.
3. Ethie Haven, at the south end of the bay, NO 699488. Again, narrow roads and limited space make parking awkward.

The southern end of the bay is probably the best area, but the easiest access is via the public car park, setting up a 'scope on the dunes nearby. Early morning visits are fraught with difficulty owing to visibility problems against the light.

Species and Calendar

There is year-round bird interest at Lunan Bay. From late July, up to 2,000 scoters (mostly Velvet) gather in the bay. One or two Surf Scoter are usually present in this flock. In late summer and early autumn large numbers of Gannet, Kittiwake and terns can be seen offshore, with a few Arctic, Great and, occasionally, Pomarine Skuas. Little Gull also occur.

Numbers of Red-throated Diver and Great Crested Grebe build up at this time, with about 100 of each present. Other diver and grebe species are occasionally seen, especially in winter. Scoter numbers decline after October, but numbers of Long-tailed Duck increase, usually to a maximum of around 100 birds.

In spring and summer the bay is busy with fishing Gannet and terns; a few Red-throated Diver, Great Crested Grebe, Common and Velvet Scoter may still be found.

The woodland around Lunan Water is good for passerine migrants in spring and autumn. Kingfisher occur on the river in autumn.

Short-eared Owl often hunt over the dunes in winter and Snow Bunting may be present.

T8 FISHTOWN OF USAN

OS ref.: NO 726546
OS map: sheet 54

Habitat and Access

This is the best seawatching site in Angus and is a relatively easy area to work. Follow unclassified roads through the farm of Seaton of Usan and park by the road (dead end) overlooking the bay. The promontory to the south of the small bay is a good vantage point.

From May to October there is plenty to see; northerly winds are best for seabird passage, whilst in spring, a south-easterly is best for passerine migrants.

Species

Passage seabirds are the main attraction. Arctic and Great Skua are numerous, whilst Pomarine are annual. Manx Shearwater are common in the autumn and a few Sootys are annual; sea-duck (especially Eider) and waders provide interest in the winter.

Willows growing around the sloping ground and cliffs surrounding the bay provide cover for some spring and autumn passerine migrants. The small boats, piles of creels and drying nets which litter the slopes are also used. The limited amount of cover provides only temporary shelter for migrant passerines and these tend to move inland to the woods surrounding Usan House (NO 723553) after maiing landfall. Many good birds have been found adjacent to the unclassified road passing through this area.

Autumn Bluethroat

In addition to the more expected species, several less common birds have occurred, such as Yellow-browed Warbler and Red-breasted Flycatcher, whilst rarities like Aquatic and Arctic Warblers have been recorded.

T9 MONTROSE BASIN

OS ref.: NO 695575
OS map: sheet 54

Habitat

A large enclosed estuary immediately inland from Montrose and fed by the River South Esk. The basin comprises extensive tidal mud/sand flats, with a fringe of reed beds, wet pasture and riverine habitats to the west. Montrose Basin is a Local Nature Reserve and Site of Special Scientific Interest covering 1,012 hectares, administered by Angus District Council and managed by the Scottish Wildlife Trust, the major landowner within the reserve.

Unlike many of the productive and sheltered inlets on the Scottish east coast, which have suffered from pollution and industrial development, Montrose Basin is a relatively clean and unspoilt estuarine area. The inter-tidal mud is exceptionally rich in invertebrates, particularly the *Hydrobia* snail, and this attracts very large numbers of waders. Glasswort and eelgrass bring in important populations of wintering dabbling duck, whilst the mussel beds in the river channel support Eider throughout the year.

Controlled wildfowling is allowed under a permit system. Shooting takes place between one hour before and two hours after sunrise and sunset, 1 September to 20 February.

A Visitor Centre is planned for near Rossie Braes, on the south shore.

Species and Calendar

In winter, Montrose Basin hosts a major roost of Pink-footed Geese. The main roost occurs in the east-central part of the basin and can be seen

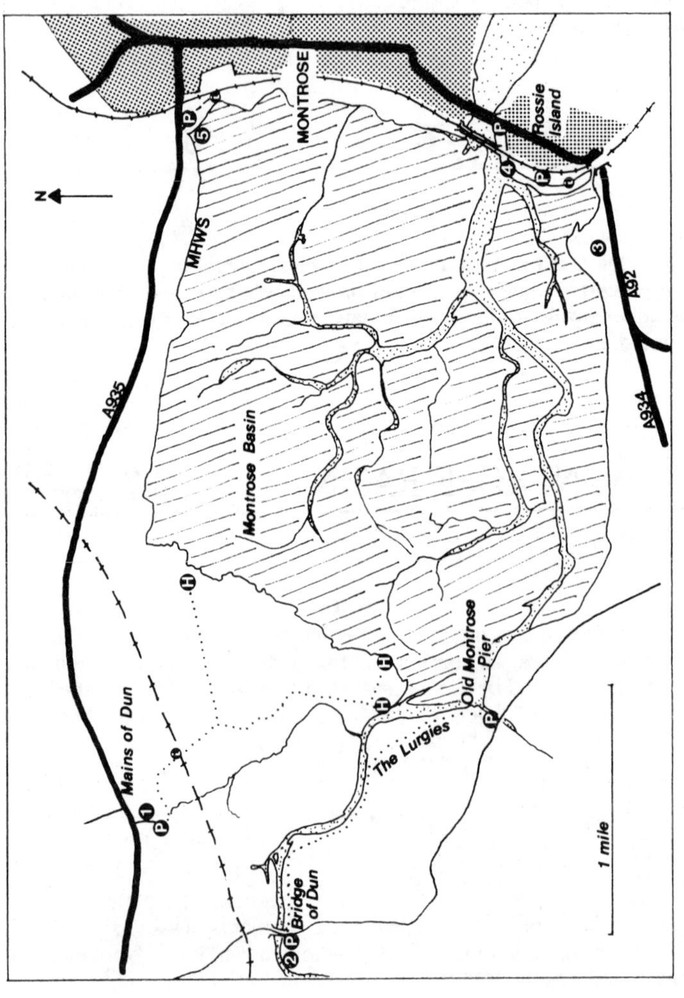
MONTROSE
MHWS
Rossie Island
A92
A934
A935
N
Montrose Basin
Old Montrose Pier
The Lurgies
Mains of Dun
Bridge of Dun
1 mile

from the railway station and Rossie Island. Numbers peak in October and November, when between 20,000 and 30,000 birds may be present. In very cold conditions, up to 3,000 Greylag Geese roost in the main channel at the western end of the basin.

Around 5,000 Wigeon occupy the basin in early winter, with approximately 1,000 Mallard and 2,000 Eider. Other wintering wildfowl include 300 to 400 Shelduck, *c*. 120 Pintail and small numbers of Shoveler, Teal, Red-breasted Merganser and Goosander. Scaup and Tufted Duck sometimes occur in freezing conditions.

Sparrowhawk, Merlin, Peregrine and Short-eared Owl all hunt over the basin regularly in winter.

Waders can include up to 4,000 Oystercatcher, large numbers of Dunlin, 10,000 Knot (more usually 2,000–3,000) 1,000 Golden Plover and 1,500+ Redshank. Knot numbers generally peak in January and Dunlin in February.

There is an excellent wader passage at the basin, particularly between July and September. Birds that are seen regularly at this time include Green and Wood Sandpipers, Spotted Redshank, Ruff and both godwit species. Spring passage is at its peak in May. There are strong passages of Curlew in March and August, of Redshank in March and September, and of Oystercatcher in October and November.

Terns use the basin extensively, post-breeding and often build up to become several thousand strong, including Common, Arctic, Sandwich and a few Little Terns. Osprey can often been seen fishing for flounders in late summer.

More than 200 pairs of Eider nest around the basin. Other breeding birds include Oystercatcher, Redshank and Lapwing. Sedge Warbler and Reed Bunting nest in the reedbeds.

Access

1 Mains of Dun

OS ref.: NO 669592

A car park at the old mill, just off the reserve, is the starting point for a track leading to the three hides overlooking the west side of the basin (see map). These hides are kept locked, however, and the keys must be obtained in advance from the SWT Ranger/Naturalist, Rick Goater (address below). A deposit of £5 (for life) per key is levied. The most northerly of these hides overlooks the corner of the basin which is the last part to flood, so is best visited near high tide, when large numbers of roosting waders may be seen.

2 Bridge of Dun – Old Montrose Pier

OS ref.: NO 663585 to 676572

Walk down the south side of the river to the old pier. There is limited parking possible at either end. The pier is a good general viewpoint for the south-eastern basin: best at low water of mid-tide.

3 Rossie Braes

OS ref.: NO 703565

The A92 roadside here is a good vantage point for the south side of the basin. There is a high tide wader roost at Rossie Point.

4 Railway viaduct

OS ref.: NO 707568

The eastern basin can be viewed from the 'no-through road' on the west side of Rossie Island, approached either on foot from the parking area immediately south of New Bridge, or by driving under the south span of the viaduct to a small car park west of the railway. Visit at low water for feeding waders.

5 Tayock Burn

OS ref.: NO 708590

Take the A935 Brechin road west out of Montrose and turn south onto the old town rubbish dump immediately after crossing the railway. This is an excellent vantage point for the north-east basin. Ideally, visit one hour either side of high tide, when close views of feeding waders should be possible. This area had the best selection of waders, as well as most of the basin's Shelduck. Roosting geese may be found here very early on winter mornings. Observation becomes tricky around midday, due to strong backlight.

Montrose is connected by bus and rail services to Aberdeen and Dundee.

Timing

No season is a dull one at Montrose Basin. Wildfowl provide the main winter interest and waders dominate the attention in spring and autumn. In summer, breeding Eider and gatherings of post-breeding terns are of note.

Wader activity is often most easily observable, especially from the south, when the river channels are full of water but there are still plenty of exposed mud-flats.

Dawn and dusk observation is inadvisable at the west end of the basin during winter, due to wildfowling activity (see above).

SWT Ranger/Naturalist

Full information on parking, access and the birdlife of the basin can be obtained from Rick Goater, The Towans, Tayock, Montrose, Angus DD10 9LE. Tel: 0674 76336.

T10 KINNABER LINKS

OS ref.: NO 738620
OS map: sheet 45

Habitat and Access

This area lies immediately south of the North Esk estuary, two miles from St Cyrus in the neighbouring Grampian Region.

Access is via the A92, turning off east onto a minor road 3 miles (4.8 km) north of Montrose (NO 724616). Park at the bend in the road at Fisherhills and walk downstream alongside the North Esk towards the coast.

Species

The river is good for Dipper, Grey Wagtail and Red-breasted Merganser (a moulting flock of around 400 birds gather at the mouth of the river in late summer).

Tidal pools at 736622 are very good for autumn waders, including less common species such as Curlew Sandpiper, Wood Sandpiper and Spotted Redshank.

Autumn passerines include Wheatear, Whinchat and (after easterly winds) Black Redstart.

Short-eared Owl frequently hunt over the Links in winter.

Offshore, a range of sea-duck similar to that seen at Lunan Bay occurs and there may be much interchange of divers, Long-tailed Duck and scoters between the two bays.

T11 BALGAVIES LOCH

OS ref.: NO 535508
OS map: sheet 54

Habitat

This 46-hectare Scottish Wildlife Trust reserve is one of a series of wetlands in the Upper Lunan Valley, situated to the east of Forfar. The loch is fringed by reed beds and woodland; to the west there is an extensive area of fen. Unfortunately, the run-off of dissolved phosphates and nitrates from the surrounding agricultural land is having a detrimental effect on the aquatic life of the loch.

Access

Take the A932 from Forfar towards Arbroath/Montrose and turn off into a parking layby that overlooks the loch 5 miles (8 km) later. This commands a good general view; there is also a hide at the south-west corner of the loch, accessible from a small car park ¼ mile (0.4 km) to the west. This is open to the public from 1 pm to 4 pm on the first Sunday of each month, but is otherwise normally locked – SWT members can obtain a key (£5 deposit) from the warden (see below), or Rick Goater, The Towans, Tayock, Montrose DD10 9LE. Permits to visit any other part of the reserve are issued by the warden (free of charge).

Species

Balgavies Loch is mainly of interest to birders between October and March, when moderate numbers of wintering wildfowl, including Wigeon, Shoveler, Pochard, Tufted Duck, Goldeneye and Goosander can be seen. Large numbers of Greylag and Pink-footed Geese roost on the loch; Heron and Cormorant roost in the trees around the shore and on a large island; Water Rail, Woodcock, Snipe and Kingfisher are sometimes seen. Little Grebe are frequently present and Great Crested Grebe breed. Long-tailed, Great, Blue and Coal Tits are usually to be seen around the hide during the winter months, whilst Bullfinch frequent the hide car park.

Warden

Charlie Riddell, Weilstaves Cottage, Balgavies, near Forfar, Angus DD8 2SD. Tel. 030 781 355.

T12 ANGUS GLENS

OS map: sheets 43 & 44

Habitat and Species

The glens of Isla, Prosen, Clova and Esk, together with their numerous minor side valleys cut deep into the Grampian plateau. The hills at the head of these glens rise steeply to well over 800 metres – high enough for birds such as Ptarmigan and Dotterel. Lower moorland terrain supports large numbers of Red Grouse, breeding Hen Harrier, Merlin, (both at lower densities than one might expect, given the quality of the habitat), Golden Plover, Dunlin and Short-eared Owl. The steep corries and craggy hillsides hold populations of crag nesting species such as Golden Eagle, Peregrine and Raven; Ring Ousel are not uncommon amongst the scree slopes.

Wheatear and Whinchat are reasonably numerous; Dipper and Grey Wagtail frequent the burnsides; Siskin and Crossbill can be found in some of the woods.

The Caenlochan National Nature Reserve, stretching from the Devil's Elbow to the heads of Glens Isla and Clova, covers 3,639 hectares of the upland plateau and steep glens.

Access

This is an immense area and accessible really only to dedicated hill-walkers. There are restrictions upon access to many upland areas between 1 June and 20 October. However, one of the attractions of these glens to the birdwatcher is that a good cross-section of species typical of upland eastern Scotland can be seen from the roads that wind up the valleys. Golden Eagle, in particular, can be seen relatively easily by regularly scanning the skylines with binoculars. Glen Isla is one of the better glens to explore in this way: it is remote and sparsely populated, with a good mix of habitats and species.

Short-eared Owl – display

Glen Esk is particularly noted for its Buzzards and also as a place to see Black Grouse.

Glen Clova is the only glen where Twite are regularly recorded, especially in the arable fields around Braedownie near the head of the glen. The adjacent woods hold Siskin and Crossbill.

April and May are probably the best months to visit, although October is often a good month for soaring eagles. Please park considerately and do not obstruct access.

T13 LOCH OF KINNORDY

OS ref.: NO 361539
OS map: sheet 54

Habitat

Loch of Kinnordy is an 81-hectare RSPB reserve consisting primarily of open water and freshwater marsh habitats. Willow and alder scrub fringe much of the loch, with some mature Scots pine on the drier ground. The loch is extremely nutrient rich, due to the combination of the underlying geology, drainage from the surrounding farmland and the enrichment effects of the droppings from the large bird population. The reserve is a Site of Special Scientific Interest.

Timing

Access is restricted to between the hours of 9 am and 9 pm (or sunset if earlier), April to August inclusive. During the period September through to November, the reserve is open similar hours on Sundays only. It is closed from December to March.

In addition to the breeding birds of April to July, the reserve can be good for passage waders during autumn and for wintering wildfowl from October onwards.

Access

The reserve lies 1½ miles (2.4 km) west of Kirriemuir, adjacent to the B951 road to Glen Isla. There is a regular bus service from Dundee to Kirriemuir. Paths lead from the car park to the two hides, a short distance away. Please do not venture beyond these hides.

There is a warden present from April through to August, usually based at Kinnordy Home Farm, Kirriemuir DD8 5ER.

Species

Great Crested, Black-necked and Little Grebe all breed on the loch and are usually easy to see from the hide. Eight species of duck have bred, including Wigeon, Gadwall, Shoveler, Pochard and, since 1979, Scotland's first Ruddy Ducks. The latter appear to have had poor fledging success so far, however.

A Black-headed Gull colony, numbering almost 7,000 pairs, breed on the islands of floating vegetation.

Water Rail, Snipe, Curlew and Redshank breed in the marshy areas; Sedge Warbler and Reed Bunting nest in the scrub vegetation.

Sparrowhawk regularly hunt over the reserve and Marsh Harrier summer. Osprey are regularly seen in late summer.

The woodlands hold Blue, Great, Coal and Long-tailed Tits, Treecreeper, Goldcrest, Great Spotted and Green Woodpeckers.

Calendar

Some of the more interesting species likely to be seen.

April–July: Breeding grebes and wildfowl, Water Rail, Moorhen, Coot, Snipe, Redshank and passage waders such as Ruff, Black and Bar-tailed Godwits and Greenshank. Breeding passerines include Sedge Warbler, Goldcrest, Spotted Flycatcher and Long-tailed Tit.

August–November: Several species of migrant wader may pass through during August and September, feeding on any exposed mud around the edge of the loch. Ruff, Greenshank and Spotted Redshank are all possibilities. Greylag Geese start to appear from October onwards – up to 5,000 use the loch as a roost during winter. An increasing number of Pink-footed Geese and occasional Barnacle Geese also occur. Short-eared Owl and Hen Harrier often hunt over the reserve in autumn and winter.

T14 LOCH OF LINTRATHEN

OS ref.: NO 278550
OS map: sheet 53

Habitat

This 162-hectare Scottish Wildlife Trust reserve is situated in the foot-hills of the Braes of Angus, to the north of the A926 Rattray–Kirriemuir road. The loch was created in the nineteenth century by damming Melgam Water and is the principal water supply for Dundee and Angus. Fertile farmland surrounds the loch, which is largely fringed by coniferous woodland.

Access

Loch of Lintrathen is reached by taking either the B951 from Kirriemuir, which runs along the north shore some 7 miles (11.3 km) later, or via the B954 from Alyth, turning off right at Bridge of Craigisla onto the minor road that circumnavigates the loch.

The loch is best viewed from a layby on the south-eastern shore. The SWT has a hide on the peninsula which juts out into the north-western loch but this is kept locked – keys are available to SWT members only – contact Rick Goater, The Towans, Tayock, Montrose DD10 9LE (£5 deposit).

Species

Of most interest here are the large numbers of Greylag Geese that roost on the loch in autumn and winter – up to 5,000 can be seen arriving from the adjacent farmland at dusk during late October and through November. Other wintering wildfowl include large numbers of Mallard, several hundred Tufted Duck and modest numbers of Goldeneye. Whooper Swan are regularly present often in large numbers, and Teal and Wigeon occur in small numbers.

In summer, Great Crested Grebe, Mallard and Tufted Duck can be found, Heron nest nearby and Osprey occasionally fish the loch. If the water level is low, the exposed mud can attract large numbers of Lapwing and a few passage Dunlin and Redshank.

T15 LOCH OF THE LOWES

OS ref.: NO 050440
OS map: sheets 52 or 53

Habitat

This Scottish Wildlife Trust reserve comprises the shallow, reed-fringed and inter-connected Loch of Lowes and Loch of Craiglush. Both lochs are bordered by mixed woodland, which includes Scots pine, juniper, oak, bird cherry and ash. The reserve covers 135 hectares and is designated a Site of Special Scientific Interest. It is famed for its nesting Ospreys, a new pair of which took up residence in 1991, after an absence of 8 years.

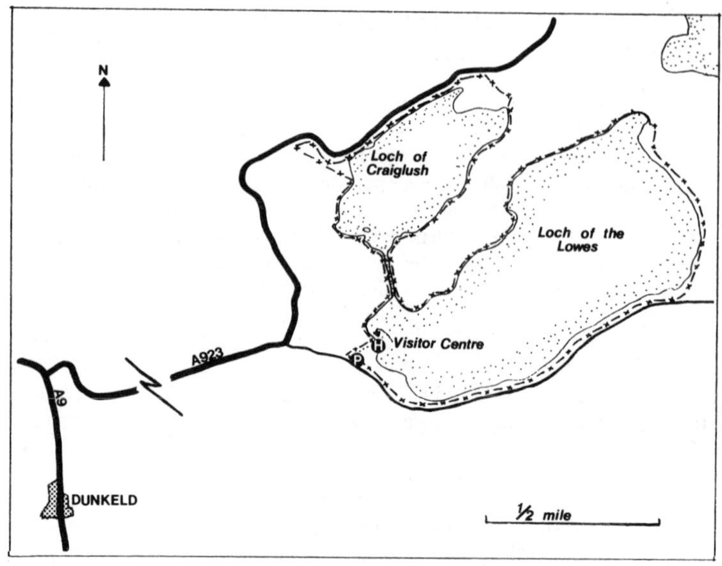

Species

During the spring and summer, the Ospreys are a major attraction, and excellent views of the nest can be obtained from the SWT hide on the loch shore. The reserve is also of interest for many other species. Little and Great Crested Grebes breed in the reed beds at the west end of the loch; Teal, Mallard and Tufted Duck are resident, except if the loch freezes in winter. Common Sandpiper, Sedge Warbler and Reed Bunting also breed. Over 1,000 Greylag Geese use the loch as a roost during the autumn: Canada Geese breed and are seen regularly.

The surrounding woodland holds Woodcock, Green and Great Spotted Woodpeckers, Treecreeper, Siskin and Redpoll. Breeding visitors include Tree Pipit, Redstart and Garden Warbler.

Access

Access to the reserve and visitor centre is from the unmarked road off the A923 Dunkeld–Blairgowrie road about 1½ miles (2.4 km) east of Dunkeld. The hide is equipped with optics during the opening hours of the visitor centre and is accessible to wheelchair users. Further along the road to the car park, a number of laybys allow the southern shore of the loch to be scanned but the observation hide is by far the best vantage point. The visitor centre contains displays explaining the conservation importance of the reserve; audio-visual programmes are shown on request. Ranger staff and volunteers are on hand to answer questions relating to the reserve or the Scottish Wildlife Trust. A limited amount of foreign language information is available.

Timing

Loch of the Lowes is important for breeding birds and wintering wildfowl: visits are therefore recommended between April and June or October and March.

The observation hide is open at all times and a visitor centre is open daily from April to September 10 am to 5 pm except mid-July to mid-August when it is open 10 am to 6 pm.

Calendar

Some of the more interesting species likely to be seen.

April–June: Osprey usually arrive back in late March or early April; Great Crested Grebe can be seen displaying during April. Woodland migrants, such as Willow Warbler, start to arrive in mid-April, although species like Sedge Warbler and Spotted Flycatcher are not usually seen until late May.

October–March: Wintering wildfowl include Goosander, Greylag Geese, Wigeon, Pochard and Goldeneye.

Reference

Loch of Lowes, compiled by Valerie M. Thom. Revised by A.H. Barclay (1990)

Reserve Ranger

Dr Alan Barclay, Loch of Lowes Visitor Centre, Dunkeld. Tel: Dunkeld 727337, April–September.

T16 LOCH FASKALLY

OS ref.: NM 930584
OS map: sheet 52

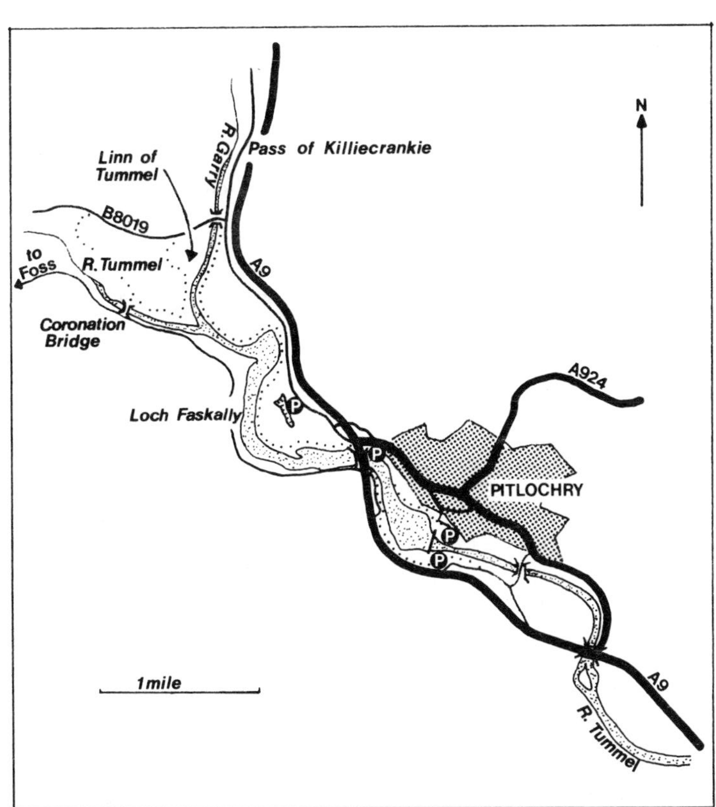

Habitat

Loch Faskally was created in the late 1940s when the River Tummel was dammed at Pitlochry for hydro-electric power generation. The loch is bordered by mature woodland, dominated by oak and beech. The policy woodlands near Faskally House are a diverse and rich songbird habitat, currently managed by the Forestry Commission.

Species

Buzzard, Green and Great Spotted Woodpeckers, Siskin and Redpoll are present all year in the woodlands. Crossbill are sometimes seen, whilst strong populations of Wood and Garden Warblers, and small numbers of Tree Pipit and Chiffchaff occur in the summer.

Red-breasted Merganser, Common Sandpiper, Grey Wagtail and Dipper frequent the loch and lochshore during summer. Kingfisher are seen in most autumns. In winter, locally important concentrations of wildfwl occur, including Little Grebe, Greylag Goose, Wigeon, Teal, Mallard, Pochard, Tufted Duck, Goldeneye and occasionally, Smew. A few Cormorant over-winter.

Access

There are car parks at the following points: (1) South of the dam at Pitlochry, next to the fish ladder (NN 935577). (2) North of the dam, signposted from the town centre (NN 936579). (3) Near the boating station beyond the Green Park Hotel, north of the town centre (NN 928587).

Loch-side paths lead off from all of these car parks. In summer, it is probably better to park at the Forestry Commission's visitor centre off the old A9, north of Pitlochry (NN 922592), where a number of waymarked paths give access to the policy woodlands and the loch side.

A circular walk around the loch can be made from any of these car parks, by making use of the paths and the minor road to Foss. The River Tummel should be crossed at the Coronation Bridge (a footbridge) and the River Garry at the old bridge at the foot of the Pass of Killiecrankie. This route takes in the Linn of Tummel (see separate entry). Alternatively, the south basin of the loch (south of the A9 bridge) can be easily circuited on paths.

T17 BEN VRACKIE

OS ref.: NN 951633
OS map: sheets 43 & 52

A reasonably accessible mountain summit approached through mainly coniferous woodland and managed heather moorland. Although the area is not exceptional for birds, it has a good range of species typical of upland east-central Scotland. Sparrowhawk and Buzzard may be seen in the woodland, whilst Kestrel, Red Grouse and Short-eared Owl occur on the moorland. Few birds are to be found at the summit, although Ring Ousel and Twite are possibilities. There are fine views of the surrounding terrain, however.

From the centre of Pitlochry, take the A924 Braemar road, turning off

Wheatears, spring

left in Moulin (behind the Moulin Inn). Follow this road for approximately 1/4 mile (0.4 km), without deviation, to a small car park (NN 945598 (Sheet 52). Allow about an hour and a half for the ascent from here to the summit of Ben Vrackie.

T18 KILLIECRANKIE

OS ref.: NN 906628
OS map: sheet 43

Habitat

The Killiecrankie RSPB reserve comprises 465 hectares of oak-dominated woodland, pastureland and birchwood, rising from the gorge of the River Garry to the crag and heather moorland 300 metres above. The area is designated a Site of Special Scientific Interest. The oak-woods which also contain ash, wych elm and alder, are of considerable botanical interest, containing a variety of ferns and mosses. Flowers such as yellow mountain saxifrage, globe flower and grass of parnassus, together with several species of orchid, are common in calcareous flushes on the hill.

Timing

The reserve is mainly of interest during the nesting season, May to July.

Access

Directions to the reserve are a little complicated. Travelling from the south, visitors should exit from the A9 immediately north of Pitlochry, onto the B8079. Follow this for 3 miles (4.8 km) through the wooded Pass of Killiecrankie. Turn left in Killiecrankie onto an unclassified road that crosses the railway and the river. Fork left up the hill and branch right after 200 metres to the car park at Balrobbie Farm. From the north, leave the A9 1½ miles (2.4 km) beyond Blair Atholl, and take the B8079 south to Killiecrankie (1½ miles (2.4 km)). Turn right onto an unclassified road and follow the directions as above.

The nearest railway station is at Pitlochry, 4 miles (6.4 km) away, on the Edinburgh to Inverness line. Buses run infrequently from Pitlochry to Killiecrankie.

Access to the waymarked trails is possible at all times. However, further exploration of the reserve requires prior arrangement with the warden (address below), who will escort parties for a modest charge.

Calendar

Some of the more interesting species likely to be seen.

All year: Sparrowhawk, Buzzard, possible long-eared Owl, Green and Great Spotted Woodpeckers in the Oak woodland; Siskin and Redpoll frequent Birch areas, whilst Black Grouse may be seen on the moorland fringe. At least one pair of Kestrel occupies the crags each year, but Raven are becoming less frequent. Golden Eagle and Peregrine are seen occasionally over the high ground.

May–July: Curlew, Tree Pipit, Redstart, Whinchat, Garden Warbler and Wood Warbler. Small numbers of Pied Flycatcher breed and have been further encouraged by the provision of nest boxes. Crossbill are occasionally seen.

Warden

Martin Robinson, Balrobbie Farm, Killiecrankie, Pitlochry PH16 5IJ. Tel: 0796 473200.

Wren

T19 LINN OF TUMMEL

OS ref.: NN 91/60
OS map: sheet 43

This area, owned by the National Trust for Scotland, lies downstream from the Pass of Killiecrankie, at the confluence of the Rivers Garry and Tummel (see map of Loch Faskally, site T16). Access is free at all times. The mainly deciduous woodland here has a good variety of breeding birds, including those to be found at the RSPB's Killiecrankie reserve.

Along the riversides, Red-breasted Merganser, Goosander, Common Sandpiper, Grey Wagtail and Dipper can be seen.

There is a visitor centre, open from April to October, at the Pass of Killiecrankie, signposted off the B8019 some 4 miles (6.4 km) north of Pitlochry.

Dippers at nest site

ADDITIONAL SITES

Site and Grid Reference	Habitat	Main Bird Interest	Peak Season
a. Arbroath NO 643405 Sheet 54	Fishing harbour – best on weekdays, when boats are returning to port	Glaucous & occasional Iceland Gulls	Oct.–May.
	Rocky shore between here & Whiting Ness (660410)	Good for Purple Sandpiper & Turnstone	Aug.–Apr.
b. Auchmithie NO 683443 Sheet 54	Beach & harbour	Kittiwake, terns & auks commuting offshore	Apr.–Aug.
	Cliffs to north	Breeding Fulmar & Puffin	May–Aug.

Site and Grid Reference	Habitat	Main Bird Interest	Peak Season
c. Carnoustie NO 560340–583352 Sheet 54.	Coast of Carnoustie, West Haven & Penbride	Passage & wintering waders	Aug.–May.
	Pitairlie Burn outflow	Large numbers of Little Gull	July.
	Craigmill Den/Penbride House grounds	Migrant warblers such as Chiffchaff, Willow Warbler & Blackcap	Apr.–May.
	Craigmill Burn (579353)	Dipper & Grey Wagtail	All year
d. East Haven NO 591362 Sheet 54	Beach car park on seaward side of railway line (reached via tunnel)	Offshore divers Little Gull often present	Oct.–May.
	Bushes & waste ground	Passerine migrants have included Yellow-browed & Barred Warblers	Sept.–Oct.
e. Forfar Loch NO 440505 Sheet 54	Small loch immediately west of the town of Forfar	Wintering wildfowl, inc. roosting Greylag, Shoveler, Tufted Duck, Pochard	Oct.–Mar.
		Build up of Coot	July–Aug.
		Migrant waders	Aug.–Oct.
f. Montreathmont Forest FC NO 575545 Sheet 54	Extensive area of old conifer plantations	Small numbers of Capercaillie (north-central sector best). Chiffchaff LE Owl, GS & Green Woodpeckers	All year
g. Rannoch Forest FC NN 58/55 Sheet 51	Birch & Caledonian pine woods on south shore of Loch Rannoch	Black Grouse, Siskin & Scottish Crossbill	All year
	A series of walks from 1 to 5½ miles (1.6–8km) long lead through the woods & along the burnsides	Breeding visitors inc. Tree Pipit, Redstart, Spotted Flycatcher	May–July.
h. Rannoch Moor Sheets 41, 42, 50 & 51	Vast area of bogs, lochans & wet moorland	Divers, Merlin, Peregrine, Greenshank & other moorland birds	May–Aug.
i. Seaton Cliffs SWT reserve No 665415 Sheet 54	Sandstone cliffs with many caves, arches & stacks	Spring & autumn migrants	Mar.–May.
		Cliff-nesting H. Martins	May–Aug.
		Good seawatching pt	May–Sept.
j. Stormont Loch SWT reserve NO 193422 Sheet 53	Inland loch with fringing fen, willow scrub & woodland	Wintering wildfowl, esp. Wigeon, Teal and Goldeneye; smaller nos of Shoveler & Tufted Duck. Breeding duck inc. Pochard & Ruddy Duck. Small no. of resident Canada Geese.	Oct.–Mar.
k. The Hermitage NTS NO 01/42 Sheet 53	Mixed conifer & deciduous woodland, steep gorge of River Braan	Common woodland species. Dipper & Grey Wagtail	Apr.–Oct.

WESTERN ISLES

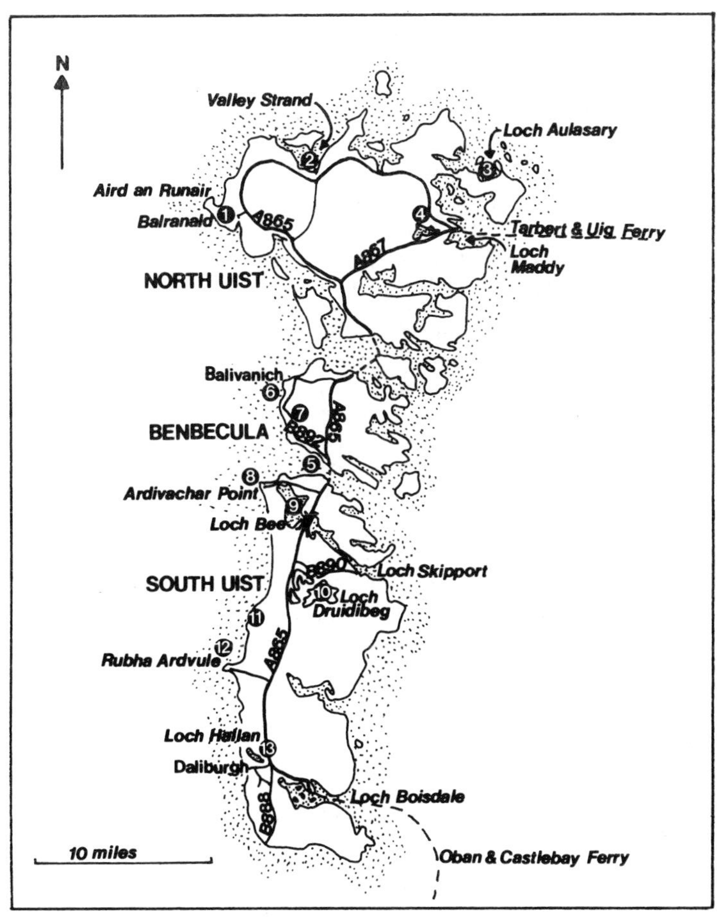

Sites

1 Balranald
2 Vallay Strand
3 Loch Aulasary
4 Loch Skealtar
5 South Ford
6 Balivanich
7 Stinky Bay and West Benbecula Lochs
8 Ardivachar Point and North Bay
9 Loch Bee
10 Loch Druidibeg
11 Peninerine
12 Rubha Ardvule
13 Loch Hallan

WI1 NORTH AND SOUTH UIST

OS map: sheets 18, 22 & 31

Habitat

This group of islands embodies the quintessence of the Hebridean environment. Two causeways nowadays link the islands of North Uist, Benbecula and South Uist, making a discrete 'unit' ideal for bird exploration. The islands are arranged in a chain just over 40 miles (64 km) long from north to south. Travelling along the main north–south road, one passes through large tracts of essentially similar habitat, but a cross-section of the islands reveals a striking zonation of habitats from the low-lying western seaboard to exposed peatlands, upland moor and blanket bog, then finally the more remote eastern coast, deeply indented with intricate sealochs. The habitat that is probably of most value to birdlife occurs as a narrow band immediately inland from the sandy beaches of the Atlantic. This area is broadly termed 'machair', and basically comprises level grasslands formed from a mixture of wind-blown sand and peat. The drier machair is generally cultivated, the crops providing cover for many nesting species. Inland of this lie the permanently wet grasslands, shallow machair lochs and grazed 'blackland' which between them hold the highest densities of breeding waders in Britain.

Species

Some of the more interesting species likely to be seen throughout the year: Little Grebe, Heron, Mute Swan, Greylag Goose, Shelduck (except autumn), Teal, Eider, Red-breasted Merganser, Hen Harrier, Buzzard, Golden Eagle, Merlin, Peregrine, Red Grouse, Golden Plover, Snipe, Redshank, Greenshank, Black-headed and Common Gulls, Black Guillemot, Rock Dove, Short-eared Owl, Rock Pipit, Stonechat, Wheatear, Raven, Twite, Reed Bunting, Corn Bunting.

Calendar

March–May: Red-throated and Black-throated Divers appear offshore by early March and quickly move inland to take up territories. By mid-March the first Lesser Black-backed Gulls are arriving. Corncrake can be heard calling from late April: between midnight and 3 am is the best time. In late April/early May the first Common Sandpipers arrive at their breeding lochans. Small numbers of Arctic Skua take up territories in the first part of May. At around this time, Common, Arctic and Little Terns start to arrive. Passage birds likely to be seen during this period include Pink-footed Goose, Greenland White-fronted Goose, Barnacle Goose, Pintail, Knot and Bar-tailed Godwit.

June–July: Great Northern Divers may linger inshore until early June, Whimbrel passage generally continues until the end of the month. Little Tern have usually departed by the end of July. Swift may occasionally be seen at this time. Southward wader passage commences, with the possibility of birds such as Quail, Knot, Sanderling and Black-tailed Godwit.

Corncrake

August–November: Autumn wader passage continues, with the possibility of Little Stint, Curlew Sandpiper, Dunlin, Ruff, Bar-tailed Godwit and Whimbrel becoming more likely. There has been a good passage of Grey Phalarope from mid-September to early October off the west coast off the west coast of South Uist in recent years. Wintering species start to arrive in October and November.

December–February: Great Northern Diver, Slavonian Grebe and possibly Scaup, Long-tailed Duck and Common Scoter may be seen offshore. Whooper Swan, Wigeon, Pochard, Tufted Duck and Goldeneye are all generally present on the freshwater lochs. Water Rail sometimes skulk in vegetated wetlands, whilst Jack Snipe and Woodcock might be found on the lower moorlands. Wintering shorebirds include Grey Plover, Purple Sandpiper, Dunlin, Bar-tailed Godwit and Turnstone. Fieldfare and Snow Bunting sometimes feed on the machair.

Seawatching calendar: Seawatching can be excellent, either from promontories such as Rubha Ardvule, Aird an Runair, or from the deck of the ferries to and from the Uists. Gannet and Kittiwake can be seen for much of the year, between March and November. From April until August large numbers of Manx Shearwater should be observable, together with a few Sooty Shearwater from June onwards, the latter often seen well into October. Arctic and Great Skuas occur throughout the period April to October and those moving off the west coast are joined during the May/June and July/August migrations by the rarer Pomarine and Long-tailed Skuas. Large numbers of the latter two species have been recorded in recent years, especially during strong westerly winds around the middle of May. Passage Leach's Petrel are regular just offshore at Rubha Ardvule in autumn, often in very good numbers.

Access

There are two car ferries operating to the Uists: (a) A service connecting Lochmaddy (North Uist), Tarbert (Harris) and Uig (Skye). (b) To Lochboisdale (South Uist) from Oban. This sailing also connects Lochboisdale with Castlebay (Barra). Check frequency of service with Caledonian MacBrayne, Ferry Terminal, Gourock PA19 1QP (tel: 0475 33755).

It is also possible to fly: (a) Via Loganair from Glasgow to Barra, and Barra to Benbecula. Contact Loganair Ltd, Glasgow Airport, Abbotsinch,

Renfrewshire (tel: 041 889 3181). (b) via British Airways from Glasgow to Benbecula. Contact British Airways, 134 Renfrew St, Glasgow (tel: 041 332 9666).

Public transport is rare and infrequent – contact the Tourist Office in Lochboisdale for details.

The uniformity of much of the moorland habitat, in particular, makes it difficult to single out specific birdwatching sites – basically the whole area is good for birds and diligent observation of the various habitat-types will eventually be rewarded by views of most of the area's 'specialities'. Most of the birds mentioned here can be best viewed from the roadside. Birds of prey, such as Golden Eagle, are most likely to be found by regularly scanning the skylines; look for Red-throated Divers flying overhead between their breeding lochans and the sea; check the fringes of lochs and marshy pools for waders; inspect the isolated stands of trees at places like Clachan, Ben Aulasary and Newton House (North Uist) and those on the B890 Lochskipport road (South Uist) for migrants; and scan the flocks of gulls at Lochmaddy and Lochbuisdale harbours and at sewage outlets such as the one at Balivanich (Benbecula) for Glaucous and Iceland Gulls. For waterfowl observation and seawatching, a telescope is almost essential.

Above all, please remember that many of the nesting birds on the Uists are extemely rare in national terms and may also be very intolerant of disturbance. Nesting divers are especially at risk, since their behaviour can be very deceptive when disturbed and this may mislead an observer into thinking that the bird is not in fact breeding at all; if you come across a diver on an inland loch, please view it *briefly* and from a safe distance before quickly moving away again.

A few outstanding areas, representative of the whole, are detailed on the following pages.

Red-throated Divers – display

NORTH UIST

1 Balranald

OS ref.: NF 70/70

This important reserve on the west coast of North Uist has been managed by the RSPB since 1966. Much of the area is croftland, using traditional farming methods which have created an ideal environment for many species of bird. To the west lies a rocky headland with sandy beaches, backed by marram-stabilised coastal dunes which shelter the arable land. Behind the dunes lies the machair, planted with oats and rye as winter feed for cattle, and providing cover for many nesting birds. Inland of this is a large tract of marshland with shallow acidic pools fringed by dense emergent vegetation. Here, sedges, rushes and iris beds all provide good nesting cover for wildfowl and waders. The reserve covers 658 hectares and has been designated a Site of Special Scientific Interest.

The entrance to Balranald is signposted 'RSPB', 2 miles (3.2 km) north-west of Bayhead, on the A865 Lochmaddy–Benbecula road. A mile (1.6 km) after taking this turn, fork left to the reception cottage at Goular. No permits are required, but visitors are asked to keep to the marked paths and to respect the crofting ground. The reserve is open year-round, but a warden is present only from April to August inclusive.

Over 180 species have been recorded on the reserve, about 50 of which breed each year. Foremost amongst these is the Corncrake, a bird which is declining throughout most of Britain: between 10 and 15 pairs can be heard each summer at Balranald. On the lochs and marshes, dense populations of duck breed, comprising mostly Mallard and Teal, but including Shoveler, Gadwall, Wigeon and Tufted Duck. Waders are particularly well represented, with about 300 pairs of Lapwing, 100 pairs each of Redshank, Oystercatcher and Ringed Plover and over 80 pairs of Dunlin nesting on the reserve. On the drier machair, Corn Bunting and Twite breed.

The headland of Aird an Runair is an excellent seawatching point, especially in spring, extending further west than any other place in the Outer Hebrides. During spring and autumn, Fulmar, Manx Shearwater, petrels, Gannet, Arctic and Great Skua, and various auks can be seen. More unusual passage seabirds also occur, such as Sooty Shearwater, Pomarine Skua and the much rarer Long-tailed Skua (see Calendar). In autumn, the best seawatching can be had from Rubha Ardvule, where large passages of petrels and shearwaters can sometimes be seen; many of these birds appear to pass west of the Monach Isles, thus missing Aird an Runair.

2 Vallay Strand

OS ref.: NF 78/74

This is perhaps the most accessible of the larger inter-tidal areas. It is most productive during autumn and winter, when large numbers of passage and wintering waders can occur. Good views over the Strand can be obtained from the main A865 road, some 10 miles (16 km) west from Lochmaddy.

3 Loch Aulasary

OS ref.: NF 95/74

Both this loch and Loch an Duin are important winter roost sites for Mute Swan. Approach along the unclassified road which leads east from the A865, 4 miles (6.4 km) out of Lochmaddy.

4 Loch Skealtar

OS ref.: NF 89/68

This is one of the most convenient lochs on which to see Red- and Black-throated Divers. The loch can be 'scoped from the A867 immediately west of Lochmaddy.

BENBECULA

5 South Ford

OS ref.: NF 77/47

Of the fords which connect Benbecula with the Uists, the South Ford is the best both in terms of numbers of waders and viewing opportunities. Birds can be watched from the causeway, or, better still, from the track which leads west, immediately south of the causeway. This joins the Ardivachar Point road at the 'Hebridean Jewellery' shop. The locality is very good from approximately 2 hours before high tide, when the waders start to get 'pushed-up' into the area between the track and the island of Gualan (NF 776470).

6 Balivanich

OS ref.: NF 76/54

The Atlantic foreshore, accessible from the B892, holds a wide variety of divers, sea-duck, waders and gulls in season.

7 Stinky Bay and West Benbecula Lochs

OS ref.: NF 77/52 etc.

These lochs have good wildfowl interest, whilst the surrounding terrain is recommended for general birding. Stinky (NF 760525) and Coot (NF 768510) Lochs are both highly recommended.

SOUTH UIST

8 Ardivachar Point and North Bay

OS ref.: NF 74/46

This headland in the north-west of the island is a good seawatching location. The point is about 4 miles (6.4 km) along the unclassified road leading westwards off the A865 just south of the Benbecula–South Uist causeway. In spring and autumn the whole of North Bay beach is also worth a look.

9 Loch Bee

OS ref. NF 77/44
A very large loch extending both sides of the A865, in the north-west of the island. More than 500 Mute Swans have been recorded using the loch in winter, and other wildfowl are often numerous. Best viewed from the main road crossing the loch.

10 Loch Druidibeg

OS ref.: NF 79/37
This important National Nature Reserve covers 1677 hectares and includes not only Loch Druidbeg itself, but the surrounding moorland and adjacent cultivated machair. The loch has an irregular outline, is shallow in profile and is studded with islands. Although the bleak surrounding terrain appears tree-less, a variety of scrub woodland thrives, especially on the islands, despite exposure to the salt-laden wind. The main A865 Lochbiosdale–Benbecula road divides this moorland part of the reserve from the more cultivated western section. This area encompasses the duneland, machair, shallow lagoons and marshes so typical of the western Uists.

The reserve can be adequately viewed from the A865, by which there is a wooden watch tower overlooking the loch, and the B890 turn-off to Lochskipport. During the breeding season closer access is permissible only to holders of a permit, issued by Scottish Natural Heritage.

Loch Druidibeg is principally renowned for its colony of breeding Greylag Geese: this has declined in the last decade, but there has been a corresponding increase in North Uist and Benbecula, where almost 250 breeding pairs were counted in 1982. In addition to the geese, the reserve holds important breeding populations of wildfowl and waders; the area is also good for watching divers, raptors such as Golden Eagle, Hen Harrier and Merlin, as well as Short-eared Owl. Corncrake, Twite and Corn Bunting frequent the dry machair west of the main road.

A small mixed wood on the B890 is worth checking for migrant and vagrant passerines.

SNH Warden
Stilligary, South Uist, Outer Hebrides.

11 Peninerine

OS ref.: NF 73/34
The coast at Peninerine and Loch a'Mhoil are good areas for migrant duck and waders. Quail can sometimes be heard in the rough grazing by the loch.

12 Rubha Ardvule

OS ref.: NF 71/29

An excellent seawatching peninsula in the centre of the west coast. It is particularly noteworthy in late summer/autumn when petrels – mainly Leach's – pass by, sometimes only a few metres offshore in good south-westerly winds. An added advantage is that these can be watched from your vehicle! Turn west onto an unclassified road, 8 miles (13 km) north of Lochboisdale on the A865. Rubha Ardvule is a further 2½ miles (4 km). Access is very occasionally restricted by military use.

13 Loch Hallan

OS ref.: NF 74/22

A rich, shallow, loch fringed with reeds in the south-west, near to the junction of the A865 and B888. Various species of wildfowl occur, often including summering Whooper Swan. The birds can be viewed without disturbance from Daliburgh cemetery, reached by taking the road westwards from the crossroads in the village and turning north onto a track after 1 mile (1.6 km).

Timing

The Uists have something to offer at any time of year, although May and June are probably the best months to visit. Spring and autumn passage can be good on both land and at sea, whilst a variety of interesting wildfowl over-winter.

References

Outer Hebrides Bird Report, nos. 1 and 2, Tim Dix and Peter Cunningham (eds.).
Birds of the Outer Hebrides, Peter Cunningham, (1983).

Recorder

Lewis, Harris, North Rona & Sula Sgeir, Flannan Isles, Shiant Isles and Rockall: Peter Cunningham, 10 Barony Square, Stornoway, Isle of Lewis PA87 2TQ.
North Uist, Benbecula, South Uist, Barra, Mingulay, Berneray, St Kilda and Monach Isles: Tim Dix, 2 Drimsdale, South Uist, Western Isles, PA 81 5RT.

ORKNEY

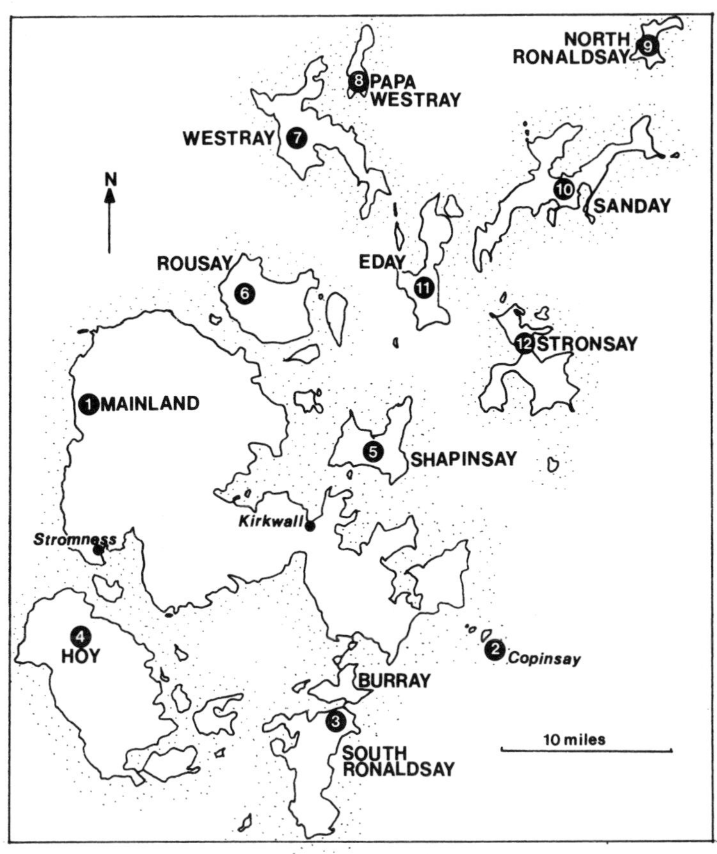

Main Sites
01 Mainland
02 Copinsay
03 Burray and South Ronaldsay
04 Hoy
05 Shapinsay
06 Rousay and Egilsay
07 Westray
08 Papa Westray
09 North Ronaldsay
010 Sanday
011 Eday
012 Stronsay

INTRODUCTION TO ORKNEY

OS map: sheets 5, 6 & 7

Orkney comprises an archipelago of 75 islands, 20 of them inhabited, covering a total of 376 sq. miles (974 sq. km). At their nearest point, the Orkney islands are only 6 miles (9.7 km) from the mainland, yet extend north-eastwards for 53 miles (85 km) and span 23 miles (37 km) from west to east.

Apart from Hoy, the islands are mostly low-lying and characterised by fertile farmland and moorland. Maritime heath is found only in relatively small parts of the west of the islands.

The islands can fairly claim to be an ornithological paradise; over 330 species have been recorded, many of them rare and recorded on only a handful of occasions within the British Isles.

We are grateful to Eric Meek, RSPB Orkney officer for supplying most of the details incorporated in this account.

Access

By sea: P&O Ferries operate a two-hour roll-on/roll-off service from Scrabster to Stromness, on the Orkney Mainland. There is a Sunday sailing from April to October, but otherwise a six-day week schedule. P&O also do a twice weekly voyage from Aberdeen to Stromness and then on to Shetland, returning to Aberdeen via Stromness again. Tel: 0856 850655 for details of the Scrabster–Stromness route; 0224 572615 for the Aberdeen–Orkney–Shetland service.

A new roll-on/roll-off service operates between Invergordon and Kirkwall six days a week – contact Orcargo Ltd., 10A Junction Road, Kirkwall, Orkney KW15 1LB. Tel. 0856 87 3838.

Alternatively, there is a passenger-only service from John O'Groats to Burwick, on the southern tip of South Ronaldsay. This 40-minute trip is run by Thomas and Bews from 29 April to 25 September, including all Sundays. Tel: 0955 81353 for details.

By air: Both British Airways and Loganair fly daily (except Sundays) to Kirkwall from Glasgow, Edinburgh and Inverness. In addition, BA have flights from Aberdeen, Loganair from Wick. Telephone the BA desk at Kirkwall airport (0856 87 3359), or Loganair (0856 87 3457) for details.

Inter-island transport: The northern isles are serviced by ferries from Kirkwall, operated by Orkney Islands Shipping Company (tel: 0856 87 2044).

Rousay, Egilsay and Wyre can be reached by roll-on/roll-off ferry from Tingwall with Orkney Islands Shipping Company.

There is a daily passenger ferry from Stromness to Moness, on Hoy (tel: 0856 850 624). In addition, a roll-on/roll-off service operates from Houton on Mainland to Lyness in southern Hoy and to nearby Flotta (tel:0856 81397).

Public transport is limited to bus routes from Kirkwall to Stromness, Kirkwall to Houton and Kirkwall to Tingwall. Details from James Peace and Co., tel: 0856 87 2868. There is a mini-bus service, 'Go-Orkney', which specialises in tours of ornithological, botanical and archaeological interest. Contact David Lea, tel: 0856 87 4260, for details of schedule.

The Orkney Tourist Board, 6 Broad St, Kirkwall, Orkney KW15 1NX will be able to help with travel information, car hire and accommodation options.

Timing

No season is a dull one on Orkney. Breeding birds dominate the interest between May and early July, with the additional bonus of spring migrants moving through during April, May and early June. Autumn passage is best from late August until mid-October; wintering species start to build up in late October and are present through until March/April, with a few lingering into early May.

Calendar

May–July: The moorlands, maritime heaths and sea-cliffs are the most obvious centres of activity at this time, although wetland and scrub habitat shouldn't be neglected either. Whimbrel and Greenshank pass through during May and early June, together with a few less common waders such as Black-tailed Godwit, Spotted Redshank and Green Sandpiper. A number of rare migrants have been recorded on Orkney during the spring in recent years, including Black Stork, Little Bustard, Terek Sandpiper, Laughing Gull, Needle-trailed Swift, Collared Flycatcher, Trumpeter Finch and Pallas's Rosefinch.

August–October: This is the peak migration period and the time when some hapless vagrant or other is most likely to make landfall. The eastern islands in the Orkney group are probably those with the highest chance of producing a rarity, particularly during a south-east wind. The passage waders mentioned for spring are also regularly seen during autumn. A wide variety of chats, warblers, flycatchers, buntings and other passerine migrants can occur, sometimes including species that are extremely rare. Some of the more regular excitements are Wryneck, Bluethroat, Yellow-browed Warbler, Red-breasted Flycatcher, Red-backed Shrike, Scarlet Rosefinch and Ortolan Bunting.

Seawatching can be excellent, with a large passage of Sooty Shearwater being especially noteworthy; the rarer shearwaters and skuas are possibilities.

October–April: Winter is a generally unproductive time of year on the moors, although Red Grouse and Short-eared Owl should be visible, whilst a visiting Rough-legged Buzzard may put in an appearance.

Wildfowl numbers greatly increase in winter, with the arrival of northern breeding birds; Loch of Harray and Loch of Stenness on the Mainland of Orkney are particularly good areas. Skeins of Greylag and other geese can be seen flying south during October. Barnacle Geese (*c.* 600–800) can be found on Switha, Swona and in the South Walls area. They also occasionally visit South Ronaldsay and Flotta. There are three flocks of Greenland White-fronted Geese: *c.* 100 at Birsay (north-west Mainland), *c.* 50 on Stronsay and *c.* 30 on East Mainland. Offshore, major concentrations of sea-fowl can be found in Scapa Flow, including large numbers of Eider and Red-breasted Merganser. Around 2,500 Long-tailed Duck feed in the relatively shallow inshore waters here during the day and fly out to roost communally in deeper waters at night. In addition, *c.* 200 Great Northern Diver and small numbers of Slavonian Grebe and Velvet Scoter are usually present. A few Little Auk winter around the islands. Waulkmill Bay, a part of the Hobbister RSPB reserve, is an ideal location from which to see a selection of these offshore species. Here, as in many other situations on Orkney a telescope can be a great advantage.

The islands are of considerable importance for winter waders; huge numbers of Curlew, nearly a quarter of the British wintering population, occupy Orkney at ths time, using the fields and shoreline. Among the other wintering shorebirds, Grey Plover, Knot, Sanderling, Purple Sandpiper and Turnstone are of especial interest, the last two species reaching numbers that qualify for national significance.

Iceland and Glaucous Gulls can often be found in the harbours at Stromness and Kirkwall.

Small numbers of Long-eared Owl are sometimes present, whilst Snow Bunting is a regular winter visitor.

O1 MAINLAND

OS map: sheet 6

Mainland is by far the largest of the Orkney islands. Irregularly shaped, it measures just less than 25 miles (40 km) at its widest and a maximum of slightly over 15 miles (24 km) north to south. It is best considered in two parts, east and west, divided by a line through Kirkwall, since each are important, but different, bird regions.

WEST MAINLAND

Habitat

The breeding bird interest here is concentrated upon three areas of heather moorland, totalling some 39 sq. miles (100 sq. km), which between them support one of the finest moorland bird communities in Britain. Numerous freshwater lochs adorn the West Mainland landscape and, despite much drainage, a number of important wetland areas survive, providing nesting habitat for ducks and waders. Another important haunt of breeding birds are the Old Red Sandstone cliffs of the west and north, which hold large colonies of nesting seabirds. Elsewhere, West Mainland is characterised by fertile fields of sown grass, grazed by cattle in summer and supporting an abundance of waders and gulls in winter.

Species

The moorland lochans support breeding Red-throated Diver, Wigeon, Teal and Red-breasted Merganser.

Hen Harriers are a speciality of the moors of West Mainland – they are generally polygamous here, with up to 100 females breeding in some years. Important populations of another vole predator, the Short-eared Owl, also occur. Small numbers of Red Grouse and several pairs of Merlin nest. Both Arctic and Great Skua breed, as do a wide range of waders, including Golden Plover, Dunlin, Snipe and exceptionally high densities of Curlew. Breeding passerines include Reed Bunting, which are common and smaller numbers of Wheatear, Stonechat, Sedge Warbler and Twite. In the absence of ground predators such as Fox, Stoat and Weasel, individuals of species such as Kestrel, Woodpigeon and Hooded Crow regularly nest on the ground.

On the larger lochs and in areas of wetland, Mallard are the most numerous of the breeding wildfowl, but Shelduck, Wigeon, Teal, Pintail, Shoveler, Tufted Duck and Red-breasted Merganser also breed. Several species of wader nest, including Dunlin, Snipe and Redshank. Rushy areas, iris beds and the more cultivated ground are the haunt of the few Corncrake that occur on West Mainland and of the more widespread Sedge Warbler and Reed Bunting.

Wildfowl numbers greatly increase in winter, with the arrival of northern breeding birds, whilst a wide variety of waterfowl and waders occur on passage.

Breeding seabird activity is concentrated on the west coast at Marwick Head, where large colonies of Kittiwake and Guillemot occur, with lesser numbers of Fulmar, Razorbill, and a few Puffin. Substantial colonies also exist at Costa Head and Row Head.

In winter the West Mainland coast is the home of a variety of visiting shorebirds. Turnstone and Purple Sandpiper feed on the rocky shores, whilst Dunlin, Bar-tailed Godwit, Redshank and Curlew are found in the more estuarine areas. Inland, Curlew are undoubtedly the most con-

Male and female Hen Harriers

spicuous of the waders using the fields as feeding and roosting sites. Peregrine and Merlin can sometimes be seen hunting over both coastal and farm habitats.

Access

1 Birsay Moors and Cottascarth RSPB reserve

OS ref.: HY 37/19

This is a 2,340-hectare moorland reserve in the north of the island. It can be reached by turning left off the A966 Finstown–Evie road, just north of Norseman Garage, 3 miles (4.8 km) from Finstown. Turn right along the track signposted Cottascarth and follow this to the hide. Further north, a second hide on Burgar Hill, near the wind generators, overlooks Lowrie's Water, where Red-throated Diver and other waterfowl can be watched. To reach this, turn off the A966 at Evie, 1½ miles (0,8 km) north-west of the B9057 junction. The Birsay moors are perhaps best viewed from the B9057 Evie to Dounby road. In the west of the area, access can be gained to the Dee of Durkadale by turning right along a rough track at the south end of Loch Hundland and following this to the ruined farm of Durkadale.

Hen Harrier and Short-eared Owl both breed; there are a few pairs of Merlin and small colonies of Arctic and Great Skua. The reserve is best visited between mid-April and mid-July.

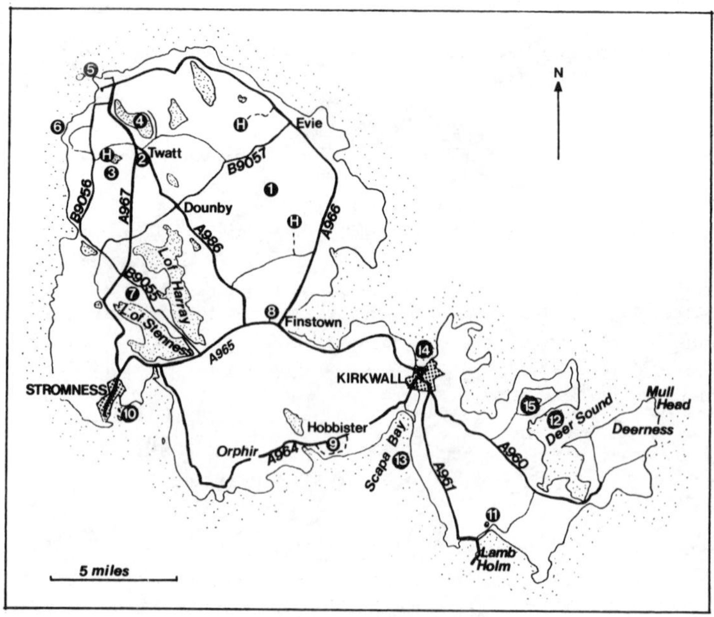

2 Loch of Banks

OS ref.: HY 27/23

This is a roosting site for Hen Harrier from October through to March and has a wildfowl and wader interest throughout the year. It is best observed from the A967/A986 roads on either side, thus reducing disturbance. Please park considerately.

3 The Loons RSPB reserve

OS ref.: HY 27/23

Located adjacent to the Loch of Ibister in the north-west of Mainland. The 64-hectare reserve, a Site of Special Scientific Interest, is basically a waterlogged marsh within a basin of Old Red Sandstone hills. It can be approached along the unclassified road leading west off the A986, just north of Twatt and 3 miles (4.8 km) from Dounby. There is a hide, open at all times, on the west side of the reserve, but access to the remainder of the area is not permissible. Emergent vegetation provides nesting habitat for both wildfowl and waders, including Wigeon, Pintail, Shoveler, Snipe and Redshank. Arctic Tern and Sedge Warbler also breed. In winter, visiting wildfowl include a flock of about 100 or so Greenland White-fronted Geese.

4 Loch of Boardhouse

OS ref.: HY 27/25

Located in the north-west of the island; the loch can be 'scoped from the A967 along the western shore and an unclassified road to the east. It is an important winter wildfowl site, especially for Pochard.

5 Brough of Birsay

OS ref.: HY 23/28

This headland at the extreme north-west of Mainland can be reached by a pedestrian causeway (closed for three hours either side of high water). Many birds can be seen from the car park on Mainland, however. It is a good sea-watching point: July to October is the best time, especially in a north-westerly wind. Species include shearwaters, petrels, skuas, gulls, terns and auks. Note: when visiting the Brough, be very watchful of the tides closing the causeway.

6 Marwick Head RSPB reserve

OS ref.: HY 22/24

A mile-long (1.6 km) cliff reserve on the west coast, including a part of Marwick Bay. The Old Red Sandstone cliffs rise to almost 100 metres and have weathered to produce abundant flat ledges for nesting seabirds. Access is possible at all times, from either the end of the minor road off the B9056 to Marwick Bay, or from the car park at Cumlaquoy, also reached by minor road off the B9056, 1 mile (1.6 km) north of the Marwick turning. There are several good viewpoints overlooking the breeding ledges, but a large part of the cliffs are not visible from land and care should be taken when near the cliff edge.

Approximately 5,000 pairs of Kittiwake and 32,000 Guillemot nest; other breeding species include Fulmar, Razorbill, a few Puffin, Rock Dove and Raven.

7 Loch of Harray and Loch of Stenness

OS ref.: HY 29/15 & 28/12

These two lochs, the largest in Orkney, are separated by a narrow peninsula which carries the B9055 road. The lochs can be viewed from surrounding roads and tracks. The car park at Ring of Brodgar is a good general observation point. Between them, the lochs hold a breeding population of around 30 pairs of Mute Swan. In winter, Greylag Geese and Whooper Swan can be seen in the fields between the lochs and those adjacent to Loch of Skaill to the north-west. Loch of Harray can hold over 10,000 wintering duck on occasion, and is one of Britain's most important sites for over-wintering Pochard. By contrast, Loch of Stenness is tidal and therefore attracts birds such as Long-tailed Duck and Goldeneye.

8 Binscarth Wood

OS ref.: HY 348140

Apart from areas of willow scrub and a few scattered bushes and stunted trees, the only woodland on West Mainland is at Binscarth, near Finstown. A track though the wood leaves the A965 on the western outskirts of Finstown. Essentially a mixture of sycamores and conifers, the wood can be attractive to passerine migrants. It contains a large rookery and often holds a winter roost of Long-eared Owls.

9 Hobbister RSPB reserve

OS ref.: HY 38/06

Although primarily a moorland reserve, Hobbister is more diverse than the Birsay and Cottascarth moors and includes elements of cliff, sand-flats and saltmarsh habitat. Access to this 759-hectare reserve is possible at any time, but is restricted to the area between the A964 and the sea. It is located 4 miles (6.4 km) south-west of Kirkwall, on the A964 road to Orphir and is entered either via the minor road on the east side of Waulkmill Bay, or along a rough track at HY 396070. The area is one of the best in Orkney for moorland breeding species and is also of interest in autumn and winter, when passage waders and wintering seafowl can be watched in Waulkmill Bay.

10 Stromness Harbour

OS ref.: HY 25/09

Considerable numbers of gulls feed in the harbour, often including 'white' gulls, such as Glaucous and Iceland Gulls in winter, with the possibility of Ring-billed Gull also.

EAST MAINLAND

Habitat and Species

The East Mainland landscape is more cultivated than that of the West. Only a narrow band of moorland remains, plus some coastal heathland areas such as those at Rose Ness and at the Mull Head in Deerness. Despite this restricted habitat, small numbers of moorland breeding birds still breed, although Herring and Lesser Black-backed Gulls tend to predominate.

Virtually all of the remainder of the area is farmed and apart from the large seabird colonies at Mull Head and the Cliffs of Noster, East Mainland has relatively limited breeding bird communities. It is however, of great significance for migrants, and rarities are regularly recorded amongst the large flocks of commoner species, such as thrushes and warblers, which sometimes arrive. Due to the extent of available habitat, however, passerine migrants tend not to be concentrated into any particular area and it is advisable to check all suitable areas of scrub, crop and other vegetation in spring and autumn.

In common with West Mainland, the coastline is an important winter habitat for visiting waders; the 1983 winter shorebird count recorded a total of 21,000 waders around the Mainland coast, dominated by the huge numbers of Curlew.

Access

11 Graemeshall Loch

OS ref.: HY 489020

Located immediately north-east of Churchill No. 1 barrier, which connects East Mainland with Lamb Holm, this inland loch can be easily viewed from the road. Several species of duck and wader breed and the extensive reed bed is good for Sedge Warbler.

12 Deer Sound

OS ref.: HY 53/07

Large inlet in the north-east, separating Deerness from the rest of East Mainland. This is an excellent area for wintering Great Northern Diver and sea-duck.

The following shallow bays/inlets in Deer Sound are good places for migrant waders between April and September: Mill Sands (HY 515080) –

view from the minor road from Tankerness to Toab, Bay of Suckquoy (HY 52/04) and St Peter's Pool (HY 54/04). The latter two can be seen from the main A960.

13 Scapa Bay

OS ref.: HY 43/07

Inlet on the south coast dividing East from West Mainland. This area can be viewed from the B9053 Scapa road at the head of the bay, just over 1 mile (1.6 km) from Kirkwall. Similar range of species as Deer Sound, with wintering seafowl providing the main interest.

14 Kirkwall Harbour

OS ref.: HY 45/11

As with Stromness harbour, large numbers of gulls can be found, often including Glaucous and Iceland Gull. The abbatoir on the Hatston Industrial Estate, to the west of the harbour, is also useful in this respect. Immediately inland from the harbour lies the enclosed Peedie Sea – a good place to watch Long-tailed Duck and Goldeneye in winter.

15 Loch of Tankerness

OS ref.: HY 51/09

A large inland loch situated on the wide peninsula which separates Inganess Bay and Deer Sound. The loch can be viewed from the road at its north-east corner. Permission from local farmers must be sought in order to cross the fields to reach the shore.

The loch is good for wildfowl from August to March and attracts migrant waders between April and September.

Timing

The bird interest of Mainland is sustained throughout the year; from May through to July, the activity is focused upon the moorland and sea-cliffs, then from August to October, wetland habitats and areas of crops or scrub become the all-important places, with coastal and offshore areas holding the main interest from late October until early May.

O2 COPINSAY

OS ref.: HY 60/01
OS map: sheet 6

Habitat and Species

The 152-hectare island of Copinsay lies some 2 miles (3.2 km) off the coast of the East Mainland. The south-east cliffs, nearly a mile (1.6 km) long and reaching about 75 metres in height, hold approximately 10,000 pairs of Kittiwake, 30,000 Guillemot and 1,000 Razorbill. Large numbers of Fulmar nest; Eider, Ringed Plover, Rock Dove, Raven and Twite also breed.

Three adjacent holms, accessible from Copinsay at low tide, have good numbers of Arctic Tern, Puffin and Black Guillemot, together with a few pairs of Common Tern. The Horse, ½ mile (0.8 km) to the north-east holds more gulls and auks.

Access

It is possible to visit Copinsay by making arrangements with the local boatman at Skaill in Deerness, East Mainland (contact S. Foubister, tel: 085 674 252). Nesting seabirds can be seen well from various cliff top vantage points, or by getting the boatman to take you underneath the cliffs.

Timing

The optimum time to visit would be between May and July, although an autumn trip could turn up any number of migrant species.

O3 BURRAY AND SOUTH RONALDSAY

OS map: sheet 7

Habitat and Species

Burray and South Ronaldsay are similar in character and birdlife to the East Mainland, to which they are attached by the Churchill Barriers. Vestiges of the former heathland support small gull and tern colonies, plus a few pairs of skuas; the remaining small lochs and wetland areas hold nesting duck and waders and on South Ronaldsay, moderately large seabird colonies exist on both the east and west coasts. For the most part, however, farming dominates the scene and the islands are of note for migrant, rather than breeding birds. In common with East Mainland, a number of rarities have occurred in recent years.

Access

The Churchill Barriers

The A961 road over these four causeways offers unrivalled opportunities for watching offshore wintering divers, grebes and sea-duck. Late April and early May is probably the best time to visit here, since birds like Great Northern Diver and Slavonian Grebe should still be present and will have moulted into their summer plumage. This is the most likely time of year to find Black-throated Diver too, an otherwise scarce bird on Orkney.

Echnaloch Bay

OS ref.: ND 47/97

An open bay on the west coast of Burray which, like the barriers, can be 'scoped from the A961. Again, sea-fowl provide the main interest.

Timing

It is probably during the autumn and winter that this area offers the best opportunities for birdwatching. A visit between late October and early May is recommended.

O4 HOY

OS map: sheet 7

Habitat

Hoy is a sparsely populated island largely dominated by heather moorland. It is the most hilly of the Orkney isles, reaching a maximum height

Great Skua harrying Arctic Tern

of nearly 500 metres at Ward Hill, in the north. The 300-metre-high sea cliffs at St John's Head, in the north-west, are amongst the highest in Britain and the rock architecture includes the spectacular 150-metre sea stack, the Old Man of Hoy.

A limited amount of arable land exists in one or two areas along the east coast and on South Walls.

Species

The moorland birdlife of Hoy is characterised by species such as Red Grouse, Golden Plover, Dunlin, Snipe and Curlew. Small numbers of Hen Harrier, Merlin and Short-eared Owl breed, whilst the island has some of the most important populations of skuas in Britain; 210–220 pairs of Arctic and circa 1,750 pairs of Great Skua were censused in 1992. In addition, the hill lochans of Hoy account for about a half of the 110 pairs of Red-throated Diver that nest on Orkney. Stonechat, Wheatear, and Twite enhance the bird interest of the island's interior.

On the cliffs, large numbers of Fulmar, Kittiwake, Guillemot, Razorbill and Puffin breed, together with many Shag, Black Guillemot and Rock Dove. Other cliff-nesting species include Buzzard, Peregrine and Raven;

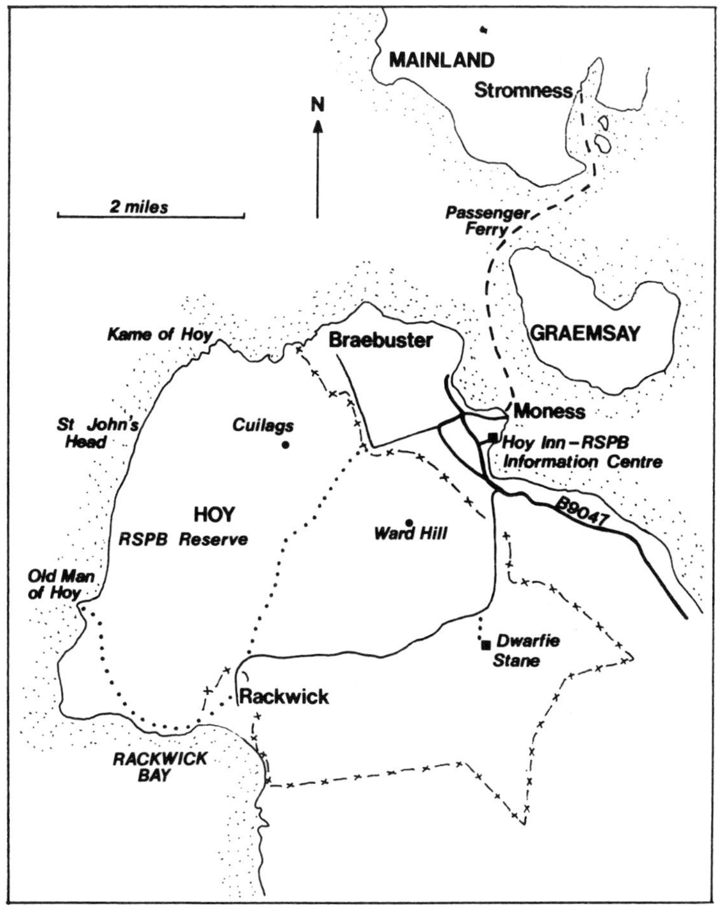

Golden Eagle have not bred since 1982, however, and are now very rarely recorded. A small but significant woodland bird community inhabits the patches of woodland/scrub (willows, birch, rowan and aspen) on Hoy, most notably at Berriedale, the most northerly native wood in Britain.

Connected to the south of Hoy is the more agricultural island of South Walls, notable for a visiting flock of over 1,000 Barnacle Geese in late winter.

Access

North Hoy RSPB reserve

OS ref.: HY 20/03

This 3,926-hectare reserve occupies the entire north-west of Hoy and includes both the summit of Ward Hill and the immense sea cliffs of St John's Head. The moorland habitats are best explored via a footpath through the glen that leads to Rackwick. From Rackwick, a second footpath heads towards the Old May of Hoy and affords fine views from the cliff top. There are no access restrictions, but visitors are asked to take especial care near the cliff edge, since it is very loose in places.

During the spring and early summer, it should be possible to see most of the moorland and coastal species mentioned above.

Small numbers of Manx Shearwater often gather off Rackwick Bay late in evening prior to coming ashore to their nesting burrows.

Timing

The ideal time to visit is from May through to July for breeding species. Hoy also attracts many migrant birds in the autumn, including the odd rare vagrant; offshore movements of the rarer shearwaters and skuas are possible. An 'out of season' trip to Hoy can therefore be very worthwhile.

Warden

Tom Prescott, Ley House, North Hoy, Orkney. Tel. Hoy 298.

O5 SHAPINSAY

OS map: sheet 6

Habitat and Species

Shapinsay is almost entirely given over to agricultural activity, with only a small remnant of moorland surviving in the south-east. Oystercatcher, Lapwing and Curlew nest on the farmland, but apart from a few skuas, gulls and terns in the south-east, the inland habitats are disappointing for breeding species.

Access

The Ouse

OS ref.: HY 505190

This shallow tidal inlet in the centre of the north coast is an important late winter gathering ground for Shelduck returning from their moulting grounds.

Mill Loch

OS ref.: HY 510190

This loch is primarily notable for the large herd of Whooper Swan that visit Shapinsay in winter. In spring, the surrounding wetlands hold breeding waders, such as Snipe and Redshank plus several species of duck, including Pintail.

Balfour Castle

OS ref.: HY 47/16

The general paucity of woodland habitats in Orkney mean that woods such as the one in the grounds of Balfour Castle are extremely significant in broadening the diversity of breeding birds. In addition, they provide shelter for a variety of migrant species.

Timing

The most interesting time to plan a trip to Shapinsay is probably the winter or early spring, when visiting swans, duck and shorebirds are present, and breeding duck and waders have returned.

O6 ROUSAY AND EGILSAY **OS map: sheet 6**

Habitat and Species

Rousay is a hilly and generally uncultivated island. The breeding bird community of the island's interior is impressive, with Red-throated Diver on the hill lochs and Hen Harrier, Merlin, Curlew, Golden Plover, five species of gull and Short-eared Owl on the heather moor. The numerous small crags have encouraged Fulmar to nest inland. A few Common Sandpiper nest – a relatively scarce breeding bird on Orkney.

Woodland at Trumland House and Westness serves to further diversify the bird interest of the island.

Egilsay, 1 mile (1.6 km) to the east of Rousay, is particularly notable for its many small lochs, which hold breeding ducks, waders and Black-headed gulls. In winter, the coastline of Egilsay can support up to 1,000 waders, including large populations of Purple Sandpiper and Turnstone. Large numbers of divers and sea-duck also winter, using the relatively sheltered sounds between Rousay, Egilsay and Wyre. This has been the wintering area for a single adult White-billed Diver in recent years.

Access

A fery service operated by Orkney Islands Shipping Company connects Tingwall (Mainland) with Rousay, Egilsay and Wyre (see Introduction)

Quandale and Brings Heathlands

OS ref.: HY 38/34

These two maritime heaths in the north-west of Rousay are the breeding haunt of up to 4,000 pairs of Arctic Tern and 100 pairs of Arctic Skua. A few Great Skua also nest. The western cliffs here hold large numbers of seabirds, including Fulmar, Kittiwake, Guillemot and Razorbill.

Trumland RSPB Reserve

OS ref.: HY 430280

This 433-hectare moorland reserve lies in the south of the island, above Trumland House. Access is possible at all times, but between April and August visitors are requested to contact the summer warden at Trumland Mill Cottage, who will escort them around the reserve. Red-throated Diver, Hen Harrier and Golden Plover breed, whilst Merlin, Arctic and Great Skua, plus Short-eared Owl may be seen.

Eynhallow Sound

OS ref.: HY 38/27

The mile-wide (1.6 km) sound between Rousay and Mainland is an important wintering area for Great Northern Diver, Eider and Long-tailed Duck; smaller numbers of Velvet Scoter and Red-breasted Merganser are also usually present.

The sound can be 'scoped from either the Brock of Gurness (HY 382269) on Mainland, or from the south Rousay coastline. The ferry also makes a good observation platform.

Timing

The best time for moorland species and seabirds is from mid-May until July, but the chance of a rare migrant might make a September/October visit worthwhile. Wintering seafowl and shorebirds complete the year-round attractions of these islands. Great Northern Diver and Long-tailed

Duck numbers build up considerably in late April, prior to their northward departure.

O7 WESTRAY

OS map: sheet 5

Habitat and Species

The breeding bird interest of Westray is dominated by the huge seabird colonies on the island's west coast, between the RSPB's reserve at Noup Head and the headland of Inga Ness, some 5 miles (8 km) to the south. Around 60,000 Guillemot, 3,000 Razorbill and 30,000 pairs of Kittiwake are estimated to nest on these cliffs, as well as smaller numbers of Shag, Puffin and Black Guillemot.

Immediately inland from these cliffs, an area of maritime heath supports populations of up to 2,000 pairs of Arctic Tern and 50 pairs of Arctic Skua. In addition, Eider, Oystercatcher, Ringed Plover and four species of gull breed.

Several freshwater lochs and associated wetland areas have breeding wildfowl and waders and these are good areas for over-wintering birds. A few Corncrake still call from suitable habitat.

Coastal waders are numerous in winter, especially Purple Sandpiper and Turnstone on the rocky shorelines and Sanderling on the sandy bays.

Access

Westray can be reached by both passenger ferry and air from Kirkwall. (See Introduction).

The following locations are recommended for initial exploration:

Noup Head RSPB reserve

OS ref.: HY 39/50

This western promontory is approached from Pierowall by following the minor road to Noup Farm and then the track to the lighthouse – a total distance of just over 4 miles (6.4 km). The RSPB owns 1½ miles (2.4 km) of cliff, designated a Site of Special Scientific Interest, which hold one of the highest densities of nesting seabirds in Britain. Inland, just off the reserve, Arctic Skua and Arctic Tern breed on the heathland.

Despite its westerly position, Westray occasionally picks up continental migrants and these tend to get concentrated at Noup Head.

Stanger Head

OS ref.: HY 511428

A broad headland in the south-east of the island. It is perhaps the easiest place on Westray to see Puffin.

A track leads to the coast here from Clifton, near the B9066, just over 6 miles (9.7 km) south of Pierowall.

Aikerness Peninsula

OS ref.: HY 45/52

The most northerly part of Westray, upon which is situated the airstrip. Follow the minor road north from Pierowall towards the airfield, branching north to the triangulation point above the coast 3 miles (4.8 km) later. Black Guillemot are relatively easy to watch along the north-west shore here.

Loch of Burness

OS ref.: HY 429481

An inland loch situated immediately west of Pierowall and visible from several surrounding tracks. This is one of the most productive of Westray's freshwater lochs, inhabited by Britain's northernmost Little Grebe and the haunt of Mute Swans, Teal, Shoveler, Tufted Duck, Moorhen and Coot. Around the margins can be found waders such as Snipe and Redshank.

Timing

A spring visit is recommended, between mid-May and mid-July.

O8 PAPA WESTRAY

OS map: sheet 5

Habitat

Papa Westray, or 'Papay' amongst Orcadians, is Westray's diminutive north-eastern satellite, separated from it by just over a mile (1.6 km) of water.

Species

The bird interest is focused upon the maritime heathland at the north of the island, which is managed as a reserve by the RSPB under an agreement with the local crofting community. This area holds one of Britain's largest Arctic Tern colonies, with an average of around 6,000 pairs attempting to nest in most years. Other large tern colonies, often including small numbers of Common and Sandwich Terns, are located in the south of the island at Sheepheight and Backaskaill.

Most of the remainder of Papay is cultivated ground and until recently, the traditional crofting practices that are employed here maintained a healthy population of Corncrake, perhaps numbering as many as 15 pairs. In 1988, however, no pairs were recorded.

Access

Papa Westray can be reached by both passenger ferry and by air from Kirkwall and Westray. (See Introduction).

North Hill RSPB reserve

OS ref.: HY 49/54

This 206-hectare Site of Special Scientific Interest occupies the northern-most quarter of Papay, and represents one of the best examples of maritime heath in Scotland. The reserve is flanked by low cliffs on its east coast – possibly the last breeding site in Britain for the now extinct Great Auk – and is otherwise bordered by a low-profile, rocky shoreline.

North Hill is reached by following the island's principal road northwards to its end. Between mid-April and mid-August, visitors are requested to contact the warden in advance of their arrival to arrange an escorted tour of the nesting colonies, which may be viewed well from the perimeter path. On arrival on the island, the warden can be found at Rose Cottage.

As a consequence of its huge Arctic Tern population, North Hill supports a colony of 150 or so pairs of Arctic Skua, which specialise in pirating the terns' prey. Eider, four species of gull and several species of wader also breed. The highest section of cliff, Fowl Craig, holds a respectably sized seabird colony of approximately 2,000 Guillemot, 1,500 Kittiwake and lesser numbers of Razorbill and a few Puffin. Up to 80 pairs of Black Guillemot nest in the boulder beach surrounding the reserve.

Mull Head, at the northern tip of Papay, can be an excellent sea-watching vantage point in late summer and autumn – Sooty Shearwater and Long-tailed Skua have been regularly recorded in recent years.

RSPB Warden: c/o Rose Cottage, Papa Westray KW17 2BU. Present from mid-April to August.

Holm of Papa

OS ref.: HY 51/52

The Holm is a small island situated mid-way down Papay's east coast and only a few hundred metres offshore. Its ornithological significance lies in the 130 or so pairs of Black Guillemot that breed on its north-eastern shore – probably the largest colony in Britain. Many gulls, terns and a small colony of Storm Petrel also breed.

Loch of St Tredwell

OS ref.: HY49/51

A large loch in the south-east of the island. This was a former breeding site of Red-necked Phalarope. It is still good for a variety of breeding wildfowl and waders.

Timing

Mid-May to July is the ideal time to visit for the breeding species, but August through to mid-October could prove interesting for sea-watching and for migrants. Papay is well situated to receive spring and autumn migrant birds and easterly winds, in particular, have produced some good rarities. Diligent searching of scrub vegetation and other cover is recommended.

O9 NORTH RONALDSAY

OS map: sheet 5

Habitat

North Ronaldsay is the most north-easterly of the islands in the Orkney archipelago and is separated from neighbouring Sanday by 3 miles (4.8 km) of open water. Measuring about 3 miles by 1 mile (4.8 by 1.6 km), the island has an area of approximately 5 square miles (13 sq. km). The coastline is predominantly rocky, with the exception of sandy beaches on the east and south shores. Inland, the ground rises to a maximum of 18 metres above sea level and is largely cultivated, the agricultural land being enclosed within a wall known as the Sheep Dyke. The island has six main lochs, some of which have fringing vegetation and associated wetlands. Overall, there are many similarities (in size, population and land use) with Papa Westray.

In 1987 the North Ronaldsay Bird Observatory was established in a modern, energy conserving building heated entirely by solar and wind energy, located in the south-west of the island. The upgrading of the present dormitory accommodation will be complete by spring 1993. This will provide five four-bedded dormitories and four twin/double rooms, including one with en-suite facilities suitable for use by the disabled.

Species

A total of 51 breeding species have been recorded, of which 34 currently breed regularly. A survey of breeding birds in 1987 recorded over 200 Fulmar nests, approximately 700 pairs of Black-headed Gull, around 1,000 pairs of Arctic Tern and over 450 Black Guillemot (individuals). A colony of over 50 pairs of Cormorant can be found on Seal Skerry, Orkney's most northerly extremity. Other confirmed breeding species included Mute Swan, Shelduck, Gadwall, Teal, Mallard (*c.* 50 pairs), Pintail, Shoveler, Eider, Water Rail, Moorhen, Coot, Oystercatcher, Ringed Plover, Lapwing, Snipe, Curlew, Redshank, Common and Herring Gulls, Sandwich Tern, Rock Dove, Skylark, Meadow and Rock Pipits, Pied Wagtail, Wren, Blackbird, Hooded Crow, Starling, House Sparrow, Twite and Reed Bunting. In addition, Raven have bred annually in recent years. Corncrake were at one time abundant, but are now rare and breeding has not been confirmed since 1981.

The accidental introduction of the hedgehog to the island in 1972 has led to declines in the populations of a number of ground nesting birds. Scores of hedgehogs have now been deported from the island (mostly to

SWT mainland reserves) in order to reduce nest predation.

A good variety of wildfowl and waders 'stage' on the island during the autumn. Particularly obvious are the large number of Golden Plover which are present from July–April. In recent years these have included a few vagrant Pacific and American Golden Plovers. North Ronaldsay is ideally situated to receive continental passerine migrants. Large 'falls' are possible in south-easterly winds and rarities are regularly found amongst the more predictable passage migrants such as pipits, warblers, chats and flycatchers. Reliable scarce migrants include Icterine, Barred and Yellow-browed Warblers, Red-breasted Flycatcher, Red-backed Shrike and Common Rosefinch. In recent years, rarities such as Great Snipe, Pechora, Red-throated and Olive-backed Pipits, Blyth's Reed Warbler, Sardinian Warbler, Isabelline Shrike, Spanish Sparrow, Pallas's Rosefinch and Pine Bunting have all been recorded. During a 'fall', birds can be everywhere, taking shelter in the Sheep Dyke, crops and croft gardens. The wind-lashed sycamores and fuchsias of the walled garden at Holland House tend to concentrate migrants and this is a particularly likely location for rare birds.

Sea-watching can be very productive, especially from the old beacon in the north-east of the island. Large passages of Fulmar have been witnessed, Sooty Shearwater are regular in autumn and Leach's Petrel, Long-tailed Skua and Sabine's Gull also occur.

For details of accommodation, contact: The Warden, North Ronaldsay Bird Observatory, Orkney KW17 2BE. Tel: 08573 267.

References

'The Breeding Birds of North Ronaldsay', M.G. Pennington, *Scottish Birds*, vol. 15 (1988).

O10 SANDAY

OS map: sheet 5

Habitat

Sanday, the largest of the northern Orkney isles, has a predominantly low-profile coastline backed by dunes and machair. Inland, the sandy soils support an agricultural regime based largely upon beef production. Althouth the big sea cliffs that are such a feature of many other islands are conspicuous by their absence on Sanday and only a very limited area of moorland exists, the island is none the less an important place for birds.

Species

The coastal habitats support large numbers of breeding Ringed Plover and there are substantial colonies of Arctic Tern at Westayre Loch, Start Point, and Els Ness. Small numbers of Corncrake and a few Corn Bunting remain.

Access

Lady Parish

By virtue of its position in the Orkney archipelago, the island's north-eastern arm attracts a considerable number of migrants and a close scrutiny of the available cover during spring and autumn could be well worthwhile.

The shallow lochs around Northwall (HY 75/44) are good for breeding wildfowl, including Teal, Wigeon, Shoveler, Tufted Duck, Red-breasted Merganser and Eider. Waders, such as Snipe, Redshank and Dunlin also breed. North Loch is often host to large numbers of visiting Whooper Swan in the early winter, as well as a variety of other northern wildfowl.

Gump of Spurness

OS ref.: HY 60/35

This hill is situated in the extreme south-west of Sanday and is the only remaining area of heather moor on the island. It holds in the order of 25 pairs of Arctic Skua. Short-eared Owl may be found hunting here and over the dunes.

Timing

Sanday is probably of greatest interest for its visiting birds; spring and particularly autumn are likely to be productive for migrants, whilst in winter, the shoreline of Sanday can hold over 7,500 waders, including Grey and Golden Plovers, Turnstone, Purple Sandpiper, Sanderling and Bar-tailed Godwit.

O11 EDAY

OS map: sheet 5

Habitat

The moorland-dominated island of Eday, some 8 miles (13 km) long and a maximum of 2½ miles (4 km) wide, lies centrally between the extremities of Westray and Sanday.

Species

The moors hold over 100 pairs of Arctic and a few pairs of Great Skua. Curlew, Snipe and occasionally Golden Plover also nest. A half dozen or so pairs of Whimbrel are of especial interest – Eday is one of only two Orkney breeding sites.

Large numbers of Fulmar and Herring Gull nest at Red Head, at the north of the island, although the best seabird colonies are on The Calf, notably at Grey Head, where Guillemot, Razorbill and Kittiwake breed and at the southern end, where a large Cormorant colony is established. Black Guillemot breed around the rocky shoreline of Eday and the small islands off the west coast; there is a small Cormorant colony on the Green Holms.

Access

During general exploration of the island, check the following localities in particular:

Mill Loch

OS ref.: HY 565368

This probably has the highest concentration of Red-throated Diver in Britain – at least eight pairs attempt to nest each year.

Carrick House

OS ref.: HY 567384

Two small woods near to the house provide ideal cover for migrants.

Timing

Visit between May and July for the moorland and coastal breeding birds; either a spring or autumn visit might produce good migrant birds.

O12 STRONSAY

OS map: sheet 5

Habitat and Species

With the exception of an area of moorland on the south-west peninsula of Rothiesholm, Stronsay is very much an agricultural island. Although the moorland bird community is one of the island's principal attractions, Stronsay also has considerable colonies of seabirds, concentrated on the east coast between Odness and Lamb Head.

Many of the island's lochs and associated wetlands are breeding haunts for wildfowl and waders, including Pintail, Shoveler, Snipe and Redshank. Corn Bunting, a species very much associated with traditional land use practices, still occurs on Stronsay, but is probably declining. Corncrake have not been heard for two years, however. Quail nest in some years.

Due to increased coverage by birders, Stronsay has recently gained a reputation as an excellent place for migrants. The island's wetland habitats are extremely valuable for passage waders in spring and autumn, whilst the fuchsia hedges that grow both within and outside the island's gardens, provide excellent cover for some migrant passerines. Amongst an impressive list of recently recorded rarities are records of American Golden Plover, Snowy Owl, Bee-eater, Olive-backed Pipit, Pied Wheatear, Subalpine, Greenish, Pallas's and Radde's Warblers, Rose-coloured Starling, Arctic Redpoll, Rustic and Little Buntings and two new species for Orkney: White's Thrush and Tawny Pipit.

The island boasts a large wintering population of wildfowl, including up to 250 Whooper Swan and 50 Greenland White-fronted Geese, in addition to large numbers of dabbling and diving duck.

Visiting shorebirds, including important populations of Ringed Plover, Purple Sandpiper and Turnstone, are a conspicuous feature of the winter scene on Stronsay.

Access

There is a twice daily place service (not Sundays) to Stronsay. In addition, a twice daily Ro-Ro ferry service operates from Kirkwall (not Sundays in winter).

Rothiesholm peninsula

OS ref.: HY 61/22

(Pronounced 'Rowsum'.) During the breeding season, the moorland is the domain of some 40 pairs of Arctic and several pairs of Great Skua, five species of gull, several hundred pairs of Arctic Tern and various species of wildfowl and wader. Red-throated Diver and Twite also nest, making this one of the best areas in the northern group of islands for moorland birds.

The surrounding cliffs are tenanted by Fulmar, Black Guillemot and small numbers of Shag, Guillemot and Razorbill.

Leave the B9061 at the old school. Access permission should be sought at Bu Farm. Park and follow the track east of the school for 400 metres south to gain access to the moorland. There are some electrified fences in this area at present, so caution is required!

Two excellent wader lochs, Mount Pleasant Loch and Bu Loch, lie adjacent to the B9061 and can be viewed en route to Rothiesholm.

Mill Bay/Meikle Water

OS ref.: HY 66/26 & 66/24

The sheltered waters of Mill Bay are excellent for sea-duck and divers, whilst the sandy beach is good for waders such as Bar-tailed Godwit and Sanderling. The area near the old mill is very good for migrant passerines and is most picturesque. Meikle Water holds duck throughout the year and plays host to a large winter population of Whooper Swan, White-fronted and Greylag Geese, as well as over 1,000 duck. Large numbers of waders also winter in the area.

To reach Mill Bay, leave the main road opposite the old mill and visit the private Stronsay Bird Reserve for local bird news. Meikle Water is best viewed from the main road which runs around its perimeter.

Timing

Visit between May and July for the moorland and coastal breeding birds; either a spring or autumn visit should produce good migrant birds.

Note: Guided bird tours, boat trips and various types of accommodation can be arranged by contacting John and Sue Holloway, 'Castle', Stronsay. Tel: 08576 363.

RSPB Orkney Officer

Eric Meek, Smyril, Stenness, Stromness, Orkney, KW16 3JX. Tel: 0856 850176.

Managing Warden, RSPB Orkney

Keith Fairclough, Viewforth, Swannay, by Evie, Orkney, KW17 2NR. Tel. 0856 72 210.

References

Birds of Orkney, C. Booth, M. Cuthbert and P. Reynolds (1984).
Islands of Birds: A Guide to Orkney Birds, Eric Meek (1985).
The Orkney Islands Reserves, RSPB leaflet.
The Birds of Stronsay, J. Holloway (1991).

SHETLAND

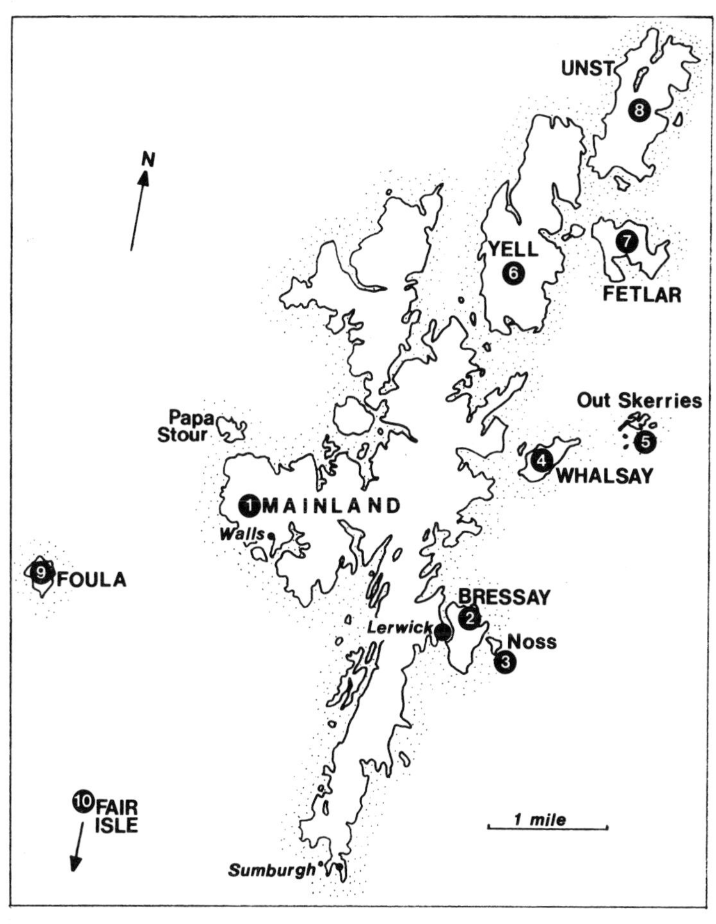

Main Sites

SH1 Mainland
SH2 Bressay
SH3 Noss
SH4 Whalsay
SH5 Out Skerries
SH6 Yell
SH7 Fetlar
SH8 Unst
SH9 Foula
SH10 Fair Isle

INTRODUCTION TO SHETLAND

OS map: sheets 1, 2, 3 & 4

Shetland comprises an archipelago of over 100 islands, for the most part north of 60°N latitude. Its topography is characterised by long peninsulas and deeply penetrating inlets (voes), firths and sounds, most of which are old river valleys drowned when the sea rose after the last ice age. There are many scattered sandy and gravel beaches in the sheltered 'inner' coastline and in places these have formed spits, bars and tombolos which jut out into the sea, occasionally extending across the entrances of voes to completely enclose them, as at Loch of Spiggie in the south Mainland. Apart from these beaches, the coast is predominantly rocky and there are several outstanding sea cliffs, some rising to over 300 metres.

Inland, the rugged moorland terrain rises to an average maximum of around 250 metres, the two obvious exceptions being the summits of Ronas Hill and Foula, which both exceed 400 metres. Innumerable peaty lochans fragment the landscape, which is exposed and largely treeless, with the exception of a few small areas of planted woodland, scrub and bushes. The weathering of exposed limestone outcrops and the accumulation of wind-blown sand containing shell fragments have produced patches of relatively fertile ground, enabling many areas to be cultivated.

Access

P&O operate a passenger and vehicle ferry service from Aberdeen to Shetland almost daily. Departure from Aberdeen and Lerwick is at 6 pm, arriving at 8 am the following morning. From the end of May through to mid-September, there is a weekly service between Shetland and Orkney. Details are available from P&O Ferries, PO Box 5, Jamieson's Quay, Aberdeen AB9 8DL. Tel: 0224 572615.

British Airways operate four flights a day from Aberdeen to Sumburgh Airport, on the southern tip of Shetland, Monday to Friday, with reduced service on Saturday and Sunday. The journey time is a little less than one hour. BA also operate a flight from Inverness via Orkney. Telephone British Airways at Sumburgh (0950 60345) for details.

Loganair also fly to Shetland, operating a daily service from Edinburgh and Glasgow to Sumburgh. From mid-May to October, the service operates via Fair Isle and Orkney on Saturdays. Contact Loganair at Tingwall for details. Tel: 059584 246/7.

Public transport on Shetland is very limited, although much of Mainland can be explored in this way; personal transport is preferable, however, since it affords the opportunity to stop and scan roadside lochans, investigate patches of scrub for possible migrants, or deviate from planned routes. Cars make excellent mobile hides, both for bird photography and general birdwatching. Car hire is available as an alternative to bringing a car across on the ferry, although neither option is cheap.

There are frequent ferries to most of the other inhabited islands with drive-on/drive-off services to the islands of Unst, Yell, Whalsay, Fetlar, Out Skerries and Bressay. Advance booking is advisable, especially in summer. Loganair operate a daily (except Sunday) inter-island air service from Tingwall Airport to Whalsay, Fetlar and Unst, with weekly flights to Foula and Out Skerries, plus three flights per week to Fair Isle.

An inexpensive Inter-Shetland Transport Timetable is published by the Shetland Tourist Organisation; this contains details of all air, sea and road services. Contact STO, Market Cross, Lerwick ZE1 0LU. Tel: 0595 3434.

Timing

Shetland is a magical place in any season and there is certainly much to see throughout the year. Breeding birds are best seen between late May and mid-July, migrants mid-April to early June and mid-August to the end of October, whilst wintering sea- and wildfowl are present from October through to March. Rarities are probably most likely in May, September and October, depending on weather conditions. Easterly and south-easterly winds are essential for good 'falls' of migrants, whereas north-westerlies are virtually useless.

Day length is a major asset in the spring and summer, when the sun is above the horizon for almost 19 hours a day, but by December this is reduced to less than six hours and this fact should be an important consideration when planning a winter visit.

Species

An increasing population of Fulmar (currently around 150,000 pairs) breed; modest numbers of Manx Shearwater, thousands of Storm Petrel and small numbers of Leach's Petrel also breed (the latter on Foula and Ramna Stacks); Gannet first bred in 1914 and now number well over 10,000 pairs, mainly at Hermaness and Noss; there are an estimated 10,000 pairs of Shag breeding and 400 pairs of Cormorant; six species of gull nest, including large numbers of Herring and Great Black-backed Gulls and circa 45,000 pairs of Kittiwake; approximately 150,000 Guillemot, 20,000 Razorbill, 250,000 Puffin and 2,000 Black Guillemot breed. In addition, over 5,600 pairs of Great and 1,900 pairs of Arctic Skuas nest on the maritime heathlands and 30,000 or more pairs of Arctic Tern and smaller numbers of Common Tern nest.

The inland lochans hold more than 600 pairs of Red-throated Diver, around 15,000 Eider and small numbers of Teal, Tufted Duck and Red-breasted Merganser also breed. Between one and five pairs of Common Scoter regularly attempt to breed.

Breeding waders include large numbers of Oystercatcher, around 500 pairs of Ringed Plover, many hundred Golden Plover, Lapwing, Snipe, Curlew and Redshank, *c* 400 pairs of Whimbrel and smaller numbers of Dunlin and Common Sandpiper. There is a small population of breeding Red-necked Phalarope and one or two pairs of nesting Black-tailed Godwit.

Merlin breed in small numbers, but Peregrine have not bred in recent years. Hen Harrier and Buzzard are irregular visitors but have been recorded in all months except July. Snowy Owl last bred in 1975, but one or two birds are still resident and can usually be found on Fetlar or Unst.

Breeding passerines include strong populations of Skylark, Rock and Meadow Pipits, Blackbird, Wheatear and the Shetland subspecies of Wren and Starling. Rook breed at Kergord and Raven and Hooded Crow are both common. Twite frequent the cliffs and a few pairs of Reed Bunting breed in areas of adjacent meadow.

Species that occasionally over-summer include Great Northern Diver, Whooper Swan, Pintail, Wigeon (breed), Shoveler (breed), Long-tailed Duck, Velvet Scoter, King Eider, Purple Sandpiper, Turnstone, Long-eared Owl, Redwing and Fieldfare (both have bred) and Snow Bunting.

Calendar

May–July: The peak period for spring migrants is from April to early June, otherwise it is the breeding birds of the moorlands and sea cliffs which are the most obvious attractions at this time of year (see above).

Passage raptors such as Sparrowhawk and Kestrel occur, with occasional records of Honey Buzzard, Marsh Harrier, Osprey and even Red-footed Falcon and Hobby.

Knot, Dunlin, Bar-tailed Godwit, Curlew, Redshank, Common Sandpiper and small numbers of Sanderling pass through in May/early June; there are also passages of Purple Sandpiper and Snipe in April/May. Other migrating waders include scarcer species such as Temminck's Stints, Ruff, Black-tailed Godwit, Spotted Redshank, Greenshank and Green and Wood Sandpipers.

Arctic and Great Skuas return from April onwards, whilst Pomarine and Long-tailed Skuas can very occasionally be seen offshore, sometimes in very large numbers.

Lesser Black-backed Gull return in late March/early April, followed by Common and Arctic Terns in May.

Small numbers of Long-eared and occasional Short-eared Owls move through from April to early May.

South-easterly winds produce the best number and variety of passerine migrants. These include large numbers of thrushes, chats, warblers, flycatchers and buntings, although autumn passage is generally more impressive. The occurrences of some species, however, are more frequent in the spring. These include common migrants such as Tree Pipit, Dunnock, Whitethroat and Spotted Flycatcher, less numerous ones such as Grasshopper and Sedge Warblers, and scarcer species like Hoopoe, Bluethroat, Golden Oriole, Red-backed Shrike and Ortolan Bunting.

August–October: This is the peak migration period and a time when almost anything can turn up; again, south-easterly winds are usually required.

Whooper Swan passage usually begins in late September, together with flocks of Greylag and Pink-footed Geese plus a few Barnacle and (rarely) Brent Geese.

As in spring, migrants raptors are again likely – Rough-legged Buzzard frequently occur in October and may linger through the winter.

Passage waders include all those mentioned for spring, with departing Oystercatcher, Ringed Plover, Golden Plover and Lapwing being joined by passage birds. Sightings of Dotterel are not unusual during August; Common Sandpiper, Whimbrel and Red-necked Phalarope depart in late July/early August; a few Little Stint and Green Sandpiper usually pass through soon afterwards, with the bulk of wader passage occurring in September and October. These include small numbers of Grey Plover, Knot, Sanderling, Curlew Sandpiper, Ruff, Black-tailed Godwit, Spotted Redshank and Greenshank as well as the more numerous Dunlin, Bar-tailed Godwit, Whimbrel, Curlew, Redshank and Turnstone. There is a small Woodcock passage in mid-October. Over-wintering Purple Sandpiper arrive in late September.

A wide variety of chats, warblers, flycatchers, buntings and other passerine migrants can occur, including Yellow and White Wagtails, Dunnock, Robin, Redstart, Stonechat, Wheatear, Ring Ousel, Reed Warbler, Garden Warbler, Blackcap, Chiffchaff, Willow Warbler, Goldcrest, Spotted Flycatcher, Chaffinch, Brambling, Greenfinch, Siskin, Twite, Redpoll, Snow Bunting and Reed Bunting. In addition, large flocks of Blackbird, Fieldfare, Song Thrush and Redwing pass through in September–November.

Some of the more regular scarce migrants are Wryneck, Icterine, Barred and Yellow-browed Warblers, Red-breasted Flycatcher, Lapland Bunting and Scarlet Rosefinch. Shetland is renowned for its rare migrants, but these can be difficult to predict – almost anything is possible! All potential cover should be checked for birds: rarities recorded in recent years include Black-throated Thrush, White's Thrush, Lanceolated, Aquatic, Booted, Radde's, Dusky, Ruppell's, Yellow, Blackpoll and Chestnut-sided Warblers, Isabelline and Brown Shrikes and White-throated Sparrow.

Sea-watching in autumn can be good, with a large passage of Sooty Shearwater in late August and September being especially noteworthy; the rarer shearwaters and skuas are also possibilities.

November–April: Offshore, up to 400 Great Northern Diver, small numbers of Red-throated Diver and occasional Black-throated and even White-billed Divers occur. An individual of the latter species which returned to the Whalsay ferry area for nine successive winters was last seen in the winter of 1990/1. Slavonian Grebe can be seen in some of the voes and other grebe species are sometimes recorded. Large numbers of Eider and Long-tailed Duck over-winter; smaller populations of Goldeneye and Red-breasted Merganser are also present. Very small numbers of Common and Velvet Scoter are present and King Eider are recorded in most winters. Wintering Guillemot and Black Guillemot occur in many voes and Little Auk can be numerous in some years.

Wildfowl numbers greatly increase in winter, with the arrival of northern breeding birds; birds seen on inland waters at this time include Whooper Swan, small numbers of Greylag Geese, 200–300 Wigeon, Teal, Mallard, 300–500 Tufted Duck, Goldeneye and Red-breasted Merganser. Odd Shoveler over-winter, whilst Pintail and Scaup are seen occasionally. Flocks of Pink-footed, Greylag and sometimes Barnacle Geese are likely on passage in March/April.

Purple Sandpiper and Turnstone are numerous, but only moderate numbers of other species over-winter. Most Oystercatcher, Ringed Plover and Lapwing start to return to Shetland in mid-February and there is a marked passage of Golden Plover from March onwards.

Iceland and Glaucous Gulls can often be found in the harbours at Lerwick and Scalloway, as well as other coastal locations.

Small numbers of Long-eared Owl over/winter and Rough-legged Buzzard are sometimes present.

Snow Bunting and Twite regularly over-winter, but otherwise there are very few notable passerines present in winter.

Access

1 Sumburgh Head

OS ref.: HU 40/08

This is the southern-most point of mainland Shetland and is an excellent place for watching breeding seabirds. In autumn, some 2,000–3,000 moulting Eider gather offshore, whilst passage seabirds include regular Sooty Shearwater, Pomarine Skua and occasionally, Long-tailed Skua.

Park near the lighthouse (take care not to obstruct access) at the end of the minor road from Grutness. The cliffs at the head reach 80 metres in height and care is needed along the cliff top, especially in strong winds.

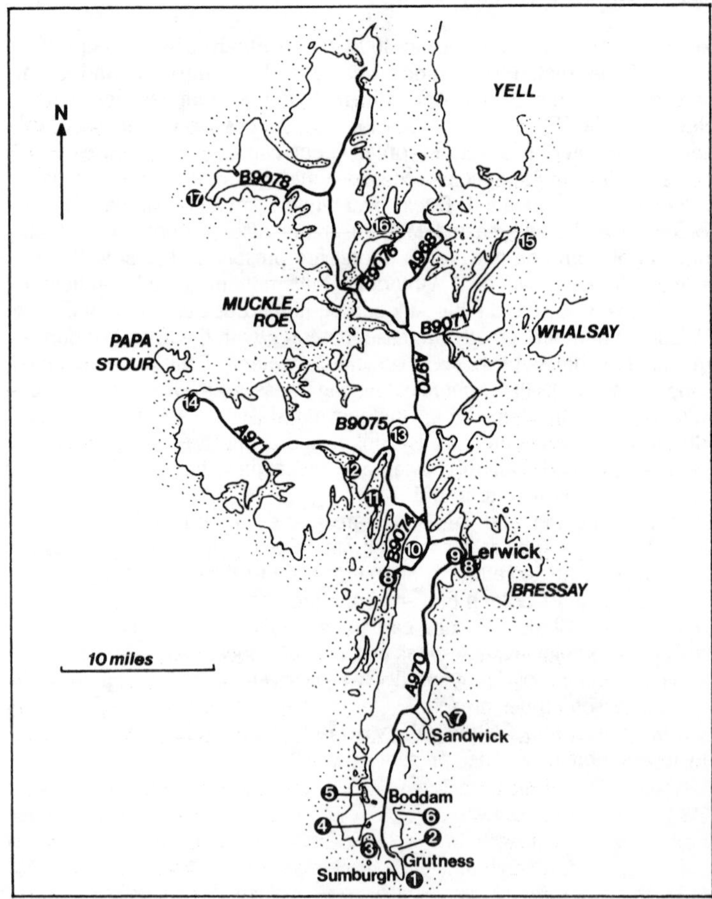

Sumburgh Head is a good location for migrant passerines, although there is little cover to hold them. It is worthwhile checking the two small quarries. The shrub gardens of Sumburgh Hotel and Grutness provide very adequate shelter, and the stone walls on the road to the lighthouse can be productive.

2 Pool of Virkie

OS ref.: HU 39/11

The sheltered tidal basin of Pool of Virkie lies immediately north of Sumburgh Airport. The inter-tidal sand and mud flats are of great importance for wintering and migrant shorebirds. Unfortunately. extensions to the airport have reduced its importance for breeding birds, especially Shelduck. The north shore, which can be worked from a minor road off the A970 to Eastshore, is the most useful vantage point. The gardens in this area are very good for migrant passerines.

3 Quendale Bay

OS ref.: HU 37/12

An extensive area of sand, backed by dunes and machair vegetation. The bay is very good for wintering divers and sea-duck and can be easily viewed from the minor road on the west side.

4 Loch of Hillwell

OS ref.: HU 376140

A machair loch with marshy fringes situated ½ mile to the north of Quendale Bay. This is an important breeding site for several species of wildfowl and in winter holds a large number and variety of species. Corncrake can occasionally be heard here. View from the road on the north or west side – do not go down to the loch.

5 Loch of Spiggie RSPB reserve

OS ref.: HU 373176

A large, productive water body, blocked off from Scousburgh Bay by a sand bar with a dune and machair system. The 115-hectare reserve includes part of the neighbouring Loch of Brow, which is separated from the main loch by an area of floating marshland which is important for breeding waders.

Shelduck, Teal, Oystercatcher and Curlew nest in the area, whilst Great and Arctic Skuas, Kittiwake and Arctic Tern often bathe on the lochs. Spiggie and the neighbouring Brow form the most important winter wildfowl site on Shetland. Up to 300 Whooper Swan regularly pass through in autumn, as well as Greylag Geese, Wigeon, Tufted Duck,

Pochard and Goldeneye. In the spring, Spiggie is a gathering site for up to 50 Long-tailed Duck. Loch of Brow is a less important winter wildfowl site, although it does attract many Pochard.

The lochs are a regular staging site for migrant duck and geese, whilst the surrounding farmland holds many birds during migration periods.

Loch of Spiggie lies at the southern end of Mainland and can be reached by taking the B9122 at Boddam, turning left onto the unclassified road that follows the north shore of the loch a mile and a half later. Good views of the loch can be obtained from this road. Please park considerately and note that the reserve may not be entered.

6 Boddam Voe

OS ref.: HU 40/15

A deep inlet in the south-east coast, Boddam Voe holds wintering divers, grebes and sea-duck and can be good for gulls and waders. The slaughterhouse attracts good numbers of Great Skua and Raven, whilst the adjacent gardens provide good migrant cover.

7 Mousa

OS ref.: HU 46/23

This attractive 180-hectare island lies just over ½ mile (0.8 km) off the east coast of Mainland, opposite Sandwick. Notable breeding species include Fulmar, Storm Petrel, Eider, Great and Arctic Skuas, several hundred Arctic Tern and many Black Guillemot. Several of the island's small pools are good for migrant waders.

Mousa is reached by shall boat from Leebitton, Sandwick – contact the tourist office at Lerwick for details.

8 Scalloway and Lerwick harbours

OS ref.: HU 40/39 & 47/41

Large numbers of gulls frequent the harbours and Black Guillemot can be seen throughout the year. White-winged gulls are often seen in winter, although Glaucous have been recorded in all months of the year. In the towns, garden shrubbery provides good shelter for migrant passerines.

9 Loch of Clickimin

OS ref.: HU 465410

On the western fringe of Lerwick, this loch is a very accessible wintering wildfowl site and can be viewed from surrounding roads and a track around the north-east shore.

10 Loch of Tingwall

OS ref.: HU 415425

Both this and Loch of Asta (HU 413415) are easily viewable from the adjacent B9074. The lochs lie in a limestone valley and are good for wintering wildfowl, especially Pochard and Tufted Duck. The crofts on the west side of the road are good for migrant birds.

11 Weisdale Voe

OS ref.: HU 38/49

This voe can be worked from the A971 along the east shore or an unclassified road from the head of the loch down the west shore. The range of species is similar to that for Sandsound Voe and includes wintering divers, grebes and sea-duck and Goldeneye.

12 Sandsound Voe and Tresta

OS ref.: HU 350490

Sandsound Voe can be 'scoped from the minor road that heads south off the A971 Walls road at Tresta. It is a particularly good area for wintering divers, grebes and sea-duck.

At Tresta itself, check the gardens and sycamore trees by the chapel for migrant birds.

13 Kergord

OS ref.: HU 395542

A series of mixed coniferous and broadleaved shelterbelts flanking the B9075 in the Weisdale Valley. These plantations are the longest established on Shetland and provide important cover for nesting birds including Rook and Goldcrest. It is also an excellent site for migrant and wintering woodland/shrub species.

Do not enter the garden area of Kergord House.

Other plantations which regularly attract migrant birds include Catfirth (HU 450542), Voxter (HU 368701), Sullom (HU 350727) and Strand (HU 432460); the latter belongs to the Shetland Bird Club.

14 Sandness

OS ref.: HU 19/57

This is a fertile crofting area with scattered lochs that hold good numbers of wintering wildfowl. The coast here can be good for sea-watching.

15 Lunna Ness

OS ref.: HU 50/70

This exposed peninsula in the north-east of Mainland is accessible via an unclassified road at Lunnasting, at the end of the B9071. The many lochans support breeding Red-throated Diver, whilst sycamore trees on the left of the road just before Lunna House and the gardens at the head of Swining Voe to the west of Lunna Ness are very good for migrants.

16 Sullom Voe

OS ref.: HU 380740

This large inlet holds good numbers of wintering Great Northern Diver, Slavonian Grebe, Eider, Long-tailed Duck and Velvet Scoter. Houb of Scatsa, immediately north-east of the airfield on the B9076, is a good wader feeding area.

Sullom Voe can be 'scoped from the B9076 along the south shore, the A970 at the head of the voe and the unclassified road to Sullom along the north shore.

17 Esha Ness

OS ref.: HU 21/79

West-facing Old Red Sandstone cliffs holding Guillemot and Kittiwake colonies. The nearby Loch of Houlland has breeding terns, whilst the surrounding maritime moorland supports breeding Whimbrel and skuas. Red-throated Diver breed on the small lochans. Esha Ness is reached by the B9078 to Stenness, of the A970.

SH2 BRESSAY

OS map: sheet 4

Habitat and Species

Bressay is the large inhabited island facing Lerwick, separated from Mainland by ½ mile (0.8 km) of deep water: Bressay Sound. The island is characterised by high moorland ground in the south and east (including the 226-metre-high Ward of Bressay) and lower cultivated ground in the west.

The crofts in the west are very good for migrants and can be easily worked from the various unclassified roads. A colony of Arctic Skua nest in the south-east.

Bressay is connected to Lerwick by a regular vehicle and passenger ferry service.

Habitat

The island of Noss is a 313-hectare National Nature Reserve lying immediately east of Bressay and separated by a narrow sound. Sandstone cliffs rise to nearly 200 metres in the east/south and from these summits the island slopes down to the low cliffs of the west coast.

Rock Doves

Noss is important because of its huge seabird colonies: a total exceeding 80,000 birds breed here, including nearly 7,000 pairs of Gannet, 10,000 pairs of Kittiwake, 15–20 pairs of Arctic and 200 pairs of Great Skua, 65,000 pairs of Guillemot and large numbers of Fulmar, Eider, Great Black-backed Gull and Puffin.

Access

Access is by ferry from Lerwick to Bressay, then by car or on foot across Bressay (4 miles (6.4 km)) to the ferry point on the east coast. Noss is reached by inflatable dinghy by arrangement with the Scottish Natural Heritage summer warden. The island is open to visitors from mid-May through to the end of August, 10 am to 5 pm daily except Monday and Thursday. There is a regular boat from Lerwick in summer which takes visitors around the island and underneath the cliffs – an excellent way to see the seabird colonies. Check these details with the Lerwick Tourist Office before visiting.

Once on Noss, visitors are requested to keep to the cliff-top path.

SH4 WHALSAY

OS map: sheet 2

Habitat

Whalsay is a relatively compact island off the east Mainland coast. It is mostly low-lying with many freshwater lochs and marshes. There is a small wader houb at Kirk Ness. Modest numbers of Kittiwake and Puffin nest at the south end of the island and the moors and lochans hold breeding Red-throated Diver, Whimbrel, Arctic Tern and Arctic Skua.

Whalsay is an important island for migrant birds owing to its easterly location; the crofts in the Skaw area in the north-east are particularly good, as are those on the seaward side of Isbister in the east and around Brough in the west. A fish factory at Symbister attracts good numbers of gulls in winter.

A car ferry operates from Laxo (Mainland) and there are daily flights (except Sundays) from Lerwick, operated by Loganair.

SH5 OUT SKERRIES

OS ref.: HU 68/71
OS map: sheet 2

Black Guillemots and breeding cliffs, spring

This small group of exposed rocky islands lie some 4 miles (6.4 km) north-east of Whalsay and are the eastern-most point in Shetland. They are extremely well placed to receive continental migrants in easterly winds and the scarcity of cover means that birds are relatively easy to find.

Breeding birds include small colonies of Eider, gulls, terns and Black Guillemot. Out Skerries are served by a passenger ferry from Lerwick (a three-hour trip) on Tuesdays and Fridays (and from Whalsay on Sunday if booked in advance). There are also weekly flights in summer from Lerwick, operated by Loganair.

SH6 YELL

OS map: sheets 1 & 2 (13)

Yell is the second largest island in the Shetland Archipelago and is dominated by extensive tracts of moorland terrain, rising to a maximum of just over 200 metres in the south.

Access

Access from Mainland is by car ferry across Yell Sound.

Lumbister RSPB reserve

OS ref.: HU 509974

This 1,720-hectare reserve is situated on the west side of Yell, between Whale Firth and the A968 to Gutcher. The moorland is dotted with many small lochans and a steep gorge which leads to the grass-topped cliffs and rocky shore of Whale Firth.

The breeding species are typical of many areas of Shetland: Red-throated Diver, Red-breasted Merganser, Eider, Merlin, Golden Plover, Curlew, Lapwing, Snipe, Dunlin, Arctic and Great Skuas, Great Black-backed Gull, Wheatear, Raven and Twite. On the coast, Oystercatcher, Ringed Plover, Black Guillemot and Puffin breed.

The reserve can be viewed from the A968 and access into the area is possible at all times from a layby 4 miles (6.4 km) north of Mid-Yell. Please take great care not to disturb breeding birds, especially divers. A summer warden is usually present.

Yell Sound

OS ref.: HU 43/80

This sound is an important wintering area for divers, Eider and Long-tailed Duck. Puffin and Storm Petrel breed on the islands in the sound, several of which are owned by the RSPB (no visiting arrangements).

SH7 FETLAR

OS ref.: HU 60/91
OS map: sheet 1 or 2

Habitat

This diverse island is the smallest of the three inhabited northern Shetland isles. Fetlar is separated from Yell by the $2\frac{1}{2}$-mile (4 km) wide Colgrave Sound and is reached by vehicle ferry from Gutcher on Yell, or Belmont on Unst.

The western part of Fetlar, especially around Lamb Hoga, is dominated by heather moorland and peat bog; to the east, the landscape is one of grassy moorland and dry heath, punctuated by many lochans, marshes and patches of cultivated land. The irregular coastline is a varied mix of cliff and beach with boulder shores in places.

The RSPB manage 690 hectares of the northern part of Fetlar as a reserve. This includes the summits of Vord Hill (158 metres) and Stackaberg, plus the coastline between East Neap and Urie Ness. Most of the reserve consists of serpentine heathland bordered by high sea cliffs to the north. This unique substrate (occurring only on Fetlar, Unst and at Lizard Point in Cornwall) is characterised by extremely short, herb-rich vegetation. The presence of Whimbrel and Snowy Owl here can presumably be attributed to this tundra-like habitat. The reserve and other areas have been designated a Site of Special Scientific Interest.

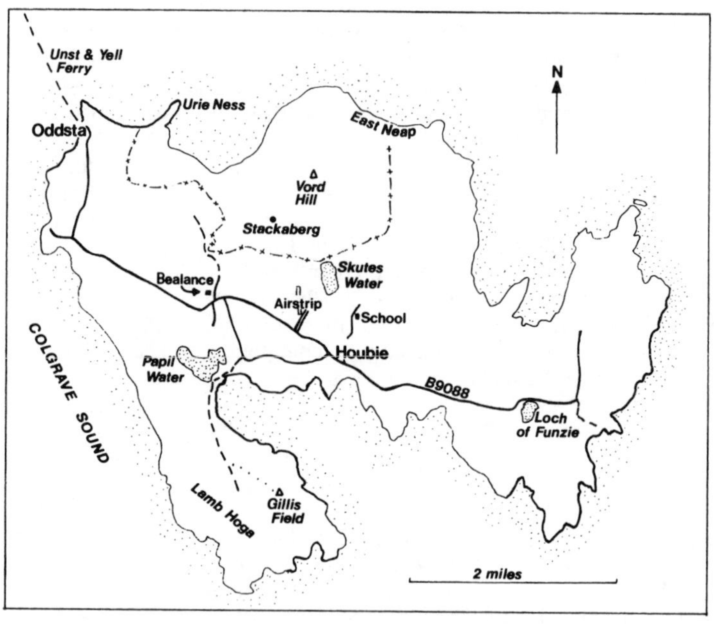

Species

Fetlar is outstanding for breeding waders. Ten species breed annually: Lapwing, Oystercatcher and Ringed Plover breed near the cultivated ground, whilst Golden Plover, Dunlin, Curlew and many Whimbrel nest on the moorland. Snipe and Redshank can be found in the wetter areas and Red-necked Phalarope occur on some lochans. Whimbrel are quite widespread – the roadside moorland west of Loch of Funzie and moorland west of the airstrip and east of the school are the best places to see them. Red-necked Phalarope generally return to Fetlar in the last week in May and can be seen feeding on roadside lochs, especially Loch of Funzie. Pools and marshland are being constructed to improve phalarope habitat. A hide has been erected overlooking the Mires of Funzie.

The island is also important for breeding seabirds. Lamb Hoga, in the south-west of the island, holds breeding Manx Shearwater and a large colony of Storm Petrel, in addition to breeding seabirds such as Shag, Kittiwake, Guillemot and Puffin.

Great and Arctic Skua breed on the moors; around the coast 300 Arctic and a few Common Tern breed. Tern breeding success has been very poor in recent years, although the situation improved considerably in 1991 and 1992.

Fetlar is much famed amongst birders for its Snowy Owls, which nested between 1969 and 1975. Since this time, only female owls have been resident, ocasionally visiting Unst, where there are abundant rabbits.

Around 15 pairs of Red-throated Diver breed and these birds can be easily watched on Loch of Funzie or Papil Water.

Other notable breeding species include Eider, Raven (9 pairs) and Twite.

Fetlar is very well placed to receive spring and autumn migrants; the crofts around the east of the island and the Old Manse garden (do not enter) regularly turn up rare birds. In 1987 these included Two-barred Crossbill and Greenish Warbler. Very large 'falls' of Fieldfare and Redwing usually occur in mid-October.

Papil Water is locally important as a wintering wildfowl site.

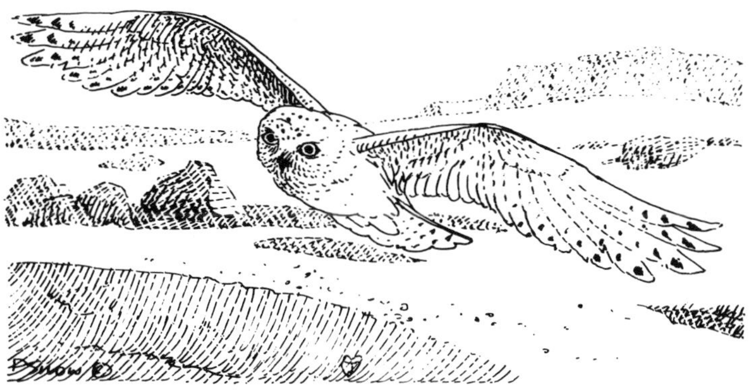

Male Snowy Owl, spring

Access

Access is by ferry from Yell (Gutcher) or Unst (Belmont) then to Fetlar (Oddsta). Advance booking of vehicles on this ferry is advisable (tel: Burravoe 259/268). A bus service from Lerwick connects with the ferry, but does not cross to Fetlar. Flights from Lerwick to Fetlar can be chartered with Loganair.

The RSPB employ a summer warden from April through to September and during this time the reserve area is accessible only by arrangement with the warden, who will escort parties. Visitors should report at Bealance Croft, signposted 2½ miles (4 km) from the Oddsta ferry terminal (HU 604916).

Please respect the property of farmers and crofters on the island and do not disturb birds thought to be breeding.

RSPB Warden

Bealance, Fetlar, Shetland ZE2 9DJ. Tel: 095783 246.

SH8 UNST

OS map: sheet 1

Habitat

Unst is the northernmost main island and is separated from neighbouring Yell by Bluemull Sound. It is a large and diverse island with a sharp ridge of high ground running north–south backing the Atlantic coastline and lower, more rounded hills to the east. The moorland terrain provides breeding habitat for many of the birds characteristic of Shetland, especially waders and skuas. The coast holds large populations of breeding seabirds, particularly at Hermaness. Snowy Owl are regular visitors to the island. The serpentine heathland holds good numbers of breeding waders, Arctic Skuas and Terns. There is an interesting Sycamore plantation at Halligarth, near Baltasound and migrants are often recorded in the gardens of Norwick, Uyeasound and Baltasound. The marsh at Norwick is worth checking, as is Easter Loch in Uyaesound.

Access

There is a frequent car ferry service to Unst from Yell and Loganair flies daily (except Sunday) from Lerwick.

Hermaness National Nature Reserve

Os ref.: HP 60/16

This 964-hectare reserve is located on the northernmost peninsula of Unst and overlooks Muckle Flugga and Out Stack, the most northerly point in Britain. The cliffs rise to between 70 and 200 metres high and hold, in conjunction with those at Saxavord, one of the largest seabird colonies in Britain.

Fourteen species of seabird breed, including 10,000 pairs each of Fulmar and Gannet, 5,000 pairs of Kittiwake, 16,000 pairs of Guillemot, 2,000 pairs of Razorbill and an immense number (approximately 25,000 pairs) of Puffin. About 800 pairs of Great and small numbers of Arctic Skua breed.

Hermaness has become well known amongst birders for its Black-browed Albatross, which returned to the cliffs annually between 1970 and 1987; since then its appearance has been more erratic, with early spring being the most likely time.

The area is accessible via the B9086 at Burrafirth – there is a limited amount of parking space near the road end. The main sea-cliffs are reached by a 3-mile (4.8-km) walk from Burrafirth along a well-marked path through rough terrain inhabited by breeding Dunlin, Golden Plover, Snipe and around 800 pairs of Great Skua.

A Scottish Natural Heritage summer warden lives in the ex-lighthouse buildings (shore station) at Burrafirth, where there is a visitor centre for visitors to Hermaness.

Bluemull Sound

OS ref.: HP 55/00

Very large passages of seabirds from Hermaness pass through the sound, especially in winter and early spring. Large numbers of Eider and Black Guillemot are often present in winter.

SH9 FOULA

OS ref.: HT 96/39
OS map: sheet 4

Habitat and Species

Foula is a remote 1,380-hectare island situated approximately 14 miles (22.5 km) west of Mainland. The topography of the island is dominated by the Kame cliffs in the west of the island, which soar to the stupendous height of 370 metres above sea level and are even more precipitous than those of St Kilda. A ridge of high ground extends south-eastwards from these cliffs, incorporating the Sneug, at 418 metres the highest point on Foula, then the ground slopes steeply down to low-lying croftland around Ham. A second summit, The Noup, lies in the south of the island, reaching 248 metres.

Foula is an internationally important seabird station with over 125,000 pairs of breeding birds comprising 12 species, including the largest colony of Great Skua in the North Atlantic. The sheer cliffs of the north coast have few ledges suitable for nesting seabirds, although Fulmar and small numbers of Razorbill and Puffin nest here. There is a very large Guillemot colony to the north-west, however, at Nebbiefield. Puffin nest in large numbers on the grassy slopes of Little Kame, along the west coast and on The Noup. Lower cliffs on the east coast have several small mixed seabird colonies, as have the few stacks off Ristie and below The Kame. The majority of cliff nesting seabirds nest in the boulder fields, along with large numbers of Shag, notably from Wester Hoevdi to The Noup and at Heddlicliff.

The small, peaty inland pools are used by breeding Red-throated Diver and bathing Great Skua and gulls. The Great Skuas mostly occupy the higher, western moors, leaving the lower crofting ground to the Arctic Skuas.

The south-east of the island has been virtually stripped of peat and the barren ground is now inhabited by high densities of nesting Oystercatcher, Ringed Plover, Arctic Skua and Arctic Tern.

The more luxuriant vegetation is principally confined to a few sheltered areas such as The Sneck, Hametoun and the mouth of Ham Burn. It is this cover and also the stone walls and cliff tops that inevitably tend to attract migrant birds.

The island's huge seabird colonies include 40,000 or more pairs of Fulmar, small numbers of Manx Shearwater, thousands of pairs of Storm Petrel, small numbers of Leach's Petrel, *c.* 200 pairs of Gannet, 3,000 pairs of Shag, 3,000 pairs of Great Skua, around 270 pairs of Arctic Skua, 6,000 pairs of Kittiwake, 30,000 pairs of Guillemot, 5,000 pairs of Razorbill, 60 pairs of Black Guillemot and 35,000 pairs of Puffin.

Access

Foula is served by a mail boat cum passenger ferry which sails from Walls on the west Mainland on Tuesdays and Fridays, weather permitting. In addition, there are weekly flights from Lerwick in the summer.

References

The Birds of Foula, R.W. Furness (1983).

SH10 FAIR ISLE

OS ref.: HZ 20/70
OS map: sheet 4

Habitat

Fair Isle is an isolated island situated more than 24 miles (39 km) southwest of Sumburgh Head, Mainland. The island covers 765 hectares and measures about 3 miles by 1½ miles (4.8 by 2.4 km). Steep sandstone cliffs, reaching 200 metres in places, enclose sheep-grazed heather and grass hill land in the north and croftland in the south, comprising mainly improved grazing land for sheep with some cultivated areas of crops such as turnip and oats.

The island is owned by the National Trust for Scotland and is designated a Site of Special Scientific Interest.

Access

Fair Isle can be reached by sea or air: between May and September the mail boat, *Good Shepherd IV*, sails from Grutness, Mainland, at 1130 hrs. on Tuesdays, alternate Thurssdays and Saturdays. On alternate Thursdays (ie. the days the boat does not leave from Grutness), the *Good Shepherd IV* sails from Lerwick. In winter, the service operates on Tuesdays only. Note that rough weather frequently disrupts this schedule. Advance booking is essential – contact Mr J.W. Stout, Skerryholm, Fair Isle, Shetland. Tel: 03512 222.

Loganair fly from Tingwall, Mainland, on Monday, Wednesday, Friday and Saturdays between May and October, and Monday and Fridays only for the rest of the year. There are connecting services between Tingwall and mainland Scotland. Contact Loganair – tel: 059584 246 (Tingwall) or 031 344 3341 (Edinburgh) for details.

Accommodation is available at the Fair Isle Lodge and Bird Observatory from April to late October. Contact Booking Dept, Fair Isle Lodge and Bird Observatory, Fair Isle, Shetland ZE2 9JU (Tel: 03512 258).

A number of crofts also cater for visitors – contact the Shetland Tourist Organisation, Lerwick, Shetland ZE1 0LU (tel: 0595 3434) for details.

For car hire on Fair Isle contact Mr J.W. Stout, Skerryholm, Fair Isle, Shetland. Tel: 03512 222.

Species

The name 'Fair Isle' is synonymous with rare migrant birds for most birdwatchers. Over 345 species have been recorded here, more than at any other British location. More than 250 of these species have been ringed – a total exceeding 220,000 birds. The 'rarity-conscious' image that Fair Isle has earned, however, tends to obscure the fact that the island holds large numbers of breeding seabirds, particularly on the west and north coasts, including around 35,000 pairs of Fulmar, almost 800 pairs of Gannet, more than a 1,000 pairs of Shag and *c.* 19,000 nests of Kittiwake. Auk populations total around 33,000 Guillemot, 4,000 Razorbill, 20,000+ Puffin and about 360 breeding Black Guillemot. In addition to the Kittiwake, four other species of gull breed around the coast, whilst around 1,100 pairs of Arctic Tern and 60 pairs of Common Tern currently nest. An unknown number of Storm Petrel breed. On the moorland, around 100 pairs each of Great and Arctic Skua breed.

Approximately 100 pairs of Eider nest; breeding waders include Oystercatcher, Ringed Plover, Lapwing, Snipe and Curlew. Dunlin and Whimbrel occasionally breed.

Breeding passerines include Rock and Meadow Pipits, Skylark, White and Pied Wagtails, Wheatear, Raven, Wren, Starling, House Sparrow and Twite.

Calendar

Some of the more interesting species likely to be seen.

All year: Fulmar, Shag, Eider, Black Guillemot, Rock Dove, Rock Pipit, Wren (Fair Isle race), Raven and Twite.

March–May: Good 'falls' of thrushes and finches can occur during south-east to east winds in March/April. In May, numbers of Bluethroat, Wryneck and Red-backed Shrike often occur; other regular migrants include Icterine Warbler, Marsh Warbler, Golden Oriole and Scarlet Rosefinch. Lapland and Snow Buntings are often seen into late April/May. Dotterel, Quail and Corncrake regularly put in an appearance. Some of the more frequently recorded rarities include Subalpine Warbler, Short-toed Lark, Tawny Pipit, Red-breasted Flycatcher, Thrush Nightingale and Ortolan, Rustic and Little Buntings. Early June is a good time for 'oddities' to turn up – Lesser Kestrel, Daurian Starling and Cretzschmar's Bunting have all been recorded at this time.

June–July: Seabirds dominate the interest (see above).

August–October: 'Falls of autumn migrants can occur in August, but are more likely in September and October, though south-east/east winds are necessary. These occurrences are often very impressive: the September 'falls' are largely composed of Redstart, Whinchat, Wheatear, Garden Warbler and Willow Warbler, whilst those in October generally involve thrushes (up to 10,000 Redwing are recorded annually), finches (including Brambling), Goldcrest and Woodcock. Long and Short-eared Owls frequently occur. Migrants can turn up anywhere, but the crofting land is the best area to check.

Of the less common autumn migrants, Wryneck, Barred Warbler and Scarlet Rosefinch are regular in August, whilst Icterine Warbler, Bluethroat, Red-backed Shrike and Ortolan Bunting are probable in September. Regular vagrants include Great Snipe (late August–end of October), Short-toed Lark, Richard's Pipit, Olive-backed Pipit (October), Citrine Wagtail (late August–mid-October), Lanceolated Warbler (mid-September–mid-October), Pallas's Grasshopper Warbler (end September–mid-October), Pechora Pipit (late September–mid-October), Greenish Warbler (August), Arctic Warbler (late August/September), Pallas's Warbler (October), Yellow-browed Warbler (end September–mid-October), Red-breasted Flycatcher (September/October), Rustic and Little Buntings (end September/October) and Yellow-breasted Bunting (end August–end September)! In addition, there is always the possibility of some of the rarer Fair Isle vagrants turning up, such as Paddyfield Warbler, Blyth's Reed Warbler, Red-flanked Bluetail, Dusky or Radde's Warbler (October/November). Red-throated Pipit is possible in spring or autumn (end September).

Skeins of Pink-footed, Greylag and Barnacle Geese can be seen overhead in late September and during October. Small numbers of Whooper Swan occur.

No raptors currently breed on the island, but Sparrowhawk, Kestrel, Merlin and Peregrine are all regular spring and autumn migrants. Hen Harrier, Honey Buzzard and Osprey occasionally occur.

Late migrants include Lapland Bunting and large numbers of Snow Bunting in October. Waxwing occur in November/December during irruption years.

Seawatching can be productive, but requires both patience and luck. Small numbers of Sooty Shearwater are seen annually from early August to early October. A few Manx Shearwater are recorded in most years between May and October. Odd divers (Red-throated and Great Northern) and a few Long-tailed Duck are present offshore from mid-October. Little Auk usually occur in early spring and late autumn. On the *Good Shepherd* crossing, Storm Petrel can be seen from mid-June until mid-October. Leach's Petrel, Pomarine and Long-tailed Skuas are also occasionally seen. The crossing is a good one for views of cetaceans, including White-beaked Dolphin, Common Porpoise and Pilot Whale, with occasional records of Risso's Dolphin and Killer Whale. In addition, a number of cetaceans are recorded from the island each year.

Timing

Mid-September to late October is without doubt the prime time to visit for rare birds, although westerly winds at this time can result in great disappointment. South-easterly winds are best for migrant 'falls' and rarities, although these are never easy to predict and rarities can turn up on any wind direction.

Late May and early June is the peak time for spring vagrants, yet a number of outstanding rarities have occurred in late March and April. August, too, has produced some classic rarities.

To savour the true character of Fair Isle and still see some good birds, avoid both the spring and autumn twitching periods and visit in April, late June to early September or late October.

References

The Birds of Fair Isle, John F. Holloway and Roderick H.F. Thorne.
Fair Isle and its Birds, K. Williamson (1965).
Fair Isle Bird Observatory Reports.
Fair Isle's Garden Birds, John F. Holloway (1983).
The Natural History of Shetland, R.J. Berry and L. Johnston (1980)
Shetland Bird Report, ed. P.M. Ellis/K. Osborn.

RSPB Shetland Conservation Officer

Pete Ellis, 'Seaview', Sandwick, Shetland ZE2 9HP. Tel: 09505 506.

Shetland Bird Club

Secretary: Kim Suddaby, 92 Sandveien, Lerwick.

USEFUL ADDRESSES

British Trust for Ornithology
The Nunnery
Nunnery Place
Thetford
Norfolk IP24 2PU

Caledonian MacBrayne
The Ferry Terminal
Gourock PA19 1QP
(Tel: 0475 34531)

Forestry Commission
231 Corstorphine Road
Edinburgh EH12 7AT

National Trust for Scotland
5 Charlotte Square
Edinburgh EH2 4DU

Scottish Natural Heritage

North East Region (Grampian, Orkney, Shetland & Speyside)
17 Rubislaw Terrace
Aberdeen AB1 1XE

North West Region (Highland (except Speyside), Outer Hebrides, Skye & the Small islands)
9 Culduthel Road
Inverness IV2 4AG

South West Region (Dumfries & Galloway, Strathclyde)
Balloch Castle Country Park
Loch Lomond Park
Balloch
Dumbartonshire G83 8LX

South East Region (Borders, Central, Fife, Lothian & Tayside)
12 Hope Terrace
Edinburgh EH9 2AS

Royal Society for the Protection of Birds
17 Regent Terrace
Edinburgh EH7 5BN

North Scotland Office
Etive House
Beechwood Park
Inverness IV2 3BW

RSPB South West Scotland Office
Unit 3.1
West of Scotland Science Park
Kelvin Campus
Glasgow G20 0SP

RSPB North-east Scotland Office
4 Headland Court
Newtonhill
Aberdeen

Scottish Ornithologists' Club
21 Regent Terrace
Edinburgh EH7 5BT

Scottish Wildlife Trust
25 Johnston Terrace
Edinburgh EH1 2NH

LOCAL RECORDERS

Immature Sea (White-tailed) Eagle

All bird records should be sent to the appropriate recorder, although in cases of difficulty, they can be sent to the editor of the Scottish Bird Report, Alan Wood, 1 Rosebank Terrace, Kilmacolm, Renfrewshire, PA13 4EW. Records should be on one side of a sheet of paper, well spaced and, if possible, in Voous order (as per most current field guides).

District(s) covered in each region are given in parentheses.

Borders
(Berwickshire, Ettrick & Lauderdale, Roxburgh, Tweedale)
R.D. Murray
4 Bellfield Crescent
Eddleston
Peebles
Borders EH45 8RQ

Central
(Clackmannan, Falkirk, Stirling (Forth drainage area))
Dr C.J. Henty
7 Coneyhill Road
Bridge of Allan
Stirlingshire FK9 4EL

Dumfries & Galloway
(Nithsdale, Annandale & Eskdale)
Ken Bruce
Mallaig
Wellington Street
Glencaple
Dumfries DG1 4RA

(Stewartry & Wigtown)
Paul Collin
Gairland
Old Edinburgh Road
Minnigaff
Newton Stewart
Wigtownshire DG8 6PL

Fife
(Dumfermline, Kirkcaldy, NE Fife)
D.E. Dickson
45 Hawthorn Terrace
Thornton
Fife KY1 4DZ

(Isle of May)
Ian Darling
597 Lanark Road West
Balerno
Edinburgh EH4 7BL

Grampian
(all, except Moray)
Ken Shaw
4 Headland Court
Newtonhill
Near Stonehaven
Kincardine AB3 2SF

Grampian/Highland
(Moray/Nairn)
M.J.H. Cook
Rowanbrae
Clochan, Buckie
Banffshire AB5 2EQ

Highland
(Badenoch & Strathspey, Inverness, Lochaber, Ross & Cromarty, Skye & Lochaish)
R.H. Dennis
Innchdryne
Nethybridge
Inverness-shire PH25 3EF

(Caithness)
E.W.E. Maughan
Burnside, Harbour Road
Reay, Thurso
Caithness

(Sutherland)
A.R. Mainwood
13 Ben Bhraggie Drive
Golspie
Sutherland KW10 6SX

Lothian
Ian Andrews
15 The Parsonage
Musselburgh
Midlothian
EH21 7SW

Orkney
C.J. Booth
34 High Street
Kirkwall
Orkney KW15 1AZ

Shetland
(except Fair Isle)
Dave Suddaby
92 Sandveien
Lerwick
Shetland ZE2 9JU

(Fair Isle)
Paul Harvey
Bird Observatory
Fair Isle
Shetland ZE2 9JU

Strathclyde
(Kyle & Carrick, Cumnock & Doon Valley, Kilmarnock & Loudoun, Cunninghame)
A. Hogg
Kirklea
Crosshill, Maybole
Ayrshire KA19 7RJ

(Dumbarton, Clydebank, Bearsden & Milngavie, Stirling (Clyde drainage area), Inverclyde, Renfrew, Eastwood, City of Glasgow, Strathkelvin, Cumbernauld & Kilsyth, Monklands, Hamilton, Motherwell, East Kilbride, Clydesdale)
Iain Gibson
c/o Beck
1 Rosebank Terrace
Kilmacolm
Renfrewshire PA13 4EW

(Arran, Bute, Cumbraes)
Bernard Zonfrillo
28 Brodie Road
Glasgow G21 3SB

(Argyll & Bute – except Bute)
Mike Madders
Carnduncan
Gruinart
Bridgend
Islay PA44 7PS

Tayside
(Perth & Kinross)
Wendy Mattingley
Cluny House
Aberfeldy
Perthshire PH15 2JT

(Angus, City of Dundee)
Stuart Green
41 Laird Street
Downfield
Dundee DD3 9QF

Western Isles
(Harris, Lewis)
Peter Cunningham
10 Barony Square
Stornoway
Isle of Lewis PA87 2TQ

(Uists, Benbecula, Barra)
Tim Dix
2 Dreumasdal
South Uist PA81 5RT

SELECT BIBLIOGRAPHY

Twite, spring

Angus, S. (ed.) (1983) *Sutherland Birds*, The Northern Times

Berry, R.J. (1985) *The Natural History of Orkney*, Collins

Berry, R.J. and Johnson, L. (1980) *The Natural History of Shetland*, Collins

Booth, C.G. (1981) *Birds in Islay*, Argyll Reproductions Ltd

Booth, C., Cuthbert, M. and Reynolds, P. (1984) *The Birds of Orkney*, The Orkney Press

Collet, P.M. and Manson, S.A.M. (1987) *Birds of Caithness*, Caithness Branch SOC

Cunningham, Peter (1983) *Birds of the Outer Hebrides*, The Melven Press

Dennis, Roy (1984) *Birds of Badenoch and Strathspey*, Roy Dennis Enterprises

Elliott, Richard (1989) *The Birds of Islay*, Christopher Helm

Eggeling, W.J. (1960) *The Isle of May: a Scottish Nature Reserve*, Oliver & Boyd, repr. 1985

Fuller, R. (1982) *Bird Habitats in Britain*, T. & A.D. Poyser

Furness, R.W. (1983) *Birds of Foula*, The Brathay Hall Trust

Hogg, Angus (1983) *Birds of Ayrshire*, Glasgow University

Holloway, John (1991) *The Birds of Stronsay*

Hywel-Davies, J. and Thom, V.M. (1984) *The Macmillan Guide to Britain's Nature Reserves*, Macmillan

Jardine, D.C., Clarke, J. and Clarke, P.M. (1986) *The Birds of Colonsay and Oransay* (Pub. privately)

Lack, P. (1986) *The Atlas of Wintering Birds in Britain and Ireland*, T. & A.D. Poyser

Madders, Mike and Snow, Philip (1987) *Birds of Mull*, Saker Press

Madders, Mike; Snow, Philip and Welstead, Julia (1992) *Birds of Mid-Argyll*, Saker Press

Meek, Eric (1985) *Islands of Birds: A Guide to Orkney Birds*, RSPB

Murray, Ray (1986) *Birds of the Borders*, Borders Branch, SOC

Nethersole-Thompson, D. (1978) *Highland Birds*, Highlands & Islands Development Board

Ogilvie, Malcolm (1992) *Birds of Islay*, Lochindaal Press

Omand, Donald (ed.) (1984) *The Ross and Cromarty Book*, The Northern Times

Prater, A.J. (1981) *Estuary Birds of Britain and Ireland*, T. & A.D. Poyser

Redman, N. and Harrap, S. (1987) *Birdwatching in Britain: a Site by Site Guide*, Christopher Helm

Sharrock, J.T.R. (1976) *The Atlas of Breeding Birds in Britain and Ireland*, T. & A.D. Poyser

Smout, A.M. (1986) *Birds of Fife*, John Donald

Thom, Valerie M. (1970) *Loch of Lowes*, SWT

——— (1986) *Birds of Scotland*, T. & A.D. Poyser

BIRD REPORTS

Wood Sandpiper, spring

Most recording areas in Scotland now produce a local bird report. These are generally available from the Scottish Ornithologists' Club, 21 Regent Terrace, Edinburgh, EH7 5BT. The list below details the reports currently published and their editors/publishers. The addresses of local distributors are listed.

Region	Recording Area	Name, history and publisher	Editor Source (if different)
Borders	Borders Region	Borders Bird Report annual since 1979 Borders SOC	Ray Murray 4 Bellfield Crescent Eddleston, Peebles Borders EH45 8RQ
Central	Central Region	part of Forth Naturalist & Historian annual since 1976	L. Corbett University of Stirling Stirling FK9 4LA
Dumfries & Galloway	Dumfries & Galloway	Dumfries & Galloway Bird Report annual since 1985	SOC 21 Regent Terrace Edinburgh EH7 5BT
Fife	Fife (not Isle of May)	Fife Bird Report annual since 1980 Fife Bird Club	Douglas Dickson 45 Hawthorn Terrace Thornton Fife KY1 4DZ
Fife	Isle of May	Isle of May Bird Observatory Report annual since 1985 Isle of May Bird Observatory	Ian Darling 597 Lanark Road West Balerno Edinburgh EH4 7BL

Grampian	Grampian (except Moray)	North-East Scotland Bird Report annual since 1974 North-East Scotland Bird Club	Editor: Andy Webb Reports from: Mark Tasker 17 Rubislaw Terrace Aberdeen AB1 1XE
Grampian/ Highland	Moray & Nairn	Moray & Nairn Bird Report annual since 1985 SOC	Martin Cook Rowanbrae Clochan, Buckie Banffshire AB5 2EQ
Highland	Highland (except Caithness, Sutherland)	Highland Bird Report 1988 only Highland SOC	Roy Dennis Inchdryne Nethybridge Invernessshire PH25 3EF
Highland	Caithness	Caithness Bird Report annual since 1983 Caithness SOC	Eric Maughan Burnside Raey, Thurso Caithness KW14 7RG
Lothian	Lothian Region	Lothian Bird Report annual since 1979 Lothian SOC	
Orkney	Orkney	Orkney Bird Report annual since 1974	Editor: Chris Booth *et al* from: Mildred Cuthbert Vishabrack Evie, Orkney
Shetland	Shetland (except Fair Isle)	Shetland Bird Report annual since 1973 Shetland Bird Club	Editor: from: Ian Sandison 9 Burnside Lerwick, Shetland
Shetland	Fair Isle	Fair Isle Bird Observatory Report annual since 1949 Fair Isle Bird Obs. Trust	Editor: Paul Harvey from: FIBOT 21 Regent Terrace Edinburgh EH7 5BT
Strathclyde	Arran	Arran Bird Report annual Isle of Arran Natural History Society	Editor: Tristan ap Rheinallt
Strathclyde	Argyll	Argyll Bird Report annual since 1984 Argyll Bird Club	Editor: Clive Craik from: N.J. Scriven Ardentinny Centre Ardentinny, Dunoon Argyll
Strathclyde	Ayrshire	Ayrshire Bird Report annual since 1976 Ayr SOC	Angus Hogg 11 Kirkmichael Road Crosshill, Maybole Ayrshire KA19 7RJ

Strathclyde	Clyde Area	Clyde Bird Report annual since 1973 Clyde SOC	Iain Gibson, c/o Beck 1 Rosebank Terrace Kilmacolm Renfrewshire PA13 4EW
Tayside	Perth & Kinross	Perthshire Bird Report annual since 1974 SOC	Wendy Mattingley Cluny House by Aberfeldy Perthshire PH15 2JT
Tayside	Angus & Dundee	Angus & Dundee Bird Report annual since 1974	Stuart Green 41 Laird Street Dundee DD3 9QF
Western Isles	Western Isles	Western Isles Bird Report annual since 1989 SOC	Peter Cunningham 10 Barony Square Stornoway Isle of Lewis PA87 2TQ

CODE OF CONDUCT FOR BIRDWATCHERS

Todays birdwatchers are a powerful force for nature conservation. The number of those of us interested in birds rises continually and it is vital that we take seriously our responsibility to avoid any harm to birds.

We must also present a responsible image to non-birdwatchers who may be affected by our activities and particularly those on whose sympathy and support the future of birds may rest.

There are 10 points to bear in mind:

1. The welfare of birds must come first.
2. Habitat must be protected.
3. Keep disturbance to birds and their habitat to a minimum.
4. When you find a rare bird think carefully about whom you should tell.
5. Do not harrass rare migrants.
6. Abide by the bird protection laws at all times.
7. Respect the rights of landowners.
8. Respect the rights of other people in the countryside.
9. Make your records available to the local bird recorder.
10. Behave abroad as you would when birdwatching at home.

Welfare of birds must come first

Whether your particular interest is photography, ringing, sound recording, scientific study or just birdwatching, remember that the welfare of the birds must always come first.

Habitat protection

Its habitat is vital to a bird and therefore we must ensure that our activities do not cause damage.

Keep disturbance to a minimum

Birds' tolerance of disturbance varies between species and season. Therefore, it is safer to keep all disturbance to a minimum. No birds should be disturbed from the nest in case opportunities for predators to take eggs or young are increased. In very cold weather disturbance to birds may cause them to use vital energy at a time when food is difficult to find. Wildfowlers already impose bans during cold weather: birdwatchers should exercise similar discretion.

Rare breeding birds

If you discover a rare bird breeding and feel that protection is necessary, inform the appropriate RSPB Regional Office, or the Species Protection Department at the Lodge. Otherwise it is best in almost all circumstances to keep the record strictly secret in order to avoid disturbance by other birdwatchers and attacks by egg-collectors. Never visit known sites of rare breeding birds unless they are adequately protected. Even your presence may give away the site to others and cause so many other visitors that the birds may fail to breed successfully.

Disturbance at or near the nest of species listed on the First Schedule of the Wildlife and Countryside Act 1981 is a criminal offence.

Copies of *Wild Birds and the Law* are obtainable from the RSPB, The Lodge, Sandy, Beds. SG19 2DL (send two 2nd class stamps).

Rare migrants

Rare migrants or vagrants must not be harassed. If you discover one, consider the circumstances carefully before telling anyone. Will an influx of birdwatchers disturb the bird or others in the area? Will the habitat be damaged? Will problems be caused with the landowner?

The Law

The bird protection laws (now embodied in the Wildlife and Countryside Act 1981) are the result of hard campaigning by previous generations of birdwatchers. As birdwatchers we must abide by them at all times and not allow them to fall into disrepute.

Respect the rights of landowners

The wishes of landowners and occupiers of land must be respected. Do not enter land without permission. Comply with permit schemes. If you are leading a group, do give advance notice of the visit, even if a formal permit scheme is not in operation. Always obey the Country Code.

Respect the rights of other people

Have proper consideration for other birdwatchers. Try not to disrupt their activities or scare the birds they are watching. There are many other people who also use the countryside. Do not interfere with their activities and, if it seems that what they are doing is causing unnecessary disturbance to birds, do try to take a balanced view. Flushing gulls when walking a dog on a beach may do little harm, while the same dog might be a serious disturbance at a tern colony. When pointing this out to a non-birdwatcher be courteous, but firm. The non-birdwatchers' goodwill towards birds must not be destroyed by the attitudes of birdwatchers.

Keeping records

Much of today's knowledge about birds is the result of meticulous record keeping by our predecessors. Make sure you help to add to tomorrow's knowledge by sending records to your local bird recorder.

Birdwatching abroad

Behave abroad as you would at home. This code should be firmly adhered to when abroad (whatever the local laws). Well behaved birdwatchers can be important ambassadors for bird protection.

This code has been drafted after consultation between the British Ornithologists' Union, British Trust for Ornithology, the Royal Society for the Protection of Birds, the Scottish Ornithologists' Club, the Wildfowl and Wetlands Trust and the Editors of British Birds.

Further copies may be obtained from The Royal Society for the Protection of Birds, The Lodge, Sandy, Beds. SG19 2DL.

SYSTEMATIC LIST OF SCOTTISH BIRDS

This species list includes all species recorded during the period 1900 to 1991 inclusive. The Gaelic name is given for most species – these are taken from 'Gaelic Names of Birds' by Frank Rennie (in *Western Isles Information Note No. 2*, published by Scottish Natural Heritage NW Region). Euring and BTO codes for each species are given in the right hand columns. A brief description of the status of each species follows – this is based on the *Checklist of Scottish Birds* published by the Scottish Ornithologists' Club (1987) with additional information (covering the period 1986–8) kindly supplied by Angus Hogg. Anyone requiring a detailed account of the status of Scottish Birds should consult *Birds in Scotland* by Valerie M. Thom (Poyser, 1986). For species with local or restricted distributions, a few sites are suggested where these birds may be sought.

Red-throated Diver *Gavia stellata* Learga ruadh 0002 RH
Breeds on hill lochans in Highlands, Hebrides, Orkney & Shetland. Winters offshore, mainly east coast.

Black-throated Diver *Gavia arctica* Learga dhubh 0003 BV
Scarce breeder on larger remote lochs in NW Highlands & Hebrides. Winters offshore.
Sites: summer H15, H25, H26, H27, WI.
winter F3, G9, G13, H19, O3, T6.

Black-throated Divers

Great Northern Diver *Gavia immer* Muir bhuachaill 0004 ND
Winter visitor offshore, especially west coast. Birds often present in late spring, occasionally over-summering. Has bred.
Sites: G9, G13, H19, H25, O, S1, SH, WI.

White-billed Diver *Gavia adamsiii* Learga bhlar 0005
Scarce vagrant, occurring annually in winter & spring. Orkney/Shetland & E coast.

Pied-billed Grebe *Podilymbus podiceps* 0006
Very scarce vagrant.

Little Grebe *Tachybaptus ruficollis* Spàg-ri-tòn 0007 LG
Resident breeder, mainly in lowlands. Some immigration to sheltered coastal waters winter.

Great Crested Grebe *Podiceps cristatus* Gobhlachan laparan 0009 GG
Breeds on many lowland waters. Wintering mostly in coastal waters, especially Firth of Forth.

Red-Necked Grebe *Podiceps grisegena* Gobhlachan ruadh 0010 RX
Scarce winter visitor, mainly seen in outer Firth of Forth. Occasionally recorded in summer & has attempted to breed.
Sites: C2, L2, L3, T1.

Slavonian Grebe *Podiceps auritus* Gobhlachan mara 0011 SZ
Scarce breeding species, Highland Region only. More widespread in winter, when found in sheltered coastal waters, both east & west coasts.
Sites: summer H13.
winter C2, DG4, H17, H19, L2, O3, S3, SH, T1, WI.

Black-necked Grebe *Podiceps nigricollis* Gobhlachan dubh 0012 BN
Scarce breeding species in lowland Scotland. Small numbers winter in coastal waters.
Sites: summer T13.
winter C2, DG4, L2, L3.

Black-browed Albatross *Diomedea melanophris* 0014
Very scarce vagrant. A single bird regularly at Hermaness in Shetland until 1987.

Fulmar *Fulmarus glacialis* Eun crom 0020 F
Widespread sea-cliff nesting species, especially common in NW. Breeds at inland sites in some areas.

Cory's Shearwater *Calonectris diomedea* 0036 CQ
Annual vagrant seen in small numbers, mostly early autumn.
Sites: F7?

Great Shearwater *Puffinus gravis* Fachadh mor 0040 GQ
Vagrant, recorded most often in autumn.

Sooty Shearwater *Puffinus griseus* Fachadh dubh 0043 OT
Passage visitor generally recorded in autumn.
Sites: B1, F4, F7, G3, O, SH, WI.

Manx Shearwater *Puffinus puffinus* Fachadh ban 0046 MX
Breeds on islands in NW with very large numbers on Rhum. See offshore April–October.

Little Shearwater *Puffinus assimillis* 0048
Very scarce vagrant.

Storm Petrel *Hydrobates pelagicus* Paraig 0052 TM
Breeds on islands in NW. Seen offshore April–October.
Sites: DG5, F7, S1, SH6, SH7, SH9, SH10.

Leach's Petrel *Oceanodroma leucorhoa* Gobhlan mara 0055 TL
Breeds on a few remote islands, NW Scotland & Shetland. Occasionally seen offshore in autumn.
Sites: DG5, S1, SH9, WI.

Gannet *Sula bassana* Suilaire 0071 GX
Few but very large breeding colonies, all in N & W except for Bass Rock. Seen in coastal waters throughout the year.

Cormorant *Phalacrocorax carbo* Sgarbh 0072 CA
Breeds at widely scattered coastal colonies plus a few inland sites.

Shag *Phalacrocorax aristotelis* Sgarbh an sgumain 0080 SA
Common breeding species around rocky coasts, especially in N & W.

Magnificent Frigatebird *Fregata magnificens* Eun-chogaidh 0093
Very scarce vagrant.

Bittern *Botaurus stellaris* Corra ghrain 0095 BI
Uncommon visitor, mostly recorded in winter.

American Bittern *Botaurus lentiginosus* 0096
Very scarce vagrant.

Little Bittern *Oxybrychus minutus* Corra ghrain beag 0098
Very scarce vagrant.

Night Heron *Nycticorax nycticorax* 0104
Scarce vargrant. A free-flying colony at Edinburgh Zoo.

Green-backed Heron *Butorides striatus* 0107
Very scarce vagrant.

Squacco Heron *Ardeola ralloides* 0108
Very scarce vagrant.

Cattle Egret *Bubulcus ibis* 0111
Very scarce vagrant, with possibility of escaped birds.

Little Egret *Egretta garzetta* Corra gheal bheag 0119
Scarce vagrant.

Great White Egret *Egretta alba* Corra bhan mhor 0121
Very scarce vagrant, with possibility of escaped birds.

Grey Heron *Ardea cinerea* Corra ghritheach 0122 H
Resident & widespread, although absent as a breeding species from Shetland & scarce Orkney.

Purple Heron *Ardea purpurea* 0124 UR
Very scarce vagrant.

Black Stork *Ciconia nigra* Corra dubh 0131
Very scarce vagrant.

White Stock *Ciconia ciconia* Corra bhan 0134 OR
Annually recorded vagrant.

Glossy Ibis *Plegadis falinellus* 0136
Very scarce vagrant.

Spoonbill *Platalea leucorodia* Gob cathainn 0144 NB
Scarce vagrant.

Mute Swan *Cygnus olor* Eala 0152 MS
Resident. Widespread but not generally abundant breeding species in lowlands. Absent from Shetland & some western islands.

Bewick's Swan *Cygnus columbianus* Eala bheag 0153 BS
Uncommon & local winter visitor.
Sites: B6, DG7, T1.

Whooper Swan *Cygnus cygnus* Eala bhan 0154 WS
Widespread winter & passage visitor. A few over-summer & breeding has occurred.

Bean Goose *Anser fabalis* Muir gheadh 0157 BE
Uncommon & very local winter visitor. Most commonly seen in Castle Douglas area & at Carron Valley.
Sites: Ca, DG2.

Pink-footed Goose *Anser brachyrhynchus* Geadh gorm 0158 PG
Wintering & passage visitor, mainly to farmland habitats in S & E.

White-fronted Goose *Anser albifrons* Geadh bhlar 0159 WG
Wintering & passage visitor, mainly to W coast & islands.
Sites: DG2, S2, S3, O.

Lesser White-fronted Goose *Anser erythropus* Geadh bhlar bheag 0160
Very scarce vagrant. Possibility of escaped birds.
Sites: S3?

Greylag Goose *Anser anser* Geadh glas 0161 GJ
Resident breeder in Outer Hebrides & NW. Wintering & passage visitor elsewhere, mainly to framland in E. Feral birds breed in some areas.

Snow Goose *Anser caerulescens* Geadh ban 0163 SJ
Scarce vagrant. Possibility of escaped birds. Feral flock breeds on Mull.
Sites: DG7?, S1, S3?

Canada Goose *Branta canadensis* Geadh dubh 0166 CG
Very scarce vagrant. Feral birds established in a few locations. Moult migration of Yorkshire birds on the Beauly Firth.

Barnacle Goose *Branta leucopsis* Cathan 0167 BY
Wintering & passage visitor. Main wintering areas are the Solway & Islay/other W coast islands.
Sites: DG7, S2, S3.

Brent Goose *Branta bernicla* Geadh got 0168 BG
Passage bird with variable number of birds over-wintering.
Sites: T1.

Red-breasted Goose *Branta ruficollis* 0169
Very scarce vagrant. Possibility of escaped birds.

Ruddy Shelduck *Tadorna ferruginea* 0171
Very scarce vagrant. Possibility of escaped birds.

Shelduck *Tadorna tadorna* Cra-gheadh 0173 SU
Widespread breeding species of 'soft' coastlines, plus a few inland sites. Absent in late summer/autumn, except at Forth estuary, where increasing number now moult. Wintering concentrations on some estuaries.

Mandarin *Aix galericulata* 0178 MN
Feral birds occasionally recorded. Small feral breeding populations on R Tay at Perth.
Sites: T3, T4.

Wigeon *Anas penelope* Glas lach 0179 WN
Widespread breeding species in Highlands, local breeder elsewhere. Wintering & passage visitor, with large numbers on many E coast estuaries.

American Wigeon *Anas americana* 0180
Scarce vagrant. Possibility of escaped birds.

Gadwall *Anas strepera* Lach glas 0182 GA
Uncommon & local breeding species. Few seen in winter.
Sites: DG7, T1, T13, WI.

Baikal Teal *Anas formosa* 0183
Very scarce vagrant.

Teal *Anas crecca* Crann lach 0184 T
Widespread breeding species. Wintering & passage visitor in large numbers, but generally scattered distribution.

Mallard *Anas platyrhynchos* Lach 0186 MA
Widespread breeding species. Wintering & passage visitor in large numbers, but generally scattered distribution.

American Black Duck *Anas rubripes* 0187
Very scarce vagrant.

Pintail *Anas acuta* Lach stiuireach 0189 PT
Scarce & local breeding species. Wintering & passage visitor, especially on Solway.
Sites: C1, DG2, DG7, F1, F6, H17, O1, O12, S2, S3, T9.

Garganey *Anas querquedula* Lach crann 0191 GY
Scarce summer visitor. Has bred.

Blue-winged Teal *Anas discors* 0192
Scarce vagrant.

Shoveler *Anas clypeata* Lach a'ghuib leathainn 0194 SV
Scarce & local breeding species. Small numbers of passage birds.
Sites: B8, C1, DG7, F6, H8, L5, O1, O12, S2, S5, T1, T11, T13, WI.

Red-crested Pochard *Netta rufina* 0196 RQ
Scarce vagrant. Possibility of escaped birds.

Pochard *Aytha ferina* Lach mhasach 0198 PO
Scarce & local breeding species. Widespread wintering population.
Sites: B8, C2, F1, F2, F5, L4, L5, S2, S4, T1, T11, T13.

Ring-necked Duck *Aythya collaris* 0200
Scarce vagrant.

Ferruginous Duck *Aythya nyroca* 0202 FD
Very scarce vagrant.

Tufted Duck *Aythya fuligula* Lach thopach 0203 TU
Widespread breeding species, especially in lowland Scotland. Common wintering & passage visitor.

Scaup *Aythya marila* Lach mhara 0204 SP
Coastal winter visitor. Occasional breeding recorded.
Sites: DG4, F2, F3, F6, G10, H14, H16, H18, S3, S4, WI.

Lesser Scaup *Aythya affinis* 0205
Very scarce vagrant.

Eider *Somateria mollissima* Lach lochlannach 0206 E
Widespread coastal breeding species. Gatherings of moulting birds in summer. Local movements to wintering areas such as Firth of Clyde, mouth of Tay, etc.

King Eider *Somateria spectablis* 0207
Annual vagrant.
Sites: G6, H19, SH.

Steller's Eider *Polysticta stelleri* 0209
Very scarce vagrant.

Harlequin Duck *Histrionicus histrionicus* 0211
Very scarce vagrant.

Long-tailed Duck *Clangula hyemalis* Eun buchainn 0212 LNN
Winter visitor to coastal waters, mainly E coast. Occasionally over-summers & has bred.
Sites: F2, F3, F6, G5, G6, G11, G12, G13, H14, H16, H19, L2, L3, O3, O6, SH, T6, T7, T10, WI.

Common Scoter *Melanitta nigra* Lach bheag dubh 0213 CX
Scarce & local breeding species, mainly in NW. Large numbers of moulting birds off E coast in summer. Winter visitor, with large numbers in Moray Basin.
Sites: F2, F3, F6, G5, G10, G12, G13, H19, L2, L3, WI.

Surf Scoter *Melanitta perspicillata* 0214
Scarce vagrant.
Sites: F3, G5, G10, G12, T7.

Velvet Scoter *Melanitta fusca* Lach dubh 0215 VS
Moult flocks off E coast in summer. Winter visitor, again mainly to E coast.
Sites: F2, F3, F6, G5, G9, G10, G12, G13, H19, L2, L3, O6, T7, T10.

Bufflehead *Bucephala albeola* 0216
Very scarce vagrant.

Goldeneye *Bucephala clangula* Lach bhreac 0218 GN
Widespread wintering & passage visitor. Some birds over-summer & small breeding nucleus in Highland Region, using nest boxes.

Goldeneye family

Smew *Mergus albellus* Sioltaich breac 0220 SY
Uncommon winter visitor.
Sites: B7, F5, G7, H14, St.

Red-breasted Merganser *Mergus serrator* Siolta dhearg 0221 RM
Widespread breeding species, mainly in N & W. Present on both coastal & inland waters. Moult flocks gather in coastal waters late summer. Main wintering concentrations on E coast.

Goosander *Mergus merganser* Siolta 0223 GD
Widespread breeding species, although absent from Orkney, Shetland & Outer Hebrides, scarce or absent other W coast islands.

Ruddy Duck *Okyura jamaicensis* 0225 RY
Scarce feral species which has bred at a number of diverse sites.
Sites: T13.

Honey Buzzard *Pernis apivorus* Clamhan riabhach 0231 H2
Scarce passage visitor, mainly May–September. Has bred.

Black Kite *Milvus migrans* 0238
Scarce vagrant, mainly in spring.

Red Kite *Milvus milvus* Clamhan gobhlach 0239 KT
Scarce vagrant. Formerly bred.

White-tailed Eagle *Haliaeetus albicilla* Iolair mhara 0243 WE
Recently re-introduced to west coast and now very scarce breeding species.

Marsh Harrier *Circus aeruginosus* Clamhan loin 0260 MR
Uncommon passage visitor, mainly in May & June. Has attempted to breed.

Hen Harrier *Circus cyaneus* Breid air toin 0261 HH
Widely distributed breeding species on moorlands; absent from Shetland & parts of NW.
Sites: summer G15, H8, H13, O1, O4, O6, S1, S3, T12, WI.
winter DG2, DG7, G6, H9, O1, S1, S3, S8, T13.

Pallid Harrier *Circus macrourus* 0262
Very scarce vagrant.

Montagu's Harrier *Circus pygarus* Clamhan luch 0263 MO
Scarce vagrant. Has bred.

Goshawk *Accipiter gentilus* Glas sheabhag 0267 GI
Scarce resident breeding species.

Sparrowhawk *Accipiter nisus* Speireag 0269 SH
Widespread resident; does not breed Shetland or Outer Hebrides. Also passage & winter visitor.

Buzzard *Buteo buteo* Clamhan 0287 BZ
Widespread resident breeding species, especially in west; absent from Shetland & much of Orkney.

Rough-legged Buzzard *Buteo lagopus* Bleidir molach 0290 RF
Uncommon winter visitor, especially to Orkney, Shetland & E coast.
Sites: O, SH.

Golden Eagle *Aquila chrysaetos* Iolaire 0296 EA
Resident throughout Highlands & in Hebrides.
Sites: G15, H6, H7, H11, H12, H13, H15, H24, H25, H26, H27, S1, S3, T12, WI.

Osprey *Pandion haliaetus* Iolaire lasgaich 0301 OP
Migratory breeding species in Highlands & passage visitor.
Sites: G13, H1, H2, H3, H12, H15, T9, T14, T15.

Kestrel *Falco tinnunculus* Clamham ruadh 0304 K
Widespread resident breeding species except Shetland, Lewis & Harris. Also a passage & winter visitor.

American Kestrel *Falco sparverius* 0305
Very scarce vagrant.

Red-footed Falcon *Falco vespertinus* Seabhag dhearg chasaich 0307
Scarce vagrant.

Merlin *Falco columbarius* Meirneal 0309 ML
Partial migrant, breeding on moorland habitat in Highlands, N & W islands, Grampian & Southern Uplands. Also passage & winter visitor.
Sites: summer G15, H7, H9, H11, H12, H24, H26, O4, O6, SH, T12, WI.
winter DG7, G7, S2, S3, T9.

Hobby	*Falco subbuteo*	Gormag	0310	HY

Scarce summer visitor. Has bred.

Eleonora's Falcon	*Falco eleonorae*		0311	

Very scarce vagrant.

Gyrfalcon	*Falco rusticolus*	Seabhag mhor na seilg	0318	

Scarce winter visitor, mainly to north.

Peregrine	*Falco peregrinus*	Seabhag	0320	PE

Widespread resident breeding species except east coast.
Sites: summer G15, H1, H7, H9, H11, H12, H24, H26, H27, T12, WI.
winter DG7, S3, T9.

Red Grouse	*Lagopus lagopus*	Coileach fraoich	0329	RG

Resident moorland breeding species.
Sites: B3, G15, H24, H25, H26, O1, O4, T17, WI.

Ptarmigan	*Lagopus mutus*	Tarmachan	0330	PM

Resident breeding species mainly in NW & central highlands & some inner Hebridean islands.
Sites: G15, H5, H6, H16, H24, H25, H27.

Black Grouse	*Tetrao tetrix*	Coileach dubh	0332	BK

Resident in Highlands (except NW) & Southern Uplands; absent from N isles & most of Hebrides.
Sites: G15, H13, H15, T12, T18.

Capercaillie	*Tetrao urogallus*	Capull coille	0335	CP

Resident breeding species in central & NE Highlands.
Sites: H3, H2, H15.

Red-legged Partridge	*Alectoris rufa*	Cearc thomain dhearg chasach	0358	RL

Feral breeding species in some lowland areas.

Grey Partridge	*Perdix perdix*	Cearc thomain	0367	P

Widespread resident breeding species in lowland agricultural areas; absent from most islands.

Quail	*Coturnix coturnix*	Gearradh gort	0370	Q

Irregular summer visitor & sporadic breeding species.
Sites: SH10?, WI?

Pheasant	*Phasianus colchicus*	Easag	0394	PH

Widespread resident breeding species in lowlands; local in Highlands & islands.

Golden Pheasant	*Chrysolophus pictus*		0396	GF

Scarce & local feral breeding species.

Water Rail	*Rallus aquaticus*	Snagan allt	0407	WA

Local resident breeding species & winter visitor. Probably very under-recorded.
Sites: B8, C1 (2), DG3, G7, H8, L2, S8, S9, T5, T13, WI.

Spotted Crake	*Porzana porzana*	Traon breac	0408	AK

Uncommon & irregular summer visitor; breeds occasionally.

Sora	*Porzana carolina*		0409	

Very scarce vagrant.

Little Crake	*Porzana parva*		0410	

Very scarce vagrant.

Baillon's Crake	*Porzana pusilla*		0411	

Very scarce vagrant.

Corncrake	*Crex crex*	Traon	0421	CE

Local migratory breeding species, mainly to Hebrides & Orkney.
Sites: S2, O1, O2, O7, O8, O12, WI.

Moorhen	*Gallinula chloropus*	Cearc uisge	0424	MH

Widespread resident breeding species except in Highlands & most islands, where scarce or absent.

Coot	*Fulica atra*	Lach a bhlair	0429	CO

Widespread resident breeding species except in Highlands & most islands, where scarce or absent.

Crane *Grus grus* Corra mhonaich 0433
Scarce vagrant, most frequent in spring.

Sandhill Crane *Grus canadensis* 0436
Very scarce vagrant.

Little Bustard *Tetrax terax* Coileach Frangach bheag 0442
Very scarce vagrant.

Great Bustard *Otis tarda* Coileach Frangach 0446
Very scarce vagrant.

Oystercatcher *Haematopus ostralegus* Gille brighde 0450 OC
Widespread breeding species & passage/winter visitor.

Black-winged Stilt *Himantopus himantopus* Luigneach 0455
Very scarce vagrant.

Avocet *Recurvirostra avosetta* Gob cearr 0456 AV
Scarce vagrant, mostly recorded in spring.

Stone-curlew *Burhinus oedicnemus* Cuilbneach nan clach 0459 TN
Scarce vagrant.

Cream-coloured Courser *Cursorius cursor* 0464
Very scarce vagrant.

Collared Pratincole *Glareola pratincola* 0465
Very scarce vagrant.

Black-winged Pratincole *Glareola nordmanni* 0467
Very scarce vagrant.

Little Ringed Plover *Charadrius dubius* Trilleachan traighe bheag 0469 LP
Scarce vagrant, mainly recorded in spring. Has bred.
Sites: L2?

Ringed Plover *Charadrius hiaticula* Trilleachan traghad 0470 RP
Widespread breeding species & passage/winter visitor.

Ringed Plover

Kildeer *Charadrius vociferus* 0474
Very scarce vagrant.

Kentish Plover *Charadrius alexandrinus* 0477 KP
Very scarce vagrant.

Greater Sand Plover *Charadrius leschenaultii* 0479
Very scarce vagrant.

Caspian Plover *Charadrius asiaticus* 0480
Very scarce vagrant.

Dotterel *Charadrius morinellus* Amadan-mointich 0482 DO
Scarce & local migratory breeding species in Highlands; passage visitor in lowlands.
Sites: H5, H6.

American Golden Plover *Pluvialis dominica* 0484
Very scarce vagrant.

Pacific Golden Plover *Pluvialis fulva* 0484
Very scarce vagrant.

Golden Plover *Pluvialis apricaria* Feadag 0485 GP
Widespread breeding species in uplands & passage/winter visitor.

Grey Plover *Pluvialis squatarola* Trilleachan 0486 GV
Uncommon passage/winter visitor.

Sociable Plover *Chettusia gregaria* 0491
Very scarce vagrant.

Lapwing *Vanellus vanellus* Carracag 0493 L
Widespread breeding species & passage/winter visitor.

Great Knot *Calidris tenuirostris* 0495
Very scarce vagrant.

Knot *Calidris canutus* Luatharan gainmhich 0496 KN
Passage/winter visitor.

Sanderling *Calidris alba* Luatharan glas 0497 SS
Passage visitor; some over-winter, especially in Hebrides.

Western Sandpiper *Calidris mauri* 0499
Very scarce vagrant.

Little Stint *Calidris minuta* Liatharan beag 0501 LX
Passage visitor, most frequent in autumn.
Sites: DG7, F6, G13, L1, L2, L3, SH, T5, T13, WI.

Temminck's Stint *Calidris temminckii* 0502 TK
Uncommon passage visitor & very scarce migratory breeding species.
Sites: L3, SH.

Least Sandpiper *Calidris minutilla* 0504
Very scarce vagrant.

White-rumped Sandpiper *Calidris fuscicollis* Luatharan ban 0505
Scarce vagrant, most frequent in autumn.

Baird's Sandpiper *Calidris bairdii* Trilleachan glas 0506
Very scarce vagrant.

Pectoral Sandpiper *Calidris melanotos* 5077 PP
Scarce vagrant, most frequently recorded in autumn.

Sharp-tailed Sandpiper *Calidris acuminata* 0508
Very scarce vagrant.

Curlew Sandpiper *Calidris ferruginea* Luatharan crom 0509 CV
Passage visitor, most frequently recorded in autumn.
Sites: C1 (6), DG7, F6, G6, G13, L1, L2, L3, O, SH, T5, T9, T10, WI.

Purple Sandpiper *Calidris maritima* Luatharan rioghail 0510 PS
Winter visitor, some over-summer. Has bred.
Sites: F3, F4, G3, G9, G10, G12, H19, L1, O, S2, WI.

Dunlin *Calidris alpina* Graillig 0512 DN
Migratory breeding species, mainly in Highlands & islands. Also passage/winter visitor.

Broad-billed Sandpiper *Limicola falcinellus* 0514
Very scarce vagrant.

Stilt Sandpiper	*Micropalama himantopus*		0515	

Very scarce vagrant.

Buff-breasted Sandpiper	*Tryngites subruficollis*		0516	

Scarce vagrant, most frequently recorded in autumn.

Ruff	*Philomachus pugnax*	Gibeagan	0517	RU

Uncommon passage visitor, mainly in autumn. Has bred.
Sites: C1, DG7, F2, F6, G6, G7, L1, L2, L3, L5, S2, S9, T1, T5, T9, T13, WI.

Jack Snipe	*Lymnocryptes minimus*	Gobhrag bheag	0518	JS

Uncommon passage/winter visitor.
Sites: C1 (7), C2, S6, T5.

Snipe	*Gallinago gallinago*	Naosg	0519	SN

Widespread breeding species & passage/winter visitor.

Great Snipe	*Gallinago media*		0520	

Scarce vagrant, most frequently recorded in autumn.

Long-billed Dowitcher	*Limnodromus scolopaceus*		0527	

Very scarce vagrant.

Woodcock	*Scolopax rusticola*	Coileach coille	0529	WK

Widespread breeding species except N & W Isles. Also passage/winter visitor.

Black-tailed Godwit	*Limosa limosa*	Cearra ghob	0532	BW

Passage/winter visitor. Very scarce breeding species.
Sites: C1, DG7, F6, G6, G7, G13, H14, L2, L3, O, S9, SH, T1, T6, T9, T13, WI.

Hudsonian Godwit	*Limosa haemastica*		0533	

Very scarce vagrant.

Bar-tailed Godwit	*Limosa lapponica*	Cearra ghob mhor	0534	BA

Passage-winter visitor; some individuals over-summer.

Whimbrel	*Numenius phaeopus*	Eun bealltainn	0538	WM

Local migratory breeding species, mainly in Shetland. Also passage visitor.
Sites: C1, G6, G13, L2,L5, O, S2, T5, SH.

Curlew	*Numenius arquata*	Guilbneach	0541	CU

Widespread breeding species & passage/winter visitor.

Upland Sandpiper	*Bartramia longicauda*		0544	

Very scarce vagrant.

Spotted Redshank	*Tringa erythropus*	Gearradh bhreac	0545	DR

Uncommon passage visitor, most frequently recorded in autumn.
Sites: C1, DG7, F6, G6, G13, L2, L3, L5, O, S9, SH, T1, T9, T10.

Redshank	*Tringa totanus*	Cam ghlas	0546	RK

Widespread breeding species & passage/winter visitor.

Marsh Sandpiper	*Tringa stagnatilis*		0547	

Very scarce vagrant.

Greenshank	*Tringa nebularia*	Deoch bhuidhe	0548	GK

Local migratory breeding species in Highlands & islands. Also passage visitor.

Greater Yellowlegs	*Tringa melanoleuca*		0550	

Very scarce vagrant.

Lesser Yellowlegs	*Tringa flavipes*		0551	

Very scarce vagrant.

Solitary Sandpiper	*Tringa solitaria*		0552	

Very scarce vagrant.

Green Sandpiper	*Tringa ochropus*	Luatharan uaine	0553	GE

Uncommon passage visitor. Has bred.
Sites: C1, G6, L1, L2, L3, O, S9, SH, T1, T5, T6, T9.

Wood Sandpiper	*Tringa glareola*	Luatharan coille	0554	OD

Uncommon passage visitor. Scarce migratory breeding species in Highlands.
Sites: C1, L2, L3, S9, T1, T9, T10.

Terek Sandpiper	*Xenus cinereus*		0555	

Very scarce vagrant.

Common Sandpiper *Actitis hypoleucos* Lutharan 0558 CS
Widespread migratory breeding species & passage visitor.

Spotted Sandpiper *Actitis macularia* 0557
Very scarce vagrant. Has bred.

Turnstone *Arenaria interpres* Trilleachan beag/Gobhlachan 0561 TT
Passage/winter visitor. Some birds present over summer.

Wilson's Phalarope *Phalaropus tricolor* 0563
Very scarce vagrant, most frequently recorded in autumn.

Red-necked Phalarope *Phalaropus lobatus* Deargan allt 0564 NK
Scarce & local migratory breeding species, mainly in Shetland.
Sites: SH7, WI.

Male Red-necked Phalarope

Grey Phalarope *Phalaropus fulicarius* Liathag allt 0565 PL
Uncommon passage visitor, most frequently recorded in autumn.

Pomarine Skua *Stercorarius pomarinus* Fasgadair donn 0566 PK
Passage visitor.
Sites: B1, C1, F2, F4, G3, SH, T8, WI.

Arctic Skua *Stercorarius parasiticus* Fasgadair 0567 AC
Local migratory breeding species, mainly in N Isles. Also passage visitor.

Long-tailed Skua *Stercorarius longicaudus* Fasgadair stiureach 0568 OG
Uncommon passage/summer visitor.

Great Skua *Stercorarius skua* Fasgadair mor 0569 NX
Local migratory breeding species, mainly in N Isles. Passage visitor on coast.

Mediterranean Gull *Larus melanocephalus* 0575 MU
Scarce vagrant.
Sites: F3, S6.

Laughing Gull *Larus atricilla* 0576
Very scarce vagrant.

Franklin's Gull *Larus pipixcan* 0577
Very scarce vagrant.

Little Gull *Larus minutus* Crann fhaoileag 0578 LU
Passage visitor, most abundant in late summer & autumn off east coast.
Sites: F3, F4, T6, T7.

Sabine's Gull *Larus sabini* 0579 AB
Scarce vagrant, most frequently recorded in autumn.

Bonaparte's Gull *Larus philadelphia* 0581
Very scarce vagrant.

Black-headed Gull *Larus ridibundus* Faoileag a' chinn duibh 0582 BH
Widespread inland breeding species. Also winter visitor.

Ring-billed Gull *Larus delawarensis* 0589
Very scarce vagrant.

Common Gull *Larus canus* Faoileag 0590 CM
Widespread breeding species & passage/winter visitor.

Lesser Black-backed Gull *Larus argentatus* Faoileag bheag 0591 LB
Migratory breeding species & passage visitor.

Herring Gull *Larus argentatus* Faoileag an sgadain 0592 HG
Widespread breeding species & passage/winter visitor.

Iceland Gull *Larus glaucoides* Faoileag liath 0598 IG
Winter visitor, mainly in N.
Sites: DG4, F3, G3, G8, G9, G12, H14, H19, L3, O1, S3, S6, SH1.

Glaucous Gull *Larus hyperboreus* Faoileag mhor 0599 GZ
Winter visitor, especially to N.
Sites: C1, DG4, F3, G3, G9, G10, G11, G12, H14, H19, L3, O1, S3, S6, SH1.

Great Black-backed Gull *Larus marinus* Farspag 0600 GB
Widespread coastal breeding species & winter visitor.

Ross's Gull *Rhodostethia rosea* 0601
Very scarce vagrant.

Kittiwake *Rissa tridactyla* Ruideag 0602 KI
Widespread coastal breeding species & passage/winter visitor.

Ivory Gull *Pagophilia eburnea* 0604
Scarce vagrant, most frequently recorded in mid-winter.

Gull-billed Tern *Gelochelidon nilotica* 0605
Very scarce vagrant.

Lesser Crested Tern *Sterna bengalensis*
Very scarce vagrant.

Caspian Tern *Sterna caspia* 0606
Very scarce vagrant, most frequently recorded in summer.

Sandwich Tern *Sterna sandvicensis* Stearnag mhor 0611 TE
Local migratory breeding species.

Roseate Tern *Sterna dougallii* Stearnag stiuireach 0614 RS
Very scarce & local migratory breeding species.

Common Tern *Sterna hirundo* Stearnag 0615 CN
Migratory breeding species & passage visitor.

Arctic Tern *Sterna paradisaea* Stearnal 0616 AE
Migratory breeding species, most abundant in N Isles. Also passage visitor.

Forster's Tern *Sterna forsteri* 0618
Very scarce vagrant.

Bridled Tern *Sterna anaethetus* 0622
Very scarce vagrant.

Sooty Tern *Sterna fuscata* 0623
Very scarce vagrant.

Little Tern *Sterna albifrons* Stearnag bheag 0624 AF
Local migratory breeding species.
Sites: G6, S7, WI

Black Tern *Chlidonias niger* 0627 BJ
Uncommon passage visitor.
Sites: F4, L2.

White-winged Black Tern *Chlidonias leucopterus* 0628
Very scarce vagrant, most frequently recorded in early summer.

Guillemot *Uria aalge* Eun dubh an sgadain 0634 GU
Widespread breeding species on coastal cliffs. Also winter visitor.

Brunnich's Guillemot *Uria lomvia* 0635
Very scarce vagrant.

Razorbill *Alca torda* Falc 0636 RA
Widespread breeding species on coastal cliffs. Also winter visitor.

Black Guillemot *Cepheus grylle* Gearra-breac 0638 TY
Sedentary breeding species on rocky shores, most abundant in N Isles.

Little Auk *Alle alle* Colcach bheag 0647 LK
Winter visitor in variable numbers.
Sites: F4, F7, G9, G12, O, SH.

Puffin *Fratercula arctica* Buthaid 0654 PU
Widespread coastal breeding species, most abundant on the islands.

Pallas's Sandgrouse *Syrrhaptes paradoxus* 0663
Very scarce vagrant.

Rock Dove *Columba livia* Calman creige 0665 DV
Resident breeding species on N & W coasts.

Stock Dove *Columba oenas* Calman gorm 0668 SD
Resident breeding species, mainly in S & E.

Woodpigeon *Columba palumbus* Calman fiadhaich 0670 WP
Widespread resident breeding species & passage/winter visitor.

Collared Dove *Streptopelia decaocto* Calman a chrios 0684 CD
Widespread breeding species, especially in lowlands.

Turtle Dove *Streptopelia turtur* Calman tuchan 0687 TD
Uncommon passage visitor. Has bred.

Rufous Turtle Dove *Streptopelia orientalis* 0689
Very scarce vagrant.

Great Spotted Cuckoo *Clamator glandarius* 0716
Very scarce vagrant.

Cuckoo *Cuculus canorus* Cuthag 0724 CK
Widespread migratory breeding species & passage visitor.

Black-billed Cuckoo *Coccyzus erythrophthalmus* 0727
Very scarce vagrant.

Yellow-billed Cuckoo *Coccyzus americanus* 0728
Very scarce vagrant.

Barn Owl *Tyto alba* Cowhachag 0735 BO
Resident breeding species, mainly in S & E; absent from much of Highlands & islands.
Sites: DG2, DG3.

Scops Owl *Otus scops* 0739
Very scarce vagrant.

Snowy Owl *Nyctea scandiaca* Comhachag bhan 0749
A few resident on Shetland (has bred). Scarce irruptive vagrant elsewhere.
Sites: SH7, SH8.

Hawk Owl *Surnia ulula* Seabhag oidhche 0750
Very scarce vagrant.

Little Owl *Athene noctua* Comhachag bheag 0757 LO
Very scarce & local resident breeding species in S.

Tawny Owl *Strix aluco* Comhachag dhonn 0761 TO
Widespread breeding species; absent N & W Isles plus some Inner Hebrides.

Long-eared Owl *Asio otus* Comhachag adharcaiche 0767 LE
Resident breeding species, mainly in S & E. Passage/winter visitor.
Sites: F4, O1, SH10, T18.

Short-eared Owl *Asio flammeus* Comhachag chluassach 0768 SE
Widespread breeding species; absent from NW Highlands, parts of Outer Hebrides & Shetland. Also passage/winter visitor.

Tengmalm's Owl *Aegolius funereus* 0770
Very scarce vagrant.

Nightjar *Caprimulgus europaeus* Sgraicheag oidhche 0778 NJ
Scarce & local migratory breeding species in Dumfries/Galloway & Arran/S Argyll.

Common Nighthawk *Chordeiles minor* 0786
Very scarce vagrant.

Needle-tailed Swift *Hirundapus caudacutus* 0792
Very scarce vagrant.

Swift *Apus apus* Gobhlan mor 0795 SI
Migratory breeding species; absent from islands & parts of NW Highlands. Also passage visitor.

Pallid Swift *Apus pallidus* 0796
Very scarce vagrant.

Alpine Swift *Apus melba* Gobhlan monaidh 0798
Very scarce vagrant.

Kingfisher *Alcedo atthis* Biorra cruidein 0831 KF
Resident breeding species, mainly in S.
Sites: C1 (2), L1, S9.

Bee-eater *Meriops apiaster* 0840
Scarce vagrant, most frequently recorded in summer. Has bred.

Roller *Coracias garrulus* Cuairsgean 0841
Scarce vagrant, most frequently recorded in spring.

Hoopoe *Upupa epops* Calman cathaidh 0846 HP
Scarce vagrant, most frequently recorded in April/May & September/October.

Wryneck *Jynx torquilla* Geocair 0848 WY
Irregular passage visitor. Very scarce migratory breeding species in Highlands.
Sites: B1, F4, F7, O, SH.

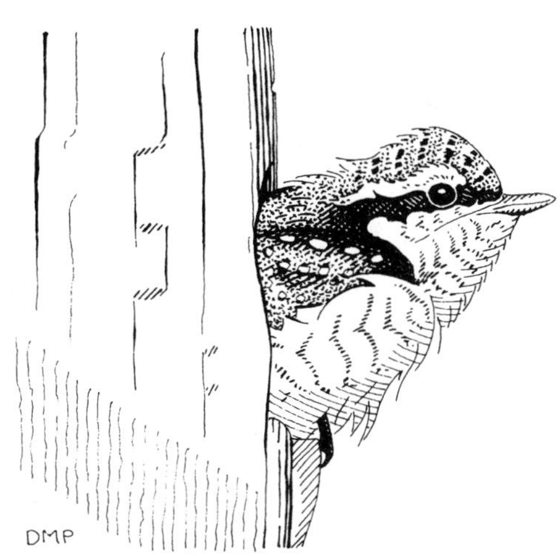

Young Wryneck at nest-hole

Green Woodpecker *Picus viridis* Snagarach 0856 G
Resident breeding species; absent from islands & N Highlands.
Sites: B2, B4, B8, H1, T18.

Great Spotted Woodpecker *Dendrocopos major* Snagan daraich 0876 GS
Widespread breeding species; absent N & W Isles. Passage/winter visitor.

Lesser Spotted Woodpecker	*Dendrocopos minor*	Snagan daraich beag	0887	LS

Very scarce vagrant. May have bred.

Calandra Lark	*Melanocorypha calandra*		0961	

Very scarce vagrant.

Bimaculated Lark	*Melanocorypha bimaculata*		0962	

Very scarce vagrant.

Short-toed Lark	*Calendrella brachyfactyla*		0968	

Scarce vagrant, most frequently recorded in autumn in N Isles.

Crested Lark	*Galerida cristata*		0972	

Very scarce vagrant.

Woodlark	*Lullula arborea*	Uiseag choille	0974	WL

Scarce vagrant.

Skylark	*Alauda arvensis*	Uiseag	0976	S

Widespread breeding species & passage/winter visitor.

Shore Lark	*Eremophila alpestris*	Uiseag dhubh	0978	SX

Scarce passage/winter visitor.

Sand Martin	*Riparia riparia*	Gobhlan gainmhiche	0981	SM

Migratory breeding species except W & N Isles. Also passage visitor.
Sites: B4, S9, T3.

Swallow	*Hirundo rustica*	Gobhlan gaoithe	0992	SL

Migratory breeding species & passage visitor.

Red-rumped Swallow	*Hirundo daurica*		0995	

Very scarce vagrant.

House Martin	*Delichon urbica*	Gobhlan taighe	1001	HM

Migratory breeding species except some W Isles.

Richard's Pipit	*Anthus novaeseelandiae*		1002	PR

Scarce vagrant, most frequently recorded in autumn.

Blyth's Pipit	*Anthus godlewskii*		1004	

Very scarce vagrant.

Tawny Pipit	*Anthus campestris*		1005	TI

Scarce vagrant, most frequently recorded in spring.

Olive-backed Pipit	*Anthus hodgsoni*		1008	

Very scarce vagrant, most frequently recorded in autumn.

Tree Pipit	*Anthus trivialis*	Riabhag	1009	TP

Migratory breeding species, except N & W Isles.

Pechora Pipit	*Anthus gustavi*		1010	

Scarce vagrant.

Meadow Pipit	*Anthus pratensis*	Snathag	1011	MP

Widespread breeding species & passage/winter visitor.

Red-throated Pipit	*Anthus cervinus*		1012	

Scarce vagrant.

Rock Pipit	*Anthus spinoletta*	Gabhagan	1014	RC

Widespread coastal breeding species. Also continental passage/winter visitor to E coast.

Yellow Wagtail	*Motacilla flava*	Breacan buidhe	1017	YW

Scarce & local migratory breeding species, mainly in central lowlands. Also passage visitor.
Sites: B4, B6, B7, B8, G4.

Citrine Wagtail	*Motacilla citreola*		1018	

Scarce vagrant, most frequently recorded in September/October.

Grey Wagtail	*Motacilla cinerea*	Breacan bain tighearna	1019	GL

Widespread breeding species except N Isles & most of W Isles.

Pied Wagtail	*Motacilla alba*	Breac an t-sil	1020	PW

Widespread breeding species. White Wagtail occur on passage & occasionally breed.

Waxwing	*Bombycilla garrulus*	Canarach dearg	1048	WX

Irruptive winter visitor.

Dipper	*Cinclus cinclus*	Gobha uisge	1050	DI

Widespread breeding species except N Isles.

Wren	*Troglodytes troglodytes*	Dreathan donn	1066	WR

Widespread breeding species.

Dunnock	*Prunella modularis*	Gealbhonn nam preas	1084	D

Widespread breeding species except Shetland. Also passage/winter visitor.

Alpine Accentor	*Prunella collaris*		1094	

Very scarce vagrant.

Robin	*Erithacus rubecula*	Bru dhearg	1099	R

Widespread breeding species except Shetland. Also passage/winter visitor.

Thrush Nightingale	*Luscinia luscinia*		1103	

Scarce vagrant, most frequently recorded in spring.

Nightingale	*Luscinia megarhynchos*	Spideag	1104	N

Scarce vagrant, most frequently recorded in spring.

Siberian Rubythroat	*Luscinia calliope*		1105	

Very scarce vagrant.

Bluethroat	*Luscinia svecica*	Oranaiche	1106	BU

Uncommon passage visitor, most frequently recorded in spring. Has bred.
Sites: B1, F4, F7, G3, O, SH.

Red-flanked Bluetail	*Tarsiger cyranurus*		1113	

Very scarce vagrant.

Black Redstart	*Phoenicurus ochruros*	Ceann dubhan	1121	BX

Passage visitor, occasionally over-winters. Has attempted to breed.
Sites: F4, T10.

Redstart	*Phoenicurus phoenicurus*	Ceann dearg	1122	RT

Migratory breeding species except N & W Isles. Also passage visitor.

Daurian Redstart	*Phoenicurus auroreus*		1126	

Very scarce vagrant.

Whinchat	*Saxicola rubetra*	Gocan	1137	WC

Migratory breeding species except N & some W Isles. Also passage visitor.

Whinchat

Stonechat	*Saxicola torquata*	Clacharan	1139	SC

Local breeding species, most abundant in W; absent from Shetland.

Isabelline Wheatear	*Oenanthe isabellina*		1144	

Very scarce vagrant.

Wheatear	*Oenanthe oenanthe*	Bru gheal	1146	W

Migratory breeding species & passage visitor.

Pied Wheatear	*Oenanthe pleschanka*		1147	

Very scarce vagrant.

Black-eared Wheatear	*Oenanthe hispanica*		1148	

Very scarce vagrant.

Desert Wheatear	*Oenanthe deserti*		1149	

Very scarce vagrant.

Black Wheatear	*Oenanthe leucura*		1158	

Very scarce vagrant.

Rock Thrush	*Monticola saxatilis*		1162	

Very scarce vagrant.

White's Thrush	*Zoothera dauma*		1170	

Very scarce vagrant.

Siberian Thrush	*Zoothera sibirica*		1171	

Very scarce vagrant.

Hermit Thrush	*Catharus guttatus*		1176	

Very scarce vagrant.

Swainson's Thrush	*Catharus ustulatus*		1177	

Very scarce vagrant.

Grey-cheeked Thrush	*Catharus minimus*		1178	

Very scarce vagrant.

Ring Ousel	*Turdus torquatus*	Dubh chreige	1186	RZ

Migratory breeding species & passage visitor.
Sites: C4, H7, H12, H24, H25, H26, T12, T17.

Blackbird	*Turdus merula*	Lon dubh	1187	B

Widespread breeding species & passage/winter visitor.

Eye-browed Thrush	*Turdus obscurus*		1195	

Very scarce vagrant.

Dusky Thrush	*Turdus naumanni*		1196	

Very scarce vagrant.

Black-throated Thrush	*Turdus ruficollis*		1197	

Very scarce vagrant.

Fieldfare	*Turdus pilaris*	Liath thruisg	1198	FF

Passage/winter visitor. Very scarce breeding species.

Song Thrush	*Turdus philomelos*	Smeorach	1200	ST

Widespread breeding species; scarce Shetland. Also passage/winter visitor.

Redwing	*Turdus iliacus*	Sgiath dhearg	1201	RE

Passage/winter visitor & scarce migratory breeding species (mainly in Highlands).

Mistle Thrush	*Turdus viscivorus*	Smeorach mhor	1202	M

Widespread breeding species except N & W Isles. Also uncommon passage visitor.

American Robin	*Turdus migratorius*		1203	

Very scarce vagrant.

Pallas's Grasshopper Warbler	*Locustella certhiola*		1233	

Very scarce vagrant.

Lanceolated Warbler	*Locustella lanceolata*		1235	

Very scarce vagrant, most frequently recorded in autumn.

Grasshopper Warbler	*Locustella naevia*	Ceileiriche leumnach	1236	GH

Migratory breeding species; absent from N & W Isles. Also uncommon passage visitor.
Sites: B4, DG2, H8, S5, S9.

River Warbler	*Locustella fluviatilis*		1237	

Very scarce vagrant.

Savi's Warbler	*Lucustella luscinioides*		1238	VI

Very scarce vagrant.

Redwing

Aquatic Warbler *Acrocephalus paludicola* 1242 AQ
Scarce vagrant, most frequently recorded in August/September.

Sedge Warbler *Acrocephalus schoenobaenus* Glas eun 1240 SW
Migratory breeding species; absent from Shetland. Also uncommon passage visitor.

Paddyfield Warbler *Acrocephalus agricola* 1247
Very scarce vagrant.

Blyth's Reed Warbler *Acrocephalus dumetorum* 1248
Very scarce vagrant.

Marsh Warbler *Acrocephalus palustris* Ceileiriche feithe 1250 MW
Scarce passage visitor, most frequently recorded in June.
Sites: O, SH.

Reed Warbler *Acrocephalus scripaceus* Cuilceag 1251 RW
Uncommon passage visitor, most frequently recorded in autumn. Has bred (once).

Great Reed Warbler *Acrocephalus arundinaceus* 1253
Very scarce vagrant.

Thick-billed Warbler *Acrocephalus aedon* 1254
Very scarce vagrant.

Olivaceous Warbler *Hippolais pallida* 1255
Very scarce vagrant.

Booted Warbler *Hippolais caligata* 1256
Very scarce vagrant.

Icterine Warbler *Hippolais icterina* 1259 IC
Scarce passage visitor.
Sites: F7, O, SH.

Melodious Warbler *Hippolais polyglotta* 1260 ME
Very scarce vagrant.

Dartford Warbler *Sylvia undata* 1262 DW
Very scarce vagrant.

Spectacled Warbler *Sylvia conspicillata* 1264
Very scarce vagrant.

Subalpine Warbler *Sylvia cantillans* 1265
Scarce vagrant, most frequently recorded in spring.

Sardinian Warbler *Sylvia melanocephala* 1267
Very scarce vagrant.

Ruppell's Warbler *Sylvia rueppelli* 1269
Very scarce vagrant.

Orphean Warbler *Sylvia hortensis* 1272
Very scarce vagrant.

Barred Warbler *Sylvia nisoria* Calleiriche srianach 1273 RR
Scarce passage visitor, most frequently recorded in autumn.
Sites: B1, F4, F7, O, SH.

Lesser Whitethroat *Sylvia curruca* Gealan coille beag 1274 LW
Scarce migratory breeding species in lowlands & uncommon passage visitor.
Sites: B1, F4, F7, L2, G3.

Whitethroat *Sylvia communis* Gealan coille 1275 WH
Migratory breeding species & passage visitor.

Garden Warbler *Sylvia borin* Ceileiriche garaidh 1276 GW
Migratory breeding species; absent from much of N & W. Also passage visitor.

Blackcap *Sylvia atricapilla* Ceann dubh 1277 BC
Migratory breeding species; absent from most of Highlands & islands. Also passage visitor.

Greenish Warbler *Phyllosopus trochiloides* 1293
Scarce vagrant, most frequently recorded in autumn.

Arctic Warbler *Phylloscopus borealis* 1295
Scarce vagrant, most frequently recorded in autumn.

Pallas's Warbler *Phylloscopus proregulus* 1298
Scarce vagrant, most frequently recorded in October.

Yellow-browed Warbler *Phylloscopus inornatus* Ceileiriche buidhe 1300 YB
Scarce passage visitor in autumn.
Sites: B1, F4, F7, G3, O, T8, SH.

Radde's Warbler *Phylloscopus schwarzi* 1301
Very scarce vagrant, most frequently recorded in October.

Dusky Warbler *Phylloscopus fuscatus* 1303
Very scarce vagrant, most frequently recorded in autumn.

Bonelli's Warbler *Phylloscopus bonelli* 1307
Very scarce vagrant.

Wood Warbler *Phylloscopus sibilatrix* Caileiriche cille 1308 WO
Migratory breeding species; absent from N & W Isles. Also uncommon passage visitor.

Chiffchaff *Phylloscopus collybita* Caifean 1311 CC
Migratory breeding species; absent from N & W Isles. Also passage visitor; some over-winter.

Willow Warbler *Phylloscopus trochilus* Crionag ghiuthais 1312 WW
Migratory breeding species & passage visitor.

Goldcrest *Regulus regulus* Crionag bhuidhe 1314 GC
Widespread breeding species & passage visitor.

Firecrest *Regulus ignicapillus* Crionag 1315 FC
Scarce vagrant.

Spotted Flycatcher *Muscicapa striata* Breacan glas sgiobalta 1335 SF
Migratory breeding species except Shetland; scarce on Orkney & W Isles. Also uncommon passage visitor.

Red-breasted Flycatcher *Ficedula parva* 1343 FY
Scarce passage visitor, most frequently recorded in autumn.
Sites: B1, F7, O, SH, T8.

Collared Flycatcher *Ficedula albicollis* 1348
Very scarce vagrant.

Pied Flycatcher *Ficedula hypoleuca* Breacan glas 1349 PF
Migratory breeding species, except N & W Isles; scarce in N. Also passage visitor.
Sites: B2, B8, C4, C6, DG2, DG3, T18.

Bearded Tit *Panurus biarmicus* 1364 BR
Very scarce visitor.

Long-tailed Tit *Aegithalos caudatus* Ciochan 1437 LT
Widespread breeding species except N & W Isles.

Marsh Tit *Parus palustris* Miontan 1440 MT
Scarce & local resident breeding species in SE.
Sites: B2, B4, B8.

Willow Tit *Parus montanus* Currac ghiuthais 1442 WT
Uncommon & local resident breeding species, mainly in SW.
Sites: DG1, DG2, DG3, S8, S9.

Crested Tit *Parus cristatus* Gulpag stuic 1454 CI
Local resident breeding species in Moray Firth catchment areas.
Sites: G10, G13, H2, H3, H4, H5, H15.

Crested Tit

Coal Tit *Parus ater* Smutag 1461 CT
Widespread breeding species except N & W Isles.

Blue Tit *Parus caeruleus* Cailleachag cheann ghorm 1462 BT
Widespread breeding species except N Isles; scarce in W Isles.

Great Tit *Parus major* Currac bhain tighearna 1464 GT
Widespread breeding species except N Isles; scarce in W Isles.

Nuthatch *Sitta europaea* Sgoltan 1479 NH
Scarce vagrant.
Sites: B8?

Treecreeper *Certhia familiaris* Snaigear 1486 TC
Widespread breeding species except N Isles; scarce in W Isles.

Golden Oriole *Oriolus oriolus* Buidheag Eirpach 1508 OL
Scarce vagrant, most frequently recorded in May–July. Has bred.

Isabelline Shrike *Lanius isabellinus* 1514
Very scarce vagrant.

Red-backed Shrike *Lanius collurio* Feoladair 1515 ED
Scarce passage visitor, most frequently recorded in spring.
Sites: B1, F4, F7, O, SH.

Brown Shrike *Lanius cristatus*
Very scarce vagrant.

Lesser Grey Shrike *Lanius minor* 1519
Very scarce vagrant.

Great Grey Shrike *Lanius excubitor* Feoladair Glas 1520 SR
Scarce passage/winter visitor.
Sites: DG2, H8.

Woodchat Shrike *Lanius senator* 1523
Scarce vagrant, most frequently recorded in spring.

Jay *Garrulus glandarius* Sgraicheag 1539 J
Resident breeding species except N Isles & most of Highlands & islands.

Magpie *Pica pica* Cadhag 1549 MG
Resident breeding species except Highlands, N & W Isles.

Nutcracker *Nucifraga caryocatactes* 1557
Very scarce vagrant.

Chough *Pyrrhocorax pyrrhocorax* Cathag dhearg chasach 1559 CF
Local resident breeding species, mainly on Islay.
Sites: S3.

Jackdaw *Corvus monedula* Gathag 1560 JD
Widespread breeding species; scarce in NW Highlands, N & W Isles. Also winter visitor.

Rook *Corvus frugilegus* Rocas 1563 RO
Resident breeding species in agricultural areas. Also winter visitor.

Carrion/Hooded Crow *Corvus corone* Feannag 1567 C
Widespread breeding species. Hooded Crow predominate in N & W. Carrion Crow in S & E. Hybrids in overlap area. Also passage/winter visitor.

Raven *Corvus corax* Fitheach 1572 RN
Resident breeding species in uplands.

Starling *Sturnus vulgaris* Druid 1582 SG
Widespread breeding species & winter visitor.

Rose-coloured Starling *Sturnus roseus* Druid dhearg 1584
Scarce vagrant, most frequently recorded in summer.

Daurian Starling *Sturnus sturninus*
Very scarce vagrant.

House Sparrow *Passer domesticus* Gealbhonn 1591 HS
Widespread breeding species.

Spanish Sparrow *Passer hispaniolensis* 1592
Very scarce vagrant.

Tree Sparrow *Passer montanus* Gealbhonn nan craobh 1598 TS
Resident breeding species in lowlands.

Red-eyed Vireo *Vireo olivaceus* 1633
Very scarce vagrant.

Chaffinch *Fringilla coelebs* Breacan beithe 1636 CH
Widespread breeding species except Shetland; scarce W Isles. Also passage/winter visitor.

Brambling *Fringilla montifringilla* Bricein caorainn 1638 BL
Passage/winter visitor. Has bred.
Sites: B4, L2, S8, T1.

Serin *Serinus serinus* 1640 NS
Very scarce vagrant.

Greenfinch *Carduelis chloris* Glaisean daraich 1649 GR
Widespread breeding species except Shetland; scarce in much of Highlands, Orkney & W. Isles. Also passage visitor.

Goldfinch *Carduelis carduelis* Lasair choille 1653 GO
Widespread breeding species except N & W Isles.

Siskin *Carduelis spinus* Gealag bhuidhe 1654 SK
Widespread breeding species except Shetland, W Isles & much of central lowlands. Also passage/winter visitor.

Linnet *Garduelis cannabina* Gealan lin 1660 LI
Widespread breeding species, especially in SE.

Twite	*Carduelis flavirostris*	Gealan beinne	1662	TW

Widespread breeding species, especially in NW & islands.
Sites: H24, H25, L2, L3, O, S2, S3, SH, T17, WI.

Redpoll	*Carduelis flammea*	Dearcan seilich	1663	LR

Widespread breeding species; scarce N & W Isles. Also passage/winter visitor.

Arctic Redpoll	*Carduelis hornemanni*		1664	

Scarce vagrant, most frequently recorded in autumn/winter.

Two-barred Crossbill	*Loxia leucoptera*		1665	

Very scarce vagrant.

Common Crossbill	*Loxia curvirostra*	Cam ghob	1666	CR

Resident breeding species & irruptive visitor.
Sites: C4, H26, S1.

Scottish Crossbill	*Loxia scotia*		1667	CY

Resident breeding species, mainly in native Scots pine forests.
Sites: G10, H2, H4, H7, H15.

Scottish Crossbill

Parrot Crossbill	*Loxia pytyopsittacus*		1668	

Very scarce vagrant.

Trumpeter Finch	*Bucanetes githagineus*		1676	

Very scarce vagrant.

Scarlet Rosefinch	*Carpodacus erythrinus*		1679	SQ

Uncommon passage visitor. Has bred.
Sites: F7, O, SH.

Pine Grosbeak	*Pinicola enucleator*		1699	

Very scarce vagrant.

Bullfinch	*Pyrrhula pyrrhula*	Corcan-coille	1710	BF

Widespread breeding species except N Isles; scarce in W Isles. Also irruptive visitor.

Hawfinch	*Coccothraustes coccothraustes*	Gobhach	1717	HF

Scarce & local resident breeding species in lowlands. Occasional passage visitor.
Sites: B8, T4.

Evening Grosbeak	*Hesperiphona vespertina*		1718	

Very scarce vagrant.

Black-and-white Warbler *Mniotilta varia* 1720
Very scarce vagrant.

Tennessee Warbler *Vermivora peregrina* 1724
Very scarce vagrant.

Yellow Warbler *Dendroica petechia* 1733
Very scarce vagrant.

Blackburnian Warbler *Dendroica fusca* 1747
Very scarce vagrant.

Cape May Warbler *Dendroica tigrina* 1749
Very scarce vagrant.

Yellow-rumped Warbler *Dendroica coronata* 1751
Very scarce vagrant.

Chestnut-sided Warbler *Dendroica pensylvanica*
Very scarce vagrant.

Blackpoll Warbler *Dendroica striata* 1753
Very scarce vagrant.

American Redstart *Setophaga ruticilla* 1755
Very scarce vagrant.

Ovenbird *Seiurus aurocapillus* 1756
Very scarce vagrant.

Common Yellowthroat *Geothlypis trichas* 1762
Very scarce vagrant.

Savannah Sparrow *Ammodramus sandichensis* 1826
Very scarce vagrant.

Song Sparrow *Zonotrichia melodia* 1835
Very scarce vagrant.

White-crowned Sparrow *Zonotrichia leucophrys* 1839
Very scarce vagrant.

White-throated Sparrow *Zonotrichia albicollis* 1840
Very scarce vagrant.

Dark-eyed Junco *Junco hyemalis* 1842
Very scarce vagrant.

Lapland Bunting *Calcarius lapponicus* 1847 LA
Uncommon passage/winter visitor.
Sites: C1 (5), F7, L3, O, SH.

Snow Bunting *Plectrophenax nivalis* Gealag an t-sneachda 1850 SB
Passage/winter visitor. Very scarce & local breeding species in Highlands.
Sites: summer H6.
winter C1 (5), F6, G5, G10, G11, H19, L1, L2, L3, O, T6, SH, WI.

Pine Bunting *Emberiza leucocephalos* 1856
Very scarce vagrant.

Yellowhammer *Emberiza citrinella* Buidheag bhealaidh 1857 Y
Widespread breeding species except Shetland; scarce Orkney & W Isles.

Cirl Bunting *Emberiza cirlus* 1858 CL
Very scarce vagrant.

Ortolan Bunting *Emberiza hortulana* 1866 OB
Scarce passage visitor, most frequently recorded in spring.
Sites: F7, O, SH.

Cretzschmar's Bunting *Emberiza caesia* 1868
Very scarce vagrant.

Yellow-browed Bunting *Emberiza chrysophrys* 1871
Very scarce vagrant.

Rustic Bunting *Emberiza rustica* 1873
Scarce vagrant, most frequently recorded in May & September/October.

Male Snow Bunting

Little Bunting *Emberiza pusilla* 1874
Scarce vagrant, most frequently recorded in autumn.

Yellow-breasted Bunting *Emberiza aureola* 1876
Scarce vagrant, most frequently recorded in autumn.

Reed Bunting *Emberiza schoeniculus* Gealag loin 1877 RB
Widespread breeding species & passage/winter visitor.

Pallas's Reed Bunting *Emberiza fallasi* 1878
Very scarce vagrant.

Black-headed Bunting *Emberiza melanocephala* 1881
Scarce vagrant/escape.

Corn Bunting *Miliaria calandra* Gealag bhuachair 1882 CB
Local resident breeding species, mainly on E coast & in W Isles.
Sites: F4, G11, O, S2, WI.

Rose-breasted Bunting *Pheucticus ludovicianus* 1887
Very scarce vagrant.

Bobolink *Dolichonyx oryzivorus* 1897
Very scarce vagrant.

Northern Oriole *Icterus galbula* 1918
Very scarce vagrant.

INDEX TO SPECIES

INDEX TO SITES

Rock Pipit